Parent–Infant Psychodynamics
Wild things, mirrors and ghosts

Dedication

To Daniel, Ingrid and Astrid and all our babies, past, present and future

Parent–Infant Psychodynamics

Wild things, mirrors and ghosts

A Reader designed for a variety of professionals working with expectant parents, babies and their families, and for parents and students in pursuit of psychoanalytic understanding.

Edited by

JOAN RAPHAEL-LEFF

Centre for Psychoanalytic Studies, University of Essex

W

WHURR PUBLISHERS
LONDON AND PHILADELPHIA

2003

© 2003 Whurr Publishers Ltd
First published 2003
by Whurr Publishers Ltd
19b Compton Terrace
London N1 2UN England and
325 Chestnut Street, Philadelphia PA 19106 USA

British Library Cataloguing in Publication Data

A catalogue record for this book
is available from the British Library.

ISBN 1 86156 346 9

Printed and bound in the UK by Athenaeum Press Ltd,
Gateshead, Tyne & Wear.

'The longer I live, the more convinced I am that we're all haunted in this world – not only by the things we inherit from our parents – but by the ghosts of innumerable old prejudices and beliefs – half-forgotten cruelties and betrayals – we may not even be aware of them – but they are there all the same – and we can't get rid of them. The whole world is haunted by these ghosts of the dead past; you have only to pick up a newspaper to see them weaving in and out between the lines – Ah! If only we had the courage to sweep them all out and let in the light!' (*Ghosts*, Ibsen, 1881, tr. Eva le Gallienne, Modern Library Books, Random House, 1957, p. 119)

Contents

Preface

In recent years governmental and UNESCO directives indicate a growing awareness of the importance of psychological issues in reproduction and parenting, and the need to provide both personalized and culturally sensitive professional care to foster infant, child and family mental health.

This Reader provides reading material for a variety of professionals engaged in such work with pregnant women, parents, babies and their carers, including midwives, health visitors, social workers, couple counsellors, child therapists, parent–infant or family therapists, general practice nurses and doctors, psychiatric nurses, fertility experts, obstetricians and gynaecologists etc.

It was originally compiled to meet the needs of students on specialist courses and summer schools run by the Centre for Psychoanalytic Studies, at the University of Essex, over the past years, relating clinical applications of psychoanalytic ideas to healthcare provisions. In consultation with local health service managers, a programme was devised consisting of a variety of theoretical seminars and clinical workshops on Family Formation, Perinatal Emotional Disturbance, Psychodynamic Observation, Groups and Organizations, Psychosis, and Work Relationships. The aim of these courses is to enhance existing service provisions by fostering emotional understanding and encouraging professionals in the field to think psychodynamically about family interrelationships and their own interaction with clients.[1]

To the best of our knowledge this comprehensive programme is unique in exploring interweaving psychic realities and unconscious dynamics between family members and the healthcare professional, alongside changing patterns of socio-cultural expectations, ethical considerations and biological realities. The broad spectrum of topics apply self-reflective thinking to the professional's role in work with families at various phases of the life-cycle, in illness and health (in particular, recognition of risk factors relating to areas of emotional vulnerability in clients and their impact on the practitioner). Thus, focus is on all those involved, noting the emergence of specific family and institutional patterns of interaction, their sources and resistance to change.

The readings in this book reflect this complex approach and, hopefully, will be a useful aid for a variety of healthcarers who are not necessarily familiar with this style of thinking.

---

[1] Details of events and courses may be viewed at http://www.essex.ac.uk/centres/psycho or by email: cpsgen@essex.ac.uk or correspondence: Administrator, CPS, University of Essex, Wivenhoe Park, Colchester CO4 3SQ; tel: 01206-873745; fax: 01206 872746.

Contributors

Stella Acquarone, is founder and Director of the School of Infant Mental Health and the Parent-Infant Clinic, London. A PhD in Clinical Psychology, for the past 30 years she has worked as a Child, Adolescent, Adult Psychotherapist in the National Health Service and privately. Over the past 18 years she has pioneered infant-parent psychotherapy, specialising in work with professionals, parents, and families in assessment and treatment of emotional damage, and understanding issues related to child genetic disorders and handicaps, about which she has published widely.

Edna Adelson, was a senior training Psychoanalyst in the British Psychoanalytical Society. She organised the Citizens' Advice Bureaux in London, and also initiated the Family Discussion Bureau (later called the Institute of Marital Studies) at the Tavistock Institute. With her husband, Michael Balint she co-founded the 'Balint Groups' for General Practitioners. Her many papers were collected by Juliet Mitchell and Michael Parsons as *'Before I was I – Psychoanalysis and the imagination*, Free Association Books, 1993.

Esther Bick, was an inspirational teacher who sadly wrote very few papers.With John Bowlby, in 1948 she started the child psychotherapy training at the Tavistock Clinic. Central to this was infant observation, her educational, research and training method which in 1960 she introduced to the training of Child Analysts at the Institute of Psychoanalysis. Her main interest lay in the boundary between sensual and mental experience, and effects of traumatic separation and loss. Published papers:Child Analysis Today (1962), Notes on Infant Observation in Psychoanalytic Training(1964), The experience of the Skin in Early Object Relations (1968) and Further Considerations on the Function of the Skin in Early Object Relations (1986).

Wilfred R. Bion, was a great psychoanalytic innovator, whose wartime work on psychiatric rehabilitation and subsequent intellectual explorations have affected the practice of group psychotherapy, grasp of psychotic processes and epistemological issues of psychoanalytic understanding and throughout the world. His many books include *Experience in Groups* (1961), *Learning from Experience* (1962), *The Elements of Psychoanalysis* (1963), *Transformations* (1965), *Second Thoughts* (1967), and a trilogy called *A Memoire of the Future* (1975, 1977, 1979).

Stanford Bourne, is both psychoanalyst and psychiatrist and was consultant at the Tavistock Clinic in London for many years until his retirement in 1993. In 1968 he wrote a paper exposing the professional attitude to still-birth as a 'non-event'. After working in the field to change maternity practices, With Emanuel Lewis, he co-founded the Perinatal Bereavement Unit at the Tavistock Clinic, London which spread understanding to psychotherapists and counselors too.

Dr. T. Berry Brazelton, is Professor of Pediatrics, Harvard Medical School and founder of the Child Development Unit, Children's Hospital Medical Center, Boston, Mass. His Brazelton Neonatal Assessment Scale is widely used throughout the world. He has authored over 200 papers and several influential books, including *Toddlers and Parents* (1989), *On Becoming a Family* (1992) and *Touchpoints* (1992)

Elizabeth M. Bryan, is Professor of Paediatrics at Queen Charlotte & Chelsea Hospital, London. She has specialised in multiple birth issues and is Medical Director of the Multiple Births Unit there.

Dilys Daws, is founder and first Chair of the Association of Infant Mental Health, UK, a multidisciplinary organisation. As a Child Psychotherapist she worked in the Under-5's section of the Tavistock Child and Family Department for many years, and with professionals in a General Practice Well-Baby Clinic, where famously she saw her role as 'standing next to the weighing scales'. She has specialised in brief interventions for disorders of early childhood and her book *Through the Night: Helping Parents and Sleepless Infants* has indeed helped many parents.

Selma Fraiberg, Psychoanalyst and Professor of Child Psychoanalysis at the University of California in San Francisco, was a world pioneer in applying psychoanalytic understanding to home-based work with parents and their infants in 'psychotherapy in the kitchen'. She supervised a team of 'scientist intermediaries' as she called them, consisting of psychologists, psychiatrists, social workers, and a pediatric nurse. In the cases presented **Edna Adelson,** staff psychologist, and **Vivian Shapiro**, staff social worker were the primary clinicians in the work that took place through the Child Development Project in Ann Arbor, Michigan. Author of *The Magic Years* and *Clinical Studies in IMH.*

Andrè Green, one of the most eminent Freudian French psychoanalysts, has written fourteen books (including *On Private Madness*, Hogarth Press, 1972 from which his contribution to this book is extracted), and some 200 papers. From 1961 to 1967 he participated in Lacan's seminars, and despite disagreements acknowledged Lacan as a 'tremendous intellectual stimulant'. A Fescrift book for Green's 70 birthday, *The Dead Mother'*, was edited by Gregorio Kohon, New Library of Psycho-Analysis, 1999.

Francis Grier, wrote this paper while training at the British Institute of Psychoanalysis. He works as senior marital psychotherapist in the Tavistock Marital Studies Institute, London and his book *'Brief Encounters with Couples – some analytic perspectives'* was published by Karnac, 2001. He is now a qualified psychoanalyst

Joanna Hawthorne, is both Research Psychologist at the Centre for Family Research at the University of Cambridge, and Coordinator of the Brazelton Centre in Great Britain, Addenbrookes NHS Trust, Cambridge where she trains professionals in the use of the NBAS.

Juliet Hopkins, is a Child Psychotherapist, formerly of the Tavistock Child and Family Department, who has done much to promote understanding of Attachment Theory and parent-infant interaction. She was instrumental in planning and teaching on the Child and Adolescent Training section of the British Association of Psychotherapists, served on the Editorial Board of the *Journal of Child Psychotherapy* and is currently Review Editor of the *Journal of Infant Observation*.

Emanuel Lewis, is a British Psychoanalyst. Together with Stanford Bourne he founded the Neonatal Bereavement Unit at the Tavistock Clinic, and together they produced the *Annotated Biography on Psychological Aspects of Stillbrith and Neonatal Death*. They have been very influential in changing professional attitudes to neonatal deaths, and developing a technique to facilitate mourning.

Dr. Mintzer, is in private practice of psychotherapy, Newton and Boston. Her colleague **Dr. Heidelise Als,** is Assistant Professor of Pediatrics (Psychology), Harvard Medical School, and Director of Clinical Research, Child Development Unit, Children's Hospital Medical Center, Boston.

Lynne Murray, is Professor of Psychology in the Winnicott Research Unit at the University of Reading. Since her earliest studies in Edinburgh with Professor Colwyn Trevarthan, she has used innovative methods to explore mother-infant exchanges. With Peter Cooper she wrote *Postpartum Depression and Child Development* in 1997 (New York: Guilford) and a picture book on infant capacities (with Liz Andrews) *The Social Baby*, 2000 which is a gem.

Joan Raphael-Leff, is a practising Psychoanalyst specialising in treating problems related to Reproductivity. She is Professor of Psychoanalysis at the Centre for Psychoanalytic Studies, University of Essex, was Chair of the International Psychoanalytical Association's Committee on Women and Psychoanalysis (1998-2001) and author of over 60 publications and seven books, including *Psychological Processes of Childbearing and Pregnancy - the inside story, Female Experience*, and *Spilt Milk-perinatal loss and breakdown*.

Isca Salzberger-Wittenberg, is a Child Psychotherapist, formerly of the

Child and Adolescent department of the Tavistock Clinic where she was also Vice Chair. She is an inspiring teacher of Infant Observation and acts as consultant to projects worldwide.

Ellen Handler Spitz, is in the department of Art & Art History at Stanford University, California. Books she has written include: *Museums of the Mind: Margrette's Labyrinth and other essays in the Arts; Image and Insight – essays in Psychoanalysis and the Arts; Art and Psyche: a study in Psychoanalysis and aesthetics* and *Inside Picture Books.*

Colwyn Trevarthen, is Professor (Emeritus) of Child Psychology and Psychobiology, and Honorary Research Fellow in the Department of Psychology at the University of Edinburgh, which he joined in 1971. He has published on neuropsychology, brain development and communication in infancy, and his research extends to sensory motor disorders, autism, Rett syndrome and to a recent focus on music and music therapy. He is a Fellow of the Royal Society of Edinburgh and a Member of the Norwegian Academy of Sciences and Letters.

Edward Z. Tronick, was Professor of Psychology, University of Massachusetts, Amherst. Today he is Program Director for the Child Development Unit, Childrens Hospital, Boston and Associate Professor of Pediatrics, Harvard Medical School.

Glen Whitney, is a London based psychologist and psychotherapist working primarily with organizational managers and their teams. His paper was written during training.

Donald W. Winnicott, is possibly the most widely know British psychoanalyst of the Independent Group and past President of the British Psychoanalytical Society. Throughout his working life he combined his two professions as a medical paediatrician and an adult psychoanalyst, during which time it is estimated he saw 60,000 cases. He was also a prolific writer with several books and about 400 published papers to his name. Among the most well known books are: *The Maturational Processes and the Facilitating Environment* (1965), *Collected Papers: Through Paediatrics to Psycho-Analysis* (1975), and *The Piggle: an account of psychoanalytic treatment of a little girl* (1977).

Ken Wright, is a British psychoanalyst in private practice, and fellow of the Centre for Psychoanalytic Studies, Essex. His book *Vision and Separation between Mother and Baby* (1991, Free Association Press) explores how symbol formation arises out of self-other differentiation. He has recently written several papers on the area of creativity which is his special interest. Over 600 publications including *Playing and Reality, Human Nature* and *Collected Papers.*

INTRODUCTION

On wild things within – an introduction to psychoanalytic thinking

JOAN RAPHAEL-LEFF

As I drove up the motorway from Colchester to London, my eye lit on a large furry animal lying face down and motionless by the edge of the road. Passing, I realized it was an oversized teddy bear. For much of the journey my mind played with stories about this far-flung toy. What wild forces had expelled it from a passing car? Who had tossed it out of the window and why? I leave you to your own fantasies about the emotional trajectory of the unfortunate teddy ... but use this unfinished story to make the point that we are all concerned with finding meaning in our internal and external worlds, and linking the two.

Searching for a way to describe the human psyche, Freud[1] likened it to something called a 'mystic writing pad' which you may remember from your childhood. When one lifted the transparent upper sheet of this little notepad, mysteriously what had been written was erased. Yet, if one looked closely at the waxed pad beneath, traces of previous inscriptions could be seen. Freud brought this metaphor of the mind as a perceptual apparatus ready for fresh encounters while unconsciously retaining traces of all that went before.

Pursuing this analogy further, as we shall see from the many people described in this book, those who are unable to clear the upper 'page' have little empty space to receive *new* messages, which get overlaid by, and confused with, the medley of previous notations. Others have such deep underpinning grooves that the 'stylus' always slips into registering the same old pattern. Yet other people are so preoccupied with deciphering the multiplicity of messages superimposed on the 'wax' underlay that they are unable to achieve surface contact at all.

However, the story is even more complicated. Our psychic 'traces' are not mere veridical inscriptions but invested with, and changed by, the meaning

---

[1] S. Freud (1925) The mystic writing pad, *Standard Edition* XIX, London: Hogarth & Institute of Psychoanalysis.

we ascribe to our own histories. Psychoanalytic understanding is based on existence of unconscious aspects of ourselves – that even as interpretations accrue and coalesce so do ambiguities and contradictions in the subjective infrastructure that informs our daily lives. Furthermore, as we interact with others, they activate dormant memories within us, releasing fantasies and re-enactments.

Wildness within and between

The collection of papers in this book has been carefully selected from a wealth of literature, to illustrate both the elusive 'intrapsychic' experiences within a person and the intricate dynamics of 'interpsychic' intertwining between intimates.

The scene is set by this Reader's subtitle, partly borrowed from Maurice Sendak's children's book *Where the Wild Things Are*. It recognizes the complexity of childhood emotions, describing how, sent to his room in the uproar of his tantrum, Max played out his own internal wild things in an imaginary rumpus with monsters who 'roared their terrible roars and gnashed their terrible teeth and rolled their terrible eyes and showed their terrible claws'. But, having become their King, he 'tamed them with the magic trick of staring into their yellow eyes without blinking once'. The story demonstrates how this ability to recognize the wild things as one's own and to master them through *in-sight* is helped by the knowledge that nevertheless one is loved 'best of all'.

This storybook acknowledges that a child engaged in the wild rumpus of a tantrum momentarily loses sight of all the good things. What is less often acknowledged is the effect of a child's emotions on the carers and the wild things they stir up within the adult.

Powerful forces create a raging momentum that escalates if a confrontation turns into a battle of wills which seems to confirm the original grievance. In both child and carer, anxiety then rises as shared wildness provides evidence of potential destructiveness, until guilt takes over from anger. What makes some parents lock horns while others, able to use ingenuity, circumvent rather than reinforce the rumpus? Why do some use diversion tactics to avert the tantrum, while others foreshorten it by *voicing*, rather than succumbing to, the underlying anxieties – about giving up control, experiencing separateness and mixed feelings. And yet others are drawn into the maelstrom. Similarly, what makes an infant's inner turmoil of inexplicable desires and wordless anxieties overpowering to a susceptible adult?

Power of the past

We all approach new situations with old trepidations, and, clearly, the more traumatic the previous situation, the greater the anxiety about current ones. Conversely, confidence in risking new and uncertain happenings is predicated by inner security – and faith in one's own resources and in the world as benign. In other words, *much of what we become as adults is rooted in the soil of earlier experiences, many from our childhoods.* During the early years, when emotions are powerful and the capacity to interpret them uninte-grated, the child (and particularly the 'infant' who lacks the organizing power of words) needs help in making sense of these. As we shall see from the stories in this book, much depends on the responsiveness of caregivers.

Babies have an innate need to socialize and even in the earliest days initiate interactions and display provocative invitations to continue the exchange. Babies are adept at reading faces, and the carer's face not only provides a key to her own emotions but also, as we shall see, acts as a first mirror, a *reflector* in which the infant sees him/herself represented for better or worse. Indeed, a baby's sense of self is partly constituted through unconscious experience of him/herself in the mind of the original carer(s). And we may say that a child's sense of security comes from being reflected and 'held' securely in a whole-some way. This is the mirror of the subtitle. As to the 'ghosts' – this concept will become clearer anon. I provide an overview for each of the four sections, introducing the main themes.

PART I

Face to Face – Containment and Early Exchange

Neonatal research over the last thirty years has demonstrated how, far from being a passive recipient in the early exchange, the infant often determines the form interactions take. Minutes after birth, an undrugged newborn is capable of coordinated responses-fixating, tracking and performing controlled 'pre-reaching' movements, but the most deliberate efforts relate to evoking and initiating intimate contact. It seems that the baby exhibits an innate desire for human connection and intersubjectivity. Some of this groundbreaking research appears in this Reader.

In the first chapter psychoanalyst Ken Wright focuses on the importance of the face and facial expressions in our perceptions of the other, and seeing ourselves through their eyes. He reviews some of the evidence from neonatal research and developmental theorists, referring to pertinent literature. Among these is Winnicott's classic paper, which appears here as Chapter 2. In it he elucidates how the mother's face acts as a 'mirror' through which the child's self-image is actually constructed out of the initial mirroring and elaborated from what he sees in his mother's gaze and experiences in her 'holding' him in mind. Winnicott focuses on what happens if the mother is too preoccupied with herself to mirror her infant. In Chapter 3, Colwyn Trevarthen continues the theme of mirroring, relating evidence from his studies showing that from early days the discriminating infant relates differently to people and objects. He begins communicating in response to the special high-pitched, rhythmic 'intuitive motherese' spoken by his carers, which draws on an innate 'pre-speech' repertoire, unconsciously influenced by the 'baby-talk' of their own infancy. With increasing technological sophistication, including split-screen videoing, neonatal research can now illustrate the precise nature of dialogic exchanges and underpinning physiological changes in both partners. Minutiae of the early exchange can be demonstrated in split-screen videos, showing the infant engaging in 'protolanguage' patterns, foreshadowing rudimentary conversation, including cross-modal imitation, turn-taking and an innate repertoire of gestures. By 4–6 weeks, engaging all senses simultaneously, infants demonstrate patterns of 'conversational' turn-taking with appropriately responsive smiles, cooing vocalizations and lip and tongue 'pre-speech' patterns. They await a reply and revel in the other's enjoyment of the exchange. However, such preverbal dialogue is fraught with difficulties, and in Chapter 4 Ed Tronick brings findings from his video research, showing that, far from being the perfect empathic 'dance' we imagine, only some 30 per cent of moments of emotional exchange between parents and their infants are perfectly matched. He describes the work under-taken by infant as well as carer to repair misunderstandings and coordinate affective goals. This reparation is possible through emotional appreciation of the other's expression and maternal sensitivity. However, once again, in some cases, repair may be disrupted by the parent's disturbance, as unresponsive-ness curtails the evaluative information needed by the infant to pursue devel-opmental tasks. (Both Trevarthen and Tronick have generously updated their classic papers for this Reader, the latter expanding on the theme of repara-tion and uniqueness of each mutual exchange pattern.) In Chapter 5 I follow the issue of reciprocal influence in the primary exchange, exploring parental disturbance when 'wild things' within them are called forth by those in their infant, as well as some of the reasons for parental depression or persecutory feelings. I suggest these arise when their unconscious representation of the two-way exchange is modelled on faulty infantile experience. Often, the baby is ascribed idealized or repudiated aspects of the carer's own baby-self, shaped by the imagined self in the eyes of the archaic carer, and preverbal implicit memories of that caregiver's emotional receptivity or lack of it.

There are two more papers in this section. Neither is easy reading, but both are extremely rewarding and repay the effort. The first, by Esther Bick, describes how the baby is effected when the mothering figure fails to provide the 'binding' force that enables him/her to develop a sense of his/her skin as a boundary separating 'me' from 'not me' (as Winnicott might say). Ordinarily, through identification with the maternal function, the infant can overcome the initial unintegrated state and gradually evolve a sense of self, relating to both external and internal 'spaces'. In the absence of this maternal binding function, the baby has to establish an artificial 'second skin' through use of musculature, clothes or a verbal 'shell'. The consequent fragility will be apparent in later life in the lack of integrated body, posture, motility or mind, illustrated by Bick in four examples from psychoanalysis in relation to problems of dependence and separation in the transference.

In Chapter 7 (especially paragraphs xiv–xxi), Wilfred Bion, also a psycho-analyst, in a paper written six years earlier than Bick's, conveys how initially, lacking distinction between self and other, the baby 'sends' pain, frustrations and fears into the mother by 'projective identification' – 'evacuating' feelings into her. Ideally, she responds by reflecting these emotions back in acceptable form. This is managed through a state of '*reverie*' – her capacity to receive, contain and transform the baby's emotional state. By converting unbearable sensations and raw sense data to 'material for dream thoughts' (which Bion calls 'alpha elements') the mother enables the baby to 'harvest' these experiences of him/herself. When the infant's desire meets with frustration, the absent gratification awakens a thought. Gradually, by internalizing the mother's containing function, the infant evolves an 'apparatus' for thinking these thoughts, that can then be utilized in the absence of the 'breast'-mother. If such external support in managing anxieties is unavailable or insensitive or distorted, rather than detoxified feelings made tolerable through maternal processing, the baby takes back a sense of (the mother's) incapacity to deal with anxiety, resulting in a 'nameless dread', or a feeling of unacceptability, which persists, often into adulthood.

These ideas about the breakdown of the early 'interplay' between maternal reverie and the baby's 'rudimentary consciousness' are complex, disturbing and extremely condensed. I urge the reader not to be put off by the difficult paper, but to reread these sections again at different times when new understanding will occur. Basically, what Bion conveys is that '*undigested' experience cannot contribute to psychic growth*. Furthermore, as we see in the next section on 'unprocessed residues', where primary containment has failed, children often grow up into seemingly rational adults, with an undertow of irrational forces. In work situations, as in daily life, people erupt in unrealistic expectations of 'perfection', disappointed yearning for 'completeness', intolerance of frustration, sudden paranoia or flaring aggression in 'road rage' or racism, or, turned back against the self, in painful bouts of depression. But, above all, vulnerable people are thrust back into primitive anxieties when parenting a baby, retriggering these wild forces. These reappear not as conscious memories but as embodied ones, compulsions to repeat unresolved issue or re-enactments, as 'ghosts' from the past revisit the home.

CHAPTER 1

Face and façade – the mother's face as the baby's mirror[1]

KEN WRIGHT

In this paper I shall focus on some early interactions between mother and baby and their potential significance for later development. Many of these early interactions involve the face, which in later life is often felt to have a special connection with the self or person. Perhaps because it is a source of information, not merely an object to be manipulated, the mother's face seems to be experienced from early on as different from other parts of the mother's body and becomes an early focus of infant attention (Wright, 1991). It retains this special significance throughout the life-cycle.

Face as core of identity

Consider the following questions: What part of the human body do we look at when we want to get to know someone? What part of the body does the passport man scrutinise at immigration? Where do lovers look during moments of closeness and intimacy? And where does a mother gaze as she tries to fathom her newborn baby?

In each case, though with differing purpose and emphasis, attention is focused on the face - the face both as locus of identity and important source of information about the other person. Human identity is often treated as though *located* in the face, so that the other person is recognised and known through their physiognomy and facial expression. To say this does not detract from the fact that we often make use of other cues. We attend to voices and the things people say, to their actions and the way they move, to their dress and the way they furnish their houses - not least, to the way they relate to those around them. Nevertheless, there remains something basic in the link between identity and the human face, such that we frequently experience the face as the 'truest' and most direct route to the inner person.

[1] Written for the CPS Summer School, University of Essex, 2001.

It is, however, a link that is often taken for granted – so basic that we think about it no more than the air we breathe. But just as we *may* become aware of breathing when there are impediments to it – as with respiratory infections or conditions of high altitude – so we *may* become aware of our faces, and uncomfortably so, when we are struggling with inner difficulties.

For example, if someone feels unsure of himself, he may become over-concerned with what others think about him, and this often translates into anxiety about appearance. There is then heightened self-consciousness and a feeling of being observed or looked at that may go counter to reason. In such moments, a person seems to regard himself from the outside, as though he were other to himself. There is a shift of focus from one's *own* experience to an *external* perspective, as though momentarily one existed only in the mirror of the other person.

The other person as mirror

The idea that the other person can be a mirror of the self is not just a poetic metaphor but a key concept in certain schools of social psychology (e.g. Cooley, 1902; Mead, 1934). To understand what this means it is helpful to consider the process of looking at oneself in an *actual* mirror. Normally, this involves a *checking-up* procedure. It is as though we check our reflections to make sure they do not differ from expectation – how we think they should look or how we want them to look. When unsure of himself, a person becomes overpreoccupied with his reflection in the mirror and may spend longer than usual checking up on it. Frequently, attempts are made to alter it, thereby creating a mask or disguise that conceals the true person. For example, a woman might spend hours at her mirror, transforming herself with 'make-up' into the 'beautiful woman' of her fantasy. Or a man might become overconcerned about his baldness and completely obsessed with trying to conceal it. Similarly, some people spend fortunes on plastic surgery – on facelifts, wrinkle removal, hair implants and so on. In such cases, one can think of the person as altering his/her appearance in order to manipulate the impression made on the other person. All this is quite normal when it remains within certain limits. But, if it becomes excessive, it can take over a person's life.

Thus it is common for plastic surgeons to see people with so-called *body dysmorphic disorder* in which the individual believes that his life has been ruined by having an organ of the wrong shape or size. The nose is too long, too short or too bumpy; the ears are too small, too big or protruding; the breasts are too big, too small or misshapen. Such individuals frequently imagine their life has been ruined by the supposed defect. They become fixated on the idea that a simple operation would make everything all right so that they could at last become the person they have wanted to be. It seems that the visible appearance of the body in such cases – often the face, or some part of it – has usurped the inner sense of self. The *external* image – the way the person looks from the outside – has superseded the inner life of feeling.

Psychological investigation frequently reveals that such people have fragile and insecure personalities. They hope to cover up or redeem their felt weaknesses by creating a different kind of external appearance. In the extreme case – for example when a young person is developing serious psychological illness – many hours a day can be spent gazing at the reflection in the mirror. Such a person may find it difficult to say what prompts such an activity, but sometimes it seems that the whole sense of self has become uncertain. The image in the mirror now somehow reassures the person, helping to bolster the feeling of crumbling identity. Perhaps, as the French psychoanalyst Jacques Lacan suggested (Lacan, 1949), it is the coherence and completeness of this image that counterbalances the sense of fragmentation so often present in psychotic illness.

There is one further situation that highlights the importance of the face to a sense of personal identity. When a person's face is severely mutilated – as, for example, by burns or injury – it creates a crisis both for the individual and for those around him. Close acquaintances may struggle to hold onto their sense of the person they once knew; casual contacts may experience a sense of disruption in the encounter. At best, there is awkwardness, a sense of derailment in normal relatedness; at worst, it may feel that the human has given way to something monstrous and strange. Invariably, the sufferer too feels dislocated from his familiar world. When he looks in the actual mirror, he perceives someone unrecognisable; when he looks in the faces of others, he perceives confusion and embarrassment. Facial injury thus radically threatens the whole sense of personal identity.

I have said enough to illustrate how the face and its expressions are interwoven with the fabric of human relatedness and underpin human identity in both its subjective and objective aspects. I now want to say something about the rather ambivalent way that psychoanalysts have regarded the face in both theory and practice.

Psychoanalysis and the face

Given its importance in human identity, it might be expected that the face would have been a major preoccupation in psychoanalytic thought. With notable exceptions this has not been the case and it is interesting to speculate on the reasons for this omission.

Freud originally developed a method of treatment in which he asked the patient to lie on a couch and sat *facing* her with a view to hypnotising her.

Gradually, however, a new and original method of treatment evolved, in which hypnosis was replaced by the patient voluntarily giving free rein to her thoughts, while Freud sat *behind* the couch, ostensibly to reduce his influence upon the patient but also to escape the feeling of being constantly looked at. This, of course, deprived him of seeing the patient's facial expressions. For the most part, psychoanalysts followed suit, thus depriving them of the single most important channel of non-verbal communication. Surely this must be part of the reason for the face being so little considered in psychoanalytic theory.

Psychoanalysis has always regarded the body as important, but, traditionally, this has been a body without a face. It possesses mouth, hands, breast, penis, vagina, these being the organs through which basic instincts are satisfied. But the face, with its rich *communicative* significance, has been largely ignored. It is paradoxical that a method of treatment so concerned with communication should so have ignored the primary channel for emotional expression (Darwin, 1872). But this is how it was, at least for the first seventy years of psychoanalytic thinking.

In the 1950s, things began to change. Perhaps this came about through psychoanalysts beginning to work in more varied situations, which now included settings in which observer and observed began to *face* each other. Some analysts, for example Rene Spitz in America, began to observe infants in their natural context – that is, in normal interaction with their mothers (Spitz, 1965). Other analysts, for example Harold Searles, also in America, began to work with psychotic patients who were often deeply regressed and sometimes mute (Searles, 1965). Both types of situation were ones in which words were no longer the primary medium of communication – indeed, for obvious reasons, non-verbal communication was often more important. Thus Spitz, observing infants and mothers smiling at each other, began to include the mother's face and the infant's smile in his formulations of infant development (e.g. Spitz and Wolf, 1946); and Searles, working *face to face* with regressed schizophrenic patients, increasingly stressed the importance of the face in communication between patient and analyst (Searles, 1963). It is thus not hard to see how setting, ways of working and types of patient may have influenced the kind of material gathered.

To illustrate this, I have given two examples of pioneer work from America. Finally, I will give an example from the highly original work of the British psychoanalyst Donald Winnicott. Winnicott was a paediatrician who only later trained as a psychoanalyst. Again, it seems, the setting had a crucial importance. Like Spitz, Winnicott worked with mothers and babies – this time in a paediatric clinic – and his work was always influenced by this experience. Winnicott's accounts of infant development differ significantly from those of his contemporaries, notably Melanie Klein, in that they give a vitally important part to the *actual* mother in the developmental process. Communication between mother and baby lies at the heart of his formulations, and the infant's relation to the mother's face as mirror to himself provides the subject of one of his most important papers (Winnicott, 1967).

To summarise: classical psychoanalysis neglected the role of the face in human development and placed the satisfaction of bodily needs at the centre of everything. Important as these needs are, it led to a bias in understanding, in which the social and relational part of the personality had somehow to be derived from the satisfaction of bodily experience. Psychoanalytic theory thus missed the primary relational core of the human personality in the same way that it failed to provide a place for the human face. This began to change as some psychoanalysts began to work with patients in face-to-face settings and directly with mothers and infants. I have given three examples of such work, but, because it is important in a different way, I want to discuss a fourth – the work of John Bowlby.

The work of John Bowlby

Most people have heard of Bowlby's Attachment Theory and his earliest accounts of this in *Child Care and the Growth of Love* (1965). Attachment Theory is spelled out and developed more fully in his three-volume major work *Attachment and Loss* (1969, 1973, 1980). *Child Care and the Growth of Love* is a study of young children who had been separated from their mothers. Reviewing the consequences of separation, Bowlby comes to the original view, at least among psychoanalysts other than the British Object Relations theorists, that the infant's need for its mother was not, as commonly stated, based on the mother being the object who satisfied the infant's bodily needs. On the contrary, the attachment need is primary – itself something like an instinct – and important in its own right. Bowlby thus comes to the view that *a primary need for the mother was there from the beginning*. He supports this view, not only with clinical material, but with evidence from *ethology*, which studies the attachment behaviour of other mammals. In short, Bowlby argues that the way the infant responds to separation from the mother is not just secondary to the loss of her bodily care and provision but results from the severing of a primary attachment bond. It is thus attachment itself that is basic and underpins the *social* nature of the human being.

If Bowlby is right – and a good deal of evidence suggests that he is – the maintenance of attachment between mother and infant is a fundamental need, as basic as the need for feeding, bodily care and sensory contact. Stemming from this is the view that the infant has built-in equipment serving this attachment need. Thus, just as a baby monkey has built-in equipment enabling it to cling physically to its mother from the beginning, so literally maintaining attachment to her, the human infant has built-in equipment enabling it to *provoke* attachment behaviour and bonding on the part of the mother. Thus, although the human infant's behaviour does not *guarantee* proximity to the mother in the way that the monkey's clinging does, it can and does help the mother to form an intense bond with the infant, so helping to ensure her continuing presence. Bowlby sees the infant's smiling response to the mother, central to Spitz's research, within this framework – as part of the infant's built-in repertoire that helps to engage the mother in nurturing and caring behaviour. (The smiling response, incidentally, is the infant's tendency to smile in response to smiles or other approaches from the caring person.)

Obviously, there are important differences between the infant's smiling response and the clinging behaviour of baby monkeys. The smiling response begins within a few weeks of birth and becomes intensified and more specific to the mother in the following weeks and months; the monkey's clinging behaviour is fully present from birth. But, whereas in monkeys attachment behaviour is relatively one-sided – the baby monkey clinging and holding onto the mother as she swings through the trees – in human babies, attachment is *interactive*. The baby's smile *elicits* a smile from the mother, and this in turn reinforces and promotes the infant's smiling. Human attachment behaviour is thus *mutually reinforcing and mutually interdependent*. For many researchers, this mutually interactive behaviour is the basis of a specifically human social relatedness. From the beginning it takes the form of *quasi*-communicative sequences which build gradually into a kind of social repertoire. Within a few months, there will have developed complex *sequences* of smiling and vocalisation between mother and infant that are highly specific to a particular mother–infant pair. They constitute a kind of *proto-conversation* and give the impression of being important and enjoyable to both participants. The idea of proto-conversation has been developed, particularly by Colwyn Trevarthen (1979).[1]

Empirical infant research

Although every psychoanalyst in training has to observe an infant in his or her home setting weekly for at least one year, psychoanalysts who observe infant behaviour in a strictly empirical fashion are extremely unusual, and in this sense, Bowlby's scientific and observational approach was atypical. However, the past 30 years or so have seen a burgeoning of *empirical*

---

[1] See Chapter 3 in this book [Ed.].

research on infant behaviour, much of it unconstrained by psychoanalytic preconceptions (Brazleton, 1976; Murray, 1988, 1992; Stern, 1985; Trevarthen, 1979). This has provided interesting data for psychoanalysts to consider. One of the things to emerge from this work is the fact that a very young infant has highly developed perceptual capacities, allowing it to follow, and often imitate, maternal behaviours in extraordinary detail. Video-recording techniques have demonstrated many different examples, often difficult to detect with the naked eye. These have been classified and sequenced in various ways, and cumulatively create a picture of infancy that is far more complex than was once envisaged. The details are less important than the principle, which is that mother and infant are intensely enmeshed with each other in highly specific ways that have been built up and learned between them, and cannot be replicated by an alternative carer. It is not only the case, then, that infants of a few days have learned the smell of their mother's milk and will preferentially respond to that smell over and above the smell of other breast milk. The enmeshment is social and involves complex sequences of interlocking responses.

This research shows that what goes on between mother and baby is highly specific for any particular mother–infant pair. From the beginning, the baby is immersed in a medium of preverbal 'conversation' with the mother and almost certainly depends on this aspect of the mother at least as much as on her purely physical care. These findings lend a new dimension to the idea of attachment: Separate an infant from its mother and you break a pattern of relating that within a few weeks of birth is highly specific and personal. In this context, the idea that carers can be changed without trauma becomes hard to sustain.

To flesh out these remarks, I shall give one example from the work of Brazleton and Cramer, noted in their book *The Earliest Relationship* (1991). These authors note that many of the earlier sequences between infant and mother are based on imitative behaviour within the couple, but, as time goes on, difference and variation between the two parties begin to be important in the interactive sequences. An example of such a sequence, which involves much mutual gazing, smiling, vocalisation and looking away, they call 'entrainment'. This is how Brazleton and Cramer describe it:

> Mother and infant begin to anticipate each other's responses in long sequences. Having learned each other's requirements, they can set up a rhythm as though with a set of rules. The power of this rhythm soon establishes an expectancy ... So powerful is this [expectancy] that it seems to carry each member of the dyad along ... Like a first violinist, one member can then 'entrain' the behaviour of the other by instituting the rhythm of attention and inattention which has already been established as the base for their synchrony. (p. 124)

The musical analogy of violin players responding to each other, and drawing the other in, is highly evocative. Each mother and infant develops as a mutually interdependent dyad in which such behaviours and interactions are cued and unfold according to mutually shared, intuitive 'rules'. Each attunes and adjusts to the other, and each, presumably, depends on this capability of the other. They are like dancing partners who know each other's moves and can anticipate them. It is this sort of idea that lends depth and detail to the idea of attachment, and, equally, a poignant sense to the meaning of infant loss.

It can be seen then that observational studies of this kind have greatly enlarged our conception of what goes on between mother and baby. What they do not attempt to do, however, is to speculate about the inner experience of an infant enmeshed in such interdependent sequences. For this reason I want to discuss the work of Donald Winnicott who has tried to address this issue.

Winnicott's contribution

Infant research was in its infancy at the time Winnicott was writing in the late 1950s, and probably for this reason he paid little attention to it. He did, however, have a keenly intuitive sense of the enveloping nature of the relationship with the mother and how enmeshed the baby might feel within such an early maternal environment. He is often quoted as saying: 'There is no such thing as a baby!' – by which he meant it was nonsensical to consider a baby on its own, because there was always a mother, or mother–infant dyad, within which the baby's embryonic *emotional* self was held and nurtured. In the first few months, according to Winnicott, the baby existed in *a merged-in state* with the mother – there was no real sense of separateness from her. The mother was an 'environment' – a phase, you might say, of the infant's experience – but not someone objectively perceived as an independent source of action. In general, she fulfilled the baby's expectations – she was *in synch* with the baby's rhythms.

Initially, Winnicott had in mind the feeding situation – he thought that the post-partum mother was in a highly sensitive state that enabled her to sense, and then offer her breast in a way that more or less fulfilled the baby's anticipation. Only as she adapted less completely might the baby experience her as different or separate. (Separateness in this sense means *not* conforming to expectation, *not* providing what is needed or providing it in a way that is out of synch). It is thus not difficult to relate Winnicott's ideas to those of Brazleton and Cramer, even though Winnicott's work for the most part predated theirs.

Winnicott speculated that, when the mother behaved in this adaptive, 'in synch' kind of way, the baby had a good experience. However, this was not just because she provided what the baby wanted, but for another important reason. The fulfilment of the baby's expectation allowed the baby to feel a kind of potency in relation to the environment. It was as though the baby could feel it had *created* what the mother had given, out of its own imagining. The attunement of the mother's response enabled the baby to feel: 'I can!' 'I am!' And this, according to Winnicott, laid the foundations of a sense of self. Winnicott (1967) later extended this earlier position in interesting ways. In a paper called 'Mirror role of mother and family in child development'[2] he shifted his attention from the breast to the interaction of the infant with the mother's face. This was important because it placed the social and communicative domain at the centre of development.

'What does a baby see', asks Winnicott, 'when he or she looks into the mother's face? I am suggesting that, ordinarily, what the baby sees is himself or herself. In other words, the mother is looking at the baby, and what she looks like is related to what she sees there' (1967, p. 112). Winnicott asserts that the baby at this stage does not see the mother primarily as an object - in other words, her face indicative of *her* mood; rather, he sees it as a kind of mirror, reflecting *his* moods and expressions, her expression resonating with his own feeling. So once again the mother's response appears as a phase of the infant's emotional self. Although in reality 'out there', it realises and makes visible what is subjective and 'in here' - in other words, a part of the baby. Hence the image of the mother's face as the infant's first mirror.

Winnicott's formulation transforms a behavioural sequence - the mother's response to the infant's smiling response - into something formative of infant self-experience. Just as earlier the mother's way of giving the breast had made the baby feel good and creative, so now the mother's affirming smile catches and 'solidifies' the 'good smiling feeling' inside the infant. The infant feeling is realised and enhanced by the mother's echoing response. It is not far from this to the idea that human experience needs to be captured and reflected by another person in this way for it to be experienced as fully real. In this sense it could be said that we only come fully alive within another person - only, that is, when the other person provides a resonating confirmation of our nascent feeling.

This is not to say that in adult life each and every experience must undergo this transforming passage through another person - there are other ways of keeping experience alive. It does suggest, however, that, at least in infancy, there is a constant need for reflecting response if the young infant is to develop and maintain a lively sense of self.

---

[2] See Chapter 2 in this volume [Ed.].

Maternal attunement

No account of early mother–infant dialogue would be complete without mention of a type of interaction that has come to be known as *attunement*. This concept has been developed by Emde (1988) and Stern (1985), both neonatal researchers and psychoanalysts influential in disseminating studies on mother–infant interchanges. The concept refers to a type of maternal behaviour that occurs at its height in the period immediately preceding the onset of language. Stern describes attunement as 'the recasting of an affective state' (Stern, 1985, p. 161). It is not dissimilar to Winnicott's reflecting maternal response, but, pertaining to an older age group, it involves a more diverse range of infant behaviours and a richer repertoire of maternal responses. What in effect Stern describes is something like this: Whatever the infant does, there is always a background feeling state, a state of tension or arousal that is integral to what is unfolding. It is not necessarily part of the infant's awareness but nonetheless present in the behaviour as its affective accompaniment. Stern is clear that these affects are not the same as those normally described as the basic human emotions: joy, anger, fear, disgust and so on. They occupy a different register and wax and wane in a more continuous fashion. Whether the baby is crawling about the floor, trying to stand up, reaching for a toy, or merely pulling the cat's tail, they form a background state with a changing but specific feeling quality. One of the things we register in another human being, according to Stern, is the changing 'shapes' of such feelings – the way for example that excitement and interest surge and subside, ebb and flow, sustain themselves and fade away. Thus, if a child is reaching for a toy, we may sense his eager intensity in going towards it, his suspense in not quite reaching it, his pleasure in managing to get it and his excitement in finally playing with it. A mother, he says, is intuitively, and almost continuously, in touch with such states in her baby, experiencing them through a barely conscious identification in the tensions and rhythms of her own body. This experiencing through identification is one part of attunement. The other part is the mother's *response*, which again is intuitive and often barely conscious. Observation reveals that mothers have a way of playing back to the baby what they have experienced through identification. Such playbacks take the form of mini performances that reflect and re-enact the mother's perception of the baby's changing state. For example, as the baby reaches for the toy she may make a series of sounds that somehow capture and portray the 'shape' of the baby's experience in the moment that has just passed. The pattern of her vocalisations, or sometimes the shape and rhythm of her gestures, will vividly portray the shape and rhythm of the baby's arousal.

It is important to realise that what the mother unwittingly provides is a certain *objectification* of the baby's feeling state. It is the counterpart of

Winnicott's baby seeing itself in the smile of the mother, or finding in the mother's breast the shape of its own anticipation. In Stern's attunement response the baby can potentially see in the mother's vocalisations and gestures the 'shape' and form of its own most recent experience.

At the end of this trajectory – maternal adaptation, mirroring, attunement – we might expect to find empathy. I mean by this that, when language comes on the scene, reflection and understanding can be conveyed in words. I can tell you how I have shared in your experience. In this paper I have been concerned with something that precedes words, a dialogue around the infant's feelings that is conveyed and communicated in non-verbal forms in both directions. I am suggesting both that the roots of later empathy may lie in this dialogue and that the capacity to *have* a feeling, rather than merely to express it, is established in this reverberating circuit between mother and infant.

Maternal depression

I have discussed a type of maternal responsiveness and dialogue that appears to foster the development of the infant self. My discussion would therefore be incomplete if I failed to consider maternal depression. Postnatal maternal depression is not only extremely common but raises the spectre of an unresponsive mother. If she becomes involved with herself, and loses her keen sense of identification with her baby, it is clear that she may be impaired in her capacity to respond in a lively way. It is therefore clear that maternal depression could be devastating in its consequences. From the baby's point of view the mother is no longer a lively and resonating mirror. She is to all intents a 'dead mother',[3] either giving nothing back or emanating a feeling of lifelessness. What the baby of such a mother might feel is hard to say with certainty. But if the baby who is responded to feels an enhancement of its feeling state – a sense of 'Yes! I've done that!' or 'Yes, I am that!' – it seems probable that the baby of a depressed mother might feel something very different: 'I've done that, so what?' 'I've smiled and yet nothing happens.' According to this view, the growth of the baby's emotional self may become stunted.

There has in fact been significant research on the effects of maternal depression on infant development (see especially Murray, 1988, 1992).[4] This work not only has shown that depressed mothers do indeed respond less than their non-depressed counterparts but also has demonstrated measurable effects of such depression on a range of developmental indices. Emotional and cognitive development are significantly impaired.

[3] See Chapter 13 in this volume [Ed.].
[4] See also Chapter 20 in this volume [Ed.].

Psychoanalysts usually see patients long after childhood is over, and all we can do is imaginatively reconstruct what the past of the patient may have been like (e.g. Green, 1983). Not infrequently we see patients who seem to be emotionally stunted and dead, and often, in these cases, we seem to find evidence of a mother who was in some way emotionally removed from her child. We may not be able to reconstruct the childhood of such patients in terms of detailed interactions. But often the consulting room in such cases seems filled with a depressive and deadening presence, and the analyst then feels he knows something of what it was like to be the child of this patient's mother.

Since this paper is addressed to front-line health professionals, I shall not develop this clinical theme. It suffices to illustrate that there are casualties of maternal depression and emphasises the immense importance of primary care work. The prevention, recognition and early treatment of maternal depression therefore poses a major challenge to the primary care services.

References

Bowlby, J. (1965) *Child Care and the Growth of Love*. Harmondsworth: Penguin.

Bowlby, J. (1969, 1973, 1980) *Attachment and Loss. Vol. 1. Attachment.* [1969]; *Vol. 2. Separation* [1973]; *Vol. 3. Loss* [1980]. London: Hogarth Press and the Institute of Psycho-Analysis.

Brazleton, T.B. (1976) Early parent–infant reciprocity. In: V.C.Vaughan and T.B. Brazleton (eds), *The Family. Can It Be Saved?* New York: Yearbook.

Brazleton, T.B. and Cramer, B.G. (1991). *The Earliest Relationship. Parents, Infants and the Drama of Early Attachment.* London: Karnac.

Cooley, C.H. (1902) *Human Nature and the Social Order*. New York: Scribner's.

Darwin, C. (1872) *The Expression of the Emotions in Man and Animals*. London: John Murray.

Emde, R.N.(1988) Development terminable and interminable. Innate and motivational factors from infancy. *International Journal of Psychoanalysis*. 69: 23–42.

Green, A. (1983) The dead mother. In: *On Private Madness*. London: Hogarth Press, 1986.

Lacan, J. (1949) The mirror image as formative of the function of the 'I'. In: *Ecrits: A Selection*. Trans. A. Sheridan, pp. 1–7.

Mead, G.H. (1934) *Mind, Self and Society*. Ed. C.W. Morris. Chicago: University of Chicago Press.

Murray, L. (1988) Effect of post-natal depression on infant development: Direct studies of early mother–infant interaction. In: Brockington, I. and Kumar, R. (eds), Motherhood and Mental Illness, Vol. 2. Bristol: John Wright.

Murray, L. (1992) Impact of post-natal depression on infant development. *Journal of Child Psychology and Psychiatry*, 33(3), 543–61.

Searles, H. (1963) The place of neutral therapist responses in psychotherapy with the schizophrenic patient. In: H. Searles (1965).

Searles, H. (1965) *Collected Papers on Schizophrenia and Related Topics*. London: The Hogarth Press.

Spitz, R.A. (1965) *The First Year of Life*. New York: International Universities Press.

Spitz, R.A. and Wolf, K.M. (1946) The smiling response: A contribution to the ontogenesis of social relations. *Genetic Psychology Monograph*, 34, 57–105.

Stern, D. (1985) *The Interpersonal World of the Infant. A View from Psychoanalysis and Developmental Psychology*. New York: Basic Books.

Trevarthen, C. (1979) Communication and cooperation in early infancy: Description of primary intersubjectivity. In: M.M. Bullowa (ed.), *Before Speech: The Beginning of Interpersonal Communication*. New York: Cambridge University Press.

Winnicott, D.W. (1951) Transitional objects and transitional phenomena: A study of the first not-me possession. In: D.W. Winnicott (1958) *Collected Papers - Through Paediatrics to Psycho-Analysis*. London: Tavistock.

Winnicott, D.W. (1967) Mirror role of mother and family in child development. In: D.W. Winnicott (1971) *Playing and Reality*. London: Tavistock.

Wright, K. (1991) *Vision and Separation. Between Mother and Baby*. London: Free Association Books.

CHAPTER 2

Mirror-role of mother and family in child development[1]

DONALD W. WINNICOTT

My theme is quite simple. It is that in individual emotional development *the precursor of the mirror is the mother's face*. I wish to refer to the normal aspect of this and also to its psychopathology. Jacques Lacan's paper 'Le Stade du Miroir' (1949) has certainly influenced me. He refers to the use of the mirror in each individual's ego-development. However, Lacan does not think of the mirror in terms of the mother's face in the way that I wish to do here.

I refer only to infants who have sight. The wider application of the idea to cover infants with poor sight or no sight must be left over till the main theme is stated. The bare statement is this: In the early stages of the emotional development of the human infant a vital part is played by the environment which is in fact not yet separated off from the infant by the infant. Gradually, the separating off of the not-me from the me takes place, and the pace varies according to the infant and according to the environment. The major changes take place in the separating-out of the mother as an objectively perceived environmental feature. If no one person is there to be mother, the infant's developmental task is infinitely complicated.

Let me simplify the environmental function and briefly state that it involves:

1 holding
2 handling
3 object-presenting

---

[1] This paper first appeared in *The Predicament of the Family*, edited by Peter Lomas, pp. 26–33, London: Hogarth & Institute of Psychoanalysis, 1967, and is reprinted here by kind permission the Winnicott Trust.

The infant may respond to these environmental provisions, but the result in the baby is maximal personal maturation. By the word *maturation* at this stage I intend to include the various meanings of the word *integration*, as well as psychosomatic interrelating and object-relating.

A baby is held, and handled satisfactorily, and then is presented with an object in such a way that the baby's legitimate experience of omnipotence is not violated. The result can be that the baby is able to use the object, and to feel as if this object is a subjective object and created by the baby.

All this belongs to the beginning, and out of all this the immense complexities develop which comprise the emotional and mental development of the infant and child.

Now, at some point, the baby takes a look round. Perhaps a baby at the breast does not look at the breast. Looking at the face is more likely to be a feature (Gough, 1962). What does the baby see there? To get to the answer we must draw on our experience with psychoanalytic patients who reach to very early phenomena and yet who can verbalize (when they feel they can do this) without insulting the delicacy of what is preverbal, unverbalized and unverbalizable, except perhaps in poetry.

What does the baby see when he or she looks at the mother's face? I am suggesting that, ordinarily, what the baby sees is himself or herself. In other words, the mother is looking at the baby and *what she looks like is related to what she sees there*. All this is too easily taken for granted. I am asking that this which is done naturally well by mothers who are caring for their infants shall not be taken for granted. I can make my point by going straight over to the case of the baby whose mother reflects her own mood or, worse still, the rigidity of her own defences. In such a case what does the baby see?

Of course, nothing can be said about the single occasions on which a mother could not respond. Many babies, however, do have to have a long experience of not getting back what they are giving. They look and they do not see themselves. There are consequences. *First*, their own creative capacity begins to atrophy, and in some way or other they look around for other ways of getting something of themselves back from the environment. They may succeed by some other method, and blind infants need to get themselves reflected through other senses than that of sight. Indeed, a mother whose face is fixed may be able to respond in some other way. Most mothers can respond when the baby is in trouble or is aggressive, and especially when the baby is ill. *Secondly*, the baby gets settled into the idea that when he or she looks what is seen is the mother's face. The mother's face is not then a mirror. So perception takes the place of apperception, takes the place of that which might have been the beginning of a significant exchange with the world, a two-way process in which self-enrichment alternates with the discovery of meaning in the world of seen things.

Naturally, there are halfway stages in this scheme of things. Some babies do not quite give up hope, and they study the object and do all that is possible to see in the object some meaning which ought to be there if only it could be felt. Some babies, tantalized by this type of relative maternal failure, study the variable maternal visage in an attempt to predict the mother's mood, just exactly as we all study the weather. The baby quickly learns to make a forecast: 'Just now it is safe to forget the mother's mood and to be spontaneous, but any minute the mother's face will become fixed and her mood will then dominate, and my own personal needs must then be withdrawn otherwise my central self may suffer insult.'

Immediately beyond this in the direction of pathology is predictability that is precarious and that strains the baby to the limits of his or her capacity to allow for events. This brings a threat of chaos, and the baby will organize withdrawal, or will not look except to perceive, as a defence. A baby so treated will grow up puzzled about mirrors and what the mirror has to offer. If the mother's face is unresponsive, then the mirror is a thing to be looked at but not to be looked into.

To return to the normal progress of events, when the average girl studies her face in the mirror she is reassuring herself that the mother-image is there and that the mother can see her and that the mother is *en rapport* with her. When girls and boys in their secondary narcissism look in order to see beauty and to fall in love, there is already evidence that doubt has crept in about their mother's continued love and care. So the man who falls in love with beauty is quite different from the man who loves a girl and feels she is beautiful and can see what is beautiful about her.

I will not try to press home my idea, but instead I will give some examples so that the idea I am presenting can be worked over by the reader.

Illustration I

I refer first to a woman of my acquaintance who married and brought up three fine male children. She was also a good support to her husband who had a creative and important job. Behind the scenes this woman was always near to depression. She seriously disturbed her marital life by waking every morning in a state of despair. She could do nothing about it. The resolution of the paralysing depression: at last it was time to get up and, at the end of her ablutions and dressing, she could 'put on her face'. Now she felt rehabilitated and could meet the world and take up her family responsibilities. This exceptionally intelligent and responsible person did eventually react to a misfortune by developing a chronic depressive state, which in the end became hidden in a chronic and crippling physical disorder.

Here is a recurring pattern, easily matched in the social or clinical experience of everyone. This case only exaggerates that which is normal. The exaggeration is of the task of getting the mirror to notice and approve. The woman had to be her own mother. If she had had a daughter, she would surely have found great relief, but perhaps a daughter would have suffered because of having too much importance in correcting this woman's uncertainty about her own mother's sight of her.

The reader will already be thinking of Francis Bacon. I refer here not to the Bacon who said: 'A beautiful face is a silent commendation' and 'That is the best part of beauty, which a picture cannot express' but to the exasperating and skilful and challenging artist of our time who goes on and on painting the human face distorted significantly. From the standpoint of this paper, this Francis Bacon is seeing himself in his mother's face but with some twist in him or her that maddens both him and us. I know nothing of this artist's private life, and I only bring him in because he forces his way into any present-day discussion of the face and the self. Bacon's faces seem to me to be far removed from perception of the actual; in looking at faces he seems to me to be painfully striving towards being seen, which is at the basis of creative looking.

I see that I am linking apperception with perception by postulating an historical process (in the individual) which depends on being seen.

When I look I am seen, so I exist.

I can now afford to look and see.

I now look creatively and what I apperceive I also perceive.

In fact I take care not to see what is not there to be seen (unless I am tired).

Illustration II

A patient reports: 'I went to a coffee bar last night, and I was fascinated to see the various characters there', and she describes some of these characters. Now, this patient has a striking appearance, and, if she were able to use herself, she could be the central figure in any group. I asked: 'Did anyone look at you?' She was able to go over to the idea that she did in fact draw some of the fire, but she had taken along with her a man friend, and she could feel that it was at him that people were looking.

From here the patient and I were together able to make a preliminary survey of the patient's early history and childhood in terms of being seen in a way that would make her feel she existed. Actually, the patient had had a deplorable experience in this respect.

This subject then got lost for the time being in other types of material, but in a way this patient's whole analysis revolves round this 'being seen' for what she in fact is, at any one moment, and at times the being actually seen in a subtle way is for her the main thing in her treatment. This patient is particularly sensitive as a judge of painting and indeed of the visual arts, and lack of beauty disintegrates her personality so that she recognizes it by herself as feeling awful (disintegrated or depersonalized).

Illustration III

I have a research case, a woman who has had a very long analysis. This patient has come through, late in life, to feeling 'real' and a cynic might say: to what end? But she feels it has been worth while, and I myself have learned a great deal of what I know of early phenomena through her.

This analysis involved a serious and deep regression to infantile dependence. The environmental history was severely disturbing in many respects, but here I am dealing with the effect of the mother's depression. This has been worked over repeatedly, and, as an analyst, I have had to displace this mother in a big way in order to enable the patient to get started as a person.

Just now, near the end of my work with her, the patient has sent me a portrait of her nurse. I had already had her mother's portrait, and I have got to know the rigidity of the mother's defences very intimately. It became obvious that the mother (as the patient said) had chosen a depressed nurse to act for her so that she might avoid losing touch with the children altogether. A lively nurse would automatically have 'stolen' the children from the depressed mother.

This patient has a marked absence of just that which characterizes so many women, an interest in the face. She certainly had no adolescent phase of self-examination in the mirror, and now she only looks in the mirror to remind herself that she 'looks like an old hag' (patient's own words).

This same week this patient found a picture of my face on a book-cover. She wrote to say she needed a bigger version so that she could see the lines and all the features of this ancient landscape. I sent the picture (she lives away and I only see her occasionally now), and at the same time I gave her an interpretation based on what I am trying to say in this paper.

This patient thought that she was quite simply acquiring the portrait of this man who had done so much for her (and I have). But what she needed to be told was that my lined face had some features that link for her with the rigidity of the faces of her mother and her nurse.

I feel sure that it was important that I knew this about the face and could interpret the patient's search for a face that could reflect herself, and at the same time see that, because of the lines, my face in the picture reproduced some of her mother's rigidity.

Actually, this patient has a thoroughly good face, and she is an exceptionally sympathetic person when she feels like it. She can let herself concern herself with other people's affairs and with their troubles for a limited period of time. How often this characteristic has seduced people into thinking of her as someone to be leaned on! The fact is, however, that the moment my patient feels herself being involved, especially in someone's depression, she automatically withdraws and curls up in bed with a hot-water bottle, nursing her soul.

Illustration IV

After all this had been written a patient brought material in the analytic hour which might have been the paper that I am writing. This woman is very much concerned with the stage of the establishment of herself as an individual. In the course of this particular hour she brought in a reference to 'Mirror mirror on the wall' etc. and then she said: 'Wouldn't it be awful if the child looked into the mirror and saw nothing?'

The rest of the material concerned the environment provided by her mother when she was a baby, the picture being of a mother talking to someone else unless actively engaged in a positive relating to the baby. The implication here was that the baby would look at the mother and see her talking to someone else. The patient then went on to describe her great interest in the paintings of Francis Bacon, and she wondered whether to lend me the Bacon book.[2] She referred to a detail in the book. Francis Bacon 'says that he likes to have glass over his pictures because then when people look at the picture what they see is not just a picture; they might in fact see themselves'.

After this the patient went on to speak of 'Le Stade du Miroir' because she knows of Lacan's work, but she was not able to make the link that I *feel* I am able to make between the mirror and the mother's face. It was not my job to give this link to my patient in this session, because the patient is essentially at a stage of discovering things for herself, and premature interpretation in such circumstances annihilates the creativity of the patient and is traumatic in the

---

[2] *Francis Bacon*, Catalogue raisonne and documentation by Ronald Alley (Thames & Hudson, London, 1964). Introduction by John Rothenstein: 'to look at a painting by Bacon is to look into a mirror, and to see there our own afflictions and our fears of solitude, failure, humiliation, old age, death and of nameless threatened catastrophe.' 'His avowed preference for having his paintings glazed is also related to his sense of dependence on chance. The preference is due to the fact that glass sets paintings somewhat apart from their environment (just as his daisies and railings set his subjects apart from their pictorial environment), and that glass protects, but what counts more in this case is his belief that the fortuitous play of reflections will enhance his pictures. His dark blue pictures in particular, I heard him observe, gain by enabling the spectator to see his own face in the glass.'

sense of being against the maturational process. This theme continues to be important in her analysis, but it appears in other guises.

This glimpse of the infant's and the child's seeing the self in the mother's face, and afterwards in a mirror, gives a way of looking at analysis and at the psychotherapeutic task. Psychotherapy is not making clever and apt interpretations; by and large it is a long-term giving the patient back what the patient brings. It is a complex derivative of the face that reflects what is there to be seen. I like to think of my work this way, and to think that if I do this well enough the patient will find his or her own self and will be able to exist and to feel real. Feeling real is more than existing, it is finding a way to exist as oneself, and to relate to objects as oneself, and to have a self into which to retreat for relaxation.

But I would not like to give the impression that I think this task of reflecting what the patient brings is easy. It is not easy, and it is emotionally exhausting. But we get our rewards. Even when our patients do not get cured they are grateful to us for seeing them as they are, and this gives us a satisfaction of a deep kind.

This to which I have referred in terms of the mother's role of giving back to the baby the baby's own self has continued importance in terms of the child and the family. Naturally, as the child develops and the maturational processes become sophisticated, and identifications multiply, the child's dependence on getting back the self from the mother's and the father's face and from the faces of others who are in parental or sibling relationships lessens in importance (Winnicott, 1960). Nevertheless, when a family is intact and is a going concern, over a period of time each child derives benefit from being able to see himself or herself in the attitudes of the individual members or in the attitudes of the family as a whole. We can include in all this the actual mirrors that exist in the house and the opportunity that the child gets for seeing the parents look at themselves. It should be understood, however, that the actual mirror has significance mainly in its figurative sense.

This could be one way of stating the contribution that a family can make to the personality growth and enrichment of each one of its individual members.

References

Lacan, J. (1949) Le Stade du Miroir. In English 'The mirror stage as formative of the function of the I', pp.1-7. In: *.E.crits – A Selection*, trans. A. Sheridan. Tavistock, 1977.

Gough, D. (1962) The behaviour of infants in the first year of life. *Proceedings of the Royal Society of Medicine* 55.

Winnicott, D.W. (1960) Ego distortion in terms of True and False Self. In *The Maturational Processes and the Facilitating Environment*, pp. 140-52, London, Hogarth Press and the Institute of Psycho-analysis, 1965.

CHAPTER 3

Conversations with a two-month-old[1]

COLWYN TREVARTHEN

New preface – 2002

It is interesting to read the account of our early work on 'protoconversations', written over a quarter of a century ago. I am pleased to see that the picture drawn of young infants' expressions and emotions, and their sensitivity to a mother's affectionate talk, still seems right. I would change little, but there is much new knowledge that confirms and extends our understanding of the infant as a person seeking company, a person who is also interested in discovering experiences to explore and to 'talk about' with others.

Lynne Murray took the experimental work that John Tatuam pioneered to a classical conclusion with her beautiful analysis of the confused and unhappy responses of two-month-olds to a mother showing a 'blank face', or to a replayed video of her communication. This confirmed the infant's sense of the immediacy of a sympathetic mother's reflected feelings in chat. We carried our film work through the first year, and Penny Hubley discovered the remarkable change that occurs in a baby at about nine months old, when a curiosity dawns in the infant mind about what a companion intends, what they are interested in. This releases learning about the world of meanings, meanings of actions and things that are artificial and that can be part of a tradition or culture. Long before language, infants are, as Michael Halliday puts it, learning 'how to mean', and they are getting others' meanings too.

The story of how this interest in other persons' consciousness and purposes leads to language and, in due course, to the kind of cleverness that interests education ministers has been told in rich detail, but the psychology

---

[1] This paper originally appeared in the *New Scientist*, 2 May 1974. It is reproduced here by kind permission of the author, who has also contributed a new preface for this Reader.

of it seems very complex and rather fragmentary. We still have to work to remind the experimenters with infant cognitions that an infant is a whole and active person, with motives, moral sense and complex emotions that evaluate the appraisal of others, whoever they may be. We have to remind them of the intuitions and intentions that make cognitions useful. In the end we all still have to remind ourselves that in most important things, a young child is our teacher, knowing the direction of the adventure for which we must offer help and information.

The most recent scientific development has come from collaboration with a musician, Stephen Malloch. His theory of Communicative Musicality, built from meticulous acoustical analysis of the 'music' in speech, vocal games and songs between parents and their infants, reveals the intricate time sense and appreciation of expressive qualities that animate the narratives of human thinking and thought-sharing. Music is cultivated from an innate 'musicality' – of time and grace in moving. Without that product of our minds, our intimate shared presence for one another would be impossible.

I said before that I had no notion of the specialised nerve networks of the brain that makes communication with infants possible. I am still baffled. All the evidence of how fast children's brains grow, how 'plastic' they are in early years, does not cast light where it is needed: on the motive structures. However, it is definitely an advance that brain scientists are teaching psychologists about the inextricable relations between emotions and cognitions, in development and in consciousness, how emotions guide cognitions. The solid proof that there is a physiological mechanism of imitation makes the miracle of newborn imitations less incredible, too. But it is still the case that we do not know how the brain makes all the parts of an infant's body so wonderfully synchronous in the presentation of a delicate choreography of expressed attentions, purposes and moods. How can a conversation enrich these states of human vitality and makes them engaging, passionate, humorous and unforgettable? ... Well, we do not know.

Conversations with a two-month-old

Some years ago I began to study infants with the intention of looking for signs of what innate structure of intelligence lay dormant or weakly expressed in them. I knew that human newborns possess huge, elaborate brains, but they were credited with doing very little; this puzzled me. With the aid of modern recording techniques, but especially television and film, I soon obtained data that made me suspect that much of the innate pattern of human intention and a predisposition to perceive and use the world, including people, had been glossed over in scientific studies of infants. Most remarkable were indications that infants of a few weeks of age were showing signs of intentions to speak and that soon after this they were entering into well-organised, sometimes even witty or humorous, conversation-like exchanges with adults.

In a preliminary film study Martin Richards and I, working with Jerome Bruner at Harvard, sought to determine if and when infants developed behaviours indicating that they perceived objects and people differently. We filmed five babies once-a-week from birth until they were six months old, either with a small toy suspended nearly in front of them, or with their mother.

We saw highly elaborate activity that was specific to communicating with persons in all subjects while they were with their mothers. The mother was simply asked to 'chat with her baby'. No mother thought this an odd request. Her presence, what she looked like, the way she moved, the sounds she made, caused even babies a few weeks old to make behaviours that were different from those made a moment later to the suspended object. The infant showed two different kinds of interest, two ways of spontaneously responding; one for the object, and one for the mother. Most different were the expressions of face, voice and hands. We hypothesised two modes of psychological action: communication with persons, and 'doing' with objects. The latter included visually exploring and tracking, trying to grasp, trying to kick or step on, or trying to seize in the mouth.

Since coming to Edinburgh, I have made films with Penelope Hubley and Lynne Sheeran, detailed analysis of which reveals that the acts of two-month-olds responding to attentions of other persons outline many psychological processes of conversation between adults. Of these we have found activity which is best called 'prespeech' because both the context in which it occurs and its form indicate that it is a rudimentary form of speaking by movements of lips and tongue. These distinctive movements are often made by young infants without sound. At other times young babies are very vocal, making a variety of cooing sounds as they move mouth and tongue. We note a specific pattern of breathing with prespeech even when sounds are not made.

Also associated with prespeech are distinctive 'hand-waving' movements that are developmentally related to the gestures or gesticulations of adults in 'eager' and 'graphic' conversation. We are now sure that, notwithstanding the importance of cultural development in the formation of language, both of speech and of gestures, the foundation for interpersonal communication between humans is 'there' at birth, and is remarkably useful by eight weeks when cognitive and memory processes are just beginning.

Communication is the essence

We can now confidently say that communication activity is much more complex than any other form of activity of infants at this age. We conclude that human intelligence develops from the start as an interpersonal process and that the maturation of consciousness and the ability to act with voluntary control in the physical world is a product rather than an ingredient of this process.

Infant communication needs a partner. It depends on a number of special adaptations in the mother's behaviour. Some of these, we find, are almost automatically fulfilled by the normal rhythm and organisation of her voluntary action, others require unconscious alterations in the way the mother would normally communicate to another adult person. Changes that all unaffected mothers make to slower, more emphatic but gentle movements and to 'baby-talk' may come from a return of the mother to more elementary or basic components in her innate repertoire of social acts. It is certain that what she does to guide and sustain the sociable mood of the infant is natural and unconscious, even though mothers and psychologists may have opinions about the effects of treating a baby as a baby. Our charts of the conversation-like exchanges between mother and infants reveal regular patterns in time. By plotting the shift of the two partners up and down a few grades or levels of social animation we find that it is possible to show in a diagram the changing roles of mother and infant. That the mother provides needed stimuli in right measure is clear. Furthermore, infants at this age do not usually take time to mimic their partners – they just play their part.

That young babies will sometimes imitate acts of others appropriately, even when to do so they must move a part of their body they cannot see, has for a long time struck psychologists as mysterious and important. It seems to indicate that babies follow instructions, but it also needs an elaborate innate machinery. Even in the second month a baby may imitate a mouth movement of the mother, or protrusion of her tongue (now known to be possible within hours of birth [Ed]). To do so the baby must have a model of the mother's face in his brain, and this model must be properly mapped onto the motor apparatus of his own face. Movements of head and hands, as well as face, may elicit imitation. The baby must have models for these parts as well.

In our films we have rarely seen imitation of this kind in babies under six months age, and, when it does occur, the infant is abstracted from the conversational flow and closely regards what the instructor does for some time before acting to imitate. Moreover, the partner must try to get imitation by pointedly repeating an act in a teacher-like way that is not a common behaviour of a mother to a young infant. On the other hand, we are impressed with the elaborate and faithful mimicry of the more animated acts of the baby by the mother. Apparently, *her* imitation is an important part of the normal encouragement to conversational activity by the baby.

Psychological communication

Discovery of embryonic speaking in the social animation of infants, nearly two years before they use words to communicate, reinforces the view of psycholinguists nowadays that language is embedded in an innate context of non-verbal communication by which intention and experience are transmitted from person to person. As the Oxford philosophers Austin, Grice and Strawson have established, we speak with obvious purpose to inform, instruct, direct or in some other way influence the actions and experience of others. The meanings of single words depend on their position in such speech acts. Infants a few months old make speechlike pattern of movement when they are also clearly overcome by some rudimentary purpose to influence, impress or lead the attentions they have obtained of another. Even though no meaningful information about the world is transmitted, the act is clearly one of psychic logical communication that may be said to show 'intersubjectivity'.

Mothers 'talking with' infants of about two months of age show phrasing of their speech to allow the infant to take his turn and 'have his say' in prespeech. Much of the behaviour of the baby expressing excitement or impulse to act is followed closely by the mother, and indeed her skill and understanding of what the infant is doing enable her often to obtain synchrony of emphatic acts so the two behave in complete concert as if dancing together. But this does not apply to prespeech, which is normally watched with little sign of imitation or shadowing.

The use of speech to name and talk about experiences in the common field of things, people, one's actions, or the actions of others, comes much later in life, after a considerable development of exploratory and manipulative intelligence, and when free locomotion is beginning. Jean Piaget concludes that this proves the primacy of the development of schemata to know objects. It may, as Joanna Ryan of Cambridge proposes, indicate the need for considerable development of intersubjective communication without words, before words can be used to signify and specify.

The early appearance of communication with persons in the psychology of infants seems to provide what is needed for sharing all kinds of action and purpose with adults as more capable, more intelligent beings. At first infants seem fully occupied with the formalities of the interpersonal play. But, after four months, developments in attention and object recognition, and particularly the development of controlled voluntary reaching for and manipulating and mouthing objects, means that a conversation can become about what the infant has looked at, reached to, done. This is the beginning of games with things, or 'toys'.

Preparing the way

We believe that all play has an interpersonal element, although this may be disguised in private games when the self plays with itself. Peter Wolff of Boston has studied the earlier purely social play a mother can have in peeka-boo or pat-a-cake with infants as young as six or eight weeks. This communi-cation prepares the way for play with things.

If an infant of four months or so reacts to the attentions of an adult by looking pointedly at or deliberately reaching for or pointing to something, this thing becomes at once the centre of interest of the partner too. Around five months many of the infants we have studied have exhibited a marked increase in such deliberate bringing of a topic from the outside into a 'conver-sation'. They seem to do so more with highly familiar partners, such as their mother, than with mere friends who, unlike strangers who threaten at this age, may be treated with undivided 'conversation'.

This is the age at which it is first possible to show a baby something one is doing, and it is also the age at which strong attention to the mouth of the mother leads a baby to imitate some of her speaking movements. Clearly, such developments have great significance as preparation for the growth of language as communication about intentions and experiences with reference to people, places and things.

Many studies have sought to trace recognition of the mother as a partic-ular person, or as an object with an identity, or conversely, to find when babies will show fear of strangers. Most of these record a critical change at about four or five months, and at present psychologists usually attribute this to an advance in learning powers or cognitive processes of the infant that enables better perceptual discrimination of strangers and friends. Psychoanalysts insist that this change is also a development of the affectional process – that love of the familiar caretaker is involved.

But at this same time infants frequently do not wish to play at conversa-tion with their mothers, but will still do so with less-familiar friends. Our evidence suggests that there is a relationship between a new wilfulness in social behaviour and the emerging intentions to take hold of and manipulate things. Entirely new levels of memory and perception process develop along with the appearance of effective actions on objects, and these advances are coupled to equally significant changes in the kind of dependency the infant has on the actions of others, especially those people for whom a special attachment is forming.

A basic innateness of personal reactions in man is shown not only by the timetable of growth of functions common to all normal babies but also in individual differences. Adults differ in personality, and they behave in widely different ways with infants, some being shy and fearful of even a manifestly friendly baby, and fathers differ in important ways from mothers. We have some evidence that some fathers play a more boisterous kind of game with more jokes and mimicry of prespeech grimaces and more poking of the body than do mothers. They thereby excite infants more to calling and laughter, and to vigorous body movements. It has been found that fathers treat infant girls with more talking and gentle touching than boys with whom they are more peremptory and sometimes very vigorous. But even very young boys and girls act differently, too, showing that such sex differences are not entirely due to learning of social roles. Male babies of only two months old generally have more vigorous body movements and adopt more readily a leading place in a conversational exchange with their mothers. Female babies tend rather to watch and follow and to act in animated face and mouth displays with fine hand gesticulation.

It seems very likely, from our few case studies of individual parents with infants, that there are also large inherent personality differences between adults or babies of one sex that affect the pattern of intersubjective behaviour. We need to do much more work to describe types of personality in very young persons.

One recent outcome of our work on intersubjectivity in early infancy throws light on the relationship between emotion and the acts that infants address to persons, a topic which is of central importance in Freudian theory of infant development. An undergraduate student John Tatum has performed an experiment in my laboratory on the emotional effects on an infant when a mother acts irrelevantly. He arranged, with a partial reflecting mirror and changing lights, for the mother, while remaining visible to the baby as before, to cease seeing the baby and to see an adult in the same place. The person silently asked the mother questions by holding up cards with writing on them. The infant could see only the mother. In replying at length the mother automatically changed her style of talking to that appropriate for an adult from that proper for her baby and, of course, also stopped reacting to what the infant did.

In every case the eight- to ten-week-old infants were clearly puzzled by the change in their mother, and they made exaggerated solicitations as if to get her attention back. Some quickly became dejected-looking and withdrawn, a state of acute depression which took minutes to abate when the mother's attention returned to the infant with a change in lighting.

Dr John Bowlby of the Tavistock Institute of Human Relations, London, has collected abundant evidence since the last European war of the depressing effects of departure or loss of a mother, or other principle companion, on the health and spirits of babies and children. He believes initial attachments are innate, but based on a few social release mechanisms like those studied in animals by Konrad Lorenz and Harry Harlow. Tatum's

experiment shows how complex is the relationship between person perception and emotion while a very young baby is actually communicating with a
person. Obviously, the basis of interpersonal relationships is highly complex
and emotional from birth.

Our findings lead us to question accepted views of the socialisation of
human intelligence. Jean Piaget, who believes in a strong, developing biological determination of the human mind, conceives of infants as initially
unaware of the separateness of themselves from the world they experience.
Out of this union with experience they 'objectify' both things and persons
without distinguishing these two. *He has* said, however, that, *following* the
development of the brain schema for an object, 'objects are conceived by
analogy with the self as active, alive and conscious', and that 'this is particularly so with those exceptionally unpredictable and interesting objects –
people'. Piaget thinks that in the first few months there are no signs that
infants respond particularly to persons as such except as a reflex, and that
infant emotions are determined by affective reflexes triggered by simple
losses or gains of equilibrium. Like Sigmond Freud he attributes the foundations of human social experience to biological needs of the self.

Freud thought these needs were derived from feelings of the body important for physiological maintenance, but he also gave great importance to the
development of affectional functions that define an 'object relation' with the
mother early in the first year of life. As is stated above, John Bowlby, who is a
psychiatrist and psychoanalyst, accepts the ethologists' idea of attachment
through innate releasers in adult and baby, and imprinting of the baby to a
particular person who is usually the mother.

Rudolph Shaffer, of Strathclyde University Glasgow, says: 'An infant is
essentially an asocial being', that 'other people, he soon finds out, are fascinating things to watch, feel and listen to, but as yet they do not constitute a
class of stimuli distinct from the inanimate world' and that 'children are not
born "knowing" people'.

But our films show that infants are adapted, at the latest by three weeks
after birth, to approach persons and objects quite differently. The elaborate-
ness of their social responses and social expressions in the second and third
months, before they have begun deliberate and controlled handling and
mouthing of objects, indicates that intersubjectivity is fitted into development from the start as a determining influence. Human social intelligence is
the result of development of an innate human mode of psychological
function that requires transactions with other persons. This function
includes rudiments of the quite unique human activity of speech, which
becomes the chief medium of individual human mental growth and the
essential ingredient of civilised society.

Interaction and communication

I believe that evolution of experimental or scientific thought processes in the mind of a child, and the object-perception processes associated with them, may develop at time in competition or disequilibrium with the growth of intersubjectivity with persons. But I also feel certain that the normal development of cognitive mastery of the world is one that advances through co-operative interaction of private experiment and social communication. Neither is sufficient alone.

Humans project their minds into the world to invest objects and events with intention, not because they confuse themselves with the world but because they have such a fundamental gift for communication with intentions of persons that mirror themselves and that they may mirror in reply. That such abilities are biologically founded in man suggests they have a determining role in the plan of growth and the changes in the life of individuals. I believe this concept of growing innate social function will prove necessary to understand the co-operative efforts of humans of different ages in families in schools, in business, in sport – anywhere where people create mutual activity.

At this point neurobiological considerations which encouraged my initial enquiry into infancy have receded far into the distance. Now I am involved in psychological considerations for which known anatomical schemes are unhelpful. Specialised nerve networks in ordered arrays must be there, but I have not the remotest notion of how or where they may be specified in the brain.

References

Malloch, S. (1999) Mother and infants and communicative musicality. In: 'Rhythms, Musical Narrative, and the Origins of Human Communication'. *Musicae Scientiae*, Special Issue, 1999–2000, (pp. 29–57). Liège: European Society for the Cognitive Sciences of Music.

Murray, L. and Trevarthen, C. (1985) Emotional regulation of interactions between two-month-olds and their mothers. In T.M. Field and N.A. Fox (eds), *Social Perception in Infants* (pp. 177–98) Norwood, NJ: Ablex.

Trevarthen, C. (1993) The function of emotions in early infant communication and development. In: J. Nadel and L. Camaioni (eds), *New Perspectives in Early Communicative Development* (pp. 48–81). London: Routledge.

Trevarthen, C. (1998) The concept and foundations of infant intersubjectivity. In S. Bråten (ed.), *Intersubjective Communication and Emotion in Early Ontogeny* (pp. 15–46). Cambridge: Cambridge University Press.

Trevarthen, C. (1999) Musicality and the intrinsic motive pulse: evidence from human psychobiology and infant communication. In: 'Rhythms, Musical Narrative, and the

Origins of Human Communication'. *Musicae Scientiae*, Special Issue, 1999–2000, (pp. 157–213). Liège: European Society for the Cognitive Sciences of Music.

Trevarthen, C. (2001a) The neurobiology of early communication: Intersubjective regulations in human brain development. In A.F. Kalverboer and A. Gramsbergen (eds), *Handbook on Brain and Behavior in Human Development* (pp. 841–82). Dordrecht, The Netherlands: Kluwer.

Trevarthen, C. (2001b) Intrinsic motives for companionship in understanding: Their origin, development and significance for infant mental health. *International Journal of Infant Mental Health*, 22(1–2), 95–131.

Trevarthen, C. (2002) Origins of musical identity: evidence from infancy for musical social awareness. In R. MacDonald, D.J. Hargreaves and D. Miell (eds), *Musical Identities* (pp. 21–38). Oxford: Oxford University Press.

Trevarthen, C. and Aitken K.J. (2001) Infant intersubjectivity: research, theory and clinical applications. Annual Research Review, *Journal of Child Psychology and Psychiatry*, 42(1), 3–48.

Trevarthen, C. and Hubley, P. (1978) Secondary intersubjectivity: confidence, confiding and acts of meaning in the first year. In A. Lock (ed.), *Action, Gesture and Symbol: The Emergence of Language* (pp. 183–229). London, New York, San Francisco: Academic Press.

Trevarthen, C. and Malloch, S. (2000) The dance of wellbeing: defining the musical therapeutic effect. *The Nordic Journal of Music Therapy*, 9(2), 3–17.

Trevarthen, C., Kokkinaki, T. and Fiamenghi, G.A. Jr. (1999) What infants' imitations communicate: with mothers, with fathers and with peers. In J. Nadel and G. Butterworth (eds), *Imitation in Infancy* (pp. 127–85) Cambridge: Cambridge University Press.

Chapter 4

Emotions and emotional communication in infants

E. Z. Tronick

New thoughts on mutual regulation: co-creation and uniqueness -- 2002

There are two critical revisions in my thinking about this paper. The first is that the model as presented fails to recognize that the process of mutual regulation is a co-creative process that generates unique ways in which the mother and infant, or the infant and any other individual, are together. As presented in the paper the model of the interaction has the infant and the mother exchanging preformed messages. Infant smiles and open gestures convey the message 'continue what you are doing', angry expressions convey 'change' or 'stop'. The mother expresses similar messages, and both the infant and the mother are able to apprehend the other's messages. These messages have a fixed meaning and a fixed form. However, when examined at a micro-temporal level, I now realize that these messages as well as the interactions are *highly variable*. They do not have a fixed form and they are not tightly constrained by rules. For example, the affective configuration of 'continue' can be made up of smiles, smiles and gestures, no smiles and positive vocalizations or no smiles but vocalizations and gestures, and on and on. The same variation characterizes all forms of the ways infants and their mothers communicate how they are to be with one another. To complicate the communication further, the sequencing of behavior is also highly variable.

Thus the communication system is hardly fixed. It is sloppy, and one wonders immediately how such a sloppy system effectively regulates the interaction.

The revision I have made, in contrast to the model of fixed exchanges of meaning, for my Model of Mutual Regulation is that *the sloppiness is overcome by a process of co-creation of meanings*. Infant and mother express a meaning or a relational intention that is sloppily expressed – 'let's continue' – which the partner sloppily or sort of 'gets', and in turn responds with their own sloppy message – 'yes, but what about'. This back and forth process over time allows for the co-creation of shared meaning. The process is a kind of mutual bootstrapping of meaning about what to do and how to be together. 'I do this touching game with my father, and I *don't* do it with you!'

Co-creation is an elaboration of the idea of reparation emphasizing the active role of each partner and the possibility of some new way of being together that emerges from the interaction. There is a crucial implication of the process of co-creation of *unique ways of being together*. It is that the fact that there is no one way of being with one person, in particular the mother–infant interaction pattern, could serve as the prototype for other interactions as asserted by Attachment Theory. The mother–infant relationship is not a general form. It is co-created and will continue to co-create unique ways of being together. Their unique ways of being together cannot be transferred to being with others. No one else shares their configuration of meanings. During feeding, mother and infant implicitly know that a glance with a small smile means 'I am ready for more', but at bedtime it means 'Don't go yet.' No one else could possibly know the meaning of these affects and relational intentions. And what is true about feeding characterizes all the highly differentiated qualities of the mother–infant relationship – what I have called its *thickness* – making it 'unusable' as a model for other relationships.

There is a second revision of my Model of Mutual Regulation. It emerges from successful regulation. Successful regulation not only leads to mutual states of affective matching and synchrony, but more importantly it leads to the emergence of what I call *dyadic states of consciousness*. States of consciousness are the assemblages of the essential meanings that are mutually conveyed during the interaction. These are the meanings of what I intend and how we can be together. They can be thought of as complex and coherent states of brain organization.

Creation of this dyadic system necessitates that the infant and mother apprehend elements of the other's state of consciousness. If they did not, it would not be possible to create a dyadic state. For example, if the mother's apprehension of the infant's state of consciousness is that the infant intends to reach for a ball when in fact the infant intended to stroke her face, a dyadic system will not be created. The two systems – infant and mother – will remain separate, uncoordinated and disconnected. Thus a principle governing the human dyadic system is that successful mutual regulation of social interactions requires a mutual mapping of (some of) the meaning assemblages of each partner's state of consciousness into the other partner's brain. I mean this literally: *each individual incorporates meaning assemblages of the other into his or her own state of consciousness.*

As a consequence of this incorporation the consciousness of each of the members of the dyadic system of consciousness expands. This expansion is accompanied by a feeling of growth and being larger than oneself. Moreover, by incorporating these assemblages of meaning from the other the state of consciousness of each of the individuals increases in complexity and coherence. Thus the states of consciousness and their expansion becomes a critical feature of interactions that are unique. The states of consciousness achieved by the infant with the mother will be different than those achieved with the father and likely not ever to be approached with a stranger. Again, the co-creation of dyadic states of consciousness raises the question of how the relationship with the mother could serve as the prototype for relationships with others.

These revisions of my thinking about the Mutual Regulation Model bring the process of co-creating meanings and dyadic states of consciousness to the center of development. For me, they also bring us to a focus on the uniqueness of the ways infants are with mothers, fathers and others. Indeed, I think it makes us all aware of the uniqueness of all our relationships and perhaps even of our own uniqueness.

Emotions and emotional communication in infants[1]

Abstract

Important advances have recently been made in studying emotions in infants and the nature of emotional communication between infants and adults. Infant emotions and emotional communications are far more organized than previously thought. Infants display a variety of discrete affective expressions that are appropriate to the nature of events and their context. They also appreciate the emotional meaning of the affective displays of caretakers. The emotional expressions of the infant and the caretaker function to allow them to mutually regulate their interactions. Indeed, it appears that a major determinant of children's development is related to the operation of this communication system. Positive development may be associated with the experience of coordinated interactions characterized by frequent reparations of interactive errors and the transformation of negative affect into positive affect, whereas negative development appears to be associated with sustained periods of interactive failure and negative affect.

---

[1] This article which first appeared in the American Psychologist, 1989, 44: 112-9. Reprinted here with permission of the American Psychological Association, who hold the copyright. A. gianino is responsible for many of the formulations.

How is it that some children become sad, withdrawn, and lacking in self-esteem, whereas others become angry, unfocused, and brittlely self-assertive, whereas still others become happy, curious, affectionate, and self-confident? As clinicians, researchers, and policymakers, our goal must be to understand the processes that lead to these outcomes, not just to generate indexes of them, so that problematic and compromised developmental outcomes can be prevented and remediated. Although the nature of these processes is not yet known, an answer is taking shape on the basis of recent work on the nature of infant–caretaker emotional communication.

The emerging answer is that the infant and adult are participants in an affective communication system. A central hypothesis is that the operation of this system has a major influence on how well the infant accomplishes his or her goals, the emotions the infant experiences, and the infant's developmental outcome. If this hypothesis is correct, then the key issue is to understand how this system works. We need to explore the inextricable links among infant emotions and behavior, caretaker emotions and behavior, and the success, failure, and reparation of interactive errors that the infant experiences when striving to accomplish his or her goals. Two contrasting examples of infant–mother interaction drawn from the work of Brazelton (et al. 1974) will serve as a base for the initial exploration of the functioning of this affective communication system.

Imagine two infant–mother pairs playing the game of peek-a-boo. In the first, the infant abruptly turns away from his mother as the game reaches its 'peek' of intensity and begins to suck on his thumb and stare into space with a dull facial expression. The mother stops playing and sits back watching her infant. After a few seconds the infant turns back to her with an interested and inviting expression. The mother moves closer, smiles, and says in a high-pitched, exaggerated voice, 'Oh, now you're back!' He smiles in response and vocalizes. As they finish crowing together, the infant reinserts his thumb and looks away. The mother again waits. After a few seconds the infant turns back to her, and they greet each other with big smiles.

Imagine a second similar situation except that, after this infant turns away, she does not look back at her mother. The mother waits but then leans over into the infant's line of vision while clicking her tongue to attract her attention. The infant, however, ignores the mother and continues to look away. Undaunted, the mother persists and moves her head closer to the infant. The infant grimaces and fusses while she pushes at the mother's face. Within seconds she turns even further away from her mother and continues to suck on her thumb.

I will not yet focus on the issue of who is responsible for the interactional errors in the second example. Instead, I will focus on the critical feature in each interaction: that the affective communications of each infant and mother actually change the emotional experience and behavior of the other. In both illustrations, the infants' looking-away and thumb sucking convey the message that the infants need to calm down and regulate their emotional state. Each mother respects this message by waiting. Within seconds, the first infant looks back at his mother, communicating that he is ready to interact, and the mother responds by moving in closer with a smile, which her infant returns. Their smiles communicate their positive evaluations of what they are doing. In the second illustration, the mother waits but then disregards the infant's message and makes a vigorous attempt to solicit the infant's attention. The mother comes in closer and actively signals her infant to change what she is doing and attend to her. The infant responds by sharply turning away with strong negative affect, communicating to her mother that *she* should change what she is doing. The mother, however, ignores this message, and the infant becomes even more affectively negative as she tries to cope with her mother's continuing intrusiveness.

Now imagine that these episodes are prototypical for each dyad. That is, the first dyad routinely experiences reciprocal positive exchanges in which interactive errors are readily repaired, whereas the second dyad experiences repeated conflictual negative exchanges. There is no need to overcharacterize these interactions. Certainly, the first dyad experiences some conflictual interactions, and the second some reciprocal positive interactions. Given the difference in the balance of positive and negative exchanges in the two, however, it is hypothesized that the first infant will develop a tendency to look at his mother more, exhibit more positive affect, and experience less distress when he experiences stress than the second infant. The second infant, by contrast, will be more withdrawn and will exhibit more sadness. There is evidence to support this prediction (as I will show later), but I first will examine some of the theoretical assumptions underlying this hypothesis.

Emotions, goals, other- and self-directed regulatory behaviors

To begin with, infants, like all other creatures, have a multiplicity of goals (Bowlby, 1982; Trevarthen, 1974). These include goals for engaging the social and inanimate environments (e.g. interacting with others, maintaining proximity to the caretaker, engaging in interactions characterized by mutual delight and reciprocity, and acting on objects) and internal goals (e.g. maintaining homeostasis, establishing a feeling of security, experiencing positive emotions, and controlling negative emotions). To accomplish these goals, infants process information about their current state in relation to their goal. They evaluate whether they are succeeding or failing and then use that evaluation to guide actions aimed at accomplishing their goal or redirecting their efforts to other goals (Tronick, 1980). For instance, the first infant in the earlier example fulfills his interactive goal by affectively signaling his mother when he is ready to interact by looking at her and smiling. He also fulfills his goal to control his emotional state by turning away and sucking on his thumb. Thus, the infant is active, not passive.

Emotions play a critical part in this evaluative process. An evaluation by the infant that the goal is being accomplished results in a positive emotional state – joy or interest – motivating further engagement (e.g. the first infant smiles and continues to look at his mother). When the infant's evaluation is that the goal is not being accomplished, the infant experiences negative emotions. More specifically, if the infant's evaluation is that the obstacle blocking the achievement of the goal can be overcome, an emotional state of anger results, and the infant is motivated to try to remove the obstacle (e.g. the second infant has an angry facial expression and pushes her mother away). However, an evaluation that the obstacle cannot be overcome results in sadness and disengagement (e.g. the second infant eventually withdraws). Thus emotions motivate and organize the infant's behavior rather than disrupt it (et al., 1983; Izard, 1978).

Obviously, infants are not born fully equipped to accomplish these goals on their own. Infants' capacities are immature, limited, and poorly coordinated. Moreover, disruptions of infants' ongoing activities come from both inside and outside (e.g. from internal physiological states, such as hunger and uncontrolled affect, as well as from external obstacles). Given these limitations and disruptions, why don't infants typically fail to achieve their goals and continuously experience negative emotions?

To oversimplify, the answer is that the infant is part of an affective communication system in which the infant's goal-directed strivings are aided and supplemented by the capacities of the caretaker. An infant's affective displays function as messages that specify the infant's evaluation of whether he or she is succeeding in achieving a goal. The caretaker 'reads' this message and uses it to guide his or her actions for facilitating the infant's strivings. Gianino and Tronick (1988) label these affective displays *other-directed regulatory behaviors* to capture their function of regulating the behavior of the infant's partner.

Consider the following example, in which the infant's goal is to get a just-out-of-reach object. The six-month-old infant stretches his hands out toward the object. Because he cannot get hold of it, he becomes angry and distressed. He looks away for a moment and sucks on his thumb. Calmer, he looks back at the object and reaches for it once more. But this attempt fails too, and he gets angry again. The caretaker watches for a moment, then soothingly talks to him. The infant calms down and with a facial expression of interest gazes at the object and makes another attempt to reach for it. The caretaker brings the object just within the infant's reach. The infant successfully grasps the object, explores it, and smiles. In this illustration, the caretaker reads the infant's affective displays, uses this information to facilitate the infant's goal-directed activities, and helps to change the infant's emotional state. More specifically, the caretaker is responsible for the reparation of the infant's failure into success and the simultaneous transformation of his negative emotion into a positive emotion (Gianino and Tronick, 1988).

There is a second important feature to this illustration. The infant is not solely dependent on the caretaker to control the negative affect he experiences. He has several coping behaviors available: looking away, self-comforting, and even self-stimulation. These behaviors control the infant's negative affect by shifting his or her attention away from a disturbing event or substituting positive for negative stimulation (Rothbart and Derryberry, 1984). For example, looking away reduces infants' heart rates during stress, and thumb sucking can calm distressed infants.

Gianino and Tronick (1988) label these coping behaviors *self-directed regulatory behaviors*, suggesting that they function to control and change the infant's own affective state (Beebe and Stern, 1977). When successful, these behaviors, like the infant's other-directed regulatory behaviors, shift the infant's negative emotional state to a more positive emotional state so he or she can pursue goal-directed engagements with people and objects. In the aforementioned example, the infant attemps to reach the object again only after calming himself down by looking away and sucking on his thumb.

Clearly, the distinction between self-directed and other-directed behavior is not hard and fast. Self-directed behavior can function as communication, conveying the infant's evaluation of success or failure and his or her emotional state to a caregiver. The caregiver may then act on this communication to aid the infant's accomplishment of internal and external goals. This also occurred in the illustration.

Other-directed and self-directed regulatory behaviors are part of the infant's normal repertoire for coping with sadness, uncontrolled anger, and the extremes of positive affect, which can turn into distress. They enable the infant to control the potential disruptive effects of these emotions and their extremes on his or her goal-directed activities. These coping behaviors make it possible for the infant to accomplish the dual simultaneous tasks of controlling his or her emotional state while interacting with people or acting on the inanimate world.

Some of the most dramatic effects of regulatory behaviors on infant emotions are seen when the mother's behavior is manipulated so that the infant is prevented from successfully achieving the goal for reciprocal inter-action. Such manipulations may involve distorting the mother's affective behavior by instructing her to act in an unresponsive manner (i.e. remaining still-faced while looking at her infant) or to behave in a disruptive manner (i.e. interacting in an emotionally flat and withdrawn fashion, which simulates the disengagement of some depressed mothers; Cohn and Tronick, 1983; Tronick, 1980).

Confronted by these manipulations, most three-month-old infants initially signal to their mothers with facial expressions, vocalizations and gestures in an attempt to get their mothers to resume their normal behavior. The infants' message is that their mothers should change what they are doing. When these other-directed behaviors fail to achieve that goal, the infants express negative emotions and use self-directed regulatory behaviors in an attempt to control their emotional responses. They look away and self-comfort. These reactions occur even when the mothers are still-faced for only a few seconds. Moreover, the infants' negative affect and utilization of self-directed regula-tory behaviors do not end simply upon the resumption of normal behavior by their mothers. Rather, there is a continuation of the infants' negative mood and reduction in visual regard of their mothers for the next few minutes. This finding suggests that even three-month-old infants are not simply under the control of the immediate-stimulus situation but that events have lasting effects, that is they are internally represented. These effects will be related to defensive behavior and psychopathology later in this article. For now, I will focus on the implication from these studies that infant emotions are specific and meaningful reactions to the infant's active processing and appreciation of the mother's and others' affective behavior.

The organized nature of infant emotions

Two-month-old infants make a fundamental distinction between people and objects (Brazelton et al., 1974; Trevarthen, 1974). Prereaching infants presented with an object look intently at it, sit up straight, remain relatively still, and punctuate their fixed gaze with swiping movements and brief glances away. Presented with people, infants' posture is more relaxed, and their movements are smoother. They become active at a slower pace and then look away for longer periods of time than they do with objects. Furthermore, infants give full greeting responses to people but not to objects. Simply stated, infants communicate with people and act instrumen-tally on objects.

Young infants can also discriminate the facial expressions of others (Malatesta and Izard, 1984). For example, infants look more at facial expres-sions of joy than anger. More significantly, it appears that the emotional content of different maternal emotional expressions are appreciated by infants (i.e. they lead to different infant emotions). When newborns are in a quiet, alert state, looking at them and gently talking to them can produce a smile. Wolff (1963) describes how the infant's smile is first regularly elicited by a vocalization and then by the face. Recent research suggests that ten-week-old infants react to maternal facial and vocal displays of anger with anger but have fewer angry responses when their mothers pose sadness (Lelwica and Haviland, 1983). Moreover, infant reactions are even influenced by their appreciation of the context surrounding the event (e.g. a mother wearing a mask elicits laughter, whereas a stranger wearing the same mask elicits distress and fear, see Sroufe, 1979).

Campos and his colleagues (Campos et al., 1983) make a classic observation of how ten-month-old infants appreciate (i.e. appraise; Bowlby, 1982) the affective expressions of others and modify their own actions on the basis of that appreciation. They found that when ten-month-old infants are exploring the surface of the visual cliff (i.e. an apparatus that presents an apparent but not real drop-off), they will look to their mothers when they come to the 'drop-off' if the apparent depth is ambiguous as to its 'danger.' When their mothers pose a fearful or angry face, most infants will not cross. But when their mothers pose a joyful face, most infants will cross. Infants react similarly to maternal vocalizations conveying fear or joy. Interestingly, the expressions and vocalizations of other adults have a similar effect. It is remarkable that infants actively seek out affective information from another person not only to supplement their information about the event but even to override their own appreciation and perception of the event. Clearly, the emotional state of others is of fundamental importance to the infant's emotional state. And carefully note that this importance is not the result of passive processes such as mirroring. Rather, it results from the infant's active use of another's emotional expression in forming his or her appreciation of an event and using it to guide action.

Infants are well equipped to convey their appreciations and their emotional states. Young infants make nearly all the muscle movements that are used by adults to express the primary emotions (Ekman and Oster, 1979). Izard (1978) identifies facial expressions of interest, joy, disgust, surprise, and distress in young infants. Weinberg (1989) and Hamilton (1989) identify facial expressions of sadness and anger in three- to six-month-olds. Furthermore, a quite dramatic phenomenon is that newborns can imitate the components of the facial expressions of surprise, fear, and sadness (Field et al., 1983). Although these findings on imitation are controversial, they provide evidence of infants' ability to discriminate facial expressions and their ability to express that discrimination in differentiated ways. Hand postures and variations in motor tone are also indicative of infant affective behavioral states, as are variations of infant vocalizations (Fogel and Hannan, 1985; Papousek and Papousek, 1987).

Far less work is available on the relations among different expressive systems. However, Weinberg (1989) has found that in normal interactions, specific facial expressions are related to specific behaviors. In six-month-olds, for example, facial expressions of joy are more likely to occur when the infant is looking at the mother, positively vocalizing, and using gestural signals, whereas facial expressions of sadness occur when the infant is looking away and fussing, but not crying. This data demonstrates well the organized quality of the infant's affective system.

Varied and differentiated as the infant's affective repertoire is, it may still be underestimated. The variety and subtlety of facial expressions still elude our categorical schemes. How many types of smiles are there? How many forms are there of what we broadly label *distress*? Moreover, past research has focused too much on facial expressions and not enough on gestures, postures, and vocalizations, and their relations. Most critically, researchers need to put the infant in situations that evoke infant goals, evaluations, and strivings in order to elicit the infant's full affective repertoire. If this is not done, then the repertoire will not be available for observation. In these situations, researchers also must carefully consider moods rather than just the brief affective expressions they have concentrated on in the past. Recurrent moods, or what Emde (1983) refers to as the infant's affective core, are critical to infant functioning because they systematically modify the infant's experience of events and bias the infant's response to them.

Regardless of what the infant's affective repertoire is eventually discovered to be, it is well established that parents are acutely sensitive to their infant's emotional expressions and behavior. Parents attend to their infant's direction of gaze and modify their behavior on the basis of it. They maintain a somewhat distant (40 cm) observational distance when their infant is looking at something other than themselves, but they move to a dialogic distance of about 22.5 cm when their infant looks at them (Papousek and Papousek, 1987). Parents also frame their infant's gaze by looking at their infant until the infant looks away from them (Kaye and Fogel, 1980). Cohn and Tronick (1987) have found that, when the infant looks away, parents use facial expressions, vocalizations, and gestures to solicit their infant's attention back to themselves, but that when eye-to-eye contact is established, parents change their affective behavior. For instance, parents often give an initial greeting in which they tilt their head slightly back, raise their eyebrows, and open their eyes and mouth wide (Papousek and Papousek, 1987).

Emde (1983) has found that parents categorize infant facial expressions along three dimensions: (a) hedonic tone, from positive to negative affect, (b) activation, from sleep to excitement, and (c) orientation, from internal to external (i.e. sleepy or bored to interested or curious). Most mothers also discriminate the discrete emotions of anger, fear, surprise, joy, interest, and sadness in their one-month-old infants. The mothers use facial, vocal, and behavioral expressions to make their judgments. Malatesta and Izard (1984) found further specificity in parental responses to infants' facial expressions of emotion. Mothers respond with contingent imitation to their infants' more fully formed categorical emotional expressions (e.g. anger and joy) than to the more 'random' facial movements (e.g. twitches or half smiles). Moreover, infant expressions of sadness and anger produce affective responses of sadness or anger in their mothers.

In sum, parents and other adults appear to operate on the assumption that a child has better information about what he or she wants than they do. Consequently, they attend to and act on a wide range of affective behaviors to aid the child's accomplishment of his or her goals.

Normal and abnormal infant–adult affective communication

Infant and adult affective communicative capacities make possible mutually coordinated infant–adult interactions. After a decade of controversy, it is now well established that the face-to-face interactions of infants and adults starting as young as three months are bidirectional (i.e. mutually regulated) rather than just being the product of adult social skills. That is, infants modify their affective displays and behaviors on the basis of their appreciation of their mother's affective displays and behavior (Cohn and Tronick, 1987; Lester et al., 1985). For instance, infant smiles and vocalizations are contingent on specific maternal affective turn-taking signals (Cohn and Tronick, 1987). Of course, adults make similar modifications.

This coordination has led to characterizations of the mother–infant inter- action as typically being reciprocal, synchronous, or coherent. These terms and others like them are attempts to capture the quality of the interaction when it is going well. Methods of assessment have been developed on the basis of this type of characterization, i.e. a 'good interaction' is a coordi- nated interaction. However, such terms overcharacterize just how well the interaction typically goes. Coordination, regardless of infant age during the first year, is found only about 30% or less of the time in face-to-face interac- tions, and the transitions from coordinated to miscoordinated states and back to coordinated states occur about once every three to five seconds (Tronick and Cohn, 1989). Thus, a more accurate characterization of the normal interaction, and a better basis for assessment, is that it frequently moves from affectively positive, mutually coordinated states to affectively negative, miscoordinated states and back again on a frequent basis. But if this is the characterization of normal interaction, what is the characterization of abnormal interaction?

I (Tronick, 1980) summarize several descriptions of infants who chronically experienced miscoordinated interactions. These infants repeatedly engaged in self-directed regulatory behaviors (e.g. they turned away, had dull-looking eyes, lost postural control, orally self-comforted, rocked, and self-clasped). These cases were extreme, but in examining a more typical population of mothers with high levels of depressive symptomatology for depression, Cohn and I (Cohn and Tronick, 1989) have found that not only are the interactions of these mothers and their infants disturbed in ways similar to those seen in the extreme cases but that the affective and regulatory reactions of the infants are related to the affect and behavior of their depressed mothers.

In general, during these interactions there are few periods when infant and mother are mutually positive, and only a few of the interactions evidence any contingency between the infant's and mother's affective behavior. As a group, the depressed mothers look away from their infants more, are angrier and more intrusive, and display less positive affect than normal mothers. Cohn and Tronick (1989) found that seven-month-old infants of the most disengaged mothers show the greatest amounts of protest, that the infants of the most intrusive mothers look away the most, and that the infants of the most positive mothers, little as that is, express more positive affect. Similarly, Hamilton (1989) found that three-month-old infants' affective expressions are strongly related to maternal reports of their own affect. Three-month-old infants whose mothers reported more anger expressed more anger, whereas infants of mothers who reported more sadness expressed more distress.

My interpretation is that depressed mothers, in different ways for different mothers, fail to appropriately facilitate their infant's goal-directed activities. Their interactive behaviors and affect are poorly timed or often intrusive. Their affective displays are negative (e.g. anger, sadness, irritability), conveying the message that the infant should change what he or she is doing. This message and way of interacting is an obstacle to successful interaction, precludes the infant's achievement of his or her interactive goal, and leads to a predominance of negative affect and self-directed regulatory behavior by the infant. Thus, a general characterization of abnormal interactions is that the participants are stuck in affectively negative miscoordinated interactive states, and their messages calling for change are disregarded.

Now let me return to my opening question: How is it that some children become happy and curious, whereas others become sad and withdrawn, and still others become angry and unfocused? My answer is that these different outcomes are related to the working of the affective communication system in which the infant participates, especially to the balance of the child's experience of success or failure during his or her social-emotional interactions. Gianino and I (Gianino and Tronick, 1988) think of the normal, often-occurring, miscoordinated interactive state as an *interactive error*, and the transition from this miscoordinated state to a coordinated state as an *interactive repair*. The achievement of a coordinated state successfully fulfills the infant's interactive goal and engenders positive affect, whereas an interactive error fails to fulfill that goal and engenders negative affect.

In normal interactions, the infant experiences periods of interactive success and interactive error and frequent reparations of those errors. Emotionally, the infant experiences periods of positive affect and negative affect and frequent transformations of negative to positive affect; hence, experiences of negative emotion are brief. In abnormal interactions, the infant experiences prolonged periods of interactive failure and negative affect, few interactive repairs, and few transformations of negative to positive affect.

Gianino and I (Gianino and Tronick, 1988) argue that the experience of success and reparation of interactive errors and negative affect that typifies normal interactions has several developmentally enhancing effects that lead to positive outcomes. The experience of interactive reparation and the transformation of negative affect into positive affect allow the infant to elaborate his or her other-directed affective communicative and self-directed regulatory capacities and to use them more effectively, i.e. to be able to maintain engagement with the external environment in the face of stress. With the accumulation and reiteration of success and reparation, the infant establishes a positive affective core, with clearer boundaries between self and other (Emde, 1983). From this experience, the infant develops a representation of himself or herself as effective, of his or her interactions as positive and reparable, and of the caretaker as reliable and trustworthy.

In some initial work on normal interactions, Gianino and I (Gianino and Tronick, 1988) found that infants who experience more repairs during normal interactions are more likely to attempt to solicit their mothers' normal behavior when their mothers are acting in a disturbing, stressful manner (i.e. still-faced). These infants, on the basis of their experience of normal interactions, have a representation of the interaction as reparable and of themselves as effective in making that repair. Infants who experience fewer repairs are less likely to solicit their mothers and more likely to turn away and become distressed. In addition, infants who exhibit specific affective tendencies, such as smiling or distress, to this stressful behavior by their mothers at a first laboratory visit exhibit similar affective tendencies on a second visit two weeks later. Stability across visits was also found for such self-directed regulatory behaviors as self-comforting. Six-month-olds are already establishing an affective coping style and a representation of self and other.

By contrast, in abnormal interactions the chronic experience of failure, non-reparation, and negative affect has several detrimental effects on developmental outcome. The infant establishes a self-directed style of regulatory behavior (i.e. turning away, escaping, becoming perceptually unavailable) to control negative affect and its disruptive effects on goal-directed behavior. Indeed, regulation of negative affect becomes the infant's primary goal and preempts other possible goals. This self-directed style of regulatory behavior precludes the infant's involvement with objects, potentially compromising cognitive development, and distorts the infant's interactions with other people. With the reiteration and accumulation of failure and non-reparation, the infant develops a representation of himself or herself as ineffective and of the caretaker as unreliable.

I (Tronick, 1980) have found that those infants who chronically experienced miscoordinated interactions disengaged from their mothers and the inanimate environment and distorted their interactions with other people. Similar effects are seen in the infants of depressed mothers: They have more negative interactions with unfamiliar adults, and those infants who are more negative during face-to-face interactions are also more negative in other situations (Tronick and Field, 1986). Of course, an infant could completely give up the goal of engaging his or her mother. However, the young infant may not be able to give up this goal, and, even if he or she could, the consequences might be even more severe (Bowlby, 1982).

From this perspective, the pathways leading to the varieties of normalcy and psychopathology derive from the divergent experiences infants have with success, reparation of failure, and the transformation of negative emotions to positive emotions. Typically, there is no single traumatic juncture or special moment separating these pathways, only the slowly accumulated interactive and affective experiences with different people and events in different contexts that shape the regulatory processes and representations of the infant over time.

A major pathway leading to the variety of normal individual outcomes, one that is often disregarded, is the difference in emotional experience of individuals due to exposure to different cultural practices of socializing affect and behavior. For example, among the Gusii of Kenya, a people with strict rules about who may look at whom during face-to-face interactions, a mother is likely to look away from her infant at just that moment when the infant gets most affectively positive. In response, the infant's affect becomes more neutral, and he or she may look away. American mothers, at least the ones we study in our laboratories, almost never look away from their infants but, rather, get quite excited themselves. In response, American infants get even more excited and positive. Thus, Gusii infants internalize one set of interactive experiences and American infants another.

Framed by cultural bounds, the most important cause of the varieties of normal outcome are the strikingly different experiences individuals have with affective communication, interactive success, and emotional reparation during their reiterated daily exchanges with others. For instance, Cohn and I (Tronick and Cohn, 1989) have found large individual differences in the ability of mother–infant pairs to maintain coordinated interactive states. In addition, Cohn and I report that mother–son pairs are in well-coordinated states about 50% more of the time than mother–daughter pairs at six and nine months. These differences have important consequences for the emotional responsiveness and the formation of the self in individual males and females.

There are many pathways to psychopathology. From the perspective of mutual regulation, psychopathology is likely to arise in situations where there is persistent and chronic interactive failure. In these situations the infant is forced to disengage from people and things because the infant has to devote too much regulatory capacity to controlling the negative affect he or she is experiencing (Main, 1981). Eventually and paradoxically, to the extent that these self-directed regulatory behaviors are successful in controlling the negative affect and containing its disruptive effects, the infant begins to deploy them automatically, inflexibly, and indiscriminately. Thus, what were normal self-regulatory behaviors become pathological or 'defensive' because they are used to preclude the anticipated experience of negative affect, even in situations where negative affect might not occur. The infant gives up attempting to appreciate the nature of the immediate situation and instead approaches new situations already withdrawn and biased to act inappropriately. This severely constricts the infant's engagement with the world, future options, and even autonomy and may lead to failure-to-thrive, depression, and other forms of infant psychopathology.

But, of course, one must be cautious. Pathology is not necessarily the outcome of abnormal interactive experiences; indeed, some effects may be positive. For example, the infant of a depressed mother might become exceedingly sensitive to her emotional state in order to read her better and to better regulate the interaction. Such sensitivity may be useful when the infant interacts with others. Moreover, experience with poorly coordinated interactions is likely to have different effects at different developmental points. For example, experience with a depressed mother will have one effect during the infant's first months of life, when the mother's behavior may disrupt her infant's early emotional experience, and a different effect at the end of the first year, when depressed behavior will be more likely to disrupt the infant's newly emerging forms of autonomy.

This account has focused on the caretaker as the critical factor effecting, especially disrupting, the affective communication system. But the infant is an agent as well. Although the infant's capacities are impressive, they are still limited, so that the infant is not always able to play his or her role in the inter-action effectively. Furthermore, individual differences in temperament make different infants quite different interactive partners. In the opening examples, the first infant might be temperamentally more active and better able to control affect, whereas the second infant might be more sensitive to stimulation and more inhibited. These sorts of differences place different demands on interactive partners, make infants differentially reactive, and lead to different outcomes.

More generally and critically, many factors affect the child's develop-mental outcome. Even a partial list would include prematurity, malnutrition, illness, the infant's other interactive experiences, and factors such as social support, stress, and self-esteem that affect the mother's behavior with her infant. Indeed, the list is a long one, but the principle is that any factor, no matter how distant, that consistently modifies the infant's affective experi-ence modifies the infant's outcome to some degree.

Conclusion

This perspective on affective communication can be extended to the older child. The older child experiences new emotions – shame and guilt to name two – and has a more structured self to be affected by success and failure (Lewis, 1987). The older child also moves on to more complex and demanding tasks with people, objects, and ideas. These tasks place new demands on the child's ability to control his or her affect and on the caretaker to supplement the child's capacities. Problems children have with tantrums, impulse control, and conduct disorders, and even the risk-taking of adoles-cents, may be viewed as arising out of children's experiences with mutual regulation and their ability to self-regulate.

The regulation of emotions, self and other, interactive success, and affec-tive reparation are in fact lifetime issues (Stern, 1985). How adults manage these functions is determined in their current circumstances by their regula-tory style and their conscious and unconscious representation of their past. Given the transformational nature of development, it would be foolish to assert that the infant's regulatory style and representations determine those of the adult, but it would be equally foolish to assert that they are without long-term influence. Certainly, the way in which the adult-as-child regulated and represented the circumstances and the emotions he or she experienced accrue to the adult.

Thus, the infant, the child, and the adult act on the world, regulate emotional states, and communicate effectively. And for all of them the working of the communicative process – its degree of interactive coordina-tion and affective reparation – is what is critical to their outcome. Of course, we need to know more. To do that we need to look in great detail at the daily reiterated workings of this emotional communication system. This will take a major effort and commitment. Indeed, the time may have arrived for researchers to reinvent the systematic study of the development of individuals looked at one at a time. However, intervention need not wait for that full understanding. We already know that many interventions–from close-up ones such as interactive coaching, parental therapy, respite care for the child and parent, and daycare, to more distant ones such as prenatal care, healthcare, and jobs – will modify the child's experience and lead to positive developmental outcomes. We should put them in place.

References

Beebe, B. and Stern, D (1977) Engagement-disengagement and early object experience. In Freedman and S. Grenel (eds), *Communicative Structures and Psychic Structures* (pp. 33–55). New York: Plenum Press.

Bowlby, J. (1982) *Attachment and Loss: Vol. 1 Attachment* (2nd ed.). New York: Basic Books.

Brazelton, T.B., Koslowski, B. and Main, M. (1974) The origins of reciprocity: The early mother–infant interaction. In M. Lewis and L.A. Rosenblum (eds), *The Effect of the Infant on Its Caregiver* (pp. 49–76). New York: Wiley-Interscience.

Campos, J., Barrett, K., Lamb, M., Goldsmith, H., and Sternberg, C. (1983) Socioemotional development. In P.H. Mussen (ed.), *Handbook of Child Psychology: Vol. 2. Infancy and Developmental Psychology* (pp. 783–915) New York: Wiley.

Cohn, J.F. and Tronick, E.Z. (1983) Three-month-old infants' reaction to simulated maternal depression. *Child Development*, 54, 185–93.

Cohn, J.F. and Tronick, E.Z. (1987) Mother–infant face-to-face interaction: The sequence of dyadic states at 3, 6, and 9 months. *Developmental Psychology*, 23, 68–77.

Cohn, J. and Tronick, E.Z. (1989) Specificity of infants' response to mothers' affective behavior. *Journal of the American Academy of Child and Adolescent Psychiatry*, 28: 242–8.

Ekman, P. and Oster, H. (1979) Facial expressions of emotions. *Annual Review of Psychology*, 30, 527–54.

Emde, R. (1983) The pre-representational self and its affective core. *The Psychoanalytic Study of the Child*, 38, 165–92.

Field, T, Woodson, R., Cohen, D., Garcia, R., and Greenberg, R. (1983) Discrimination and imitation of facial expressions by term and preterm neonates. *Infant Behavior and Development*, 6, 485–90.

Fogel, A. and Hannan E.T. (1985) Manual actions of nine- to fifteen-week-old human infants during face-to-face interaction with their mothers. *Child Development*, 56, 1271–79.

Gianino, A. and Tronick, E.Z. (1988) The mutual regulation model: The infant's self and interactive regulation coping and defense. In T Field, P. McCabe, and N. Schneiderman (eds), *Stress and Coping* (pp. 47–68). Hillsdale, NJ: Erlbaum.

Hamilton, P (1989) *The interaction of depressed mothers and their 3 month old infants*. Unpublished doctoral dissertation, Boston University.

Izard, C. (1978) Emotions as motivations: An evolutionary-developmental perspective. In H.E. Howe, Jr. (ed.), *Nebraska Symposium on Motivation* (Vol. 26, pp. 163–99). Lincoln: University of Nebraska Press.

Kaye, K. and Fogel, A. (1980) The temporal structure of face-to-face communication between mothers and infants. *Developmental Psychology*, 16, 454–64.

Lelwica; M. and Haviland, J. (1983) Ten-week-old infants' react?ons to mothers' emotional expressions. Paper presented at the biennial meeting of the Society for Research in Child Development, Detroit.

Lester, B., Hoffman, J., and Brazelton, T.B. (1985) The structure of mother–infant interaction in term and preterm infants. *Child Development*, 56, 15-27.

Lewis, M. (1987) Social development in infancy and early childhood. In J.D. Osofsky (ed.), *Handbook of Infant Development (2nd ed., pp. 419-555). New York: Wiley.*

Main, M. (1981) Avoidance in the service of attachment: A working paper. In M.K. Immelmann, G. Barlow, M. Main, and L. Petrinovich (eds), *Behavioral Development: The Bielfield Interdisciplinary Project* (pp. 651-93). New York: Cambridge University Press.

Malatesta, C.A. and Izard, C.E. (1984) The ontogenesis of human social signals: From biological imperative to symbol utilization. In N.A. Fox and R.I. Davidson (eds), *The Psychobiology of Affective Development* (pp. 161-206). Hillsdale, NJ: Erlbaum.

Papousek, H. and Papousek, M. (1987) Intuitive parenting: A didactic counterpart to the infant's precocity in integrative capacities. In J.D. Osofsky (ed.), *Handbook of Infant Development* (2nd ed., pp. 669-720). New York: Wiley.

Rothbart, M. and Derryberry, D. (1984) Emotion, attention and temperament. In C. Izard, J. Kagan, and R. Zajonc (eds), *Emotion, Cognition and Behavior* (pp. 133-56). New York: Cambridge University Press.

Sroufe, L. (1979) The coherence of individual development: Early care, attachment, and subsequent developmental issues. *American Psychologist*, 34, 834-41.

Stem, D.N. (1985) *The Interpersonal World of the Infant. A View from Psychoanalysis and Developmental Psychology*. New York: Basic Books.

Trevarthen, C. (1974) Conversations with a two-month-old. *New Scientist*, 896. 230-5.

Tronick, E.Z. (1980) On the primacy of social skills. In D. Sawin, L.Q Walker, and Penticuff (eds), The Exceptional Infant. Psychosocial Risks in Infant Environment Transactions (pp. 144-58). New York: Brunner/Mazel.

Tronick, E.Z. (in press) Of course all relationships are unique: How co-creative processes generate unique mother–infant and patient–therapist relationships and change other relationships. *Psychological Inquiry*, 2002.

Tronick, E.Z. (in press) The increasing differentiation and non-transferability of ways of being together: The primary attachment is specific, not prototypical. Journal of Infant, Child and Adolescent Psychotherapy, 2002.

Tronick, E.Z. and Field, T. (1986) Maternal Depression and Infant Disturbance: New Directions for Child Development (Vol. 34). London: Jossey-Bass.

Tronick, E.Z. and Cohn, J.F. (1989) Infant–mother face-to-face interaction: Age and gender differences in coordination and the occurrence of miscoordination. *Child Development*, 60, 85-92.

Tronick, E.Z, Brushweiller-Stern, N., Harrison, A.M., Lyons-Ruth, K., Morgan, A.C., Nahum, J.P., Sander, L., and Stern, D.N. (1998) Dyadically expanded states of consciousness and the process of therapeutic change. In E.Z. Tronick (ed.), Interactions that Effect Change in Psychotherapy: A Model Used on Infant Research. *Infant Mental Health Journal* [Special issue], 19, 290-9.

Weinberg, K. (1989) *The relation between facial expressions of emotion and behavior in 6 month old infants*. Unpublished master's thesis, University of Massachusetts, Amherst.

Wolff, P. (1963) Observations on the early development of smiling. In B.M. Foss (ed.), *Determinants of Infant Behaviour* (pp. 113-38). London: Methuen.

CHAPTER 5

Where the wild things are[1]

JOAN RAPHAEL-LEFF

The 'wild things' are within each of us. They are the 'formless' things without names, the untamed, unprocessed, passionate, chaotic things that seethe deep below the civilized surface and erupt at times of greater permeability in fragments of dream imagery, inexplicable rage or tears and mood states over which we have no control. Infrequently, in adulthood, we encounter unusually arousing individuals and emotional experiences which resonate with elusive feelings deep inside ourselves, reactivating in us preverbal and non-verbal feeling states. I suggest that parents are particularly susceptible to revival of these 'wild' unprocessed residues of their own infancy and early childhood, evoked by exposure to equivalent raw emotions in their babies.

A close encounter with a baby throws us into the deep end amid the primitive wild things, by violating all the rules. An infant forces awareness of much we have defended against. Disarming adult defences, a baby compels his/her mother or father to re-experience what it is like to be helpless, needy, frustrated, enraged, tantalized, abandoned, betrayed ... and not only newborns. Therese Benedek (1959) traces how, at each stage of development, the child stirs up corresponding unconscious developmental conflicts from the parent's past, especially when these have remained unresolved. As they say colloquially, the parent 'loses it' when the child pushes their specific 'button'. But a paradox operates. To function sensitively to the infant's emotional signalling, the caretaker must remain empathically receptive and therefore keep the boundary between them open. To do so increases vulnerability. If a parent is too susceptible to the unprocessed wild things called up inside by the baby's messiness, neediness, anguish or 'greed', she (and

---

[1] Much modified in 2002 from my paper by this name which originally appeared in the *International Journal of Prenatal & Perinatal Studies*, 1: 78–89, 1989.

equally, the father) can no longer function effectively in helping the infant transform these into manageable emotions. Fury, panic, depression or persecutory anxiety arise at this junction where the wildness evoked within her meet the external provocation and the boundaries fail to contain them. This in turn alarms the unprotected infant, who may play suit to match the parental emotions, play dead to avoid them, or play up to placate them. We might say, then, that at any one time interaction between parent and infant becomes *a reciprocally negotiated compromise between the communicativeness of each one, and the other's capacity to respond.*

Emotional communication in adult encounters

Each of us inhabits a social world in which encounters with others are largely determined by interactional rituals (Goffman, 1967) that we operate without conscious attention. These rules of conduct, which impinge on us both as obligations and expectations, are imbibed from infancy in our interactions with significant others. They serve as the infrastructure for emotional expression – defining in each social exchange the perimeters of our personal space, the nature of our communications, and the code of exchange that transforms both action and inaction into meaningful expression. *In our everyday encounters we each unconsciously manipulate a pliable personal boundary – stretching its limits to take another in, tightening it to expel.*

We become aware of this system of meta-communication only when the rituals of social intercourse can no longer be taken for granted – for instance when we cross the border into another country and find ourselves unclear about ceremonial behaviour or rules of etiquette governing approved manners. In our own society, too, we may encounter individual misconduct which violates systems of decorum, deference or demeanour. We feel ill at ease when strangers talk too loud or stare, when a friend's greeting is not as warm as anticipated or their farewell too prolonged. *Intensity* is a factor: over-involvement may violate mutuality; one partner in the exchange may be too effusive or get 'carried away' emotionally; he or she may self-centredly demand more than his/her share of 'resources' by dominating the conversation, by being too passive or by incapacitating the other with subtle put-downs, or a show of cleverness or seductive persuasiveness. Similarly, on occasion the symmetry of interaction is threatened when one participant seems detached or withholding, distant, or withdrawn behind a mental barrier. If dyadic social interactions are visualized as encounters between two individuals each enclosed within a permeable boundary, *space* – both topographic and internal – enters the equation. Boundaries are felt to be overstepped when people transgress territories of personal reserve, when someone stands too close in a casual encounter, or too far in a familiar one, when an acquaintance intrudes into a private sphere reserved for intimates by gazing, physical touching, intrusive personal questions or tacit assumptions of similarity, or when someone 'dumps' their burdens on us, or steals our ideas. In addition to the external domain there is *internal space*, a complex interior world of internalized figures and happenings which continue to live on as a psychic reality inside each of us, affecting our experience of external reality. We may feel violated by a person who sucks us into their own subjective inner world, forcing us to become a figure in their past. Likewise, we may have a sense of our own innermost space being invaded by someone who worms his/her way into a secret place within, resonating with our own internal figures or strangely disturbing our tranquillity by arousing deep echoes of our own untamed wildness.

As adults, we have learned to handle many such situations between ourselves and others. However, curiously, while feeling discomfort or avoiding some such interactions, on occasion we may find ourselves actually seeking them out, precisely because they do touch on emotional areas within ourselves. We sometimes find an individual or activity that appears to offer an unusual encounter, enabling us to recognize and revitalize an elusive self that we each only dimly sense. In their presence we enter an enclave of our past, find ourselves catapulted through layers of dull defence to archaically intense emotional experience. I am suggesting that these adult encounters revive residues of '*supercharged early moments*', in Fred Pine's felicitous phrase (Pine, 1981), or what Robert Emde (1988) defines as the '*affective core of self-experience*' established in babyhood. Tapping into our own early needs enables us to recapture an old sense of wordless fusion, moments of charged preverbal exchange with loved ones who contained our raw feelings and processed them with us.

In such encounters, what is currently evoked are not only relics of sweet gratification but also undigested moments of wild rage, poignant fragility or inarticulate despair where our own primary caregivers failed us. In our yearning to release our hidden selves, as adults, at times we unconsciously seek metamorphosis. We operate on significant people in our environments to *make* them behave in ways that reactivate these preverbal experiences (see Sandler, 1976). We try to get them to articulate our alienation, seduce them to enact a longlost scene, or manipulate them to spark off a dumb and dormant feeling. Christopher Bollas notes that, in the hope of recapturing early experiences of emotional transformation, we recurrently not only pursue both people and aesthetic experiences who offer (as does psychoanalysis) the transforming qualities that our early parents possessed but also '*surrender*' ourselves to these '*transformational objects*' as to a medium than can alter us (Bollas, 1987).

Hence, we may entice someone to formulate our unspoken desires. We may try and extract a reflection of our own inchoate being that we project to reside mirror-like in someone else, or, by getting another to feel our pain or fear, rid ourselves of it or force them to act protectively or make them process ambiguous fantasies thereby enhancing our range of inner well-being. Much of the time, all this takes place without our conscious knowledge as we wordlessly register each others' states of being, intuitively read and respond to non-verbal signals – or unwittingly use others outside us to mitigate dark forces stirring within. We absorb or deflect, momentarily become receptively permeable or harden into imperviousness.

However, *the corollary of this wish to express and know our innermost selves is a desperate fear of being 'found out' and exposed to hurt.* Our yearning to liberate shackled potential struggles within each of us against defensive inhibitions, the weight of inertia and repetitive enactment of delimiting, crippling familial experiences. *Even as we seek release, anxiety about succumbing to unknown wild impulses leads to intensification of defences and avoidance of 'dangerous' triggers while a desire for 'breakthrough' mingles with a concern about breakdown.* In this context, the motivation to become a parent is often accompanied by an unconscious wish to release archaic raptures, to retrieve and rework undigested experiences and heal early scars. But the full force of a baby's impact can be too much for a parent's fragile defences, and the impact of unresolved parental wild things distorts the child's being.

The provocative exchange

However, I suggest that the threat to personal boundaries begins earlier, during pregnancy, when the expectant mother's body has *actually* incorporated another and distinctions between 'outer' and 'inner' are at risk as delineations between past and future, self and other, conscious and unconscious, order and chaos, fact and fantasy become more fluid. Pregnancy invalidates the axiom of *personal singularity*. In reality, two people now reside under her skin. Natural physical laws of bodies occupying separate spaces are dissolved when two people live inside one body. Furthermore, *gender* is violated as a male substance, a sperm penetrates deep into a female, uniting with her ovum to produce a genetically foreign body embedded within her. Like her internal figures, another exists, operates and moves within her, beyond her conscious control. In addition, a two-way system operates within her transmuting substances between mother and foetus.

In other circumstances such invasion by a semi-foreign body would be ejected or destroyed by the host's immune system but, in pregnancy, the gravida displays a superior ability to suppress the normal response through mechanisms not yet fully grasped. Similarly, to respect the child as other, the woman has to overcome psychic urges to abort her invader or to absorb it into herself. Conversely, as a mother, she temporarily must renounce the 'immunological' boundaries of her psychic separateness and resist a temptation to reject the infant's demands on her inner space and her internal resources. From my clinical experience across the 'caesura of birth', I suggest that how she does this is predicated by conceptualization of their interchange during this time when she serves as container and transformer for her baby, and recipient of his/her waste products.

My account is based on thousands of hours of listening to 150 parents seen 1–5 times per week in psychoanalysis or psychotherapy, sometimes for years, before conception, during pregnancy and early motherhood, over the past 26 years. (Earlier work was also based on questionnaire data derived from pre- and postnatal studies and three surveys of mothers attending a Community Centre Playgroup – Nov. 1980, July 1982, Nov. 1983, ($n = 81$) – and cumulative observation of 23 infant–carer pairs, for three hours a week over a period of 1–3 years, reported elsewhere; Raphael-Leff, 1985a, 1985b; 1986, 1991.

Here I wish to examine how representations of the exchange between expectant mother and foetus act as precipitants of the encounter with the infant:

- What unconscious meanings does the mother–baby exchange represent in a woman's multi-layered inner world?
- How do these expectations coincide with the reality of becoming a parent?
- What happens when the screaming infant touches on a raw nerve and unexpectedly awakens wild things residing deep inside the parent?

Placental paradigm

I am suggesting that motherhood is foreshadowed by pregnancy, the maternal holding of the baby echoing the physical containment of the embryo within the womb, the bi-directional placental system foreshadowing the two-way communicative exchange. My emphasis here is that the intra-uterine processing of nutrients and waste may be seen as an unconscious paradigm for postnatal transformational interaction – when the mediating mother is primed to remove harmful, unwanted aspects of the infant's reality and to replace them with nutritious, growth producing experiences. The foetus during gestation remains unaware that with every heartbeat his mother pumps oxygen-loaded blood and nourishment into the placenta and removes carbon dioxide to be breathed out through her lungs and nitrogen compounds to be excreted by her kidneys in her urine.

However, already in the womb, the mother serves the function of *container*, *transformer and waste disposer* to her loved/hated parasite feeding off her tissue, directing her blood to its own system and spewing out its deposits into her. In pregnancy she physically processes and transmutes good nutrients and bad waste, in the way that she will later act as metaphorical container and transformer of her baby's complex experiences and feelings. 'Metabolizing' his wild projections and feeding back a 'detoxified' processed version that can now safely be re-internalized by the infant, as Bion suggests (1962).

Most women are aware that during pregnancy transposing processes take place through the medium of the placenta. It is a commonly held belief that the generous mother grows this placenta for her baby. In actual fact, since it has evolved from the outer cells of the fertilized ovum, it may equally be said to be brought by the prudent foetus. Similarly, in viewing the placental exchange, one perspective focuses figuratively on *the mother* – either as provider of nourishment or as passive container. An alternative view converges on *the foetus* – 'merged' or growing innocently or else half-alien and/or devouring, stealing and polluting maternal resources. Indeed, some pregnant women fantasize that their entire system is being drained or undermined by the ruthless parasite. How each woman conceptualizes this interaction is determined by her inner reality and, in turn, affects her experience of pregnancy (Raphael-Leff, 1993). Hence, one pregnant woman may imagine that she feels nauseous because of foetal excretions in her body; another might welcome morning sickness as a symptom that she is indeed pregnant in the early absence of other signs; while yet another might consider the nausea to be the manifestation of her secret desire to get rid of the foetus by vomiting it out. Similarly, placental insufficiency could be interpreted either as the 'stingy' mother withholding nourishment from her child or as the 'greedy' baby's needs outstripping placental capacity.

Moreover, as we know, the placenta not only conveys substances. It acts as a *barrier* – again, depending on one's focus, protecting the mother and/or the foetus against harmful substances produced or ingested by the other. Conversely, the barrier must be permeable. 'Good' things need to cross: not only nutrients but antibodies to provide protection against diseases and placental hormones which help sustain the pregnancy. I suggest that, for the expectant mother, this imagined physiological-psychological exchange between herself and the foetus can be conceptualized as a 'Placental Paradigm', in which she imagines herself and her baby as a particular 'good', 'bad' or mixed tandem. Needless to say, at this point, when her relationship with the unknown foetus is based on her own fantasies and projections, her composite conceptualization is of the baby containing aspects of her own imagined baby self (for better or worse) and herself as mother, partly influenced by unconscious representations of her own mother in interaction with her baby self. More complicatedly, representations of the infant to be also include aspects of other internal figures. But during this time when she is carrying a baby as she herself was carried in her mother's womb, a woman's experience in pregnancy, and the early postnatal period, is largely articulated by her *relationship to her own mother* – both the real person who can offer generous help or resort to biting criticism and the internalized image of her archaic mother, providing an inner powerhouse of confidence or an undermining sense of untrustworthiness or anxiety (similarly an expectant father).

Postnatal encounter

With birth, that which was inside her is now out. The natural purposefulness of pregnancy is replaced for the woman by the shapelessness of days and nights filled with infantile demands, chaos and tiredness. Wild things which have been kept at bay now come seeping in with a vengeance.

Having a baby means contagious exposure to primitive experiences. Boundaries can no longer be effortlessly maintained. The infant, a fragile, urgent, needy creature, stirs up resonances of these sensations in the empathic caretaker, who uses her sensitivity to understand the baby's needs. During the first few weeks, the mother, still raw from her own experience of pregnancy and giving birth, is at her most sensitive and, hence, most vulnerable. Often she is isolated and lonely. Often she herself lacks support and care. As primary carer in continuous contact with her baby, she lacks the psychic space and time to restore her own emotional balance and is at risk of becoming overwhelmed by the heightened emotions aroused in her. Yet she is expected to let the baby suck juices from her body, answer urgent cries and dispose of the mess. She is immersed in primal matter – herself discharging lochia and lactating milk – and must clean away the stuff oozing out of every orifice of her baby's body including eyes, ears, navel, mouth, anus and genitals. The smells and sight of these primary substances activate preverbal bodily memories which further increase her susceptibility. Yet she is given full responsibility for her baby and designated as 'container' for the infant's unbearable anxieties. At this very time, while she is thus bombarded, she is meant to love her baby, to process reality and help him or her to make sense of the world. A mother who can risk being receptive can receive what the baby evacuates into her, and if she can reflect on these, having metabolized these anxieties, may give back safe, processed feelings for the baby to internalize, along with the capacity for thinking (Bion, 1962). However, when she herself is full of her own unbearable anxieties, there is no space to process the baby's.

MOTHER	BABY	PLACENTAL ACTIVITY
+ Safe/good *(processing/nourishing)*	**+ Safe/good** *(sustaining)*	Mutual communion
+ Safe/good *(bountiful)*	**– Dangerous/bad** *(parasite)*	Mother's defence barrier
– Dangerous/bad *(polluting)*	**+ Safe/good** *(innocent)*	Baby's defence barrier
– Dangerous/bad *(harmful)*	**– Dangerous/bad** *(harmful)*	Mutual barrier

Figure 5.1 Placental Paradigm.

Maternal experiences

Postnatally, too, mothers differ in their responses. Some experience both themselves and the baby as 'good', 'safe' and 'compatible'. During the first weeks, they surrender themselves to sweet communion as they did in pregnancy, swelling their personal boundary to encompass both. Some of these mothers sustain the dyad through the support of a good internal mother or external equivalent. Others draw on an idealized representation of mothering which denies any ambivalent feelings, vicariously nourishing their baby selves from a common pool of infantile fusion which can serve them in the early weeks but later, with the baby's growing agency, 'merger' falters. Yet others are disappointed, feeling empty and bereft of the special closeness of pregnancy. Some mothers even contemplate conceiving again immediately to reinstate the lost satisfying state of pregnancy. Others may succumb to *depression*. Feeling guilty about letting the baby down, anxious about her own ability to protect the baby from external dangers (and herself from the threat the baby may represent), for one mother, each small failure may be experienced as a tidal wave of distress, wiping out everything safe and good, as if, once started, archaic darkness will leak out from her own inner space where only desolation now reigns. This mother's bolt-hole might be an inner vortex of oblivion, alcoholism or wall-staring depression, sometimes necessitating removal of both herself and the baby to the safe environs of a containing hospital.

To another woman, the real baby may feel alien – no longer part of the self – and unlike the fantasy she held in mind. Out in the world, it may become a source of envy, now it, not she, is the centre of attention. She may feel the infant can show her up, having been inside her and knowing the worst about her. The infant may come to represent repudiated needy or greedy aspects of herself. The hallmark of the latter pattern is one of *persecution* rather than guilty or anxious depression. A woman may dread being 'sucked' into the morass of infancy, drowning in the sea of maternity and confusion. Bombarded by sentimental social and media expectations, she may feel 'bad' about her need to break free. Yet now that her life feels taken over by motherhood she may lose her familiar sense of identity and self-esteem. Submerged in trivia, bogged down in contaminating menial jobs and raw sensations, and starved of intellectual content, a woman experiences herself becoming invisible, taken over by the baby. Living in a timeless world of wasting, wanting, waiting to be saved by the ringing phone – unless she can be rescued from the tedium, she may become deeply resentful and depressed – and feeling devoid of self-expression, sucked dry by the demanding baby she is too exhausted and trapped to be responsive to the infant's emotional communications.

But it is not physical inertia. In addition to the drudgery, much energy is used by such 'persecuted' mothers to ward off terrible passions. As each new mother is plunged back into powerful naked emotions of infancy, her own repudiated reservoirs of deprivation, hurt, hatred and rage are tapped: an unhappy baby may terrify the mother into feeling that once the infant starts crying he or she will never stop. The mother fears that contagion might set in and she too may burst the floodgates of her emotion; tears and self-pity will come pouring out of an unplugged hole deep inside her and never cease flowing. She feels the need to erect a sound barrier between them, rigidifying her boundary to keep the baby out – to prevent his misery leaching into her innermost crevices and stirring up her own. Another mother may dread her baby's voracious hunger, feeling unequal to meeting the bottomless pit of his greed. Yet another fears competition with her needy baby over scarce supplies of time and inner resources, which she keeps for herself. While her adult self appreciates her partner's parenting skills, she may nevertheless feel jealous of the baby's relationship with him. Old sibling rivalries may resurface as this baby's birth dredges up jealousy experienced when a baby brother or sister was born many years ago. Detaching herself, another may feel she is slowly dying of boredom and erosion ... un-nurtured and desperately alone.

This is where external support becomes essential. Struggling on, women who wish to be good mothers and do the best for their babies may be too proud to ask for help, or even to recognize that it is needed. Where therapy is unavailable, health visitors can do much to alleviate the suffering and help restore a woman's capacity to find her own strengths.

Parental representations

Thus, the urgent pitch of a baby's cry pierces through defensive barriers, catapulting the parent back into infantile anguish. Crying might be experienced by the hypersensitive adult as a critical judgement of their parenting. An accusation that this mother or father has failed to satisfy the baby, that he or she is mean and withholding or no good – painful news to a parent who had hoped to surpass their own depriving parents. Again, what is heard is determined by the parent's own inner world and past experiences of being parented. Listening to her baby's cry, one mother might hear wild rage, hatred, blame or frustration while another hears the sound of an intolerable desolation and sadness spilling out of the baby into the mother, beseeching her to take the hurt away. The baby's speechless cry resonates with forgotten things buried deep inside herself, perforating her internal barriers.

I suggest that depending on whether she sees him (the baby – and, unconsciously, the baby she imagines herself to have been in the eyes of her own carer) as innocent and harmless or parasitical, savage and threatening, and whether she sees her current self (identified with, or in competition to, her archaic mother and other constitutional internal figures) as safe and bountiful, or empty, bad and potentially dangerous, she consolidates or dismantles the defensive barriers between them.

A mother may be so concerned to ratify herself as the sole source of 'goodness' that she is unable to allow gifts from elsewhere. She might crave to blend into her infant, vicariously gratifying the infant within her, obliterating her adult self in blissful fusion. Symbiosis is then prolonged, curtailing her growing child's drive towards independence. Where such an idealized merger is maintained, all ambivalence within the relationship must be denied. The baby is not allowed to cry, rage, question or express any negative feelings which could be experienced as rejection by the mother. However, her own unconscious grievance lurks hidden beneath her oversolicitous care and anxious monitoring, and she is unable to separate from her individuating baby in whom she has invested so much of herself.

Conversely, a woman may consciously be so frightened of the damage she could do her baby, or he/she do her, that she loses faith in the capacity for a benign exchange. Fearing contagion, she feels in danger of being turned into a harmful mother through exposure to her wild baby. Critical others will see her naughty baby as evidence that she's a 'Bad Mother', that she's no good at it, doesn't know how or, worse, they will regard this bad baby who has come out of her as a revelation of her own *hidden self*, parading her badness for all the world to see. The baby, identified with disowned aspects of herself, must be controlled. Terrified to remain on her own with the infant, fearful of losing control and becoming dangerous too, she may try to protect him/her from her own wildness and herself from his/her retaliation, by retreating behind a barrier of emotional absence, obsessionality, schizoid withdrawal or indifferent neglect.

If she has the means, she may try utilizing socially approved means of getting away – finding a childminder or crèche, going back to work or nipping out to the shops. Failing these 'legitimate' outlets, feeling desperate in her need to create a mutual boundary of space between them, she may just make a wild bolt for freedom. However, socioeconomic circumstances, lack of employment, social disapproval of working mothers, subtle influences from experts and media and internalized expectations may pressure the woman into staying put. Despairingly, she may see herself on a treadmill of demands, a martyr chained to the stake, conscientiously having to go on providing comfort and security because no one else will do so... Depression in these circumstances of 'no choice' is extremely common. Where there is no help forthcoming and no relief from her dangerous baby and from the experience of herself as a harmful, bad mother, she may resort to detachment or to punitive measures in an attempt to force her wild baby into submission to make him 'good'. In extreme cases she may act out the fantasy of ridding herself of the wilful, wild persecutor through suicide or battering her jailer.

If unresolved issues about containment, separation and resources prefigure our expectations, defensive manoeuvres originate in an attempt to protect ourselves from loss and to control resources when these seem meagre and endangered. In families, where people are interdependent, there is often an undercurrent of competition over who controls the resources and how these can be shared out. A baby's demands on the exhausted parent's energy and precious 'prime' time may feel excessive. However, because of their asymmetry, to that child the powerful parent holds the key to all resources, both to concrete goodies and to the capacity to mirror and interpret the inexplicable. The parent's ongoing love is taken on trust by the infant, but, when that trust fails, defensive options range from *freezing* in a limbo state of nothingness (or suffering), *taking flight* into fantasy (or 'away'), or *fighting it out* using the weapon of one's lungs and flailing arms to register defiance or complaint. Like their babies, some parents live in constant anxiety of loss; however, unlike this restricted repertoire of the young child, parents have a range of defences. Some compulsively control resources by hoarding them obsessionally. Others counteract fears by manic largess or regulate resources by parcelling them out with great attention to fairness. Yet others practise measured martyrdom or collapse into a sense of (manipulative) victimized helplessness or depressed worthlessness. While feeling persecuted, some panic; others erupt in ferocious demands. Psychoanalytic understanding enables us to trace common roots to different behaviours. Conversely, it allows us to see the overdetermined variety of meanings that a single symptom may express. Thus, in both adults and children, rage, anxiety, depression, and tyranny may all be related to a subjective sense of lacking agency.

```
                              'GOOD'
                              MOTHER

*Idealized Merger                   |        * Control/Martyrdom

NO BARRIERS                         |        Mother's DEFENCE BARRIER

'GOOD'                                                          'GOOD'
  BABY _____ |_____ BABY

* Guilt/Depression                  |        * Anxiety/persecution

Baby's DEFENCE BARRIER              |        MUTUAL BARRIER

                              'BAD'
                              MOTHER
```

Key
* = predominant experience

Note: Where past events have been processed, ambivalence is acknowledged and parenting can proceed without a prefigured predominantly defensive experience.

Figure 5.2 Maternal subjective experience of mother–infant interchange.

Intrafamilial forces

Undoubtedly, the experience of these early weeks is much influenced by familial factors – not only whether this baby is an only child, its gender and position in the family constellation but also whether its symbolic significance in relation to each parent's family of origin. Crucial is whether the mother has emotional and practical support, from a partner if she has one, and the degree and quality of involvement she may expect from him (or her – but lesbian couples are not the topic of this paper). Joint care for the infant and a shared emotional reality can mitigate unconscious forces within the parents and enhance their sense of adult partnership and enjoyment of the baby. However, fathers too have their internal infant-carer paradigms. And a partner who is envious of his woman's capacity to give birth and nurture – or jealous of the relationship between her and the infant, or one who withdraws to defend his own boundary against invasion by the baby's wild being – increases the burden of pressures on the new mother, making exacting, possessive, sexual, or even violent claims upon her to process *his* emotional experience and cater to *his* needs at the expense of the baby's or her own.

She then becomes caught in the double cross-fire of interpersonal and intrapsychic demands with no one to reaffirm her.

Partners become parents

Not only is the mother's or father's responsiveness to the baby affected by how well they have processed their own infantile feelings but when partners become parents it often leads to deterioration of the emotional and sexual relationship. Dependency is one issue. In couples where only he works outside the home, his attitude towards her economic dependence can make the difference between her experience of feeling as helpless and powerless as the baby (a 'stateless person colonized by a chequebook' as one mother said), or a valued, self-respecting woman doing a most important job. Debarred from adult company and denuded of non-domestic skills, she may feel reduced to a childlike existence, slipping back into dependency – not only economic but emotional, too. When the non-domestic partner retreats behind a sullen wall of silence and refuses to participate, mediate or even take in the minutiae of the primary carer's intimate adventures with the baby, this not only solidifies barriers between the couple but leaves that caregiver overexposed to dangers. Trapped in the dyadic relationship of primary identification and mirroring she/he looks to the other to triangulate the interchange. The partner who works outside could bring home the real world where these crude, concrete substances – faeces, urine, mucus – are symbolic and abstracted. Language could process some of the strange and ambiguous contradictions the primary carer feels within him/herself. Allowed to spell out their ambivalence, a dread secret might be dispelled and replaced by a mundane human feeling. However, left to stew within unvoiced terrors of the unknown and unknowable, the baby's carer often feels uncared for, forgotten, and imprisoned at home with the dangerous baby and reawakened vulnerability, caught in a round of sleepless nights, unrelieved total responsibility and heightened emotion. While true for fathers who are involuntary primary caregivers, it is particularly the case with unsupported lone parents of either sex who lack a confidant. She or he may succumb to fears of the tension building up within, feeling as if, without rigid control, the boundaries would split open, and all the accumulated internal mess and wildness would come pouring out. If there are other children in the family, they, too, may be drawn into becoming emotional mainstays to the unsupported carer, or into erecting barriers between carer and baby.

In a family with two parents, personal areas of vulnerability do not necessarily coincide and so parental reactions might clash. This is hardly surprising given that sexual partnerships are often the most complex of all chosen relationships. At times of stress or disappointed hopes, unconscious residues from early intimate relationships are played out. And, according to their own emotional resourcefulness, each partner within a couple gravitates towards his or her own fixed or fluid, meshing or contradictory resolution. Finally, I suggest that the trend towards ever-contracting family and social stratification reduces opportunities to work actively through archaic feelings in the presence of other infants (siblings, cousins, friends' children) before the birth of one's own. Indeed, the newborn for whom a Western parent is given full responsibility is often the first they have ever encountered, which further exacerbates the arousal they experience. However, it is also the case that this very revival of infantile feelings in early parenthood can be a chance to 'metabolize' what has been unprocessed, thereby leading to healing and growth.

How each partner responds to parenthood is largely determined by their own early experiences of being parented, whether their internal wildness was transformed into creative happenings by loving, nurturing carers and how well they themselves have reflected upon their own early experiences over the years and processed the unconscious tandem representation of baby in the mind of the carer. For, however bad these experiences really were, once these are processed and understood, the person can move on rather than repeat or remain at the mercy of the wild things within. If the parent has been able to forgive their own parents for being less than perfect, they can then draw on the memories of the loving and helpful metabolized experiences that they *have* retained despite the mistakes, frustrations and sad times. This will enable him or her to engage in *a real and new relationship* with their own baby, a process of reciprocal discovery through emotional receptivity, physical exchange and play.

Once archaic grievances are laid to rest and unfulfilled desires mourned as unobtainable, a parent is better able to tolerate and even enjoy the present and face the future unhampered by infantile hopes for compensation or revenge. One route to this process is through *a perinatal therapeutic relationship* in which the reactivated past can be re-evaluated and understood, alleviating the chronic sense of endangerment from without or within. Another is through the very *process of parenting a baby* oneself, fostering insights enabling a father or mother to forge a new relationship with internal figures and the past. Repeated gratifying exchanges with the baby both revitalize positive infantile experiences and make it easier to bear the pain of one's own early deficiencies and deprivations without acting them out or inflicting them on the new baby. The very *newness* of her relationship with this baby helps a mother discover facets of herself hitherto unrealized. At the same time, with support, her current position as mother enables her to actively re-experience, repeat and 'master' familiar and deeply held passive bodily and emotional experiences of having been mothered. Finally, this enables her to be receptive to the particular needs of her own baby. When a parent can hold onto the good times with the infant while not denying the bad, and can remain emotionally available without being overwhelmed, allowing the baby to be himself or herself – neither 'good' nor 'bad' but a unique 'good-enough' baby and the parent, 'good-enough' (see Winnicott, 1960) – the baby's infancy will be truly transformational, and they will all emerge with realistic self-esteem and integrated solidity.

Psychic change

In this case – for a woman – mothering will not necessitate primary identification or competition with her mother that means mindlessly repeating mother's obstetric history and her reaction to a screaming, hungry baby:

- Neither will she need to drive herself to fulfil an impossibly idealized role by trying to emulate the mother she wished she'd had.
- Nor yet will she feel forced to subjugate part of herself, attempting to subdue and conceal the wildness in herself which she felt her mother could not accept and which she now fears might be damaging to the baby.
- She need not try and change the baby into the perfect baby she believes her mother might have wished her to be.
- Nor exploit the baby to vicariously fulfil what she feels she has missed out on or now needs, to the detriment of spontaneous interaction with the baby or metabolizing his/her own unique experience.
- Nor yet will she need to turn the baby into a projection of her wildest dreams or a vicarious means of revitalizing her own dormant wildness.

In conclusion, the wild things are within us all, awaiting discovery and verbal processing to transform them into creative potential. Whether this can occur in adulthood depends on the quality of mothering we glean from our surroundings and offer ourselves. How we each contain ourselves within the holding 'womb' of our minds; how well we nourish, metabolize and rid ourselves of 'waste'; how accessible we are and how permeable or rigid we allow barriers to be both intrapsychically and with others. And, above all, growth depends on whether we can recognize and accept ownership for the wild things inside ourselves.

References

Benedek, T. (1959) Parenthood as a Developmental Phase. *Journal of the American Psychoanalytic Association*, 7, 389–417.

Bion, W.R. (1962) *Learning from Experience*. London; Heinemann.

Bollas, C. (1987) *The Shadow of the Object: Psychoanalysis of the Unthought Known*. London, Free Association Press.

Emde, R. (1988) Development Terminable and Interminable. *International Journal of Psycho-Analysis*, 69: 23–43; 283–97.

Goffman, I. (1967) *Interaction Ritual: Essays on Face-to-face Behaviour*. New York, Pantheon.

Pine, F. (1981) In the Beginning: contribution to psychoanalytic developmental psychology. *International Review of Psychoanalysis*, 8: 15–34.

Raphael-Leff, J. (1985a) Facilitators and Regulators: vulnerability to postnatal disturbance. *Journal Psychosomatic Obstetrics & Gynaecology* 4: 151–68.

Raphael-Leff, J. (1985b) Facilitators and Regulators; Participators and Renouncers: mothers' and fathers' orientations towards pregnancy and parenthood. *Psychosomatic Obstetrics & Gynaecology*, 4: 169–84.

Raphael-Leff, J. (1986) Facilitators and Regulators: conscious and unconscious processes in pregnancy and early motherhood. *British Journal of Medical Psychology*, 59: 43–55.

Raphael-Leff, J. (1991) *Psychological Processes of Childbearing*, University of Essex, 2001.

Raphael-Leff, J. (1993) *Pregnancy – The Inside Story*, Karnac, 2001.

Sandler, J. (1976) Countertransference and Role-Responsiveness. *International Review of Psycho-analysis*, 3: 43–8.

Winnicott, D.W. (1960) Ego Distortion in terms of True and False Self. In *The Maturational Processes and the Facilitating Environment*, pp. 140–52, London, Hogarth Press.

CHAPTER 6

The experience of the skin in early object relations[1]

ESTHER BICK

The central theme of this brief communication is concerned with the primal function of the skin of the baby and of its primal objects in relation to the most primitive binding together of parts of the personality not as yet differentiated from parts of the body. It can be most readily studied in psychoanalysis in relation to problems of dependence and separation in the transference.

The thesis is that in its most primitive form the parts of the personality are felt to have no binding force amongst themselves and must therefore be held together in a way that is experienced by them passively, by the skin functioning as a boundary. But this internal function of containing the parts of the self is dependent initially on the introjection of an external object, experienced as capable of fulfilling this function. Later, identification with this function of the object supersedes the unintegrated state and gives rise to the fantasy of internal and external spaces. Only then the stage is set for the operation of primal splitting and idealization of self and object as described by Melanie Klein. Until the containing functions have been introjected, the concept of a space within the self cannot arise. Introjection, i.e. construction of an object in an internal space, is therefore impaired. In its absence, the function of projective identification will necessarily continue unabated and all the confusions of identity attending it will be manifest.

The stage of primal splitting and idealization of self and object can now be seen to rest on this earlier process of containment of self and object by their respective 'skins'. The fluctuations in this primal state will be illustrated in case material, from infant observation, in order to show the difference

[1] This paper, which was read at the 25th International Psycho-Analytical Congress, in Copenhagen, July 1967, first appeared in print in the *International Journal of Psycho-Analysis*, 49: 484–6, 1968, and is reprinted here by kind permission of that journal.

between unintegration as a passive experience of total helplessness and disintegration through splitting processes as an active defensive operation in the service of development. We are, therefore, from the economic point of view, dealing with situations conducive to catastrophic anxieties in the unintegrated state as compared with the more limited and specific persecutory and depressive ones.

The need for a containing object would seem, in the infantile unintegrated state, to produce a frantic search for an object – a light, a voice, a smell, or other sensual object – which can hold the attention and thereby be experienced, momentarily at least, as holding the parts of the personality together. The optimal object is the nipple in the mouth, together with the holding and talking and familiar-smelling mother.

Material will show how this containing object is experienced concretely as a skin. Faulty development of this primal skin function can be seen to result either from defects in the adequacy of the actual object or from fantasy attacks on it, which impair introjection. Disturbance in the primal skin function can lead to a development of a 'second-skin' formation through which dependence on the object is replaced by a pseudo-independence, by the inappropriate use of certain mental functions, or perhaps innate talents, for the purpose of creating a substitute for this 'skin-container' function. The material to follow will give some examples of 'second-skin' formation. Here I can only indicate the types of clinical material upon which these findings are based. My present aim is to open up this topic for a detailed discussion in a later paper.

Infant observation: baby Alice

One year of observation of an immature young mother and her first baby showed a gradual improvement in the 'skin-container' function up to 12 weeks. As the mother's tolerance to closeness to the baby increased, so did her need to excite the baby to manifestations of vitality lessen. A consequent diminution of unintegrated states in the baby could be observed. These had been characterized by trembling, sneezing, and disorganized movements. There followed a move to a new house in a still-unfinished condition. This disturbed severely the mother's holding capacity and led her to a withdrawal from the baby. She began feeding while watching television, or at night in the dark without holding the baby. This brought a flood of somatic disturbance and an increase of unintegrated states in the baby. Father's illness at that time made matters worse, and the mother had to plan to return to work. She began to press the baby into a pseudo-independence, forcing her onto a training-cup, introducing a bouncer during the day, while harshly refusing to respond to the crying at night. The mother now returned to an earlier tendency to stimulate the child to aggressive displays which she provoked and admired. The result by six-and-a-half months was a hyperactive and aggressive little girl, whom mother called 'a boxer' from her habit of pummelling people's faces. We see here the formation of a muscular type of self-containment – 'second-skin' in place of a proper skin container.

Analysis of a schizophrenic girl: Mary

Some years of analysis, since age $3^1/_2$, have enabled us to reconstruct the mental states reflected in the history of her infantile disturbance. The facts are as follows: a difficult birth, early clenching of the nipple but lazy feeding, bottle supplement in the third week but on breast until 11 months, infantile eczema at four months and scratching until bleeding, extreme clinging to mother, severe intolerance to waiting for feeds, and delayed and atypical development in all areas.

In the analysis, severe intolerance to separation was reflected from the start as in the jaw-clenched systematic tearing and breaking of all materials after the first holiday-break. Utter dependence on the immediate contact could be seen and studied in the unintegrated states of posture and motility, on the one hand, and thought and communication, on the other, which existed at the beginning of each session, improving during the course, to reappear on leaving. She came in hunched, stiff-jointed, grotesque like a 'sack of potatoes' as she later called herself, and emitting an explosive 'SSBICK' for 'Good morning, Mrs Bick'. This 'sack of potatoes' seemed in constant danger of spilling out its contents partly due to the continual picking of holes in her skin representing the 'sack' skin of the object in which parts of herself, the 'potatoes', were contained (projective identification). Improvement from the hunched posture to an erect one was achieved, along with a lessening of her general total dependence, more through a formation of a second skin based on her own muscularity than on identification with a containing object.

Analysis of an adult neurotic patient

The alternation of two types of experience of self – the 'sack of apples' and 'the hippopotamus' – could be studied in regard to the quality of contact in the transference and experience of separation, both being related to a disturbed feeding period. In the 'sack of apples' state, the patient was touchy, vain, in need of constant attention and praise, easily bruised and constantly expecting catastrophe, such as a collapse when getting up from the couch. In the 'hippopotamus' state, the patient was aggressive, tyrannical, scathing, and relentless in following his own way. Both states were related to the 'second-skin' type of organization, dominated by projective identification.

The 'hippopotamus' skin, like the 'sack', was a reflection of the object's skin inside which he existed, while the thin-skinned, easily bruised, apples inside the sack, represented the state of parts of the self which were inside this insensitive object.

Analysis of a child: Jill

Early in the analysis of a five-year-old child, whose feeding period had been characterized by anorexia, skin-container problems presented themselves, as in her constant demand from mother during the first analytic holiday, that her clothes should be firmly fastened, and her shoes tightly laced. Later material showed her intense anxiety and need to distinguish herself from toys and dolls, about which she said: 'Toys are not like me, they break to pieces and don't get well. They don't have a skin. We have a skin!'

Summary

In all patients with disturbed first-skin formation, severe disturbance of the feeding period is indicated by analytic reconstruction, though not always observed by the parents. This faulty skin-formation produces a general fragility in later integration and organizations. It manifests itself in states of unintegration as distinct from regression involving the most basic types of partial or total unintegration of body, posture, motility, and corresponding functions of mind, particularly communication. The 'second-skin' phenomenon, which replaces first-skin integration, manifests itself as either a partial or total type of muscular shell or a corresponding verbal muscularity.

Analytic investigation of the second skin phenomenon tends to produce transitory states of unintegration. Only an analysis which perseveres to thorough working-through of the primal dependence on the maternal object can strengthen this underlying fragility. It must be stressed that the containing aspect of the analytic situation resides especially in the setting and is therefore an area where firmness of technique is crucial.

CHAPTER 7

A theory of thinking[1]

WILFRED R. BION

i. In this paper I am primarily concerned to present a theoretical system. Its resemblance to a philosophical theory depends on the fact that philosophers have concerned themselves with the same subject-matter; it differs from philosophical theory in that it is intended, like all psycho-analytical theories, for use. It is devised with the intention that practising psycho-analysts should restate the hypotheses of which it is composed in terms of empirically verifiable data. In this respect it bears the same relationship to similar statements of philosophy as the statements of applied mathematics bear to pure mathematics.

The derived hypotheses that are intended to admit of empirical test, and to a lesser extent the theoretical system itself, bear the same relationship to the observed facts in a psycho-analysis as statements of applied mathematics, say about a mathematical circle, bear to a statement about a circle drawn upon paper.

ii. This theoretical system is intended to be applicable in a significant number of cases; psycho-analysts should therefore experience realizations that approximate to the theory.

I attach no diagnostic importance to the theory though I think it may be applicable whenever a disorder of thought is believed to exist. Its diagnostic significance will depend upon the pattern formed by the constant conjunction of a number of theories of which this theory would be one.

---

[1] This paper was read at the 22nd International Psycho-Analytical Congress held in Edinburgh, 1961 and was first published in the *International Journal of PsychoAnalysis*, 43: 306–10, with whose kind permission it is reprinted here. It also appeared in Bion's book, *Second Thoughts*, published by Karnac in 1984.

It may help to explain the theory if I discuss the background of emotional experience from which it has been abstracted. I shall do this in general terms without attempting scientific rigour.

iii. It is convenient to regard thinking as dependent on the successful outcome of two main mental developments. The first is the development of thoughts. They require an apparatus to cope with them. The second development, therefore, is of this apparatus that I shall provisionally call thinking. I repeat – thinking has to be called into existence to cope with thoughts.

It will be noted that this differs from any theory of thought as a product of thinking, in that thinking is a development forced on the psyche by the pressure of thoughts and not the other way round. Psychopathological developments may be associated with either phase or both, that is, they may be related to a breakdown in the development of thoughts, or a breakdown in the development of the apparatus for 'thinking' or dealing with thoughts, or both.

iv. 'Thoughts' may be classified, according to the nature of their developmental history, as pre-conceptions, conceptions or thoughts, and finally concepts; concepts are named and therefore fixed conceptions or thoughts. The conception is initiated by the conjunction of a pre-conception with a realization. The pre-conception may be regarded as the analogue in psychoanalysis of Kant's concept of 'empty thoughts'. Psycho-analytically the theory that the infant has an inborn disposition corresponding to an expectation of a breast may be used to supply a model. When the pre-conception is brought into contact with a realization that approximates to it, the mental outcome is a conception. Put in another way, the pre-conception (the inborn expectation of a breast, the a priori knowledge of a breast, the 'empty thought') when the infant is brought in contact with the breast itself, mates with awareness of the realization and is synchronous with the development of a conception. This model will serve for the theory that every junction of a pre-conception with its realization produces a conception. Conceptions therefore will be expected to be constantly conjoined with an emotional experience of satisfaction.

v. I shall limit the term 'thought' to the mating of a pre-conception with a frustration. The model I propose is that of an infant whose expectation of a breast is mated with a realization of no breast available for satisfaction. This mating is experienced as a no-breast, or 'absent' breast inside. The next step depends on the infant's capacity for frustration: in particular it depends on whether the decision is to evade frustration or to modify it.

vi. If the capacity for toleration of frustration is sufficient, the 'no-breast' inside becomes a thought, and an apparatus for 'thinking' it develops. This initiates the state, described by Freud in his 'Two Principles of Mental Functioning', in which dominance by the reality principle is synchronous with the development of an ability to think and so to bridge the gulf of frustration between the moment when a want is felt and the moment when action appropriate to satisfying the want culminates in its satisfaction. A capacity for tolerating frustration thus enables the psyche to develop thought as a means by which the frustration that is tolerated is itself made more tolerable.

vii. If the capacity for toleration of frustration is inadequate, the bad internal 'no-breast', that a personality capable of maturity ultimately recognizes as a thought, confronts the psyche with the need to decide between evasion of frustration and its modification.

viii. Incapacity for tolerating frustration tips the scale in the direction of evasion of frustration. The result is a significant departure from the events that Freud describes as characteristic of thought in the phase of dominance of the reality principle. What should be a thought, a product of the juxtaposition of pre-conception and negative realization, becomes a bad object, indistinguishable from a thing-in-itself, fit only for evacuation. Consequently the development of an apparatus for thinking is disturbed, and instead there takes place a hypertrophic development of the apparatus of projective identification. The model I propose for this development is a psyche that operates on the principle that evacuation of a bad breast is synonymous with obtaining sustenance from a good breast. The end result is that all thoughts are treated as if they were indistinguishable from bad internal objects; the appropriate machinery is felt to be, not an apparatus for thinking the thoughts, but an apparatus for ridding the psyche of accumulations of bad internal objects. The crux lies in the decision between modification and evasion of frustration.

ix. Mathematical elements, namely straight lines, points, circles, and something corresponding to what later become known by the name of numbers, derive from realizations of two-ness as in breast and infant, two eyes, two feet, and so on.

x. If tolerance of frustration is not too great, modification becomes the governing aim. Development of mathematical elements, or mathematical objects as Aristotle calls them, is analogous to the development of conceptions.

xi. If intolerance of frustration is dominant, steps are taken to evade perception of the realization by destructive attacks. In so far as pre-conception and realization are mated, mathematical conceptions are formed, but they are treated as if indistinguishable from things-in-themselves and are evacuated at high speed as missiles to annihilate space. In so far as space and time are perceived as identical with a bad object that is destroyed, that is to say a no-breast, the realization that should be mated with the pre-conception is not available to complete the conditions necessary for the formation of a conception. The dominance of protective identification confuses the distinction between the self and the external object. This contributes to the absence of any perception of two-ness, since such an awareness depends on the recognition of a distinction between subject and object.

xii. The relationship with time was graphically brought home to me by a patient who said over and over again that he was wasting time – and continued to waste it. The patient's aim is to destroy time by wasting it. The consequences are illustrated in the description in *Alice in Wonderland* of the Mad Hatter's teaparty – it is always four o'clock.

xiii. Inability to tolerate frustration can obstruct the development of thoughts and a capacity to think, though a capacity to think would diminish the sense of frustration intrinsic to appreciation of the gap between a wish and its fulfilment. Conceptions, that is to say the outcome of a mating between a pre-conception and its realization, repeat in a more complex form the history of pre-conception. A conception does not necessarily meet a realization that approximates sufficiently closely to satisfy. If frustration can be tolerated, the mating of conception and realizations, whether negative or positive initiates procedures necessary to learning by experience. If intolerance of frustration is not so great as to activate the mechanisms of evasion and yet is too great to bear dominance of the reality principle, the personality develops omnipotence as a substitute for the mating of the pre-conception, or conception, with the negative realization. This involves the assumption of omniscience as a substitute for learning from experience by aid of thoughts and thinking. There is therefore no psychic activity to discriminate between true and false. Omniscience substitutes for the discrimination between true and false a dictatorial affirmation that one thing is morally right and the other wrong. The assumption of omniscience that denies reality ensures that the morality thus engendered is a function of psychosis. Discrimination between true and false is a function of the non-psychotic part of the personality and its factors. There is thus potentially a conflict between assertion of truth and assertion of moral ascendancy. The extremism of the one infects the other.

xiv. Some pre-conceptions relate to expectations of the self. The pre-conceptual apparatus is adequate to realizations that fall in the narrow range of circumstances suitable for the survival of the infant. One circumstance that affects survival is the personality of the infant himself. Ordinarily the personality of the infant, like other elements in the environment, is managed by the mother. If the mother and child are adjusted to each other, projective identification plays a major role in the management; the infant is able through the operation of a rudimentary reality sense to behave in such a way that projective identification, usually an omnipotent phantasy, is a realistic phenomenon. This, I am inclined to believe, is its normal condition. When Klein speaks of 'excessive' projective identification I think the term 'excessive' should be understood to apply not to the frequency only with which projective identification is employed but to excess of belief in omnipotence. As a realistic activity it shows itself as behaviour reasonably calculated to arouse in the mother feelings of which the infant wishes to be rid. If the infant feels it is dying it can arouse fears that it is dying in the mother. A well-balanced mother can accept these and respond therapeutically: that is to say in a manner that makes the infant feel it is receiving its frightened personality back again, but in a form that it can tolerate – the fears are manageable by the infant personality. If the mother cannot tolerate these projections the infant is reduced to continue projective identification carried out with increasing force and frequency. The increased force seems to denude the projection of its penumbra of meaning. Reintrojection is affected with similar force and frequency. Deducing the patient's feelings from his behaviour in the consulting room and using the deductions to form a model, the infant of my model does not behave in a way that I ordinarily expect of an adult who is thinking. It behaves as if it felt that an internal object has been built up that has the characteristics of a greedy vagina-like 'breast' that strips of its goodness all that the infant receives or gives, leaving only degenerate objects. This internal object starves its host of all understanding that is made available. In analysis such a patient seems unable to gain from his environment and therefore from his analyst. The consequences for the development of a capacity for thinking are serious; I shall describe only one, namely, precocious development of consciousness.

xv. By consciousness I mean in this context what Freud described as a 'sense-organ for the perception of psychic qualities'.

I have described previously (at a Scientific Meeting of the British Psycho-Analytical Society) the use of a concept of 'alpha-function' as a working tool in the analysis of disturbances of thought. It seemed convenient to suppose an alpha-function to convert sense data into alpha-elements and thus provide the psyche with the material for dream thoughts, and hence the capacity to wake up or go to sleep, to be conscious or unconscious. According to this theory consciousness depends on alpha-function, and it is a logical necessity to suppose that such a function exists if we are to assume that the self is able to be conscious of itself in the sense of knowing itself from experience of itself. Yet the failure to establish, between infant and mother, a relationship in which normal projective identification is possible precludes the development of an alpha-function and therefore of a differentiation of elements into conscious and unconscious.

xvi. The difficulty is avoided by restricting the term 'consciousness' to the meaning conferred on it by Freud's definition. Using the term 'consciousness' in this restricted sense it is possible to suppose that this consciousness produces 'sense-data' of the self, but that there is no alpha-function to convert them into alpha-elements and therefore permit of a capacity for being conscious or unconscious of the self. The infant personality by itself is unable to make use of the sense data, but has to evacuate these elements into the mother, relying on her to do whatever has to be done to convert them into a form suitable for employment as alpha-elements by the infant.

xvii. The limited consciousness defined by Freud, that I am using to define a rudimentary infant consciousness, is not associated with an unconscious. All impressions of the self are of equal value; all are conscious. The mother's capacity for reverie is the receptor organ for the infant's harvest of self-sensation gained by its conscious.

xviii. A rudimentary conscious could not perform the tasks that we ordinarily regard as the province of consciousness, and it would be misleading to attempt to withdraw the term 'conscious' from the sphere of ordinary usage where it is applied to mental functions of great importance in rational thinking. For the present I make the distinction only to show what happens if there is a breakdown of interplay through projective identification between the rudimentary consciousness and maternal reverie.

Normal development follows if the relationship between infant and breast permits the infant to project a feeling, say, that it is dying, into the mother and to reintroject it after its sojourn in the breast has made it tolerable to the infant psyche. If the projection is not accepted by the mother the infant feels that its feeling that it is dying is stripped of such meaning as it has. It therefore reintrojects, not a fear of dying made tolerable, but a nameless dread.

xix. The tasks that the breakdown in the mother's capacity for reverie have left unfinished are imposed on the rudimentary consciousness; they are all in different degrees related to the function of correlation.

xx. The rudimentary consciousness cannot carry the burden placed on it. The establishment internally of a projective-identification-rejecting-object means that instead of an understanding object the infant has a wilfully misunderstanding object – with which it is identified. Further its psychic qualities are perceived by a precocious and fragile consciousness.

xxi. The apparatus available to the psyche may be regarded as fourfold:

a. (a)   Thinking, associated with modification and evasion.
b. (b)   Projective identification, associated with evasion by evacuation and not to be confused with normal projective identification (para. xiv on 'realistic' projective identification.)
c. (c)   Omniscience (on the principle of *tout savoir, tout condamner*).
d. (d)   Communication.

xxii. Examination of the apparatus I have listed under these four heads shows that it is designed to deal with thoughts, in the broad sense of the term, that is including all objects I have described as conceptions, thoughts, dream thoughts, alpha-elements and beta-elements, as if they were objects that had to be dealt with (a) because they in some form contained or expressed a problem, and (b) because they were themselves felt to be undesirable excrescences of the psyche and required attention, elimination by some means or other, for that reason.

xxiii. As expressions of a problem it is evident they require an apparatus designed to play the same part in bridging the gap between cognizance and appreciation of lack and action designed to modify the lack, as is played by alpha-function in bridging the gap between sense-data and appreciation of sense-data. (In this context I include the perception of psychic qualities as requiring the same treatment as sense-data.) In other words just as sense-data have to be modified and worked on by alpha-function to make them available for dream thoughts, etc., so the thoughts have to be worked on to make them available for translation into action.

xxiv. Translation into action involves publication, communication, and commonsense. So far I have avoided discussion of these aspects of thinking, although they are implied in the discussion and one at least was openly adumbrated; I refer to correlation.

xxv. Publication in its origin may be regarded as little more than one function of thoughts, namely making sense-data available to consciousness. I wish to reserve the term for operations that are necessary to make private awareness, that is awareness that is private to the individual, public. The problems involved may be regarded as technical and emotional. The emotional problems are associated with the fact that the human individual is a political animal and cannot find fulfilment outside a group and cannot satisfy any emotional drive without expression of its social component. His impulses, and I mean all impulses and not merely his sexual ones, are at the same time narcissistic. The problem is the resolution of the conflict between narcissism and social-ism. The technical problem is that concerned with expression of thought or conception in language, or its counterpart in signs.

xxvi. This brings me to communication. In its origin communication is effected by realistic projective identification. The primitive infant procedure undergoes various vicissitudes, including, as we have seen, debasement through hypertrophy of omnipotent phantasy. It may develop, if the relationship with the breast is good, into a capacity for toleration by the self of its own psychic qualities and so pave the way for alpha-function and normal thought. But it does also develop as a part of the social capacity of the individual. This development, of great importance in group dynamics, has received virtually no attention; its absence would make even scientific communication impossible. Yet its presence may arouse feelings of persecution in the recipients of the communication. The need to diminish feelings of persecution contributes to the drive to abstraction in the formulation of scientific communications. The function of the elements of communication, words, and signs is to convey either by single substantives, or in verbal groupings, that certain phenomena are constantly conjoined in the pattern of their relatedness.

xxvii. An important function of communications is to achieve correlation. While communication is still a private function, conceptions, thoughts, and their verbalization are necessary to facilitate the conjunction of one set of sense-data with another. If the conjoined data harmonize, a sense of truth is experienced, and it is desirable that this sense should be given expression in a statement analogous to a truth-functional statement. The failure to bring about this conjunction of sense-data, and therefore of a commonplace view, induces a mental state of debility in the patient as if starvation of truth was somehow analogous to alimentary starvation. The truth of a statement does not imply that there is a realization approximating to the true statement.

xxviii. We may now consider further the relationship of rudimentary consciousness to psychic quality. The emotions fulfil for the psyche a function similar to that of the senses in relation to objects in space and time; that is to say, the counterpart of the common-sense view in private knowledge is the common emotional view; a sense of truth is experienced if the view of an object which is hated can be conjoined to a view of the same object when it is loved, and the conjunction confirms that the object experienced by different emotions is the same object. A correlation is established.

xxix. A similar correlation, made possible by bringing conscious and unconscious to bear on the phenomena of the consulting room, gives to psychoanalytic objects a reality that is quite unmistakable, even though their very existence has been disputed.

PART II

Unprocessed Residues

It is the key to this book that many early feelings remain dormant but are retriggered by particular life-events. *Childbearing is a most potent experience, thrusting the new parent back into the primitive space of powerful raw emotions and primal substances, which reactivate unprocessed preverbal experiences, and presymbolic embodied memories.*

I suggest that geographical mobility and smaller families reduce opportunities to re-engage with one's own archaic feelings in the presence of infants before the birth of one's own, which leaves new parents more vulnerable to this reactivation.

When archaic representations of our own baby-self in the mind of the carer have remained unchanged in adulthood, they dominate our own caregiving capacities for better or worse. As noted, early parenthood is a time of great vulnerability as it re-exposes new mothers and/or fathers to infantile issues, revitalizing these unprocessed residues from their own infancies. Simultaneously, it is a time of susceptibility for the vulnerable infant. Indeed, the wild things within an individual are often manifestations of transgenerational residues. In Chapter 8, in a paper which has become a treasured classic, Selma Fraiberg and her colleagues show how reactivated 'ghosts' from the caregiver's own troubled past threaten to intrude into the new baby's nursery. The authors find that once these have established their 'residence privileges' in a family for three or more generations the ghosts of the past are extremely difficult to expel, even with professional assistance, as they in turn treat helpers as intruders rather than allies. In this book, professionals working to dispel the unconscious wild things in families demonstrate this invasion in action – how old trespassers take possession of the parent, leaping across body-boundaries to take up residence in the baby's developing mind.

For each new parent, there comes a time when a particular developmental issue in their child resonates with the weakest links from their own childhoods. As we shall see, what presses their own 'button' is specific to each parent and may range from separation, night disturbance, and toilet training to feeding issues, sibling rivalry, tantrums or masturbation ...

A crying baby unites all these – re-evoking painful childhood feelings in parents as well as older siblings, which distort the current interaction. Wailing and screaming, whining, apathy and withdrawal in infants may thus reflect not just their own misery but *family* malfunctioning, as child psychotherapist Juliet Hopkins reminds us in Chapter 9, as may a range of psychosomatic and other disorders of eating, toilet training and speech development. Revisiting the work of Selma Fraiberg, she illustrates the distinction between developmental guidance and parent–infant therapy in her work with crying babies. Sleep problems are probably the most common of all, and Dilys Daws brings some of her extensive experience at the Tavistock Under-5s clinic and elsewhere to illustrates in Chapter 10 how sleep disturbances too are not only a cause but a manifestation of distress in the family as a whole. Ranging from nightmares to insomnia, bedtime and night distress, these tend to cluster around a 'key theme', like separation, resentment, parental sexuality or 'wild things', the meaning of which differs for each family. This chapter is followed by Ellen Handler Spitz, who also writes about bedtime preoccupations – and how, before facing the night separation and exclusion from loved ones, children's books may help parents to provide a young child with the extra containment against their unprocessed residues and anxieties about inner wild things and their external counterparts.

In general, these pages hold many poignant examples of ways in which we all *externalize our innermost wishes*, unconsciously roping others into playing out roles from our own unresolved scenarios, and *unwittingly take part in*, and contribute to, playing out the emotional scripts of our other people and their significant internal figures. In families, as all these papers illustrate, this unconscious transmission between generations may take many forms. Once again, the section ends with two more classic but difficult papers illustrating the remarkable interaction between the unconscious of one human being with that of another (commented on by Freud), illustrated here by intergenerational transmissions. In a case that spans four generations, Enid Balint utilizes her countertransferential feelings aroused in the analysis of a woman to locate the 'leap' of unconscious feelings from her grandmother's infancy, bypassing the mother's conscious awareness, reappearing as a 'foreign body' and dread of loss in the grandchild, now a mother herself. In Chapter 13 André Green describes how, even in a healthy relationship, life-events can affect the next generation. Confronted with a bereaved mother, having in vain tried to repair her, an infant will unconsciously identify with the depressed mother's emotional absence, replacing the live and responsive mother in his mind with a 'dead' internal counterpart. In an attempt to master the traumatic situation, the emptiness of this internalized 'hole' in the psyche is then filled with a precocious and compulsive intellectual quest for lost meaning, which persists into adulthood. These papers, too, will reward the reader's effort.

CHAPTER 8

Ghosts in the nursery: a psychoanalytic approach to the problems of impaired infant–mother relationships[1]

SELMA FRAIBERG, EDNA ADELSON AND VIVIAN SHAPIRO

In every nursery there are ghosts. They are the visitors from the unremembered past of the parents, the uninvited guests at the christening. Under favorable circumstances, these unfriendly and unbidden spirits are banished from the nursery and return to their subterranean dwelling place. The baby makes his own imperative claim upon parental love and, in strict analogy with the fairy tales, the bonds of love protect the child and his parents against the intruders, the malevolent ghosts.

This is not to say that ghosts cannot invent mischief from their burial places. Even among families where the love bonds are stable and strong, the intruders from the parental past may break through the magic circle in an unguarded moment, and a parent and his child may find themselves re-enacting a moment or a scene from another time with another set of characters. Such events are unremarkable in the family theater, and neither the child, his parents nor their bond is necessarily imperiled by a brief intrusion. It is not usually necessary for the parents to call upon us for clinical services.

In still other families there may be more troublesome events in the nursery caused by intruders from the past. There are, it appears, a number of transient ghosts who take up residence in the nursery on a selective basis. They appear to do their mischief according to a historical or topical agenda, specializing in such areas as feeding, sleep, toilet training or discipline, depending upon the vulnerabilities of the parental past. Under these circumstances, even when the bonds between parents and child are strong, the

[1] The paper by this name first appeared in *Journal of the American Academy of Child Psychiatry*, 14(3): 387–422, 1975. This later version is from Selma Fraiberg's *Clinical Studies in Infant Mental Health – the First Year of Life*, Tavistock Publications.
Reprinted by permission.

parents may feel helpless before the invasion and may seek professional guidance. In our own work we have found that these parents will form a strong alliance with us to banish the intruders from the nursery. It is not difficult to find the educational or therapeutic means for dealing with the transient invaders.

But how shall we explain another group of families who appear to be possessed by their ghosts? The intruders from the past have taken up residence in the nursery, claiming tradition and rights of ownership. They have been present at the christening for two or more generations. While no one has issued an invitation, the ghosts take up residence and conduct the rehearsal of the family tragedy from a tattered script.

In our infant mental health program we have seen many of these families and their babies. The baby is already in peril by the time we meet him, showing the early signs of emotional starvation, grave symptoms or developmental impairment. In each of these cases the baby has become a silent actor in a family tragedy. The baby in these families is burdened by the oppressive past of his parents from the moment he enters the world. The parent, it seems, is condemned to repeat the tragedy of his own childhood with his own baby in terrible and exacting detail.

These parents may not come to us for professional guidance. Ghosts who have established their residence privileges for three or more generations may not, in fact, be identified as representatives of the parental past. There may be no readiness on the part of the parents to form an alliance with us to protect the baby. More likely it is we, and not the ghosts, who will appear as the intruders.

Those of us who have a professional interest in ghosts in the nursery do not yet understand the complexities and the paradoxes in the ghost story. What is it that determines whether the conflicted past of the parent will be repeated with his child? Is morbidity in the parental history the prime determinant? This strikes us as too simple. Certainly, we all know families in which a parental history of tragedy, cruelty, and sorrow have *not* been inflicted upon the children. The ghosts do not flood the nursery or erode the love bonds.

Then, too, we must reflect that, if history predicted with fidelity, the human family itself would long ago have been drowned in its own oppressive past. The race improves. And this may be because the largest number of men and women who have known suffering find renewal and the healing of childhood pain in the experience of bringing a child into the world. In the simplest terms – we have heard it often from parents – the parent says, 'I want something better for my child than I have had.' And he brings something better to his child. We have all known young parents who have suffered poverty, brutality, death, desertion, and sometimes the full gamut of childhood horrors, who do not inflict their pain upon their children. History is not destiny, then, and whether parenthood becomes flooded with griefs and injuries or whether it becomes a time of renewal cannot be predicted from the narrative of the parental past. There must be other factors in the psychological experience of that past which determine repetition in the present.

In therapeutic work with families on behalf of their babies we are all the beneficiaries of Freud's discoveries before the dawn of this century. The ghosts, we know, represent the repetition of the past in the present. We are also the beneficiaries of the method Freud developed for recovering the events of the past and undoing the morbid effects of the past in the present. The babies themselves, who are often afflicted by the diseases of the parental past, have been the last to be the beneficiaries of the great discoveries of psychoanalysis and developmental psychology. These patients, who cannot talk, have had to await articulate spokesmen.

During the past three decades, a number of psychoanalysts and developmental psychologists have been speaking for the babies. What the babies have been telling us is sobering news indeed. This story you already know, and we will not attempt to summarize the vast literature that has emerged from our studies of infancy.

In our own work at the Child Development Project we have become well acquainted with the ghosts in the nursery. The brief intruders, which we describe above, or the unwelcome ghosts who take up temporary residence, do not present extraordinary problems to the clinician. The parents themselves become our allies in banishing the ghosts. It is the third group, the ghosts who invade the nursery and take up residence, who present the gravest therapeutic problems for us.

How is it that the ghosts of the parental past can invade the nursery with such insistency and ownership, claiming their rights above the baby's own rights? This question is at the center of our work. The answers are emerging for us, and in the closing section of this chapter we return to the question and offer a hypothesis derived from clinical experience.

In this chapter we will describe our clinical study and our treatment through two of the many imperiled babies who have come to us. As our work progressed, our families and their babies opened doors to us which illuminated the past and the present. Our psychoanalytic knowledge opened pathways into understanding the repetition of the past in the present. The methods of treatment we developed brought together psychoanalysis, developmental psychology, and social work in ways that will be illustrated. The rewards for the babies, for the families, and for us have been very large.

In this collaborative work, Edna Adelson, staff psychologist, was the therapist for Jane and her family, Vivian Shapiro, staff social worker, was therapist for Greg and his family, and Selma Fraiberg served as case supervisor and psychoanalytic consultant.

Jane

Jane, who came to us at $5^{1}/_{2}$ months, was the first baby referred to our new infant mental health project. Her mother, Mrs. March, had appeared at an adoption agency some weeks earlier. She wanted to surrender her baby for adoption, but adoption plans could not proceed because Mr. March would not give his consent. Jane's mother was described as 'a rejecting mother'.

Now, of course, nobody loves a rejecting mother, in our community or any other, and Jane and her family might at this point have disappeared into the anonymity of a metropolitan community, perhaps to surface once again when tragedy struck. But chance brought the family to one of the psychiatric clinics of our university. The psychiatric evaluation of Mrs. March revealed a severe depression, an attempted suicide through aspirin, a woman so tormented that she could barely go about the ordinary tasks of living. The 'rejecting mother' was now seen as a depressed mother. Psychiatric treatment was recommended at a clinical staffing. And then one of the clinical team members said, 'But what about the baby?' Our new project had been announced and scheduled for opening the following day. There was a phone call to us, and we agreed to provide immediate evaluation of the baby and to consider treatment.

Early observations

From the time Jane was first seen by us we had reason for grave concern. At $5^{1}/_{2}$ months she bore all the stigmata of the child who has spent the greater part of her life in a crib with little more than obligatory care. She was adequately nourished and physically cared for, but the back of her head was bald. She showed little interest in her surroundings she was listless, too quiet. She seemed to have only a tenuous connection with her mother. She rarely smiled. She did not spontaneously approach her mother through eye contact or gestures of reach. There were few spontaneous vocalizations. In moments of discomfort or anxiety she did not turn to her mother. In our developmental testing she failed nearly all the personal-social items on the Bayley scale. The test could not be completed. Jane was badly frightened by the unexpected sound of the test bell. After only a few more items her threshold of tolerance was shattered, and she collapsed into prolonged screaming.

The mother herself seemed locked in some private terror, remote, removed, yet giving us rare glimpses of a capacity for caring. For weeks we held onto one tiny vignette captured on videotape, in which the baby made an awkward reach for her mother and the mother's hand spontaneously reached toward the baby. The hands never met each other, but the gesture symbolized for the therapists a reaching out toward each other, and we clung to this symbolic hope.

There is a moment at the beginning of every case when something is revealed that speaks for the essence of the conflict. This moment appeared in the second session of the work when Mrs. Adelson invited Jane and her mother to our office. By chance it was a moment captured on videotape, because we were taping the developmental testing session as we customarily do. Jane and her mother, Mrs. Adelson, and Mrs. Evelyn Atreya, as tester, were present.

Jane begins to cry. It is a hoarse, eerie cry in a baby. Mrs. Atreya discontinues the testing. On tape we see the baby in her mother's arms screaming hopelessly; she does not turn to her mother for comfort. The mother looks distant, self-absorbed. She makes an absent gesture to comfort the baby, then gives up. She looks away. The screaming continues for five dreadful minutes on tape. In the background we hear Mrs. Adelson's voice, gently encouraging the mother: 'What do you do to comfort Jane when she cries like this?' Mrs. March murmurs something inaudible. Mrs. Adelson and Mrs. Atreya are struggling with their own feelings. They are restraining their own wishes to pick up the baby and hold her, to murmur comforting things to her. If they should yield to their own wishes, they would do the one thing they feel must not be done. For Mrs. March would then see that another woman could comfort the baby, and she would be confirmed in her own conviction that she was a bad mother. It is a dreadful five minutes for the baby, the mother, and the two clinicians. Mrs. Adelson maintains composure, speaks sympathetically to Mrs. March. Finally, the visit comes to an end when Mrs. Adelson suggests that the baby is fatigued and probably would welcome her own home and her crib, and mother and baby are helped to close the visit with plans for a third visit very soon.

As we watched this tape later in a staff session, we said to each other incredulously, 'It's as if this mother doesn't *hear* her baby's cries.' This led us to the key diagnostic question, *'Why doesn't this mother hear her baby's cries?'*

The mother's story

Mrs. March was herself an abandoned child. Her mother suffered a postpartum psychosis shortly after the birth of Mrs. March. In an attempted suicide, she had injured herself and was horribly mutilated for life. She had then spent nearly all of the rest of her life in a hospital and was barely known to her children. For five years Mrs. March was cared for by an aunt. When the aunt could no longer care for her, she was shifted to the house of the maternal grandmother, where she received grudging care from the burdened, impoverished old woman. Mrs. March's father was in and out of the family picture. We did not hear much about him until later in the treatment.

It was a story of bleak rural poverty, sinister family secrets, psychosis, crime, a tradition of promiscuity in the women, of filth and disorder in the home, and of police and protective agencies in the background making futile uplifting gestures. Mrs. March was the cast-out child of a cast-out family.

In late adolescence, Mrs. March met and married her husband, who came from poverty and family disorder not unlike her own. But he wanted something better for himself than his family had had. He became the first member of his family to fight his way out of the cycle of futility, to find steady work, to establish a decent home. When these two neglected and solitary young people found each other, there was mutual agreement that they wanted something better than what they had known. But now, after several years of effort, the downward spiral had begun.

There was a very high likelihood that Jane was not her father's child. Mrs. March had had a brief affair with another man. Her guilt over the affair, her doubts about Jane's paternity, became an obsessive theme in her story. In a kind of litany of griefs that we were to hear over and over again, there was one theme. 'People stared at Jane,' she thought. 'They stared at her and knew that her father was not her father. They knew that her mother had ruined her life.'

Mr. March, who began to appear to us as the stronger parent, was not obsessed with Jane's paternity. He was convinced that he was Jane's father. And anyway, he loved Jane and he wanted her. His wife's obsession with paternity brought about shouting quarrels in the home. 'Forget it!' said Mr. March. 'Stop talking about it! And take care of Jane!'

In the families of both mother and father illegitimacy carried no stigma. In the case of Mrs. March's clan, the promiscuity of their women over at least three or four generations cast doubt over the paternity of many of the children. Why was Mrs. March obsessed? Why the sense of tormenting sin? This pervasive, consuming sense of sin we thought belonged to childhood, to buried sins, quite possibly crimes of the imagination. On several occasions in reading the clinical reports, we had the strong impression that Jane was the sinful child of an incestuous fantasy. But, if we were right, we thought to ourselves, how could we possibly reach this in our once-a-week psychotherapy?

Treatment

The emergency phase

How shall we begin? We should remember that Jane and Mrs. March were our first patients. We did not have treatment models available to us. In fact, it was our task in this first infant mental health project to develop methods in the course of the work. It made sense, of course, to begin with a familiar model, in which our resident in psychiatry, Dr. Zinn, worked with the mother in weekly or twice-weekly psychotherapy, and the psychologist, Mrs. Adelson, provided support and developmental guidance on behalf of the baby through home visits. But, within the first sessions, we saw that Mrs. March was taking flight from Dr. Zinn and psychiatric treatment. The situation in which she was alone with a man brought forth a phobic dread, and she was reduced to nearly inarticulate hours or to speaking of trivial concerns. All efforts to reach Mrs. March, or to touch upon her anxieties or discomfort in this relationship, led to an impasse. One theme was uttered over and over again. She did not trust men. But also, we caught glimpses in her oblique communications of a terrible secret that she would never reveal to anyone. She broke appointments more frequently than she kept them. With much difficulty, Dr. Zinn sustained a relationship with her. It was nearly a year before we finally heard the secret and understood the phobic dread that led to this formidable resistance.

There are no generalizations to be drawn from this experience. We have been asked sometimes if women therapists are more advantaged in working with mothers who have suffered severe maternal deprivation themselves. Our answer, after nearly eight years of work, is, 'Not necessarily; sometimes not at all.' We have examples in our work in which the male therapist was specially advantaged in working with mothers. We tend to assign cases without too much concern about the sex of the therapist. Mrs. March must be regarded as an exceptional case. But now we were faced with a therapeutic dilemma. Mrs. Adelson's work was to center in the infant–mother relationship through home visits. Mrs. March needed her own therapist, Dr. Zinn, but a morbid dread of men, aroused in the transference, prevented her from using the psychiatric help available to her. With much time and patient work in the psychiatric treatment, we would hope to uncover the secret that reduced her to silence and flight in the transference to Dr. Zinn.

But the baby was in great peril. And the baby could not wait for the resolution of the mother's neurosis. Mrs. Adelson, we soon saw, did not arouse the same morbid anxieties in Mrs. March, but her role as the baby–mother therapist, the home-based psychologist, did not lend itself easily to uncovering the conflictual elements in the mother's relationship to the child and the treatment of the mother's depression.

Since we had no alternative, we decided we would use the home visits for our emergency treatment. What emerged, then, was a form of *psychotherapy in the kitchen* so to speak, which will strike you as both familiar in its methods and unfamiliar in its setting. The method, a variant of psychoanalytic psychotherapy, made use of transference, the repetition of the past in the present, and interpretation. Equally important, the method included continuous developmental observations of the baby and a tactful, non-didactic education of the mother in the recognition of her baby's needs and her signals.

The setting was the family kitchen or the living room. The patient who couldn't talk was always present at the interviews – if she wasn't napping. The patient who could talk went about her domestic tasks or diapered or fed the baby. The therapist's eyes and ears were attuned to both the non-verbal communications of the baby and the substance of the mother's verbal and non-verbal communications. Everything that transpired between mother and baby was in the purview of the therapist and in the center of the therapy. The dialogue between the mother and the therapist centered upon present concerns and moved back and forth between the past and the present, between this mother and child and another child and her family in the mother's past. The method proved itself and led us, in later cases, to explore the possibilities of the single therapist in the home-based treatment.

We shall now try to summarize the treatment of Jane and her mother and examine the methods that were employed.

In the early hours of treatment, Mrs. March's own story emerged haltingly, narrated in a distant, sad voice. It was the story we sketched earlier. As the mother told her story, Jane, our second patient, sat propped on the couch or lay stretched out on a blanket, and the sad and distant face of the mother was mirrored in the sad and distant face of the baby. It was a room crowded with ghosts. The mother's story of abandonment and neglect was now being psychologically re-enacted with her own baby.

The problem, in the emergency phase of the treatment, was to get the ghosts out of the baby's nursery. To do this we would need to help the mother to see the repetition of the past in the present, which we all knew how to do in an office that was properly furnished with a desk and a chair or a couch, but which we had not yet learned to do in a family living room or a kitchen. The therapeutic principles would need to be the same, we decided. But, in this emergency phase of the treatment, on behalf of a baby, we would have to find a path into the conflictual elements of the mother's neurosis which had direct bearing upon her capacity to mother. The baby would need to be at the center of treatment for the emergency period.

We began, as we said, with the question to ourselves: '*Why can't this mother hear her baby's cries?*'

The answer to the clinical question is already suggested in the mother's story. This is a mother whose own cries have not been heard. There were, we thought, two crying children in the living room. The mother's distant voice, her remoteness and remove we saw as defenses against grief and intolerable pain. Her terrible story had been first given factually, without visible suffering, without tears. All that was visible was the sad, empty, hopeless look upon her face. She had closed the door on the weeping child within herself as surely as she had closed the door upon her crying baby.

This led to our first clinical hypothesis: *When this mother's own cries are heard, she will hear her child's cries.*

Mrs. Adelson's work, then, centered upon the development of a treatment relationship in which trust could be given by a young woman who had not known trust, and in which trust could lead to the revelation of the old feelings which closed her off from her child. As Mrs. March's story moved back and forth between her baby, 'I can't love Jane,' and her own childhood, which can be summarized, 'Nobody wanted me,' the therapist opened up pathways of feeling. Mrs. Adelson listened and put into words the feelings of Mrs. March as a child. 'How hard this must have been ... This must have hurt deeply ... Of course, you needed your mother. There was no one to turn to ... Yes. Sometimes grown-ups don't understand what all this means to a child. You must have needed to cry ... There was no one to hear you.'

The therapist was giving Mrs. March permission to feel and to remember feelings. It may have been the first time in Mrs. March's life that someone had given her this permission. And, gradually, as we should expect – but within only a few sessions – grief, tears, and unspeakable anguish for herself as a cast-off child began to emerge. It was finally a relief to be able to cry, a comfort to feel the understanding of her therapist. And now, with each session, Mrs. Adelson witnessed something almost unbelievable happening between mother and baby.

You remember that the baby was nearly always in the room in the midst of this living-room-kitchen therapy of ours. If Jane demanded attention, the mother would rise in the midst of the interview to diaper her or get her a bottle. More often, the baby was ignored if she did not demand attention. But now, as Mrs. March began to take the permission to remember her feelings, to cry, and to feel the comfort and sympathy of Mrs. Adelson, we saw her make approaches to her baby in the midst of her own outpourings. She would pick up Jane and hold her, at first distant and self-absorbed, but holding her. And then one day, still within the first month of treatment, Mrs. March, in the midst of an outpouring of grief, picked up Jane, held her very close, and crooned to her in a heartbroken voice. And then it happened again, and several times in the next sessions: an outpouring of old griefs and a gathering of the baby into her arms. The ghosts in the baby's nursery were beginning to leave.

These were more than transitory gestures toward rapprochement with the baby. From all evidence to Mrs. Adelson's observing eyes, mother and baby were beginning to find each other. And, now that they were coming into touch with each other, Mrs. Adelson did everything within her capacity as therapist and developmental psychologist to promote the emerging attachment. When Jane rewarded her mother with a beautiful and special smile, Mrs. Adelson commented on it and observed that she, Mrs. Adelson, did not get such a smile, which was just the way it should be. That smile belonged to her mother. When a crying Jane began to seek her mother's comfort and found relief in her mother's arms, Mrs. Adelson spoke for Jane. 'It feels so good when mother knows what you want.' And Mrs. March herself smiled shyly, but with pride.

These sessions with mother and baby soon took on their own rhythm. Mr. March was often present for a short time before leaving . (Special sessions for father were also worked out on evenings and Saturdays.) The sessions typically began with Jane in the room and Jane as the topic of discussion. In a natural, informal, non-didactic way, Mrs. Adelson would comment with pleasure on Jane's development and weave into her comments useful information about the needs of babies at six months or seven months and how Jane was learning about her world and how her mother and father were leading her into these discoveries. Together the parents and Mrs. Adelson would watch Jane experiment with a new toy or a new posture and, with close watching, could see how she was finding solutions and moving steadily forward. The delights of baby-watching, which Mrs. Adelson knew, were shared with Mr. and Mrs. March, and, to our great pleasure, both parents began to share these delights and to bring in their own observations of Jane and of her new accomplishments.

During the same session, after Mr. March had left for work, the talk would move at one point or another back to Mrs. March herself, to her present griefs and her childhood griefs. More and more frequently now, Mrs. Adelson could help Mrs. March see the connections between the past and the present and show her how 'without realizing it', she had brought her sufferings of the past into her relationship with her own baby.

Within four months Jane became a healthy, more responsive, often joyful baby. At our ten-month testing, objective assessment showed her to be age-appropriate in her focused attachment to her mother, in her preferential smiling and vocalization to mother and father, in her seeking of her mother for comfort and safety. The Bayley developmental testing showed uneven but impressive progress. Jane was two months advanced on social interaction items and at age level for fine motor performance for her corrected age. Lags of from one to two months on vocalization and gross motor items placed her below her corrected age, but still within the normal range.

Mrs. March had become a responsive mother and a proud mother. Yet our cautious rating of the mother's own psychological state remained: 'depressed'. It was true that Mrs. March was progressing, and we saw many signs that the depression was no longer pervasive and constricting, but depression was still there, and, we thought, still ominous. Much work remained.

What we had achieved, then, in our first four months' work was not yet a cure for the mother's illness, but a form of control of the disease, in which the pathology which had spread to embrace the baby was now largely withdrawn from the child; the conflictual elements of the mother's neurosis were now identified by the mother as well as ourselves as 'belonging to the past' and 'not belonging to Jane'. The bonds between mother and baby had emerged. And the baby herself was insuring those bonds. For every gesture of love from her mother, she gave generous rewards of love. Mrs. March, we thought, may have felt cherished by someone for the first time in her life.

All this constitutes what we would call 'the emergency phase of the treatment'. Now, in retrospect, we can tell you that it took a full year beyond this point to bring some resolution to Mrs. March's very severe internal conflicts, and there were a number of problems in mother–child relationships which emerged during that year, but Jane was out of danger, and even the baby conflicts of the second year of life were not extraordinary or morbid. Once the bond had been formed, nearly everything else could find solutions.

Other conflictual areas

We shall try to summarize the following months of treatment. Jane remained the focus of our work. And, following the pattern already established, the therapeutic work moved freely between the baby and her developmental needs and problems and the mother's conflicted past.

One poignant example comes to mind. Mrs. March, in spite of newfound pleasure and pride in motherhood, could still make casual and unfeeling plans for babysitting. The meaning of separation and temporary loss to a one-year-old child did not register with Mrs. March. When the mother took part-time work at one point (and the family poverty gave some justification for additional income), Mrs. March made hasty and ill-thought-out sitting arrangements for Jane and then was surprised, as was Mr. March, to find that Jane was sometimes 'cranky' and 'spoiled' and 'mean'.

Mrs. Adelson tried in a number of tactful ways to help the Marches think about the meaning to Jane of her love for mother and her temporary loss of mother during the day. She met a blank wall. Both parents had known shifting and casual relationships with parents and parent substitutes from their earliest years. The meaning of separation and loss was buried in memory. Their family style of coping with separation, desertion, or death was 'Forget about it. You get used to it.' Mrs. March could not remember grief or pain at the loss of important persons.

Somehow once again we were going to have to find the affective links between loss and denial of loss, for the baby in the present, and loss in the mother's past.

The moment came one morning when Mrs. Adelson arrived to find the family in disorder: Jane crying at the approach of a now-familiar visitor, parents angry at a baby who was being 'just plain stubborn'. Thoughtful inquiries from Mrs. Adelson brought the new information that Jane had just lost one sitter and started with another. Mrs. Adelson wondered out loud what this might mean to Jane. Yesterday she had been left, unexpectedly, in a totally new place with a strange woman. She felt alone and frightened without her mother and did not know what was going to happen. No one could explain things to her; she was only a baby, with no words to express her serious problem. Somehow, we would have to find a way to understand and to help her with her fears and worries.

Mr. March, on his way to work, stopped long enough to listen attentively. Mrs. March was listening too, and before her husband left she asked him to try to get home earlier today so that Jane would not be too long at the sitter's.

There followed a moving session in which the mother cried, and the baby cried, and something very important was put into words. In a circular and tentative way, Mrs. March began to talk about Aunt Ruth, with whom she had lived during her first five years. There had not been a letter from Aunt Ruth for some months. She thought Aunt Ruth was angry at her. She switched to her mother-in-law, to thoughts of her coldness and rejection of Mrs. March. Then came complaints about the sitters, with the theme that one sitter was angry because Jane cried when her mother left. The theme was 'rejection' and 'loss', and Mrs. March was searching for it everywhere in the contemporary scene. She cried throughout, but somehow, even with Mrs. Adelson's gentle hints, she could not put all this together.

Then at one point Mrs. March left the room, still in tears, and returned with a family photograph album. She identified the pictures for Mrs. Adelson. Mother, father, Aunt Ruth, Aunt Ruth's son who had been killed in the war. Sorrow for Aunt Ruth. Nobody in the family would let her grieve for her son. 'Forget about it' is what they said. She spoke about her father's death and her grandfather's death in the recent past. Many losses, many shocks, just before Jane's birth, she was saying. And the family always said, 'Forget about it.' And then Mrs. Adelson, listening sympathetically, reminded her that there had been many other losses, many other shocks for Mrs. March long ago in her infancy and childhood. The loss of her mother, which she could not remember, and the loss of Aunt Ruth when she was five years old. Mrs. Adelson asked how Mrs. March had felt then, when she was too young to understand what was happening. Looking at Jane, sitting on her mother's lap, Mrs. Adelson said, 'I wonder if we could understand how Jane would feel right now if she suddenly found herself in a new house, not just for an hour or two with a sitter, but permanently, never to see her mother or father again. Jane wouldn't have any way to understand this; it would leave her very worried, very upset. I wonder what it was like for you when you were a little girl.'

Mrs. March listened, deep in thought. A moment later she said, in an angry and assertive voice, 'You can't just replace one person with another ... You can't stop loving them and thinking about them. You can't just replace somebody.' She was speaking of herself now. Mrs. Adelson agreed, and then gently brought the insight back on behalf of Jane.

This was the beginning of new insights for Mrs. March. As she was helped to re-experience loss, grief, and feelings of rejection in childhood, she could no longer inflict this pain upon her own child. 'I would never want my baby to feel that,' she said with profound feeling. She was beginning to understand loss and grief. With Mrs. Adelson's help, she now began to work out a stable sitter plan for Jane, with full understanding of the meaning to her child. Jane's anxieties began to diminish, and she settled into her new regime.

Finally, too, we learned the dread secret which had invaded the transference to Dr. Zinn and caused her to take flight from psychiatric treatment. The morbid fear of being alone in the same room with the doctor, the obsessive sense of sin which had attached itself to Jane's doubtful paternity, had given us the strong clinical impression that Jane was 'an incestuous baby', conceived long ago in childhood fantasy, made real through the illicit relationship with an out-of-wedlock lover. By this we meant nothing more than 'an incestuous fantasy', of course. We were not prepared for the story that finally emerged. With great shame and suffering, Mrs. March told Mrs. Adelson in the second year of treatment her childhood secrets. Her own father had exhibited himself to her when she was a child and had approached her and her grandmother in the bed they shared. Her grandmother had accused her of seducing her elderly grandfather. This Mrs. March denied. And her first intercourse at the age of 11 took place with her cousin, who stood in the relationship of brother to her, since they shared the same house in the early years of life. Incest was not fantasy for Mrs. March. And now we understood the obsessive sense of sin which had attached itself to Jane and her uncertain paternity.

Jane at two years of age

During the second year of treatment, Mrs. Adelson continued as the therapist for Mrs. March. Dr. Zinn had completed his residency, and Mrs. March's transference to Mrs. Adelson favored continuity in the work with the mother. William Schafer, psychologist on our staff, became the guidance worker for Jane. (We no longer have separate therapists for parent and child, but in this first case we were still experimenting.)

It is of some considerable interest that in the initial meetings with Mr. Schafer, Mrs. March was again in mute terror as her morbid fear of 'a man' was revived in transference. But this time Mrs. March had made large advances in her therapeutic work. The anxiety was handled in transference by Mr. Schafer and brought back to Mrs. Adelson where it could be placed within the context of the incestuous material that had emerged in treatment. The anxiety diminished, and Mrs. March was able to make a strong alliance with Mr. Schafer. The developmental guidance of the second year brought further strength and stability to the mother–child relationship, and we saw Jane continuing her developmental progress through her second year, even as her mother was working through very painful material in her own therapeutic work.

Were there residues in Jane's personality from the early months of neglect? As a two-year-old, Jane was an attractive, busy little girl who presented no extraordinary problems in development. The only residue we could detect was a momentary stoppage of play at times when Mrs. March became temporarily uncomfortable, as in an unfamiliar social setting or when recalling particularly painful memories.

For the rest, Jane was a bright, vocal, sociable child. Her affectionate ties to her mother and father appeared to us as appropriate for her age. She was remarkably free from signs of withdrawal, self-absorption, or separation anxiety. In spontaneous doll play we saw a strong positive identification with her mother and with acts of mothering. She was a solicitous mother to her dolls, feeding, dressing them with evident pleasure, murmuring comforting things to them. Bayley developmental testing showed continued progress. She had retained her age adequacy on social interaction and fine motor items. Gross motor development was now also at age level. Language, which had previously been a major area of concern, now showed only a slight delay of one month.

It was in doll play at one year ten months that Mr. Schafer first heard Jane speak a full sentence. Her doll was accidentally trapped behind a door with a spring catch, and Jane could not recover it. 'I want my baby. I want my baby!' she called out in an imperative voice. It was a very good sentence for a two-year-old. It was also a moving statement to all of us who knew Jane's story.

For us the story must end here. The family has moved on. Mr. March begins a new career with very good prospects in a new community that provides comfortable housing and a warm welcome. The external circumstances look promising. More important, the family has grown closer; abandonment is not a central concern. One of the most hopeful signs was Mrs. March's steady ability to handle the stress of the uncertainty that preceded the job choice. And, as termination approached, she could openly acknowledge her sadness. Looking ahead, she expressed her wish for Jane: 'I hope that she'll grow up to be happier than me. I hope that she will have a better marriage and children who she'll love.' For herself, she asked that we remember her as 'someone who had changed'.

Greg

Within the first weeks of our new program we were asked to make an urgent call and an assessment of Greg, then $3^1/_2$ months old. His 16-year-old mother, Annie, refused to care for him. She avoided physical contact with the baby; she often forgot to buy milk for him, and she fed him Kool-Aid and Tang. She turned over the baby's care to her 19-year-old husband, Earl.

Annie's family had been known to social agencies in our community for three generations. Delinquency, promiscuity, child abuse, neglect, poverty, school failure, and psychosis had brought every member of the family to our community clinics and courts. Annie Beyer at 16 now represented the third generation of mothers in her family who actually or psychologically abandoned their babies. Annie's mother had surrendered the care of her children to others. As did her mother. And it was, in fact, Greg's grandmother, Annie's mother, who called our agency for help. She said, 'I don't want to see what happened to me and my babies happen to Annie and her baby.'

Vivian Shapiro of our staff called for an appointment and made a home visit immediately. Mother, father, and Greg were present. Mrs. Shapiro was greeted by a cold and silently hostile adolescent mother, a sad, bewildered boy who was the father, and a solemn baby who never once in that hour looked at his mother. Greg was developmentally adequate for his age, Mrs. Shapiro estimated, and her impressions were later sustained by our developmental testing. This spoke for some minimum adequacy in care, and we had good reason to believe that it was Earl, the father, who was providing most of Greg's care. At nearly every point in the one-hour session when Greg required care, Annie summoned her husband or picked up the baby and gave him to his father. He settled comfortably with his father and, for father, there were smiles.

During most of this session, and for many others that followed, Annie sat slumped in a chair. She was obese, unkempt, and her face registered no emotion. It was a mask which Mrs. Shapiro was to see many times, but, when Annie brought herself to speak, there was barely controlled rage in her voice. She did not want our help. There was nothing wrong with her or her child. She accused her mother of a conspiracy against her and, in her mind, Mrs. Shapiro was part of the conspiracy. Winning Annie's trust was to become our most arduous therapeutic task of those first weeks. To maintain the trust, after it was given, was equally difficult. It was a great advantage to Mrs.

Shapiro, as it has been for all of us who have come to this work with broad clinical experience with children and adolescents. An adolescent girl who defies her would-be helpers, who challenges, provokes, tests mercilessly, breaks appointments, or disappears to another address, will not cause an experienced social worker to turn a hair. Mrs. Shapiro could wait to earn Annie's trust. But there was a baby in peril, and, within only a few visits, we understood how great the peril was.

We began with the question to ourselves, *'Why does Annie avoid touching and holding her baby?'* To find the answers, we would need to know more about Annie than she was willing to give in those early hostile hours. And always there was Greg, whose own needs were imperative, and who could not wait for his teenage mother to make the therapeutic alliance, which is slow-paced in adolescence. It was surely not ignorance of the needs of babies that distanced Annie from her child. Doctors and public health nurses had given wise counsel before we even met the Beyer family. She could not use the good advice.

An illuminating hour

In the sixth home visit, something of the therapist's caring for Annie as a lonely and frightened child came through. Annie began to speak of herself. It made her angry, she said warily, when her husband, when people, thought she wasn't doing enough for her baby. She knew she was. Anyway, she said, she had never liked holding a baby very much ... ever since she was a little girl. When she was little, she had had to take care of her younger sister. She would be given the baby and told to hold her. She much preferred leaving the baby on the couch.

And then, led on by tactful questions, she began to speak of her childhood. We heard about Annie, as a nine-year-old girl, responsible for the cleaning, cooking, and care of other siblings – after school hours. For any negligence in duties, there were beatings from her stepfather, Mr. Bragg. Annie spoke of her childhood in a flat, dull voice, with only an edge of bitterness in it. She remembered everything, in chilling detail. And what Annie told the therapist was not a fantasy and was not distorted, since the story of Annie's family had been factually recorded by protective agencies and clinics throughout her community. There was the mother who periodically deserted her family. There was the father who died when Annie was five years old. And there was Mr. Bragg, the stepfather, alcoholic, probably psychotic. For trivial misdemeanors he dragged Annie off to the woodshed and beat her with a lath.

When Mrs. Shapiro spoke to the feelings of Annie as a child, of anger, fear, helplessness, Annie warded off these sympathetic overtures. She laughed cynically. She was tough. Her sister Millie and she got so they would just laugh at the old man when it was over.

In this session, in the midst of Annie's factual account of childhood horrors, Greg began a fretful cry, needing attention. Annie went to the bedroom and brought him back with her. For the first time in six visits Mrs. Shapiro saw Annie hold Greg closely cuddled in her arms.

This was the moment Mrs. Shapiro had been waiting for. It was the sign, perhaps, that, if Annie could speak of her childhood sufferings, she could move protectively toward her baby. The baby clutched his mother's hair as she bent over him. Annie, still half in the past and half in the present, said musingly, 'Once my stepfather cut my hair to here,' and pointed to her ears. 'It was a punishment because I was bad.' When Mrs. Shapiro said, 'That must have been terrible for you!' Annie, for the first time, acknowledged feelings. 'It was terrible. I cried for three days about it.' At this point, Annie began to talk to the baby. She told him he was smelly and needed to be changed. While Annie was changing him, Greg seemed to be looking for something to play with. There was a toy beside him on the couch. It was, of all things, a toy plastic hammer. Annie picked up the toy hammer and tapped it, gently, against the baby's head. Then she said, 'I'm gonna beat you. I'm gonna beat you!' Her voice was teasing, but Mrs. Shapiro sensed the ominous intention in these words. And, while still registering, as therapist, the revealed moment, Mrs. Shapiro heard Annie say to her baby, 'When you grow up, I might kill you.'

It was the close of the session. Mrs. Shapiro said those things that would quiet the turbulence in Annie, supporting the positive strivings toward motherhood, allying herself with those parts of the ego of this girl-mother that sought protection against the dangerous impulses.

But this, we knew, as we talked together in an emergency session back at the office, would not be enough to protect the baby from his mother. If Annie had to rely upon her therapist as an auxiliary ego, she would need to have her therapist in constant attendance.

Emergency clinical conference

The question was, how could we help Annie and her baby? We now knew why Annie was afraid to be close to her baby. She was afraid of her own destructive feelings toward him. But we had read these signs from the break-through of unconscious impulses in the tease games with the baby. We could not interpret sadistic impulses which were not yet conscious to Annie herself. If we cooperated with the ego to maintain these sadistic impulses in repression, Annie would have to distance herself from her baby. And the baby was our patient too, our most vulnerable patient.

We were attentive to small positive signs in this session. After talking about her childhood terrors, even though the affect was flat in the telling, Annie did pick up her baby and hold him close and cuddle him. And this was the first time we had seen closeness between mother and baby in six sessions. If Annie could remember and speak of her childhood suffering, could we open pathways which would free her baby from her own past and enable her to mother Greg? If Annie could be helped to examine her feelings toward the baby, if we could elicit the unspeakable thoughts, would Annie be able to reach out to her baby?

From the standpoint of an exercise in pure theory and method, we were probably on the right track in our thinking. The case considerations were derived from psychoanalytic experience. But this was not a psychoanalysis. As psychoanalytic consultant, Selma Fraiberg recalls that she suddenly found herself bereft of all the conditions and the protections against error which are built into the psychoanalytic situation.

First of all, the conditions of this therapy on behalf of a baby and his adolescent mother made it imperative to move quickly to protect the baby. Under all normal circumstances in therapy, we believe in cautious exploration: an assessment of the ego's capacity to deal with painful affects, an assessment of the defensive structure of the patient. Also, as experienced therapists with adolescents, we knew that to win the trust of this hostile girl might easily take months of work. And the baby was in immediate danger.

We were attentive to the defenses against painful affect which we saw in Annie. She remembered, factually, the experiences of childhood abuse. What she did not remember was her suffering. Would the liberation of affect in therapy increase the likelihood of acting out toward the baby or would it decrease the risks? After thorough discussion of alternatives, we decided, with much trepidation, that the chances of acting out toward the baby would be greater if the anxiety and rage were not elicited in treatment. Selma Fraiberg recalls: 'Speaking for myself, I clung to the belief that it is the parent who cannot remember his childhood feelings of pain and anxiety who will need to inflict his pain upon his child. And then I thought: "But what if I am wrong?"'

Then we would also be confronted with another therapeutic problem in this once-a-week psychotherapy. If we worked within the realm of buried affects, we could predict that the therapist who conjures up the ghosts will be endowed in transference with the fearsome attributes of the ghost. We would have to be prepared for the transference ghosts and meet them squarely every step of the way.

As we reviewed these conference notes one year later, we were satisfied that our treatment formulations had stood up well in the practical test. We now know, through the progress of our treatment, that the main lines of the work were well considered. But now we shall have to take you with us on a detour from the treatment that turned out to be as important for the outcome as the psychotherapeutic plan.

Before any part of this treatment plan could be put into effect, Annie took flight from the therapist.

Annie locks the door: a flight from treatment

You remember that our emergency conference had followed the critical sixth session interview in which Annie began to speak of her childhood beatings. The seventh session was a home visit in which a number of Annie's relatives came to visit, and there was no opportunity to speak with Annie alone. In the eighth session, Mrs. Shapiro arranged to speak with both Annie and Earl about continuing visits and to invite them to raise questions with her about how we might best be able to help the Beyers. Earl said emphatically that he wanted Mrs. Shapiro to continue visiting them. He said that he felt Mrs. Shapiro was helping them to see things about Greg's development that they would never have been able to see themselves. Annie remained silent. Then, when Mrs. Shapiro inquired about Annie's wishes, Annie said, with some hesitation, that she would like Mrs. Shapiro to continue to come. She would like to be able to talk about the baby and about herself.

In this hour Annie herself picked up the narrative which had begun in the sixth session. She began, however, by speaking of her fears that Earl drove too fast, that he might have an accident. A child needed a father. Greg needed a father. This led her to speak of her own father, her natural father, with some affection. After her father died when Annie was five years old, nobody ever really cared for her. There had been several men in the household who lived with Annie's mother. There were six children, born to four different fathers. Millie was her mother's favorite. Annie said bitterly, 'They didn't want me. I didn't want them. I didn't need anybody.' She spoke again of Mr. Bragg and the beatings. At first she used to cry, but he wouldn't stop. Then later, she would laugh, because it didn't hurt any more. He beat her with a lath. He would beat her until the lath broke.

After her father died, Annie's mother disappeared. She went to work in another city, leaving the children with an old woman. To punish the children, the old woman locked them out of the house. She remembered one night when she and Millie were locked out in the freezing cold and huddled together. Her mother never seemed to know what was going on. Even when she returned to her family, she went to work, and, even when she wasn't working, she didn't seem to be around.

To all this Mrs. Shapiro listened with great sympathy. She spoke of a child's need for protection. How frightening to a child to have no one to protect her. How much Annie missed her mother and a mother's protection. Perhaps she would be a different kind of mother to Greg. Would she feel she had to protect him? 'Of course,' Annie replied. And, very gently, Mrs. Shapiro spoke of the deep unhappiness and loneliness in Annie's childhood and of how difficult it was to be a young mother who had missed so much in her own childhood. Together, Mrs. Shapiro and Annie would talk about these things in their future visits.

It was, Mrs. Shapiro felt, a good visit: clarification of the role of the therapist, an acknowledgment that Annie and Earl wanted help for themselves and for their baby; for Annie, the beginning of the permission to feel along with remembering. A permission that she was not yet ready to take. But this would come.

And then, following this visit, Annie refused to see Mrs. Shapiro. There were numerous broken appointments. Appointments would be made, but Annie would not be at home. Or Mrs. Shapiro would arrive, with all signs of activity in the house, and Annie would refuse to answer the door. Annie literally locked the door against Mrs. Shapiro. It was no consolation during a period like this to understand the nature of transference resistance while the patient barricades the door against the therapist. It is far worse to know that there are two patients behind the door and that one of them is a baby.

As the memories of childhood terrors emerged in that last session, the original affects must have emerged – not in the treatment hour, but afterward – and the therapist became the representative of fears that could not be named. Annie did not remember or experience her anxiety during the brutal beatings by Mr. Bragg, but anxiety attached itself to the person of the therapist, and Annie took flight. Annie did not remember the terror of being locked out of the house by the woman who cared for her when her mother deserted the family, and to make sure that she would not remember, the ghosts and the ego conspired to lock Mrs. Shapiro out of the house. Annie did not remember the terror of abandonment by her mother, but she re-enacted the experience in transference, creating the conditions under which the therapist might have to abandon her.

We were, ourselves, nearly helpless. But this is not to say that the psychoanalytic insight was without value. To understand all this gave us a measure of control in the countertransference. We were not going to abandon Annie and her baby. We understood the suffering behind the provocative, tough, and insolent adolescent posture and could respond to the anxiety and not the defense.

The only thing we lacked was a patient who could benefit from the insight. And there was the baby who was more imperiled than his mother.

During the two-month period in which Mrs. Shapiro was locked out of the house, reports from grandparents, a visiting nurse, and others increased our alarm. Annie showed phobic symptoms. She was afraid to be alone in the house. And she was pregnant again. Greg looked neglected. He was suffering from recurrent upper respiratory illness and was not receiving medical care. The paternal grandparents were alarmed for Greg and reported to

Mrs. Shapiro that Annie was playing rough games with Greg, swinging him from his ankles. Our own alarm for Greg brought us to a painful decision. In our hospital and in our community we are ethically and legally bound to report cases of neglect and suspected or actual abuse to Protective Services.

In a case where treatment alternatives are rejected by the family (as in Annie's case) the report is mandatory. The law is wise, but in the exercise of our legal responsibility we would bring still another tragedy to the Beyer family. This was a critical moment, not only for the family but for Mrs. Shapiro and for our entire staff. There is no greater irony for the clinician than that in which he possesses the knowledge and the methods to prevent a tragedy and cannot bring this help to those who need it. Clinically speaking, the solution to the problem resided in the transference resistance. Exploration of the negative transference with Annie would prevent further acting out. We all know how to deal with transference ghosts in an office with a patient who gives even grudging cooperation with our method. How do we deal with the negative transference when the patient has locked herself in a house with her baby and their ghosts and will not answer the door?

The considerations for Greg were paramount now. Mrs. Shapiro wanted to prepare Annie and Earl for the painful alternative which lay before us, a referral to Protective Services. But Annie refused to answer the door when Mrs. Shapiro called. As a sad alternative, Mrs. Shapiro prepared a letter which was sent to Annie and Earl and to both sets of grandparents. It was a letter which spoke for our concern and deep caring for both of the young parents and for their baby. It cited the many attempts we had made to reach the family with our help and our wish, still, to help this young family. If they felt we could not help them, we would need to seek help for them elsewhere, and we would request the help of Protective Services. A reply was requested within the week.

We learned within a few days of the impact of this letter on Annie and Earl and the grandparents. Annie cried for the entire weekend. She was angry at Mrs. Shapiro. She was frightened. But on Monday she called Mrs. Shapiro. Her voice was exhausted, but she managed to say that everything in Mrs. Shapiro's letter was true. She would see Mrs. Shapiro.

Extended treatment

This was the beginning of a new relationship between Annie and Earl and Mrs. Shapiro. Step by step, Mrs. Shapiro dealt with Annie's distrust, her anger toward Mrs. Shapiro and all 'helping people' and clarified her own role as a helping person. Mrs. Shapiro was on the side of Annie and Earl and Greg and wanted to do everything possible to help them to find the good things they wanted and deserved in life, and to give Greg all the things he needed to become a healthy and happy child.

For Annie, the relationship with Mrs. Shapiro became a new experience, unlike anything she had known. Mrs. Shapiro began, of course, by dealing openly with the anger which Annie had felt toward her, and she made it safe for Annie to put anger into words. In a family pattern where anger and murderous rage were fused, Annie had only been able to deal with anger through flight or identification with the aggressor. In the family theater, anger toward the mother and desertion by the mother were interlocking themes. But Annie learned that she could feel anger and acknowledge anger toward her therapist, and her therapist would not retaliate and would not abandon her.

It was safe to experience anger in transference to the therapist, and *within* this protected relationship the pathways of anger led back to childhood griefs and terrors. It was not an easy path for Annie. Yes, she acknowledged in a session soon after Mrs. Shapiro began visiting again, yes, she had felt bad about the therapist coming to see her. Yes, she resented her. 'But what's the use of talking? I always kept things to myself. I want to forget. I don't want to think.'

Mrs. Shapiro, with full sympathy for Annie's suffering and the need to forget, discussed with Annie how trying to forget did not get rid of the feelings or the memories. Annie would only be able to make peace with her feelings by talking about them to Mrs. Shapiro. Together through talking, the therapist would be able to help Annie feel better. Annie did not reply in words. At this point in the session she picked up Greg and held him very close, rocking him in her arms. But the tension within her was transmitted to Greg; she was holding him too tightly and the baby began to protest. Yet we had seen Annie reach *spontaneously* for her baby, and this was a favorable sign. (Her awkwardness was to diminish over time, and we were later to witness a growing pleasure in physical intimacy with her baby.)

In successive sessions, Annie took the permission to speak of her feelings. And the story of childhood privations, of brutality and neglect, began to emerge once again, as if the narrative begun two months ago could now be resumed. But this time Mrs. Shapiro knew what had caused Annie to take flight from treatment two months ago, and her own insight could be employed in a method which would prevent flight or acting out and would ultimately lead to resolution. It was not the telling of the tales which had caused Annie to take flight, but the unspoken affect which had been maintained in isolation from the memories. Annie, you remember, had described her stepfather's beatings in exact and chilling detail, but the affect was isolated. She laughed cynically throughout that early session. Somewhere between the factual reporting of beatings and neglect and the flight from Mrs. Shapiro, affect which had been maintained in partial repression had emerged, and anger, fear, simple terror sought an object, a name for itself, and the name was Mrs. Shapiro.

This time, with the start of treatment, properly speaking, Mrs. Shapiro elicited affect along with the telling and made it safe to remember. When the story of childhood horrors emerged now, Mrs. Shapiro offered her own commentary. 'How frightening to a child. You were only a child then. There was no one to protect you. Every child has a right to be taken care of and protected.' And Annie said, with bitterness, 'The mother is supposed to protect the children. My mother didn't do that.' There was a refrain in these early hours which appears in the record again and again. 'I was hurt. I was hurt. Everyone in my family is violent.' And then another refrain. 'I don't want to hurt anybody. I don't want to hurt anybody.' Mrs. Shapiro, listening attentively, said, 'I know you don't want to hurt anybody. I know how much you have suffered and how much it hurt. As we talk about your feelings, even though it is painful to remember, it will be possible to find ways to come to terms with some of these things and to be the kind of mother you want to be.'

Annie, we saw, got both sides of the message. Mrs. Shapiro was on the side of the ego which defended against the unconscious wish to hurt and to repeat the hurts with her own child. At the same time, Mrs. Shapiro was saying, in effect, 'It will be safe with me to speak of the frightening memories and thoughts, and when you speak of them you will no longer need to be afraid of them; you will have another kind of control over them.'

Mrs. Shapiro also anticipated with Annie the possibility of negative transference feelings that might arise during sessions where painful memories would be revived. Mrs. Shapiro said to Annie, 'It may be that in talking about the past, you will feel angry toward me, without knowing why. Perhaps you could tell me when this happens, and we can try to understand how your feelings in the present are connected to memories in the past.'

For Annie, however, it was not easy to tell anyone she was angry. And she resisted putting into words her affect, so clearly evident in her face and body language. When Mrs. Shapiro asked Annie what she thought Mrs. Shapiro might do if Annie became angry with her, Annie said, 'Sometimes I get close to people – then I get mad. When I get mad, they leave.' Mrs. Shapiro reassured Annie that she could accept Annie's angry feelings and that she would not leave. With permission now to express anger, Annie's rage emerged in succeeding sessions, often in transference, and very slowly anger toward the objects of the past was re-experienced and put into proper perspective so that Annie could relate to her present family in a less conflicted way.

During all of these sessions, Mrs. Shapiro's watchful eye was upon Greg, always in the room. Would the rage spill over and engulf Greg? But once again, as in the case of Jane, we became witness to extraordinary changes in the young mother's relationship with Greg. In the midst of anger and tears, as

Annie spoke of her own oppressive past, she would approach Greg, pick him up, enclose him in her arms, and murmur comforting things to him. We knew then that Annie was no longer afraid of her destructive feelings toward the baby. The rage belonged to the past, to other figures. And the protective love toward Greg, which now began to emerge, spoke for a momentous shift in her identification with the baby. Where before she was identified with the aggressors of her childhood, she now was the protector of her baby, giving him what had not been given, or rarely given, in her own childhood. 'Nobody', said Annie one day, 'is ever going to hurt my child the way I have been hurt.'

Mrs. Shapiro, in her work, moved back and forth between the story of Annie's past and the present. She helped Annie see how fear of the parental figures of her childhood had led her to identify with their fearsome qualities. And, as Annie moved toward a protective relationship with her own baby, Mrs. Shapiro fortified each of these changes with her own observations. Sometimes, speaking for Greg, Mrs. Shapiro would say, 'Isn't it good to have a mommy who knows just what you need?' As Greg himself, now mobile, began to approach his mother more and more for affection, for comfort, for company, Mrs. Shapiro drew Annie's attention to each move. Greg, she pointed out, was learning to love and trust his mother, and all of this was due to Annie and her understanding of Greg. Annie was holding Greg now, cradling him protectively in her arms. We saw no more 'playful' threats of beating and killing, such as we had witnessed months before. Annie was feeding the baby and using Mrs. Shapiro's tactful suggestions in providing the elements of good nutrition in the baby's diet.

In this family without traditions in child rearing, Mrs. Shapiro often had to be the tactful educator. In Annie's and Earl's families, even a seven-month-old baby was regarded as being capable of malice, revenge, and cunning. If a baby cried, he was 'being spiteful'. If he was persistent, he was 'stubborn'. If he refused to comply, he was 'spoiled rotten'. If he couldn't be comforted, he was 'just crying to get someone's goat', Mrs. Shapiro always asked the question 'Why?' Why is he crying, why is he being stubborn, what could it be? Both parents, perhaps initially surprised by this alien approach to a baby, began to assimilate Mrs. Shapiro's education. More and more, as the weeks and months progressed, we saw the parents themselves seeking causes, alleviating distress by finding the antecedent conditions. And Greg began to flourish.

This is not to say that within a few months we had undone the cruel effects of Annie's own childhood. But we now had access to this past. When Annie's voice sometimes became shrill and she gave brusque treatment to Greg, Annie knew as well as Mrs. Shapiro that a ghost from Annie's childhood had invaded the nursery again. And together they could find meaning in the mood that had suddenly overpowered her.

As the baby progressed and Annie's conflicted past became sorted out, we began to see one figure emerge in Annie's childhood who stood for protection, tolerance, understanding. This was Annie's natural father, who had died when Annie was five. In Annie's memory he was kind and fair. He never beat her. He would never have allowed other people to be cruel to her, if only he had remained with the family. And, as she spoke of her own father, love and a remembrance of his loss overwhelmed her. Whether Annie's memory of her father was accurate or not does not matter, of course. What does matter is that in the chaos and terror of her childhood there had been one person who gave her a sense of love and protection. In searching her past for something good, for some source of strength, this is what she found, and Mrs. Shapiro kept this good memory alive for Annie. We now understood another part of the puzzle. When we had first known the Beyer family, you remember, Annie had not only refused to care for her baby but regularly turned him over to her husband, the baby's father, for care. All of this had changed in the intervening months as Annie learned, through her therapist, how a mother too can be a protector to her child.

Greg himself began to show a strengthening of his bond to his mother within the early months of work. At ten months of age, just before Mrs. Shapiro left for vacation, his behavior toward his mother showed selective response and seeking of her, much smiling and seeking contact with her, approaches to mother for comfort and for company. But there was still some fear of mother, we saw, when her strident voice stopped him in the middle of some trivial misdemeanor.

During these months, we should now recall, Annie was pregnant. She rarely spoke of the coming baby to Mrs. Shapiro. It was as if the pregnancy was not real to her. There were no fantasies about the baby. She was fully preoccupied with her own self and with Greg, who was becoming the center for her.

In July, when Mrs. Shapiro was on vacation, Annie delivered a stillborn child. When Mrs. Shapiro returned, Annie was sad and burdened with guilt. The death of the baby she thought was a punishment to her. She had not wanted the baby, and she thought God did not want a baby to come into the world who would not be loved. Many hours were spent in putting together the experience of loss and self-reproach.

It was during this period too that Annie began to understand with help why she had not been ready for another baby. She was, indeed, drawing upon all of her impoverished emotional resources to give care and love to Greg, and in giving she felt depleted. Many times we had the impression that she was sustaining herself through the warmth and caring of her therapist, borrowing strength, augmenting the poverty of her own experience in love through the relationship to her therapist. This was always a professional relationship, of course, but, for a girl who had been emotionally starved and brutalized, this professional caring and understanding seemed to be experienced as the giving of love.

The unsatisfied hungers of childhood were persistent ghosts in this household. Often when the therapist arrived, Annie and Earl were watching television. Their favorite TV shows were children's programs and animated cartoons. This was not for Greg's sake, we must assure you, since Greg himself had no interest in these shows. During the summer of the Watergate hearings, which were carried on nearly every channel, of course, Mrs. Shapiro saw Annie and Earl switch from channel to channel until they found a program they liked. It was *The Jolly Green Giant*.

When Mrs. Shapiro brought carefully selected toys for Greg (as we always do for our children when we know that the parents cannot provide them), Annie wore a conflicted look on her face. It was envy, Mrs. Shapiro realized, and longing. On one occasion, when Mrs. Shapiro brought some simple plastic toys for the baby, Annie said, in a voice full of feeling, 'It's my birthday next week. I'll be seventeen.' Mrs. Shapiro understood, of course. Annie wished the present were for her. The therapist, quickly responding, spoke of Annie's coming birthday and her wish that it be a very special day. Annie said, 'I never had a birthday. I never had a party. I'm planning to have one for Greg in August. My mother will probably forget my birthday.' (Her mother did forget.) And for Annie's birthday, Mrs. Shapiro brought a small, carefully chosen present for her.

On Greg's birthday, Mrs. Shapiro brought a toy bus for the baby. Annie opened the package. She was enraptured. She examined each of the little figures, opened the bus door, placed all the little people on the seats, and only when she had finished playing with it did she give it to Greg and share her excitement with him.

The last ghost: the most obstinate one

The last ghost to leave the nursery was also the first ghost to enter it. And its name, of course, was 'identification with the aggressor'. Even in its most formidable aspect after the first months of therapeutic work this ghost no longer threatened the baby. That is to say, there was no longer serious danger of abuse of Greg by his mother. We saw how the strengthening of the love bonds between Annie and her baby protected the child from physical abuse. We also saw how Annie's remembrances of her own suffering became a form of protection to her baby. She would no longer inflict her pain upon her child.

At the end of the first year of treatment, then, Greg showed favorable signs of developmental progress and attachment to his mother. But the ghost still lingered, and we saw it in many forms that still endangered Greg's development.

As Greg became active, independent, curious, and mischievous in his second year, Annie's repertoire of disciplinary tactics appeared ready-made from the ruins of her childhood. Maternal and protective and affectionate as she could be when Greg was quiet, obedient, and 'good', there was a voice for disobedience or ordinary toddler mishaps which was strident, shrill, and of a magnitude to shatter the eardrums. Greg at these moments was frightened, and Mrs. Shapiro drew Annie's attention to the baby's reactions on many occasions. And then very quickly, it seemed to us, Greg acquired a defense against the anxiety produced in him by mother's anger. He would laugh, giddily, a little hysterically, we thought. And this, of course, was exactly the defense which his mother had acquired in her childhood. Greg was 16 months old when we witnessed the appearance of this defense.

Very clearly, an important component of Annie's defense – 'identification with the aggressor' – had not yet been dealt with in the therapy. Annie had not yet fully experienced in therapy her childhood anxiety and terror before the dangerous, unpredictable, violent, and powerful figures of the past. From analytic experience we knew that the pathogenesis of the defense known as identification with the aggressor is anxiety and helplessness before the attackers. To reach this stratum of the defense structure through psychoanalysis is often a formidable task. How shall we reach it through our once-a-week psychotherapy-in-the-kitchen?

We examined the pathways available to us. Annie's voice, Mrs. Shapiro had observed, would shift in a single moment from a natural conversational voice, which was her own, to the strident, ear-shattering voice which seemed to be somebody else's. But Annie seemed not aware of this. The alien voice was also incorporated in her personality. Could we employ the on-the-spot manifestations of this pathological identification in a two-phase interpretive process? First, to make the voice ego-alien, identify it; then, to interpret it as a defense against intolerable anxiety and lead Annie to re-experience her own childhood sense of terror and helplessness?

There was no difficulty finding the occasion in a home visit. The occasion, as it happened, appeared with startling clarity in a visit shortly after we examined the technical problems in our conference.

Greg, 17 months old, was in his high chair, eating his breakfast. Mother kept up a stream of admonitions while he ate: 'Don't do that. Don't drop the food off.' Then suddenly, responding to some trivial mishap in the high chair, Annie screamed, 'Stop it!' Both Greg and Mrs. Shapiro jumped. Annie said to the therapist, 'I scared you, didn't I?' Mrs. Shapiro, recovering from shock, decided this was the moment she was waiting for. She said, 'Sometimes, Annie, the words and sounds that come out of your mouth don't even sound like you. I wonder whom they do sound like.' Annie said immediately, 'I know. They sound just like my mother. My mother used to scare me.' 'How did you feel?' Annie said, 'How would you feel if you were in with a bull in a china shop? ... Besides, I don't want to talk about that. I've suffered enough. That's behind me.'

But Mrs. Shapiro persisted, gently, and made the crucial interpretation. She said, 'I could imagine that as a little girl you might be so scared that in order to make yourself less scared, you might start talking and sounding like your mother.' Annie said again, 'I don't want to talk about it right now.' But she was deeply affected by Mrs. Shapiro's words.

The rest of the hour took a curious turn. Annie began to collapse before Mrs. Shapiro's eyes. Instead of a tough, defiant, aggressive girl, she became a helpless, anxious little girl for the entire hour. Since she could find no words to speak of the profound anxiety which had emerged in her, she began to speak of everything she could find in her contemporary life that made her feel afraid, helpless, alone.

In this way, and for many hours to come, Mrs. Shapiro led Annie back into the experiences of helplessness and terror in her childhood and moved back and forth, from the present to the past, in identifying for Annie the ways in which she brought her own experiences to her mothering of Greg, how identification with the feared people of her childhood was 'remembered' when she became the frightening mother to Greg. It was a moment for therapeutic rejoicing when Annie was able to say, 'I don't want my child to be afraid of me.'

The work in this area brought about profound changes in Annie and in her relationship with Greg. Annie herself began to leave behind her tough, street-child manner, and the strident voice was muted. As the pathological identification with her own mother began to dissolve, we saw Annie seeking new models for mothering and for femininity, some of which were easily identified as attributes of Mrs. Shapiro.

And Greg himself began to respond to the changed climate of his home. As we should expect, the fear of mother and the nervous laugh as a defense against anxiety began to disappear. Since there were, in fact, strong bonds between mother and baby, there was much that Annie could now employ in an education of her son without fear.

Mrs. Shapiro enlisted the mother as observer of Greg's attempts to communicate with her. Concrete suggestions and demonstrations were offered in a supportive, non-critical way. This time Annie was able to use the developmental guidance in a less defensive and more constructive way, working in alliance with the therapist on behalf of Greg. Within a month of the time Greg's need for help in language was first identified, he began to use language expressively and was soon well within the normal range of the Bayley Scale.

Treatment continued for two years, which is some time beyond the point where Greg had achieved adequacy in all areas of functioning, and Annie and Earl themselves had become competent and devoted parents. In large measure, the work of those two years was supportive of the two young parents who were coping with the stresses of 'growing up' themselves, of completing their own adolescence, at the same time as they were learning to become parents of a kind they had never known in their own experience. Annie and Earl continued to seek guidance from Mrs. Shapiro in many areas of child rearing and yet were making good and wise decisions on their own as Greg moved into each new developmental stage. Treatment was terminated when Greg was three years old, when Annie herself told Mrs. Shapiro that she now felt good about her ability to manage without help. It was understood that at any time in the future that she needed to call Mrs. Shapiro or visit she would always be most welcome.

Follow-up

Since Annie and Earl kept in touch with Mrs. Shapiro from time to time, we have a follow-up report augmenting the story of this family.

The outcome of treatment for Annie, for Earl, and for Greg has been hopeful. In 1977, Greg – now close to five years of age – is seen in follow-up as a healthy, buoyant little boy, affectionate and endearing. A new baby brother, now two years old, testifies to the good mothering he is receiving and the good climate of his home. The marriage of Annie and Earl has become stable – and it is the only stable marriage in both their extended families. Annie herself is a proud and competent young woman. Last year Annie, the high-school dropout, enrolled in a class in child development. She was surprised, she told Mrs. Shapiro, to discover how much she knew.

She is consulted by all members of her family, including her mother, as family crises continue to occur. She dispenses wise counsel and keeps her own head. She thinks her mother and sisters all need therapy and has done her earnest best to persuade them, but not yet with success.

The questions – and a hypothesis

We began this chapter with a question: *'What is it, then, that determines whether the conflicted past of the parent will be repeated with his child?'* Morbidity in the parental history will not in itself predict the repetition of the past in the present. The presence of pathological figures in the parental past will not, in itself, predict identification with those figures and the passing on of morbid experience to one's own children.

From the clinical studies of Mrs. March and Annie Beyer, and from many other cases known to us in which the ghosts of the parental past take possession of the nursery, we have seen a pattern which is strikingly uniform: These are the parents who, earlier, in the extremity of childhood terror, formed a pathological identification with the dangerous and assaultive enemies of the ego. Yet, if we name this condition in the familiar term, 'identification with the aggressor', we have not added to the sum of our knowledge of this defense. Our literature in this area of defense is sparse. Beyond the early writings of Anna Freud, which name and illuminates this defense in the formative period of childhood, we do not yet know from large-scale clinical study the conditions which govern the choice of this defense against other alternatives, or the dynamics which perpetuate an identification with the enemy, so to speak.

We are on sound grounds clinically and theoretically if we posit that a form of repression is present in this defense which provides motive and energy for repetition. But what is it that is repressed? From a number of cases known to us in which identification with the aggressor was explored clinically as a central mechanism in pathological parenting, we can report that memory for the events of childhood abuse, tyranny, and desertion was available in explicit and chilling detail. *What was not remembered was the associated affective experience.*

Annie, for instance, remembered her childhood beatings by her stepfather, and she remembered her mother's desertion. What she did not remember was terror and helplessness in the experience of being abused and deserted. The original affects had undergone repression. When the therapeutic work revived these affects, and when Annie could re-experience them in the safety of her relationship with the therapist, she could no longer inflict this pain upon her child. Mrs. March could remember rejection, desertion and incestuous experience in childhood. What she could not remember was the overwhelming anxiety, shame, and worthlessness which had accompanied each of these violations of a child. When anxiety, grief, shame, and self-abasement were recovered and re-experienced in therapy, Mrs. March no longer needed to inflict her own pain and her childhood sins upon her child. With the re-experiencing of childhood suffering along with the memories, each of these young mothers was able to say, 'I would never want that to happen to my child.'

These words strike a familiar note. There are many parents who have themselves lived tormented childhoods but who do not inflict their pain upon their children. These are the parents who say explicitly, or in effect, 'I remember what it was like ... I remember how afraid I was when my father exploded ... I remember how I cried when they took me and my sister away to live in that home ... I would never let my child go through what I went through.'

For these parents the pain and suffering have not undergone total repression. In remembering, they are saved from the blind repetition of that morbid past. Through remembering, they identify with an injured child (the childhood self), while the parent who does not remember may find himself/herself in an unconscious alliance and identification with the fearsome figures of the past. In this way the parental past is inflicted upon the child.

The key to our ghost story appears to lie in the fate of affects in childhood. Our hypothesis is that access to childhood pain becomes a powerful deterrent against repetition in parenting, while repression and isolation of painful affect provide the psychological requirements for identification with the betrayers and the aggressors. The unsolved mystery is why, under conditions of extremity, in early childhood, some children who later become parents keep pain alive; they do not make the fateful alliance with the aggressor which defends the child ego against intolerable danger and obliterates the conscious experience of anxiety. We hope to explore these problems in farther study.

The theory posited here, however incomplete, has practical implications for psychotherapy with parents and children in those families where the ghosts of the parental past have taken up residence in the nursery. In each case, when our therapy has brought the parent to remember and re-experience his/her childhood anxiety and suffering, the ghosts depart and the afflicted parents become the protectors of their children against the repetition of their own conflicted past.

CHAPTER 9

Therapeutic interventions in infancy: two contrasting cases of persistent crying[1]

JULIET HOPKINS

Infants are liable to many symptoms of emotional disturbance. However, it is now widely agreed that there is no such thing as individual psychopathology in infancy. Infantile disturbances are considered to be a function of current relationships. The paper briefly summarizes available psychodynamic approaches to problems in infant relationships. It argues that more case studies of therapeutic interventions in infancy are needed to increase our understanding of early disturbances and of their treatment. Two contrasting case studies of intervention in persistent crying attempt to understand what may sustain this distressing problem. In each case the possible meaning of the crying both to the babies and to their families is considered.

Introduction

Can babies be maladjusted? Certainly, disturbances in the first year of life are legion. Babies can suffer from 'behaviour disorders': sleeping problems, incessant rocking, breath-holding, persistent masturbation, head-banging and other forms of self-harm. They are susceptible to 'disorders of mood': persistent crying and screaming, whining and misery, apathy and withdrawal. They may show autistic features or even merit the diagnosis of autism. A range of feeding disorders can also be added to the list of potential problems: failure to thrive, food refusal, pica (eating non-food substances) and rumination (chewing regurgitated food). Finally, there are illnesses which have been traditionally termed 'psychosomatic disorders': vomiting,

---

[1] This paper first appeared in *Psychoanalytic Psychotherapy*, 8: 141-52, 1994. It is reprinted by kind permission of the journal and of the author.

diarrhoea, constipation, asthma, eczema, some allergies and unusual susceptibility to infectious illness. In the second year of life all the disorders associated with toilet training and speech development can be added to in this
catalogue of woe.

In spite of this impressive array of available symptoms, babies have defied
attempts to fit their ills into psychiatric categories. Indeed, recent opinion in
the field of infant psychiatry is that 'there is no such thing as individual
psychopathology in infancy' (Sameroff and Emde, 1989). This is obvious if
we agree with Winnicott that 'There is no such thing as a baby', only a
mother–baby couple. Infants' symptoms can only be understood as a
function of their current relationships. However, this does mean that babies
do not contribute problems from their side of the relationship. It is of course
well known that moments differ widely in temperamental endowment. It
does mean that the treatment of infant symptoms is often best conducted via
the infant–parent relationship, rather than either with the infant or parent
separately. The exact age at which infantile problems become internalized to
be susceptible to individual psychoanalysis remains uncertain and may well
be variable. However, clinical experience shows that infants under the age of
about two to two-and-a-half years are usually quickly responsive to changes in
their parents' feelings and behaviour towards them. Early intervention reaps
this great advantage.

Psychotherapy with infants and their parents

The work of Selma Fraiberg (1980) in America marks the start of systematic
thinking about psychotherapeutic approaches to infancy. Fraiberg introduces
two terms to describe her work: 'developmental guidance' and
'infant–parent psychotherapy' (also known as 'parent–infant psychotherapy').

Developmental guidance consists of supportive counselling in which
advice is very rarely given. Parents are helped to observe and think about
their baby while coming to recognize their own unique importance to their
child. This approach is often sufficient to resolve minor difficulties, and the
restrictions of this method are necessary for parents who are not ready to
consider the role that their own relationships may play in their baby's current
difficulties.

Infant–parent psychotherapy goes further. The method involves an interpretative approach aimed at understanding the way that the parental past
may be interfering with the parent's capacity to relate to the baby in the
present. Fraiberg believes that this was the treatment of choice whenever the
baby had come to represent an aspect of the self which was repudiated or
negated, or had become the representation of figures from the past, 'the

ghosts in the nursery'.[2] This method and its further development by psycho-analysts B. Cramer, D. Stern and R. Emde is described elsewhere (Hopkins, 1992).

Therapeutic approaches to infants and their parents have also developed in this country. Winnicott (e.g. 1941, 1971) reports working with the baby in the presence of the mother. Daws (1989) developed a psychodynamic approach within a GP practice.[3] Byng-Hall has used Attachment Theory to develop his approach to families with non-verbal infants (Byng-Hall and Stevenson-Hinde, 1991)

Another relevant development has been the growth of practice of *infant observation* (Bick, 1964).[4] Experience of this method of observing babies in their families is an excellent background for training in therapeutic work with infants (Miller, 1992).

Therapeutic intervention in infancy can make a significant contribution to understanding the genesis of psychopathology. It helps to disclose the factors sustaining deviant development by changing them. More individual studies are needed, both as a source of hypotheses about infancy and as an addition to general knowledge available to the clinician. This paper aims to add to this literature by describing intervention in two cases of persistent crying.

Persistent infant crying

Studies suggest that at least 10% of healthy infants suffer from this problem (e.g. St James-Roberts et al., 1993). Severe cases of crying in the early months are often labelled 'colic', although there are no accepted clinical criteria for this term. Persistent crying and colic do not occur in very depriving institu-tions for infants (e.g. Provence and Lipton, 1962); babies simply give up. This is a reminder that crying is always a function of a relationship, as well as of the baby's endowment.

Crying is an intensely powerful communication. It expresses strong feelings and it arouses them. The reaction of parents to persistent crying depends upon the meaning which they ascribe to it. This in turn will depend in part upon the nature of their baby's cry, its intensity, its emotional tone (anger, misery or fear) and its particular aversive qualities. Persistent crying makes most parents desperate. It is not surprising that it is associated with abuse. Clearly, someone or something is felt to be to blame and it may seem to be the fault of a monster baby. Scapegoating can start from here. In

---

[2] See Chapter 8, this volume [Ed.].
[3] See Chapter 10, this volume [Ed.].
[4] Infant observation is also used in training for adult psychoanalysis. Chapter 16 is an example of this [Ed.].

contrast to, and often along with, their feelings of fury and frustration with their baby, parents experience themselves as helpless and rejected failures. Compassion for the baby is normally mixed with both anger and self-doubt. It can be a great relief to hold 'colic' responsible.

What does crying mean to the baby? This question is usually avoided. Babies are simply described as having 'low thresholds of irritability', 'difficult temperaments' or 'problems with state regulation'. It can be hard to imagine that they are crying about something when all their needs appear to have been met. No doubt some babies are prone to cry much more easily than others. They bring their own genetic endowment and their own histories of pre-natal life, birth and early experience. For example, one group of infants especially prone to persistent crying is identified by Brazelton (1985).[5] These are babies who are born small for gestational age and have been malnourished in the womb. Whereas 'colicky' babies usually stop crying at around three – four months, these babies continue with their aversive cry until five months. Parents who are sensitive enough to discover that they require particularly calm, quiet and steady care are able to soothe them.

Since so many babies cry excessively in the early months, they cannot all be offered specialized therapeutic help, nor do they need it. Most families get by with the support of grandparents, friends and health visitors or the help of voluntary organizations, like CRY-SIS. Happily, crying is usually outgrown, although the association of early persistent crying with later behaviour problems (Forsyth and Canny, 1991) suggests that disturbed relationships may persist. Certainly, professional help is needed when crying is combined with other signs of infantile disturbance, when abuse threatens or when parents are distraught. In the two case examples which follow, the extremity of these infants' crying and of its effect on their parents is indicated by the fact that both infants were admitted to hospital for investigations of their distress before they were referred for psychological help. Both families were seen under the auspices of the Under-Fives Counselling Service of the Tavistock Clinic, an NHS psychiatric outpatient clinic. The Service aims to offer families an appointment within a week or two of referral. It provides up to five sessions, which may take place weekly or be spaced over several months according to need. Audit has shown that the majority of problems improve markedly within five meetings, but in some cases further work is needed.

---

[5] See Chapter 19 in this volume for a description of Brazelton's Neonatal Behavioural Assessment Scale [Ed.].

Case example: Hannah

Hannah was referred by a paediatrician at the age of six months. She was said to suffer from persistent crying and would not make eye contact. The paediatrician gave the following history. Hannah had been born to a single schizophrenic mother with whom she had spent her first three days in maternity hospital. She was then transferred to a paediatric ward where she spent a month until her move to a foster home. During that month in hospital, she developed a reputation as 'a screamer'. Her foster parents had two little girls of their own, but, in spite of their conflicting demands for attention, the foster mother, Martha, had done her best to try to comfort Hannah, to no avail. When Hannah was still screaming at six months old, Martha persuaded the paediatrician to admit Hannah to hospital to establish whether anything was wrong with her. All tests were negative, but it was noticed that Hannah was hypertonic when held and would not make eye contact either with the nurses or with her foster family. The paediatrician knew that this was characteristic of autism and feared that Hannah might have inherited a psychotic constitution from her mother.

I invited the whole foster family to bring Hannah to meet me, since it is usually valuable to begin by exploring how an infant's problem affects everyone in the family and to observe how each affects the infant. However, only the foster mother, Martha, and her two-year-old daughter, Mary, were able to come with Hannah. Hannah was asleep in her buggy and Mary settled easily to play while Martha eagerly grasped the opportunity to share her distress about the pain of this, her first experience of fostering. She was evidently a warm-hearted woman, who had been extremely distressed by Hannah's screaming, which occurred daily and sometimes persisted for up to four hours at a time. 'It's worse than crying. It's piercing screams,' she said.

I acknowledged how desperate she must have felt and explored how she had dealt with her own exasperation and anger. This is always a crucial issue for the parents of crying babies. When she hesitated, I acknowledged what any mother might feel in the circumstances, and she admitted that she had come close to battering Hannah. She had not been able to tell the social worker this in case she took her away. She had always loved Hannah and wanted to help her become a normal, happy child like her two daughters, but she felt that the task might be beyond her and that she might have to give Hannah up. Both her husband and her mother had said she would never be able to cope with three little children, and she feared they were right. Moreover, her husband disliked the idea of her working for money and had not supported her plan to foster, although he was gradually growing fond of Hannah. Whenever Hannah screamed, she worried that he would either insist that she gave up fostering or would divorce her. In view of Hannah's screaming, they were both afraid she would become psychotic like her mother.

At this point in our meeting Hannah awoke with an abrupt startle, which Martha said was how she always awoke. Martha lifted her gently onto her lap while talking kindly to her and showed me how Hannah sat stiffly, not moulding to Martha's body. Most striking to observe, Hannah held her legs raised above Martha's lap, and Martha explained that Hannah never let her legs rest on Martha's body. Hannah had always rejected cuddling, and Martha showed me how Hannah strained away from her chest when she drew her towards her. She told me that holding her when she screamed made her cry more. Babies like this, who seem to need holding but reject it, pose a particular problem that would benefit from a growing literature of case studies.

Next, Martha laid Hannah on a rug on the floor and knelt beside her. They played together in a lively way, involving Mary in bringing toys for Hannah. Hannah smiled, vocalized and laughed, especially to Mary, but although her eyes swept across both their faces she never allowed a moment of sustained contact.

Martha gave a very good impression as a foster mother, being caring, concerned, sensitive and observant, and had a happy, affectionate relationship with her own attractive little girl. She had observed with pain that Hannah had seemed to prefer the isolation in hospital, had screamed much less there than at home and had drunk more milk from a propped bottle than she did on Martha's lap. She was surprised that Hannah loved the swing on the ward when she had always resisted being rocked in arms.

Together we built up a picture of Hannah as a baby very different from her own: a nervous, hypersensitive baby, who had had a bad start in life, who felt overwhelmed and frightened by people when exposed to face, voice and physical contact all together, but who clearly enjoyed relationships with her family when they were modulated. Martha was pleased that I felt it would be all right to continue the propped bottle, to leave Hannah alone in her cot and not to try to cuddle her when she resisted. She thought she would buy her a rocking chair.

Martha left saying she was much relieved that I appreciated her efforts and had not blamed her. I was aware that I had also given her permission to take her cues from the baby. We agreed to meet again three weeks later, together with her husband.

A week later Martha phoned to say that, although she would have liked another appointment, in view of the very difficult journey, she would not come as there was no further need. Hannah had made eye contact both with her and her husband on the day of our consultation, she was continuing to do so and had become more smiley and friendly. She had screamed much less and was not so jumpy, but she still kept her legs lifted off the lap and did not want to be cuddled.

We kept in touch by phone until Hannah was 11 months old, when Martha reported that Hannah now enjoyed and initiated cuddles. She had only had one screaming fit in the past month, when a stranger visited and made too rapid overtures; after that she had 'screamed all night'. Otherwise all was well, and Martha was confident that she could help Hannah through any remaining difficulties. I was sorry that Martha felt no further need for contact since Hannah's recent screaming fit alerted me to her persisting vulnerability. There is often a conflict for therapists in infant–parent work between supporting parents' autonomy and self-esteem by encouraging them to help their children themselves and the therapist's wish to be their most effective. In this fascinating case, I was deprived of first-hand follow-up, but was informed by the family's health visitor that Hannah had indeed made all the beneficial changes which Martha had reported. She thought that without intervention Martha would have abandoned her attempt to foster Hannah.

Hannah's capacity to change was a surprising endorsement of the claim that there is no such thing as individual psychopathology in infancy. Forgetting this, I had supposed, as the referring paediatrician had done, that the presenting problems were best understood as Hannah's. Only when Hannah changed in response to the consultation did it emerge that there had been relationship factors sustaining her problems. The initial causes of Hannah's screaming must remain obscure. Perhaps there were constitutional factors and/or perhaps she had been traumatized. Winnicott believes that, when babies appear hypersensitive and paranoid from birth, environmental factors could be to blame. If this were so, then in Hannah's case, a recovery proved possible through an environmental change. When Martha changed so did Hannah.

What had enabled the foster mother to change? During our meeting, Martha had been able to face her underlying anger, guilt and sense of failure and her distress at her husband's and her mother's disapproval of her fostering. She said she had not realized how upset she was until she talked to me. Afterwards, she felt relieved of her emotional burden and less determined to prove that she could cure Hannah. She gave me details of how this change of attitude enabled her to adapt herself to Hannah's needs instead of trying to coax her to become like her own children. Babies who have had a muddled start like Hannah seem to need a period of maximal adaptation before they settle down, but instead, in the kindest possible way, Hannah had found herself required to comply. She could not make eye contact until Martha saw her through more accepting eyes.

Hannah also illustrated the amazing speed and ease with which change can take place in infancy. Selma Fraiberg (1980) was so impressed by this that she writes, 'When a baby is at the centre of treatment something happens which has no parallel in any other form of psychotherapy. It's like having God on your side.'

The intervention used by Martha and Hannah would have been classified by Selma Fraiberg as *developmental guidance*. My second case example concerns a family for whom it was not sufficient to explore the reasons in the present for their mutual distress. They needed the interpretative approach of *infant-parent psychotherapy* to discover its origins in the past.

Case example: Betty

Betty was referred when eight weeks old by a paediatrician who had admitted her to hospital for a week because her mother could not stand her crying any more. Her first baby had also cried persistently until the age of over a year, and the mother felt she could not bear 'a repeat performance'. She had scarcely visited Betty in hospital where Betty continued to cry persistently.

The family came to see me a week later. Both parents, Tim and Tracey, were accountants. Their son Terry was aged three years and Betty was nine weeks old. Betty was crying as they entered and continued to cry throughout, with a steady, protesting cry. Tracey responded by offering her appropriate comfort, cradling, patting and rocking, and occasionally putting her down in the buggy or passing her to Tim, all to no avail. Terry busied himself throughout with a succession of scribble drawings which he took to his mother, with smiles and kisses. This little boy, who himself had cried for sixteen months, appeared to have become a compulsive caregiver and this was confirmed in later meetings.

The parents took the opportunity to have a major row. Tracey accused Tim of not wanting the baby, refusing to help at home and even getting ill himself. She readily agreed with my half-humorous suggestion that she must have wished that the paediatrician had also admitted him to hospital, and she spoke bitterly of the need for divorce. Tim accused Tracey of refusing to appreciate everything he *did* do to help, which he listed at length. They both shouted above the baby's cries. I could scarcely think: I wanted to scream too. Naturally, I wondered whether Betty could not be comforted because of the extreme tension in this unhappy household. I acknowledged that they all had a great deal to cry about so it was not surprising that Betty had the same problem. And I asked about sources of support; this is always a crucial issue with young families. Although both parents were English, neither parent had family currently living in England. No grandparents had yet to come to visit the baby. Talking about their shared isolation seemed to bring them somewhat together, and we were then able to give some attention to Betty.

Tracey explained that, although she could not stand Betty's crying, she always stayed with her, held her and rocked her, so Betty would know she was trying to help; this meant pacing the floor most of the night. Although she was exhausted, she felt sure she would not hurt her. It was her husband whom she wanted to attack.

Tim said that Betty *is* sometimes peaceful while awake and that Tracey exaggerated the amount that she cried. Tracey admitted, 'She is always crying in my mind.' I wondered what this perpetual crying represented. I enquired about the parents' childhoods. Tim knew nothing of his infancy. Tracey knew that she too had been a crying baby and had been left to scream sometimes for hours. I acknowledged that she was determined not to give Betty the same unhappy experience of crying alone. I said that Betty's cries must have evoked painful memories of her own childhood, cries which were never comforted. Tracy was pleased to have a plausible explanation of her own distress, but she did not respond to this with any depth of feeling, and I was not surprised that Betty's crying continued. Perhaps, I had made this intervention too early, before a more solid working alliance with the family had been established. Unfortunately, with this family an alliance was slow to form since Tim's work and an illness of Terry's both intervened to postpone what were intended to be weekly appointments.

At our second meeting, three weeks later, when Betty was twelve weeks old, she still cried most of the time. There were undercurrents of hostility between the parents, but no open warfare. During this session, I realized why I had felt uncomfortable about Tracey's relationship with Betty, in spite of her evident concern for her and her appropriate handling: even when Betty was not crying Tracey did not make eye contact with her or talk to her. When I invited her to do so, she could not think of anything to say except, 'I don't want to see your tonsils.' She told me she did not feel rewarded by Betty's smiles, they simply made her feel, 'So what?' Tim, too, seemed at a loss to talk to Betty and said that he preferred older children like Terry.

The first session had helped the parents to recognize the possible significance of their own childhoods, which they now spontaneously recalled. Tracey was reluctant to blame her own mother, but Tim recounted how Tracey's mother had said she hated small children, had sent Tracey to a day nursery as soon as possible and had determined never to have another child. Tracey explained how her mother had depended upon her emotionally as she grew up. Her parents' marriage was stormy; they divorced when Tracey was thirteen years old, and Tracey was left alone with her mother who then suffered a depressive breakdown.

The family seemed calmer, but more storms were to come. It was not until our fourth meeting, when Betty was nearly five months old, that Betty's persistent crying finally stopped. No sooner had the family arrived, than another furious row developed. Tracey was again irate that Tim would not help. She was totally incensed by the fact that he 'escaped' from the house every day to go to work and enjoy 'one long holiday', while she was trapped with the children. She became irrational to the point of delusional about Tim's daily absences, and I feared that this time she, not the baby, would need hospitalization. This reminded me of her own mother's depressive breakdown. I asked whether the present desperate situation reminded Tracey of the terrible time her father had walked out and left her to cope with her mother's tears. Tracey wept as she recalled her own helplessness to comfort her mother. She talked at length about this terrible experience. She had never been able to satisfy her mother's demands and had left home at the age of 16. Both she and Tim could recognize the parallels with Tracey's current situation.

This proved to be a turning point in the therapy. As soon as Tracey had finished her recollections, Betty stopped crying and Tracey spontaneously related to her as a person, smiling and talking and asking her how she was. 'Do you feel better, Betty? I think you do.' It was evident that at least Tracey did. After this session Betty stopped her persistent crying and Tracey dropped her irrational accusations of Tim. At two follow-up meetings during Betty's sixth month, Tracey was happy that she was enjoying Betty at an age when Terry had still been a 'tyrant'. Although Betty no longer cried and was happily responsive when Tracey initiated conversations with her, I noticed that Betty did not initiate conversations with either of her parents, but instead attempted across the room to initiate smiling and talking with me. Clearly, problems remained, and I was willing to continue meeting, but Tracey vetoed further help. She felt that only her return to full-time work would remove her envy of her husband and so save her sanity.

This brief intervention was not a therapeutic miracle. Tracey remained burdened by her unhappy past and still at risk of acting it out with Betty, as she already seemed to be doing in a different way with her son Terry, whose need to look after her probably mirrored her own childhood attempt to care for her own depressed mother. What had happened is what Cramer and Stern (1988) call '*a dynamic disconnection*' between Tracey's past and Betty's present. Betty's cries no longer touched off Tracey's childhood anguish – Betty had been unhooked from Tracey's hang-ups, and Tim could now be appreciated for his contribution, instead of being attacked for absconding as Tracey's father had done.

When a dynamic disconnection happens, parental behaviour changes without ever having been a focus of therapy. As long as Betty represented

Tracey's own childhood screams and the insatiable demands of her own mother, Tracey could not comfort her or respond to Betty as a separate person in her own right. After Tracey's own cries had been heard, she could feel empathy for Betty instead of hostility, and Betty responded with contentment. As Fraiberg (1980) writes, '*remembering saves a parent from blind repetition because it enables identification with the injured child*'. Until Tracey changed, Betty's angry crying had probably indicated her sensitivity to Tracey's hostility, reflected in Tracey's bodily tension and in her failure to engage in social interaction with her daughter. Research has shown that one- and two-month-old babies have innate expectations of relationships and that they manifest distress when their mothers unexpectedly ignore them for brief periods (Cooper et al., 1991).[6] Their facial expressions show that they attribute meaning to this experience. It seems possible to suppose that babies are liable to respond to prolonged periods of social rejection with distress, which they may loudly express in protest as long as active parental involvement keeps their hopes for more social contact alive.

Discussion

These two contrasting cases of persistent crying illustrate the need for every case to be considered in its own right. However, in spite of many obvious differences, both babies illustrate extreme sensitivity to feelings. Both mothers had tried their utmost to comfort their babies, but they could not succeed until their own underlying distress had been heard. Only then could they relinquish their personal preoccupations and respond appropriately to their babies' needs.

Although interpreting infants' behaviour is inevitably highly speculative, it seems that, in the first case, Hannah's need was to have her fears of intimacy accepted and to have her own cues followed. Winnicott (1962) would say she needed the recognition of her 'spontaneous gesture'. Until this happened her withdrawal and her prolonged bouts of screaming indicated that she was in the grip of 'unthinkable anxieties', such as going to pieces, falling for ever, having no relationship to the body and no orientation! Once she felt herself to be existentially confirmed, through contingent responsiveness to her own cues, she could turn to her foster parents for comfort and her unthinkable anxieties could be mitigated.

As for Betty, it seemed that what she had needed was for her mother to withdraw her hostile projections, to empathize with her and to welcome her socially as a person. Until then her angry protest proclaimed her sense of rejection and her demand for the right attention.

---

[6] See Chapter 20 in this volume for Lynne Murray's presentation of her research [Ed.].

The role of eye contact is of particular interest in both cases. Direct eye contact allows an intimate appreciation of facial expression. Hannah avoided it until Martha ceased to pursue it. As Martha reported on the telephone, 'It's funny, but, when we stopped worrying about it, she looked at us.' Presumably, Martha's and her husband's pursuit of eye contact had been felt by Hannah as a persecuting demand. When Hannah felt accepted, she could enjoy looking back. And, once she had discovered that she could initiate contact on her own terms, her acceptance of physical contact soon followed. What had been developing as an extremely avoidant pattern of attachment (Ainsworth, 1985) gave hope of becoming gradually secure.

In Betty's case it was her parents who quite unconsciously avoided eye contact with her, while offering plenty of physical contact. Tracey must have been unable to look Betty in the eye because she feared to see projected there the insatiable demands of her own mother and of her own infant-self. Once she had recalled and contained some of these painful memories, she did not need to project them. Betty could then be seen by her as more appealing than demanding.

Projections do not pass by magic through the air. They are subtly conveyed to babies by eye contact, facial expression, tone of voice, holding and handling. Video can reveal some of the details which pass too swiftly to observe. However, video cannot adequately convey the emotional impact which we as therapists receive. Our capacity for emotional attunement to details too fine for conscious processing contributes to the countertransference which informs our thinking. For example, while meeting with Martha and Hannah, I found myself responding with unusual therapeutic zeal to their plight. It was through recognizing my sense of effort that I became aware of Martha's effort and so could wonder whether Hannah needed a more accommodating approach. Unfortunately, countertransference can also be a source of difficulty in this work, especially when therapist's feelings become split between parent and infant. This happened with Betty's family when I found myself exasperated with Tracey and identified with Betty's cries. Tracey was rightly angry with me when I briefly took sides and treated her as the patient. I had to remind myself that *one family member can express feelings on behalf of another*. Since babies are so palpably open to their parents' feelings, this is probably more convincingly apparent in infancy than at any subsequent stage of development.

Fraiberg (1980) observes that, like their babies, parents of infants are particularly flexible in their capacity to change. Perhaps this is because there has been less time to establish a history of antagonism; perhaps also the fresh start, which a baby's new life connotes, inspires determination to make a fresh start in their parents. The capacity of both infants and parents to respond to intervention is naturally rewarding for the therapist. The preventive aspects of the work are obvious and, in addition, its refreshing and rewarding nature is likely to prove therapeutic for overburdened therapists. More time could be given to preventive intervention in infancy by the staff of child mental health clinics. It should amply repay the resources given to it.

References

Ainsworth, M.D.S. (1985) Patterns of infant-mother attachment. *Bulletin New York Academy of Medicine* 6, 771–91.

Bick, E. (1964) Notes on infant observation in psychoanalytic training. *International Journal of Psychoanalysis* 45, 558.

Brazelton, T.B. (1985) Application of cry research for clinical perspectives. In B.M. Lester and C.F.Z. Boukydis (eds), *Infant Crying*. New York: Plenum.

Byng-Hall, J. and Stevenson-Hinde, J. (1991) Attachment relationships within a family system. *Infant Mental Health Journal* 12, 187–200.

Cooper, P., Murray, L., Stein, A. (1991) Postnatal depression. In *The European Handbook of Psychiatry Disorders*. Zaragos: Antropos.

Cramer, B. and Stern, D.N. (1988) Evaluation of changes in mother–infant brief psychotherapy: a single case study. *Infant Mental Health Journal* 9, 20–45.

Daws, D. (1989) *Through the Night: Helping Parents and Sleepless Infants*. London. Free Association Books.

Forsyth, B.W.C. and Canny, P. (1991) Perceptions of vulnerability $3^1/_2$ years after problems of feeding and crying behaviour in early infants. *Journal Pediatrics* 88, 757–63.

Fraiberg, S. (ed.) (1980) *Clinical Studies in Infant Mental-Health: The First Year of Life*. Tavistock Publications. London, New York.

Hopkins, J. (1992) Infant–parent psychotherapy. *Journal of Child Psychotherapy* 18, 5–18.

Miller, L. (1992) The relation of infant observation to clinical practice in an under five's counselling service. *Journal of Child Psychotherapy* 18, 19–32.

Provence, S. and Lipton, R.C. (1962) *Infants in Institutions*. New York. International Universities Press.

St James-Roberts, I., Harris, G. and Messer, D. (1993) *Infant Crying, Feeding and Sleeping. Development, Problems and Treatments*. Harvester Wheatsheaf London.

Sameroff, A.J. and Emde, R.N. (eds) (1989) *Relationship Disturbances in Early Childhood: A Developmental Approach*. Basic Books Inc. New York.

Winnicott, D.W. (1941) Observations of infants in a set situation. Chapter IV in *Collected Papers. Through Paediatrics to Psychoanalysis*. London. Tavistock 1958.

Winnicott, D.W. (1962) Ego integration in child development. In *The Maturational Processes and the Facilitating Environment*. London. Hogarth Press.

Winnicott, D.W. (1971) Playing: a theoretical statement. Chapter 3 in *Playing and Reality*. London. Tavistock.

CHAPTER 10

Sleep problems in babies and young children[1]

DILYS DAWS

In a preceding article, I described my work in the baby clinic of a general practice. Some of my time there is spent in consulting with the GPs and health visitors who run the baby clinic about the emotional aspect of the problems they are concerned with in the babies they see.

The work

In the actual clinical work I undertake myself I see families where there is a feeling of not being able to manage a particular state of a baby's or small child's development. The most pressing of these are often presented as sleeping problems. I have seen a number of these and found that about half can be noticeably helped in a short time. One or two consultations allow some change in the parents' approach to the baby that breaks the deadlock between them.

My technique is to combine a structured questioning about the details of the baby's timetable – taking the mother through the minutiae of both day and night – with a free-ranging look at the history of the pregnancy and birth, with the mother's relationship with the father and with her own parents. My impression is that, if there is a good marriage or stable relationship, this work is effective if carried out either with the mother alone or with both parents. With an unsatisfactory relationship the mother alone can be helped, but, with this particular technique, taking on two disharmonious parents is not usually effective in the short-term. It can, however, be a focus and starting-off point for parents who are looking for marital help. At times, sleeping

[1] This paper, given at a meeting for the Association of Child Psychology and Psychiatry in 1985, is reprinted with permission from the *Journal of Child Psychotherapy*, 11(2).

problems in their baby appear to expose a lack of real commitment to a long-term relationship in two young unmarried parents.

What strikes me in this work is that, by offering a free-floating attention, a particular arresting theme often emerges – a connection that has a compulsive attraction. I am never sure that this is what the problem is 'really' about, but pinpointing it seems to be of significance both for the mother and myself at the time. This is possibly more likely to happen if I see the mother alone. An unconscious thread builds up between the mother and myself so that my line of questioning is informed by the clues she has been giving me and cumulative evidence is built up.

Separation

Often this theme is of separation, frequently tied to problems about weaning. A mother who had only recently weaned her demanding 16-month-old boy, Duncan, was also having difficulty in getting him to sleep at night. He needed to be held in her arms and to stroke her breast until he fell asleep. We looked at how *she* was holding onto him as much as he was holding onto her. The next week she reported that instead of holding him in her arms to go to sleep she had been able to put him into the cot and hand him a teddybear for *him* to hold. It amazes me how quickly the transition from understanding a connection to some effective form of action can be made. It is almost if my words were as useful a transitional object for this mother as the teddybear was to the little boy.

Quite often, babies have become used to falling asleep only at the breast. They have thus no opportunity to be alone in their cot, half-awake, half-asleep, savouring the memory of a feed and digesting the emotional experience along with the actual physical nourishment. Emotional growth comes from digesting such an experience and, with this, the ability to start managing on one's own. What was useful to Duncan's mother was possibly my sympathy with her identification with Duncan's difficulty in separating from her, and at the same time my conviction that separations can be survived, that independence is itself to be prized. I ask mothers stuck at this point to remember or speculate on their own experiences; perhaps weaning was an issue their own mother found difficult to negotiate. Some mothers having difficulties may feel that their own mother was unable to have a confrontation with them about separation. They are left feeling that it must be unbearable.

One such mother with severe sleeping difficulties herself remembered that her own mother had never been able to leave her to cry. The fragility she had sensed in her own mother when *she* was a child seemed to form a large part of her own sense of herself as a mother. Others have the contrary impression that their mothers handled them in too cut-and-dried a manner – that bedtimes or weaning were handled too abruptly. The lingering resentment about this is translated into a resolve to treat their own child differently, perhaps as a belated way of showing grandmother how wrong she was.

My clearest example of this interconnection was a mother whose two-year-old, Molly, was having sleeping difficulties, but the actual example concerned toilet training. Molly's mother told me at length of how untidy her house was, and how much her own mother, who was coming to stay, would disapprove. She developed this theme to tell me of how she expected her mother also to disapprove of Molly's lack of progress in toilet training. I asked her if she knew about her own toilet training and, indeed, she did. Her mother has made sure that she knew that she and her sisters had been definitively trained at about one year. I pointed out that her descriptions to me of her untidy house were not only despairing, they were also boastful. A messy baby side of herself that she felt had been cleaned up too quickly still needed to communicate with her own mother about this issue. Getting in touch with the idea of this, through the medium of our words, seemed to be sufficient to mobilize more adult motivations, and she went home intending to tidy up her kitchen before grandmother's visit. Molly's toilet training ceased to be a fraught issue and was resolved within the next few weeks.

Sleep

With sleep problems it seems to me often that what I am doing for the mother is directly containing her anxiety so that she can go back to the baby and contain the baby's anxiety. There is often some real external cause for anxiety in the mother: difficulties in the birth or early weeks that she has not recovered from and not properly absorbed. Mothers worry that their baby may die in the night, and this kind of fear is based on reality. Everyone has heard, or read in the newspapers, of such tragic events. Talking through these fears and experiences makes them much more manageable. When the mother meets the baby's anxiety in the night, it no longer connects with her own infinite experience, and she can respond to it appropriately.

Sometimes the anxiety seems to originate in the baby, and excessive anxiety may be expressed in the form of nightmares. Some mothers find it particularly hard to stand the common situation of going in to a baby crying out during a nightmare and being rejected, that is to say being treated as a part of the nightmare. I saw one mother whose one-year-old child, Joanna, slept badly, had frequent nightmares, and had frequent temper tantrums during the day. Joanna's mother, vividly described feeling that her baby saw her as a 'witch' in the night.

It seemed appropriate to go quite explicitly through a simple Kleinian version of child development and talk about the child's difficulty in managing her own aggressive and destructive impulses, and her need to project these into her mother. This mother was interested intellectually but also responded instinctively. The sleeping difficulties had started at six weeks, after a brief period when Father had to be away. We connected the sleeping difficulties with Mother's own panic at this separation and her resentment with Father for not being there to support her. After ten months of bad nights Joanna slept through the night for two weeks. After that there were some broken nights, but the relationship between mother and daughter changed dramatically from mutual fury to a loving, teasing one. By understanding the nature of her baby's fears in the night Mother was better able to respond to them. The baby now had the experience of being understood and was comforted by this understanding. She no longer needed to wake repeatedly to seek it.

Some time later this mother saw her medical notes by accident, and read the referral letter from her GP to me. In fury, she saw him to complain and threatened to take the complaint further. I offered to see her also and suggested that it was not *what* the doctor had written about her to me that rankled but the fact that he had written at all. It was like a child overhearing parents talking *about* her rather than *to* her. Perhaps an oedipal situation that had not been managed between parents and daughter was echoed in the trouble between this mother and her own daughter.

I worked with this mother alone, but it does usually seem important to see two parents together where the meaning of the baby's or child's not sleeping seems to be in a non-resolution of oedipal feelings: that is, where the reason for not sleeping seems to be an anxiety about the parents being together and excluding the child. Often the taking up of the parents' evening together can be as detrimental to a marriage as intrusion into their night. In a potentially good marriage parents are often very relieved to see how they have slipped into habits of allowing the child to dominate their time together, perhaps feeling that the partner preferred it that way. Spelling out for parents the advantage of small children in allowing a marital relationship that by definition excludes the child, and supporting them in confronting the child's jealousy, seems to be helpful.

I believe this jealousy to be a factor with quite small babies, but it is unmistakable in older children. A three-year-old boy, Adam, who had always slept badly, became even more difficult after the birth of a new baby who slept in the parents' bedroom. Every night Adam came and got into the parents' bed. In many families this would be an acceptable solution for a while, but Adam, having got into his parents' bed, was unable to settle down. He slept restlessly, kicked his parents and woke them and himself many times during the night. It seemed as though the disturbing feelings which led him to seek their bed were not relieved by being with them; they seemed in fact to be accentuated. Adam's parents decided to try to keep him in his own bed. They explained to him that Father would come to him if he called, but that he was not allowed out of his bed. They offered him a small car as a reward for staying in his bed. On the first two nights he stayed in his bed throughout the night, calling out for Father a couple of times, and falling asleep again while Father stayed with him. On the third night he slept throughout the night and came into the parents' bedroom in the morning, saying to his father, 'You've been a very good boy. You stayed in your bed all night. I shall buy you a new pair of cuff-links.' This father indeed deserved a reward for the firmness which relieved his son of the torment of jealousy of both parents and new baby, which he was unable to get away from in the parents' room.

Wild things

Often children of this age suffer from nightmares, and we might speculate that the strength of their emotions causes some of these. The book *Where the Wild Things Are* by Maurice Sendak can have an amazingly therapeutic effect on children in the grip of these feelings. Max, the hero of this book, makes so much mischief that his mother calls him a 'Wild Thing', after he says to her, 'I'll eat you up,' and is sent to bed without his supper. In bed he dreams of going to where the wild things are, tames the monsters and becomes their king. After a year of this he becomes lonely and goes home to 'where someone loved him best of all'.

What seems to work in this story for a small child is the acknowledgement of the wild feelings inside himself, making friends with them and overcoming them within himself, and getting back to a loving relationship with his mother. Having this book read to them may often help children manage their nightmares, as also may patient listening by parents to children recounting the content of these dreams. The parents' task is to help children deal with the force of these – the actual having of a nightmare may be a useful form of self-awareness and of managing the fierceness of the child's own emotions.

Fathers also can be supportive to mothers in not letting babies and small children exploit their mothering. They can help with a cut-off point. Many mothers feel unsure that they have given their babies enough good mothering during the day, and let the baby go on asking for more during the night. Helping the mother to feel that she has done what is reasonable during the day and that nothing more is owing to the baby can be startlingly effective.

Single parents may be particularly vulnerable in this area, with no one easily available to support them in this way. Many single parents are also aware that they are unsure whether they really want their small child to go off to bed and leave them alone. The parent may be torn between needing a respite from a child's demands and dreading loneliness. Sometimes difficulties in a child going off to bed may be an unconscious protest by both child and parent about the missing parent who is not there to help; perhaps what both are doing is keeping a place open for the absent parent.

Working mothers may also have difficulties of this kind. They and their babies may actually need more time together to become reunited after the day's separation, but this may merge into a guilty reluctance to face the baby's feelings about being put down. One professional mother found that her one-year-old boy, Henry, was having great difficulty in sleeping when she started back at work. She then realized that one problem was in her way of separating from him in the daytime. She had been taking him to the child-minder, waiting until he was happily settled and playing, and then slipping out of the room without saying goodbye to him. This mother had gone back to work reluctantly and found the separation from her little boy very painful. She realized she was saving herself the pain of saying goodbye to him during the day but was having to have the confrontation with him at night instead. When she managed to let him know in the mornings that she was going away, he was able to make his protest to her at the appropriate time and not displace it to the evenings. He also perhaps felt more generally secure by always knowing when his mother was leaving him, and when she was not. With this settled between them, his mother was able to look at her feelings about leaving him and found them to be more complex than she had imagined. She had previously not owned that she was leaving her son; she had thought the job was taking her away from him. Once she had worked out that this was how her son perceived the situation, it became more like that for herself. She took the responsibility for the separation. She became more able to enjoy her job while still regretting the time away from her son.

It can be very confusing for parents to deal with a baby's anger in the night and also to face the anger in themselves at their own need for rest and sleep not being met. Many parents are justifiably afraid of battering their baby in the night: how, allowing themselves to express reasonable firmness or even anger may stem from being afraid of going too far. It may help the parents to be more effective, to look at how expressing this anger within bounds may be as much a relief to the baby as to the parent.

A baby who keeps on crying in the night can undermine a parent's belief in the quality of their parenting, and undermines their judgement. One very caring mother of a slightly underweight baby felt she must pick him up every time he cried, which was sometimes hourly through the night. She was sure he needed something, though she was not sure whether this need was emotional, or for more food. I said sharply that what he needed was a good night's sleep and so did she. This mother appreciates the matter-of-factness of my comments, but has not yet trusted her baby to their implications.

Symptoms

One point that interests me is that in this brief focused work it is essential to focus on the symptom. Simply seeing the mother or both parents in a generalized supportive way, picking up anxiety in the parents, or marital conflict, does not, in my experience, affect the child's sleeping.

I saw Molly's mother, who also had three other children, unusually over a period of two years. She was a gifted and creative woman and also very anxious. During the period I saw her, fortnightly and then monthly, she and her husband made a major change in their lifestyle which brought order to a very disorganized household, and she improved her relationship with all four children. Molly, the youngest, was a few months old when I first saw the mother, and she mentioned several times in passing that this child slept badly. It seemed not unlikely in the context of the general chaos of the family. It was not until Molly was two that her mother presented Molly's sleeping problem as the most pressing one in the family. We sat down together and focused on this problem single-mindedly, and it seemed as though this was one of the cases where Mother was allowing herself to be exploited and misused. Although this was a theme we had looked at in terms of the other children and the family in general, we had not specifically connected it with the youngest child's sleeping problem. I assure you that this child started to sleep properly from that night on!

One major theme of my work with this mother was the establishing of boundaries in bringing up children. She incidentally taught me something important about the boundaries of institutions. She failed to keep an appointment and rang me next day to explain that a baby, not her own but one she was closely involved with, had died. She was distressed and my next free time at the baby clinic was nearly two weeks away. It seemed sensible to offer her an appointment next day at my Child Guidance Clinic. She knew I worked there, and she lived close by. She arrived next day and settled down to tell me the whole story of the baby's death. She mentioned the helpfulness of the doctors involved, and I realized that she was telling me about the general practice doctors as though I did not know them. I as a worker in the Child Guidance Clinic was no longer a colleague of the workers in the general practice; in fact, I was a stranger to them. By implication I at the Child Guidance Clinic was a stranger to myself at the general practice.

Resentment

Another major factor underlying sleeping problems seems to be resentment by the mother about some important aspect of her situation. This resentment can be retrospective. I saw one striking-looking Scottish woman with an equally stunning solemn-faced baby sitting upright on her lap. She had entered a relationship with a man thought to be beneath her socially and had been disowned by her mother. By a series of blunders she and her husband had ended up in 'homeless families' at the time of this baby's birth. Their living conditions were so bad that she had gone out to work to get away from it, and had been able to leave the baby with a pleasant childminder. She and her husband now had what she described as a marvellous council house; she enjoyed her job and hoped to make it up soon with her quirky mother. She felt her husband to be completely supportive, both in practical help and emotionally. I nevertheless queried strongly why they were not married and felt all was not yet properly resolved. I put into words the enormous resentment that I thought was there about the bad time she had been through when her baby was small. She was delighted to recognize a legitimate cause for the feelings she was choked with. She came again next week to tell me that the baby now slept through the night.

I see many families who are badly housed and at times have to remind myself that there is some evidence that bad housing does not in itself create emotional problems in children. What I often see is that anger in parents about their bad living conditions makes it difficult for them to bring their children up in these conditions. This anger is often constructive, the only effective weapon that might change something for them, but the fury in the family and the impotent waiting for outside bureaucracy to find a solution can make it very difficult for emotional issues to be dealt with effectively within the family unit. These include the setting of limits for sleeping.

Paradoxically, in some families limits are set too closely. One possible cause for difficulty in sleeping is where the child has been too confined during the day. Children who have not been able to get out to play may have a wound-up tension that makes it hard for them to relax into sleep. In one extreme example two unemployed parents and their two-year-old stayed at home all day. When their eight-year-old daughter returned from school, she was sent out again to do the family shopping. The two-year-old roamed aimlessly round the flat while his demoralized parents watched television. The night had as little structure as the day, and he was in and out of his cot all night.

Conversely, some very active children, who are also often very intelligent, seem unable to let go and settle into sleep. Sometimes these children have been engaged through the day only in activity that stimulates them further.

They have not let themselves relax into any kind of regressive, less high-powered pursuit. The parents of one such child thought about whether some very simple kind of play was missing from their child's day. They found that playing with sand, plasticine or water during the day made a difference to how he settled at night. All these involve a use of the body while allowing reflective thoughts to develop. Ambitious children may be calmed by such simple activities.

Dawn

One family illustrated, albeit dramatically, some of the problems of single-parent families. The sleeping problem was also an introduction to other work. Just before the summer a five-year-old girl, Dawn, and her eight months' pregnant mother were referred to me. Dawn was not sleeping and was refusing to go to school. Dawn's father had left her mother some years ago before and the expected baby's father had just left after beating the mother violently. In the first session I got the mother to tell me some of this story, in front of Dawn. I listened and commented that Dawn was also listening while she played with toys. I then asked about Dawn's sleeping difficulties and Mother told me of her reluctance to go to sleep, and of her nightmares. I talked about what I thought was Dawn's worry about Mother, after all the dreadful experiences. Dawn listened carefully. I then asked her to tell me of her recurrent nightmare. She crossed the room, stood in front of me, and told me at great length. I had not become attuned to her speech and could not understand *anything* that she had said. However, it was obvious that Mother could; she was listening as avidly as Dawn had earlier listened to her. I solemnly said that the dream *was* very frightening, and that Dawn should tell her mother every morning what her dreams had been about.

Next week they reported to me that there had been no nightmares. Dawn had gone to bed easily each night and slept well through the night. That week Dawn told me in vivid detail of the time the mother's boyfriend had smashed up the flat. Mother told me that she had not been able to get Dawn to talk about it at all before. I said it seemed to need an outside person to help them both talk about such things.

Pathetically, Dawn and her mother could both have used me, not just as an outside listener, but as the missing father. We talked about Dawn staying home from school to look after her mother, and about how omnipotent she had become. When I once said to her that she was a little girl and she didn't decide what happened, that Mummy decided, she said 'No, you decide.' Dawn was really needed too much at home and did not go back to school for the last couple of weeks of term. In addition, she had a necessary eye operation at the end of July. I believe that it was due to my encouragement that

Mother, though wearied by her pregnancy, managed to stay in hospital with Dawn. They came to see me after the operation and debriefed themselves of the experience.

The new baby, a boy, was born in August, and Dawn went quite freely back to school at the beginning of the new term. Mother called in to see me while bringing the new baby for his check-up at the clinic. Dawn came at half-term to report on her progress at school. She told me about games they play in the toilets at school. She said with great emphasis that there were signs on the boys' toilets and no signs on the girls' toilets. When I suggested that she was also thinking about the new baby being a boy, and that his willy was a sign of being a boy, and girls didn't have signs like that, Mother giggled and said that Dawn hadn't seemed to notice the baby's willy. We were able to talk about whether Dawn worried that Mother preferred the new baby to her because he was a boy. She was still very bossy at home, and we talked of her dilemma, of being neither a real grown-up like Mummy, or like the new baby who got specially looked after.

Conclusions

Looking at sleeping problems makes us aware of the complexity of the emotions involved in being a parent. We see how subtle is the process by which mothers and babies move from their early closeness to seeing themselves as two separate beings. Sleeping difficulties punctuate uncertainties at every stage. We see how receptivity to the needs of a baby, understanding of their fears, and spontaneous offering of comfort need to be tempered with a gradual setting of limits. Understanding of a baby's fears enables a parent to contain those fears. The baby gradually learns to manage them himself. A parent does not need to take on the baby's fears as though they are his own.

I sometimes suggest to parents that they read Winnicott's *The Child, The Family and The Outside World* to put them more in touch with ideas about emotional development. I also recommend Jo Douglas and Naomi Richman's *My Child Won't Sleep*. This excellent book helps parents plan their strategies for getting their child to sleep. In this paper I have described how I help parents speculate on what the sleeping problem represents in their own child's emotional life and the relationship between them and their child. Understanding this often enables parents to make effective changes.

What *I* bring to the work is an ability to listen and share parents' fascination with the minute details of their baby's life and to connect this with the background of personalities and relationships of the family he was born into. Absorbing all this is hard work; my response has to be fresh and spontaneous for each family; there are no automatic solutions. Possibly, this work can be done by many professionals with a detailed experience of babies and an interest in how family relationships develop. It cannot be done in a routine way; the worker has to be prepared to be shaken each time by the intensity of anxiety and emotion that each family's story conveys.

References

Douglas, J. and Richman, N. (1984) *My Child Won't Sleep*. London: Penguin.
Sendak, Maurice (1970) *Where the Wild Things Are*. London: Puffin Books.
Winnicott, D.W. (1964) *The Child, The Family and The Outside World*. London: Penguin.

Further Reading

Dunn, Judy (1980) Feeding and Sleeping. In: *Scientific Foundations of Developmental Psychiatry*. London: Heinemann.
Fraiberg, Selma (1950) On the Sleep Disturbances of Early Childhood, *Psycho-Analytic Study of the Child*, 5.
Haslam, D. (1985) *Sleepless Children*. London: Piatkus.
Klein, M. (1963) *Our Adult World and its Roots in Infancy*. London: Heinemann.

CHAPTER 11

Into the night: children's dream books[1]

ELLEN HANDLER SPITZ

Dusk: that delicate time suspended between wakefulness and slumber, activity and rest, interaction with others and communion with self. Suddenly, a rush of anxieties and longings may appear that were absent during the daylight hours.

Falling asleep for children often means relaxing after an action-packed day, cosy warm covers, perhaps and a goodnight kiss. It means bidding farewell to play, food and sociability. It means surrendering to the need for rest and peace. Poetry and prayer have related it metaphorically to life's final separation. The *Gates of Repentance*, for example, the Reform Jewish prayer-book for the High Holy Days, contains, in its Memorial Service, the following lines: 'Like children falling asleep over their toys, we relinquish our grip on earthly possessions only when death overtakes us' (1984, p. 480). Many Christian children learn to recite at bedtime a prayer that also relates the two: 'Now I lay me down to sleep; I pray the Lord my soul to keep/If I should die before I wake, I pray the Lord my soul to take.' Thus, falling asleep at night is an experience that can be welcomed or feared and one that is met normally with a mixture of emotions.

Going safely and calmly to sleep each night prepares a child for the more difficult and final partings that must be faced inevitably later in life. In fact, if we look at books that deal explicitly with death, we often find bedtime scenes included. It is interesting to note that the Western middle-class child, unlike children of other social classes and many other countries, is expected to sleep in a room by himself. To sleep in close quarters with other children and with other members of one's family, however, may significantly alter a child's response to bedtime and to his or her fantasies and dreams.

---

[1] This paper was especially adapted for this book from the author's *Inside Picture Books* (New Haven and London: Yale University Press, 1999).

Bedtime is negotiated peacefully by young children and their parents most of the time, but not always. When difficulties do arise, many factors may be held responsible, some specific to the individual and his or her unique situation, others more general. In this brief essay, we will explore a small number of classic picture books that deal explicitly with bedtime and that have long been read to children to ease the tensions that attend this transition into the world of sleep and dreams. Each book offers a unique perspective; each speaks subtly to underlying worries that may surface from time to time.

Darkness, by blinding children to the consoling sight of familiar surroundings and objects, may itself become a source of fear. *Goodnight Moon* (1947), by Margaret Wise Brown and Clement Hurd, acknowledges this fact; it conveys the comforting knowledge that, despite a little bunny's gradually diminishing power to see the beloved possessions in his room, he can nonetheless count on all of them to survive intact, as will he and the love of those who care for him.

Bedtime is the point when parents actively separate themselves from their offspring, and under some circumstances and from time to time, this routine parting may be perceived as an abandonment. When parents withdraw physically, they take with them, temporarily, their attention and affection, which, as children quickly perceive, they can refocus on one another or on other individuals or interests. Children left alone in their beds may understandably feel neglected and long to continue being the primary objects of their parents' love and solicitude. (A classic statement of this longing occurs in *Where the Wild Things Are* when Max, banished to his room, sits exhausted after his orgiastic romp with the monsters, his head resting dejectedly on his hand, and 'was lonely and wanted to be where someone loved him best of all'.) Enterprising young persons, finding themselves in this unwanted state, invent, as we all know well, a variety of ingenious schemes to delay the inevitable night-time parting.

Bedtime for Frances (1960), by Russell Hoban and Garth Williams, addresses this theme. Its title page reveals a little girl badger, who, with her paw in her mouth, peeks out from behind a partly open door into a room where, we can imagine, her parents are still sitting up together enjoying each other's company. She looks a bit sheepish, knowing full well that she ought not to be there, but a tiny ray of hope flickers: perhaps this time they will let her stay up and join them. The image captures those paradigm moments in childhood when, even though they know perfectly well that you are going to say 'no' to them, the children go on hoping that, just this once, you will be soft-hearted and give in. In the same way perhaps, every time I have ever seen a truly affecting performance of *Macbeth* and begun to pity the tormented murderous thane, I hope against hope that just *this time* great Birnam wood to high Dunsinane Hill will not come.

Bedtime is hard, this picture hints, because, in many Western households, it signifies the young child's separation from the company of loved ones. Not only that, but the parents themselves get to go on being with one another, possibly doing pleasurable things, secret things, night things. Frances, peeking in through the doorway, expresses a poignant sense of exclusion: bedtime means being left out.

Maurice Sendak's *In the Night Kitchen* (1970) is a book that also thematizes bedtime as exclusion from parental intimacy, but here the point of view is distinctly masculine. Gender accounts for important differences between the way Mickey, the protagonist of *In the Night Kitchen*, and Frances, the protagonist of *Bedtime for Frances*, choose to cope with and master their respective situations. Mickey creates a heroic fantasy in order to triumph over his noisy parents and prove that he can fend for himself in their absence. Frances, on the other hand, in her 'abandoned' state, bends all her cleverness not toward establishing her independence of her parents but rather toward reinserting herself into the coveted parental nest. Thus, the two books both separately and together comment on our different modes of socializing boys and girls. The former are pushed in the direction of autonomy and self-reliance; the latter, in the direction of uninterrupted human contact and interaction.

Fear of bad dreams is the subject of Mercer Mayer's *There's a Nightmare in My Closet* (1968), which may resonate especially with children who are familiar with the Frances books and with *Where the Wild Things Are*, both of which are quoted pictorially in it. Like several of the others, this book models the creation of a scary dream or fantasy, a monster (the dreaded nightmare) which can be tamed and which is even treated by its protagonist, an unnamed little boy, with the ambivalence toddlers usually reserve for their baby brothers and sisters.

Finally, children of four, five and six have the capacity to be quite independent when left alone in the dark. They may actually revel in the uninterrupted opportunity bedtime brings for exercising their imaginations and for making up night-time adventures in which they are free to face dangers, rescue themselves, and triumph gloriously over distressful events that occurred during the day. A. A. Milne's marvelous poem springs to mind:

Here I am in the dark alone,
What is it going to be?
I can think whatever I like to think,
I can play whatever I like to play,
I can laugh whatever I like to laugh,
There's nobody here but me.
I'm talking to a rabbit...
I'm talking to the sun

I think I am a hundred –
I'm one

(*Now We Are Six*, 1927, pp. 100–1)
Reproduced with permission Dell Publishers.

Similar imaginative bedtime adventures are given visual form in Crockett Johnson's inimitable picture book *Harold and the Purple Crayon* (1955). In works such as these, bedtime is portrayed as an ideal occasion for mental experimentation. Little Harold savors the pleasures of his solitude as, utterly uncensored, he 'draws' freely and wildly upon the powers of his imagination.

When Clement Hurd, the illustrator of *Goodnight Moon*, died, he was honored on Valentine's Day on the editorial page of *The New York Times* (2/14/88). Declaring that 'some things are inexplicably magical', *The Times* article went on to evoke hundreds of freshly scrubbed small children in pajamas falling peacefully to sleep in the world created by this artist. By the time of his death, *Goodnight Moon* had been in print for four decades and sold over two million copies.

The Times (1/25/89) writer's imaginary vision of children actually going to sleep in the world of *Goodnight Moon* takes on even greater specificity when we read it in the context of an anecdote reported by Clement Hurd himself. At bedtime one evening, a little boy of 18 months had heard *Goodnight Moon* five times and after the final rendition was contemplating the book as it lay open before him, its last pages revealed. These pages are the ones in which the 'great green room' has grown dark and quiet and the little bunny has closed his eyes. The words read: 'Goodnight noises everywhere.' The small boy in question stared at the open book before him and then deliberately placed one of his feet on the left-hand page and struggled to get his other foot onto the right-hand page; thereupon, he burst into tears. His mother, watching this behavior, took only a second to realize what he was doing: he was trying with all his might to transport his whole small body into the cosy, loving world of *Goodnight Moon*.

Imagery and imagination

Who can presume to account for the love inspired by a work of art? The best we can do is offer clues. In the case of these bedtime picture books, the value of such clues is that they may find their way, subtly, into our subsequent readings to children – not only of the book at hand but of others and even of other cultural objects. Clues as to why certain cultural objects are loved may thus enrich our ongoing dialogues with children. As we gain insight into the factors that seem to matter most, we can search for them and attempt to discover and recreate them elsewhere.

Let's start with a key factor: rhythm. What I mean by rhythm are both
auditory and pictorial patterns of flow and forward movement. *Goodnight
Moon* is structured by its rhythms. If you listen to the regular beats of the
accented words in its simple text and note how soothing they sound,
together with their alliteration ('great green room') and their internal rhymes
('little bears sitting on chairs' and 'brush' and 'mush' and 'hush'), you will
perceive the subtle power of this crucial element and begin to look for it in
other places. *Goodnight Moon* provides an auditory counterpart and
complement for a child's heartbeat as it calms down in the moments before
she falls asleep.

Two clocks in the bunny's room are set at seven when *Goodnight Moon*
begins. As measured by the hands on these clocks, the time has progressed to
ten past eight by the time the last page is reached; thus, an entire imaginary
hour has elapsed between the book's first and final moments. This slowing
down is exquisitely appropriate to its theme: the transition between day and
night, activity and repose.

This prolongation of time symbolizes and concretizes an antidote for
conditions even more poignant today than when the book was originally
published some fifty years ago. Today's American children are, of necessity,
clamped squirming in the vise of our rapidly paced technologically driven
culture. Paradoxically, they are being held down while being speeded up at
an ever-accelerating rate. Given little space for the growth of their own imaginations and the gradual acquisition of mastery, today's children are
bombarded with prefabricated stimuli – images, sensations, impressions –
that occur too fast and furiously. As the media disseminate 'information' in
visual terms and pictures fly past, we understand little about the long- or
short-term effects of the speed and volume of communication. What might
be its psychological consequences? To foreground fast time as an issue for
concern is to wonder about its potential for harm. Might, for instance, the
rapid processing of imagery, particularly imagery that is exciting and frightening, work to curtail rather than nurture human capacities for reflection,
containment, and nuanced emotional response? Could it be that the
cherished ancient metaphor 'to see is to know' might collapse if exposure to
visual material is too rapid? Could speed result in a decrease rather than an
increase in the virtues of delay and deliberation, not to mention empathy?
What serious human losses are implied in the shift we are witnessing from a
slower-paced narrative-verbal culture to a faster-paced image-based culture?
And especially, what are the effects of this shift on the very youngest children
whose first mission it is to find and construct for themselves a meaningful
and safe world?

Goodnight Moon absolutely refuses speed. It is not a book to hurry
through. In this sense it works as a welcome antidote. Children who have

been rushed through the day can relax into it. Confidently, they know what will come next, and yet, as they trace the antics of the little mouse, encounter a new word or observe a new form, they are learning as well. They can feel, in this imaginary space, the pleasures of satisfied expectations, the meeting of hope with fulfillment. Thus, never static, *Goodnight Moon* is also a site of exploration. It creates a world that reminds me of an artist's studio, where familiarity becomes the locus for growth. Think, for example, of Matisse's painting *The Red Studio* (1911), with its similar electric Chinese red, its touches of green and flecks of gold, its wine glass and chair and chest, its framed and unframed pictures and possible clock and window. How like an artist's studio is the bedroom of a small child? Filled with highly invested possessions, this room is also a dual locus of security and discovery, of work and of rest.

To return now to rhythm and recurrence, I want to note that these aesthetic features work pictorially as well as auditorily in *Goodnight Moon*. The repetition of imagery here is patent and wise – wise because it is reassuring. When we understand that young children are engaged in the ongoing process of forging and strengthening their nascent sense of identity and of boundaries, we can see that, as Selma Fraiberg points out in *The Magic Years* (1959, pp. 174-5), they may resist falling asleep precisely because the loss of consciousness seems to threaten their newly developing sense of identity, of who they are. If this idea seems strange to you, consider for a moment your own intermittent adult fears of falling asleep. Often these fears have to do with anxiety over giving up control and over the temporary loss of consciousness, anxiety fuelled by the symbolic alliance of sleep and death, which we have already remarked. In the wake of such dysphoria, *Goodnight Moon* works on many levels, psychologically and aesthetically, to allay fear, to forestall bad dreams. Its pictures shore up the child's sense of intactness just at the moment when that intactness seems to be slipping away. By picturing all the familiar objects of daily life, and by repeating them and naming them, its pages convey a clear message that life and self are whole and can be counted on to continue being there, even as darkness descends.

The psychological function of the surviving objects in *Goodnight Moon* is profound. They teach young children that life can be trusted, that life has stability, reliability, and durability. The youngest of us live, as it were, in a world of vanishing objects. A baby cries when its mother leaves because her absence is experienced as threatening to that infant's very existence. A crucial step in early development is therefore the establishment of what has been called 'object permanence', 'object constancy' or 'basic trust'. Essentially, these related ideas simply mean a secure knowledge that just because something cannot be seen at a particular moment it has not disappeared forever. One's loved ones are a permanent acquisition, even when lost to view; one's self is ongoing as well. Games of hide-and-seek and peek-a-boo are founded on the need for such learning. Here, the issue is patent: each object in *Goodnight Moon* can be recognized and named, and each one reappears and persists from the beginning to the end. Darkness may envelop the world but love and self endure. On the very last page, to make this point explicit, the grandmother rabbit has left for the night, and little bunny is alone. Clement Hurd, for the second time, quotes from another book he and Margaret Wise Brown wrote together, *The Runaway Bunny* (1942) in which a child and his mother are continually reunited after multiple separations. *Goodnight Moon* thus metaphorically pledges enduring love.

Goodnight Moon is, in short, an amazing work. Spine-ripped, scotch-taped and smudged, pages coming unsewn, it lies there tenderly defying all those scholars who want to historicize everything. It says: 'Look at me! I was made fifty years ago, before the mothers and fathers of today's young children were born; yet, I am loved more than ever. Despite the changes wrought by the past half-century in America – McCarthyism, Sputnik, the Civil Rights movement, Haight-Ashbury, Viet Nam, the women's movement, gay rights, Watergate, the Internet, cyber-space, the advent of a new millennium – I am still taken to bed every night by thousands of American children, to whom I belong and who still adore me.'

As a foil, perhaps, for this small masterpiece and to make one or two additional points, I would like to turn at this point to another children's bedtime storybook, *There's a Nightmare in My Closet* (1968) by Mercer Mayer, one that deals explicitly with the formation and content of children's dreams.

The first double-page spread of this popular and oft-reprinted book provides imagery that may well seem familiar to children who have already encountered *Goodnight Moon* (the little boy's bed is in the same position on the page as is the bunny's) and *Bedtime for Frances* (the curtain blowing in at the window will recall its final pages). As the story progresses, children may even recall the well-known territory of Max's wild things, as well as the lands where Dr. Seuss's fanciful hybrid creatures roam. Such associations, even when not fully conscious, work to tame a new story and its pictures and lend them an aura of underlying comfort, especially when, as here, the content may be disturbing.

Rendered in a line-driven cartoon style, similar to that of Sendak and Seuss, the pictures in *There's a Nightmare in My Closet* illuminate the text so fully that the plot-line can be read straight off the images themselves. We have the first-person story of a little boy who determines to rid himself of his night-time fears, which have assumed the form of a Nightmare that lurks in his closet. Armed with a helmet and toy gun, he threatens to shoot the beast when it emerges. When it appears in due course, however, the beast turns out to be a huge goofy monster who looks contrite and fearful rather than threatening. The little boy shoots anyway. In response to this, the enormous Nightmare begins to cry. With its finger in its mouth, it resembles a giant baby. In that guise, it manages then to mobilize the identification, pity, and scorn of many children listening to the story. Interestingly, the boy protagonist's own initial reaction is not contrition or empathy but anger. And, as we know, many parents in fact do feel and express a rush of anger when their punished children cry. So the boy's reaction here actually mirrors a parental position, albeit not a very enlightened one. He tells the bawling Nightmare to be quiet and then, his heart softening, takes him comfortingly into his own little bed – thus acting out in fantasy (from the parental side as well as his own) exactly the goal Frances tries to achieve with her bedtime shenanigans and Mickey tries to deny with his flight into the night kitchen.

Closing the closet door and lying in his bed under the covers with his Nightmare, the boy now says he knows another Nightmare may yet appear. Hopefully, he adds however, with a smile, his bed is not big enough for three. Nevertheless, on the last pages of the book, when the boy and his tamed monster have gone to sleep in the darkened bedroom, an enormous head pokes out of the closet door. Another monster has, indeed, suddenly appeared! There are no words, and the book ends.

Mulling it over, I realized gradually that my own reaction to this ending was somewhat mixed. On the one hand, *There's a Nightmare in My Closet* attempts to convey a highly sophisticated idea. By introducing the second monster at the end, it points out to children something they need to know, and, indeed, *do* know – namely, that fears, even those which have been dealt with successfully, tend to recur. A similar message is conveyed in Sendak's *Pierre*, the fourth book of his *Nutshell Library* of 1962. *Pierre*, a prototypical little ethics primer, tells the story of an *oppositional* toddler who brags 'I don't care' so often that he is eventually eaten by a lion. Just to give a sense of the psychological and aesthetic sophistication implicit in the particular story, I want to mention that Sendak places an identical border at the start and end of his text, in which the child's verbal 'no' is translated pictorially into the form 'upside down', so that the little boy is depicted turning a somersault. Pierre's parents cajole him in vain. They command and implore him and finally depart, thereby abandoning him. Left to his own negativism, he is then eaten up by a lion to whom he responds, 'I don't care.' When at length the parents return, they find this lion in Pierre's bed and vent their wrath now on him (that is on the child's and their own projected aggression). Finally, in a recap of the upside-down motif (Pierre had stood on his head to defy his father), the lion is turned upside down and spits Pierre out. The whole family rides home astride the lion, who is thereby not banished but accepted as part of the family. Aggression is in this way valorized and accepted as an ongoing issue for both parents and children. What is relevant to *There's a Nightmare in My Closet* is the last page of Sendak's story. As the family rides triumphantly home on the back of the lion, a deliciously furtive smile adorns the beast's face. He gazes up mischievously at Pierre, as if to say, 'So, you really think you are finished with me, do you? Well, you just wait and see ...' (There's another nightmare in the closet ...)

This is a highly sophisticated lesson about open-endedness. It is similar to, although perhaps somewhat more benign than, the lesson of the second monster in *There's a Nightmare in My Closet*. Some young children, however, especially at bedtime, may require greater closure, more security. Indeed, one of the most satisfying aspects of picture books at bedtime is that they possess a finite quality. Their covers open and, importantly, close. Each story has a clear beginning and a fixed end. These limits add an important dimension of order to the child's world, and children usually prefer books that have well-defined endings. For this reason, *There's a Nightmare in my Closet* worries me a bit. By introducing a scary new monster on the last page, I think it may deprive some children of the closure they crave and leave them in a state of apprehension, wondering and concerned about what might happen next. If so, instead of teaching a lesson about the normal recurrence of anxieties and bad dreams, this book might actually contribute to a child's already present stock of worries.

In order to test my hypothesis, I decided to read *There's a Nightmare in My Closet* to three-year-old Haley. When I showed the book and asked whether she had ever seen it before, she replied, 'Yes,' promptly. Then, immediately, she added: '*another* monster'. This spontaneous unsolicited bit of information seemed a wonderfully timed and ingenious counter-phobic remark – rather as though she were trying, by invoking the second monster in advance, to arm herself against it. We began the story. Haley sat quietly while I turned the pages, reading. Every now and then, she interpolated something verbal, but it was I who physically held the book and flipped each successive page – until we neared the end. Haley began to look more serious as the boy closed his closet door and then lay down in bed with his tamed Nightmare to go to sleep. At the end – the final, wordless page on which the new monster emerges from the closet – Haley looked at it for a split second and then, with a rapid gesture, took the corner of the page in her own right hand and turned it over quickly, looking hard – as if to see what would happen next. But the page, of course, was completely blank.

This small incident felt significant to me. It corroborated my hunch that, on some level, for at least some children, the ending provided by this book is inconclusive and unsatisfying. It underscores the *individuality* of children's responses to picture books and the need for parents to notice, respect, and cherish this. Haley, who had hopefully turned the last page over to see what would come next, even though she knew that the end had already been reached, did not, on the other hand, refuse to hear this book again. To the contrary, the very openness of its ending may be appealing to some children and serve as a spur to repetition and mastery. It may incline them to want to re-experience it, to pit themselves against it, as it were – their knowledge and courage versus the anxiety it evokes.

Parents reading this book may choose to pose a question or two at the end, such as: 'What do you think will happen now?' or 'If you were that little boy, what would you do now?' or entertain a little dialogue about nightmares and dreams, thus inspiring the child to invent his own personally more satisfying ending. That ending might well turn out to be another violent solution, such as shooting the second monster, or, more mildly, ordering it to go away, or, benevolently, squeezing it into bed with himself and the first monster. What matters is that stories like this, which leave unwoven threads, can become spurs to imaginative creation – story-telling, drawing, acting, singing, dancing, and eventually dreams – to an untold variety of collaborative adventures within the self and between the generations. As regards those children for whom this book does feel satisfying, I think it is because of the little boy's identification with his parents vis-à-vis the monster, courage and eventual compassion, his calm; these are the factors that make it possible for him to tame his fears so that the child experiencing the story can participate vicariously with him in that project.

Before leaving the topic of night and of these children's books, one final point deserves emphasis, namely that, when love is felt to be secure, children can allow themselves to be curious about the world, to explore mentally, to learn, to grow, and to dream. When, on the other hand, love is contingent and the world is unpredictable, anxiety gains the upper hand, and children's energies must be deployed elsewhere. We see, under those unfortunate circumstances, a waning of the lust for adventure. In choosing books to read to young children at bedtime, then, this principle may serve as a guide – modified always according to the individual, since children differ so, and by the particular context of any given evening.

References

Brown, Margaret Wise and Clement Hurd (1942) *The Runaway Bunny*. New York: Harper & Row.

Brown, Margaret Wise and Clement Hurd (1947) *Goodnight Moon*. New York: Harper & Row.

Fraiberg, Selma (1959) *The Magic Years*. New York: Charles Scribner's Sons.

Gates of Repentance: The New Union Prayerbook for the Days of Awe (1984) New York: Central Conference of American Rabbis.

Hoban, Russell and Garth Williams (1960) *Bedtime for Frances*. New York: Harper & Row.

Johnson, Crockett (1955) *Harold and the Purple Crayon*. New York: Harper & Row.
Marcus, L. (1987) 'A Moon That Never Sets', *The New York Times Book Review*, Jan. 25,
    pp. 112–19 (1/25/89, p. 22).
Mayer, Mercer (1968) There's a Nightmare in My Closet New York: Dial.
Milne, A.A. (1927) *Now We Are Six*. New York: Dell.
Sendak, Maurice (1962) *The Nutshell Library*. New York: Harper & Row.
Sendak, Maurice (1963) *Where the Wild Things Are*. New York: Harper & Row.
Sendak, Maurice (1970) *In the Night Kitchen*. New York: Harper & Row

Thanks to the publishers for permission to quote from A. A. Milne

CHAPTER **12**

Unconscious communication[1]

ENID BALINT

> Thus a child's super-ego is in fact constructed on the model not of its parents but of its parents' super-ego . . . mankind never lives entirely in the present. The past, the tradition of the race and of the people, lives on in the ideologies of the super-ego, and yields only slowly to the influence of the present and to new changes and so long as it operates through the super-ego it plays a powerful part in human life, independently of economic conditions. (Freud, 1933, p. 67)
>
> It is a very remarkable thing that the unconscious of one human being can react upon that of another without passing through the conscious . . . descriptively speaking, the fact is incontestable. (Freud, 1915, p. 194)

This paper concentrates on a particular aspect of the relationship between a mother and her child: a relationship which Freud understood, but which has subsequently been illustrated by clinical material arising out of patients from the Holocaust (e.g. Pines, 1986). There have also been empirical observations about the effect on babies of their mothers' internal world which the babies perceive before the external world has any substance for them (Stern, 1985). In this connection the mother's mood is more important than her actions, as has been noted by many analysts, perhaps most convincingly by Green (1986, ch. 7).[2] I have found that much more than the mother's general mood is absorbed by the very young infant, who reacts, for example, to her aliveness or deadness and to her unconscious anxieties, which do not necessarily arise from the relation between mother and baby. What can be perceived imaginatively by the infant and internalised by him are aspects of the mother's unconscious life, that is to say aspects of her mental life of

---

[1] This paper appeared in Enid Balint's collected papers, edited by Juliet Mitchell and Michael Parsons, *Before I Was I – Psychoanalysis and the Imagination*, Free Association Books, 1993 and appears here with their permission.
[2] See Chapter 13, this volume [Ed.].

which she herself is unaware. An analyst then has to understand parts of the mother's unconscious mind, which, because the mother is not the patient, are difficult to comprehend in a reliable way. One way of describing this is in terms of projective mechanisms. The essential point, however, is that in trying to understand a woman one has always to be in touch with three generations: the patient, the patient's parents and the parents' parents, that is, the patient's grandparents.

I shall describe a phase of analysis where I found that I could only make progress by working on the hypothesis that the unconscious mind of the mother of my patient communicated very directly with her daughter's unconscious, without the communication passing through the conscious mind of either, and that the daughter's illness, and indeed her whole life, was governed by this.

First some background data

The mother of this patient lived the apparently sedate rural life of an intelligent, educated woman, married to a successful businessman and devoted to her two children. She was probably slightly depressed and capable of some anxiety of an appropriate kind. She showed, as far as I could see, no sign of the inner chaos which might be expected from a woman who had suffered severe traumata of loss and abandonment in her own infancy. Instead, her first child, my patient, behaved as if she had been subjected to severe traumata and disturbances, and her life was anything but calm and sedate. During the early years of analysis, I did not grasp that the patient was living out, or demonstrating, her mother's catastrophes as well as her own. It was only when this became clear that real work started in the analysis and I understood both the day-to-day transference manifestations and my own feelings during the sessions, as well as the possible cause of them. I began to think that parts of the patient's unconscious mind had been reacting on mine without passing either through my conscious thoughts and feelings or through hers. I thought that something similar might have happened between mother and daughter, probably in early infancy, which could account for her intense way of living, her strivings, and her illness and also my feelings of being outside, but not useless. I had sensed danger but could not locate it in a rational way. The analysis seemed straightforward and easy, but everything of importance was bypassed, and I was left at the end of each session feeling uneasy and vaguely cheated. I made what I thought were appropriate interpretations about her relationship to me and its connections with the past, but they did not make any difference to the situation or lead to any change to either her feelings or mine, or in her life of anxiety and over-activity.

When she first came to analysis, my patient, whom I shall call Kay, was a thirty-year-old married woman with one child of 18 months. Her mother, who was illegitimate, had been put into an orphanage soon after her birth. She was adopted when she was two and a half years old. All Kay's mother's memories were about her good, caring, adoptive parents who by then were dead. My patient spoke about her mother's childhood without anxiety or unease, and her mother herself spoke of it with affection and pleasure. When I questioned this, quite early in the analysis, she could not grasp what I was saying and moved away from it. It sounded to her like analytic theory, no more. It had nothing to do with her own family.

Kay is married to a professional man; she lives comfortably and enjoys her garden, her house, and her possessions. She was able to give up work before her child was born and has devoted herself to him ever since. She came to me because she had become extremely anxious and exhausted and was advised to have analysis. I had seen her husband for a single consultation some years before they got married, and it was he who suggested she should come and see me. I had no vacancy at that time, but I offered her one in a few months, which she at first refused but later accepted.

Kay's father comes from a prosperous middle-class family from the north of England. When at last Kay thought about the possibility that her mother had had a difficult time in her early infancy and childhood, she asked her about it. Her mother said her adoptive parents had told her that she cried for the first few months of her life with them. Even this, however, did not suggest to Kay that her mother had perhaps loved or missed or been attached to the first parents she knew in the children's home, or what it meant to her that she and her mother, Kay's grandmother, had lost each other.

Kay's own dread of losing objects and of not being able to find them was shown from the beginning of her analysis. I had no impression of a mother who was living under a heavy burden of denial and depression connected with loss, but I soon knew my patient was living under such a burden. Early in the analysis I connected this with an episode when her mother had a brief illness and Kay was separated from her, being only a few weeks old at the time. I linked the experiences of the two babies, Kay and her mother, but I did not realise the enormous importance of the mother's catastrophe for Kay until much later; nor did I appreciate at this stage the crucial difference between the lives of the mother and the grandmother and the life of my patient. I saw rather the similarity that both mother–daughter couples had apparently lost each other and not found each other again. Objectively speaking, of course, Kay's mother did not disappear for ever, but for Kay, with her own sense of reality in her own world the mother who came back after the brief illness was not as the mother she had first known. That mother was lost for ever. Or was it possible that she could be re-found? As the analysis went on, it appeared that Kay was compelled to live not only her own life but also her mother's and grandmother's lives. She was trying to resolve something for them, as well as to find her own 'first' mother.

When Kay came to analysis, she was looking after her son twenty-four hours a day; she could not leave him. Both she and her baby were suffering, not from an experience of loss but from a fear of it. Whose loss was it that must be avoided at all costs?

The analysis started straightforwardly, and although Kay showed her terror of dependence and loss she coped with it well, using her relationship with her son, on whom she was totally dependent and whom she totally overshadowed, to overshadow and deny her dependence on me. She left her sessions hurriedly, usually with something humorous cropping up at the end, and rushed back to 'real life' at home with her son. Life with me did not feel real to her. She strove to find what she needed but was terrified of finding it.

After the first analytic break she came back one day late and told me that the previous day, the day she should have returned, she had lost a ring. She had searched for it everywhere, over and over again; she could not stop looking. The ring had no value, it was of no importance, it was bound to turn up anyway. In fact it was a valuable Georgian ring given to her by her husband, and it never did turn up. The horror and disbelief that this loss brought were intense. Interpretations about the holiday and the lost session brought no relief. In fact, they did not feel relevant either to my patient or to myself, in spite of seeming so obvious. Acting out can be obvious but nonetheless distressing as long as it still hides what is being denied or disavowed.

This episode was followed by two others when objects were lost. One was found again after a frantic, disorganised period in which I could again see what it was like for Kay to lose something. Both lost objects were soft toys belonging to her baby, who seemed quite calm about their loss. His calmness, though, had no effect on his mother. Kay said it drove her mad, and so it appeared. Only later were the panic and pain experienced in identification with the lost, neglected object itself, not just with the person who had lost it, and linked to Kay's fear of being lost as well as her fear of losing. Even worse was that the lost object had no value to her, and she felt guilty for not valuing it, particularly in the case of the ring her husband had given her. Presumably, this was based on the thought that her mother and grandmother had had no value for each other and nor did she and I.

Similar panic states occurred at other times, not only in connection with the loss of an object but the panic itself was usually brief and was followed by a fairly severe attack of what the patient called 'depression'. These episodes seemed to be connected to Kay's birthday, and, because of this, her family took it for granted that no birthday celebrations were possible. The 'celebration' was, in fact, the depression. This was a lifeless, immobile, agonised state, during which Kay could do nothing, looked distraught, and dressed in a particular way, in what might have been baby clothes. They were white, not soft and clinging, but starched. During the hopeless, empty depression, she spoke about loss and the sensation of things being 'all gone'. This phrase described something terrible beyond belief. Sometimes even Kay herself had to appear 'all gone' so that I would know what it was like. It was important for her not to make me feel utterly lifeless, or 'all gone', myself, but she made sure that that was how I perceived her.

We gradually saw these bouts of illness as repetitions of her own and her mother's traumatic first weeks. Kay assumed that her birth had been so terrible that her mother had nearly died. This was not true. In fact, she had had a good first few weeks with her mother, who 'recovered' her baby when she got over her illness just as in reality Kay recovered her. This was when I began to realise how different were the experiences of the two infants, Kay and her mother, because the grandmother never did recover her baby nor that baby her mother. I came to think, and to interpret, that in those states Kay was experiencing what her grandmother had felt when she lost touch with her baby and never found her again. The grandmother was lost and not found; Kay's mother was lost and not found. Analytic work succeeded only when Kay began to identify with the grandmother who lost her baby. Although Kay's mother lost her own mother and never found her, she did find a substitute home where she may have been well looked after, but when she was two and a half she lost that substitute home and remembered only how good the third home was, the home of her adoptive parents. Any feelings about these losses were disavowed or denied. But the mother handed on the disturbance, chaos and confusion to her baby, who reacted to it without knowing to what she was reacting. She received it, but without making it a part of the world she knew and had created for herself. It was not imaginatively perceived.

It was difficult to follow the repercussions of the unconscious burden which brought dread and depression to my patient and led to spontaneous, uncontrollable actions that were not linked with thought. The transference, too, was difficult to follow. I was seen principally as the grandmother or the baby who had no life and was alone. I now understood the little jokes before she left each day; they were to avoid the pain of knowing that she left me as a child who had no mother, or a mother without a child, while she went home to a child who did have a mother.

Kay's life became centred around her wishes to make life less terrible for her grandmother and her baby, to deal with her own and her mother's guilt, and to keep her 'dangerous' grandmother away from her own child. When I interpreted to Kay her pity for me because I had no child and my envy of her because she did have one, she agreed and later was able to link this to her grandmother's real experiences.

Freud (1900, p. 149) says that 'identification ... enables [patients] to suffer on behalf of a whole crowd of people and to act all the parts in a play single-handed'. This describes well what Kay was doing, but, as I shall discuss later, in her case it was because she could *not* identify with what she had introjected from her mother.

After this work which took place during the third year of her analysis, Kay began to talk about having another child. Her mother had had a second child, Kay's younger brother, but it did not seem to be this that had so far prevented Kay from thinking of having another child herself. Her fear was that, if she did so, her first child would be neglected and 'placed in a home', with the house no longer being neat, tidy, and absolutely right for him. Of course, Kay was also frightened of my envy. She conceived while I was on holiday but waited until I got back to have the abortion she had wanted from the moment she knew she was pregnant. She could not bear the idea of what would happen to her son or to me if she did have a baby. Her body, as always, reacted very strongly, and she became ill and exhausted.

During the year that followed, the analysis was occupied with panic states which expressed themselves through various physical illnesses. These were sometimes quite severe and could not be diagnosed medically. Various remedies were tried. Finally, Kay made friends with a woman who had six children and came to feel at home in a house which was messy, yet where the children seemed to thrive. She had to force herself to love it. Her feelings and her ideas about such homes made it hard for her to perceive that the children did thrive and the home was good. Soon after this happened Kay became pregnant and had her second child without undue stress.

To sum up

Some patients are affected by aspects of their parents' unassimilated unconscious life, which does not seem to affect their parents' activity or behaviour but does affect their own. In analysis it can be traced to the experience of grandparents which was bypassed by the parents, instead of being introjected and identified with, and handed on to, the children. The children do introject it, but it is not identified with and therefore cannot become conscious. I have come to see this as a foreign body inside the grandchild, which remains unconscious but gives rise to affect and action, which did not occur in the parent. Whether to describe this as negation, disavowal or in some other way needs further discussion. The patient acts compulsively, out of that part of his unconscious, when it is triggered or touched upon by certain happenings in the external world. This does not make him feel confused; that happens only when he is unable to act upon it. For instance, Kay was compelled to find lost objects and to look after and mend them. Provided she could do this, she was able to live a harmonious social life. She did not seem split into two separate people but rather as though she had two separate lives to live, which she could manage but only with some strain. If, for example, she could not find a piece of furniture she wanted to repair, then she became frantic.

As in all analyses, one is tempted to try to understand the associations and histories of such patients in relation to their own infancies. The transference usually appears to confirm such reconstructions and indicates that there was some trauma that could give rise to the patient's panic and distress. These emotions, however, are not usually felt by the analyst as they are with other patients. The analyst is not in touch, either, with the unconscious thought that underlies the patient's compulsive activity. The projective mechanisms by which one might expect the unconscious thoughts and feelings to communicate themselves to the analyst are not active in these patients. The analyst thus comes to feel more and more out of contact, and the reconstructions do not bring with them the appropriate conflict, anxiety or sense of guilt. Nor do they have any effect on the panic. The patient continues to feel dread but has no idea what it is about. She is driven into activity. If she cannot be active, she becomes confused and finds an outlet by, for instance, 'freeing' some object by buying it and trying to mend it, an attempt which often fails.

When Kay began to tell me how she looked after her house, her clothes, and the objects around her, she showed me two things. On the one hand, there was a compulsive kind of caring. It was only as she started to connect this with her grandmother's (never her mother's) tragedy that she became less driven to such activity, and stopped watching films and reading books which illustrated the kind of suffering she was trying to prevent. On the other hand, she could also be very uncaring and unfeeling, and it surprised her when she recognised this. It was noticeable, for example, that she had to be allowed to do whatever she wanted with her objects. If anybody interfered, she would get rid of the objects quite ruthlessly. If anybody actively asked her to look after someone in need, she would not do so and she was, again, quite ruthless in her ability to get rid of whoever made such a request. She would not take care of her mother if she were ill, but she would find the right kind of fittings for her mother's curtains, and, if it were her mother's puppy that was ill, she would take care of it, in her own way, twenty-four hours a day.

We are familiar with the idea that the unconscious mind of one person can communicate through the unconscious mind of the other. For instance, the choice of a partner in a marriage can often be understood only by relating it to how the unconscious wishes of both partners interact, rather than to the conscious decisions involved. We are less familiar in analysis with a situation where part of one person's unconscious mind is taken over by the unconscious mind of another and becomes subject to experiences which are not related to memory or to any objective or imaginative perception. This resembles a psychosis where the patient has no thoughts but those which are implanted in him by another. Roustang (1982) comments on this phenomenon.

Presumably, Kay's mother perceived the loss of her own mother and the loss of her first home, but the trauma of these perceptions was so great that instead of assimilating and acting upon them she disavowed them. When she had a baby she handed over to it, or projected into it, her unresolved history. The daughter, Kay, had no perception of this but acted nonetheless as though the problems were hers and strove to resolve them herself. She had no notion of why she was compelled to find damaged objects and mend, or fail to mend them, nor of why she so ruthlessly had to get rid of people who interfered with this compulsion. The wounds which could not heal or be resolved in Kay were the wounds her mother had either not felt, or felt only briefly and then disavowed, and the wounds her grandmother had suffered when she lost her baby. The unhealed scars were not Kay's own but those of her mother and grandmother. Resolution was possible only when Kay's identification with her grandmother became conscious. Then Kay's guilt and her mother's guilt became accessible, and Kay was able to contain the inevitability of her own and her mother's history.

When and under what conditions is an ego too weak to absorb the projections of another person's experience? Kay's mother became ill for the only time in her life soon after Kay's birth. This may have been the only time that she was in touch with the loss of her own mother and her guilt about that, and it was perhaps at this point that she handed her history to her baby. When such unconscious communications are transmitted from a mother to her baby's unconscious, they are not connected with the rest of the baby's life experiences. This need not be seen in terms of splitting or the breaking of links. Rather there is a set of experiences which, although introjected, cannot be identified with by the ego. Thus, they are, from the beginning, alien to the other life experiences. They do not, therefore, give rise to the kind of illness that splitting of the ego produces. Instead they produce something like a foreign body inside the ego or superego. This foreign body may have to remain in place until it can be dealt with by its 'host' when he or she is strong enough to do what the original recipient of the trauma could not do. In theoretical terms this may be related to what is known as the Area of the Basic Fault (Balint, 1968).

Such a chain of events means that one generation has to resolve traumata that another generation has failed to. This may explain situations where characteristics appear to be inherited from one generation to the next in ways which are genetically inexplicable. From a clinical viewpoint it may also shed light on certain kinds of negative therapeutic reaction.

In this analysis, work based on these hypotheses brought about a change in the patient's relationship to me. It became easier for her to know what she wanted from me, and the projective mechanisms which had been missing also became active. She was not frightened of being taken over by me. I existed for her. One might say that she was able to create me, or to let me into her creative space. She could, that is to say, imaginatively perceive me and parts of reality that had been closed to her.

References

Balint, M. (1968) *The Basic Fault: Therapeutic Aspects of Regression*. London: Tavistock.

Freud, S. (1900) *The Interpretation of Dreams*. Standard Edition of the collected works, Vol 4, london: Hogarth institute of psychoanalysis, p. 149.

Freud, S. (1915) *The Unconscious*. Standard Edition XIV, pp. 166–204.

Freud, S. (1933) *New Introductory Lectures on Psychoanalysis*. Standard Edition Vol 22, pp. 2–182.

Green, A. (1986) The Dead Mother. Chapter 7 in *On Private Madness*. London: Rebus.

Pines, D. (1986) Working with women survivors of the holocaust: affective experiences in transference and countertransference, *International Journal of Psycho-Analysis*, 67: 295–307.

Roustang, G. (1982) *Dire Mastery*. Baltimore: Johns Hopkins UP.

Stern, D. (1985) *The Interpersonal World of the Infant: A View from Psycho-analysis & Developmental Psychology*. New York: Basic Books.

CHAPTER 13

The dead mother complex[1]

ANDRÉ GREEN

The dead mother complex is a revelation of the transference.[2] When the
subject presents himself to the analyst for the first time, the symptoms of
which he complains are not essentially of a depressive kind. Most of the time
these symptoms indicate more or less acute conflicts with objects who are
close. It is not infrequent that a patient spontaneously recounts a personal
history where the analyst thinks to himself that here, at a given moment, a
childhood depression should or could have been located, of which the
subject makes no mention. This depression, which has sometimes appeared
sporadically in the clinical history, only breaks into the open in the transference. As for the classic neurotic symptoms, they are present but of secondary
value or, even if they are important, the analyst has the feeling that the
analysis of their genesis will not furnish the key to the conflict. On the
contrary, the problems pertaining to narcissism are in the foreground where
the demands of the ego ideal are considerable, in synergy with or in opposi-
tion to the superego. The feeling of impotence is evident. Impotence to
withdraw from a conflictual situation, impotence to love, to make the most
of one's talents, to multiply one's assets, or, when this does take place, a
profound dissatisfaction with the results.

When the analysis is underway, the transference will reveal, sometimes
quite rapidly but more often after long years of analysis, a singular depression. The analyst has the feeling of a discordance between the *transference*

---

[1] 'The dead mother', written in 1960 and dedicated to Catherine Parat, was translated by
Katherine Aubertin. It first appeared as 'La mère morte' in *Narcissisme de vie. Narcissisme de
mort*. Paris: Editions de Minuit, pp. 222-53. It appeared in English in 1986, in A. Green, *On
Private Madness*, London: Hogarth Press and Rebus Press, later Karnac Books. A section of it is
reprinted here by generous permission of the publisher and author.
[2] For this and other psychoanalytic concepts see glossary at the end of the book [Ed.].

162

depression – an expression that I am coining on this occasion to oppose it to *transference neurosis* – and the behaviour outside the analysis where depression does not blow up, because nothing indicates that the entourage perceives it clearly, which nevertheless does not prevent the people close to him from suffering from the object-relationship that the analysand establishes with them.

What this transference depression indicates is the repetition of an infantile depression, the characteristics of which may usefully be specified. It does not concern the loss of a real object; the problem of a real separation with the object who would have abandoned the subject is not what is in question here. The fact may exist, but it is not this that constitutes the dead mother complex.

The essential characteristic of this depression is that it takes place in the presence of the object, which is itself absorbed by a bereavement. The mother, for one reason or another, is depressed. Here the variety of precipitating factors is very large. Of course, among the principal causes of this kind of maternal depression, one finds the loss of a person dear to her: child, parent, close friend, or any other object strongly cathected by the mother. But it may also be a depression triggered off by a deception which inflicts a narcissistic wound: a change of fortune in the nuclear family or the family of origin, a liaison of the father who neglects the mother, humiliation, etc. In any event the mother's sorrow and lessening of interest in her infant are in the foreground.

It should be noted that the most serious instance is the death of a child at an early age, as all authors have understood. In particular there is a cause which remains totally hidden, because the manifest signs by which the child could recognize it, and thus gain retrospective knowledge of it, is never possible because it rests on a secret: a miscarriage of the mother, which must be reconstructed by the analysis from minute indications; a hypothetical construction, of course, which renders a coherence to what is expressed in the clinical material, which can be attached to earlier periods of the subject's history.

What comes about then is a brutal change of the maternal imago, which is truly mutative. Until then there is an authentic vitality present in the subject, which comes to a sudden halt, remaining seized from then on in the same place, which testifies to a rich and happy relationship with the mother. The infant felt loved, notwithstanding the risks that the most ideal of relationships presupposes. Photos of the young baby in the family album show him to be gay, lively, interested, carrying much potentiality, whereas later snapshots show the loss of this initial happiness. All seems to have ended, as with the disappearance of ancient civilizations, the cause of which is sought in vain by historians, who make the hypothesis of an earthquake to explain the death and the destruction of palace, temple, edifices and dwellings, of which nothing is left but ruins. Here the disaster is limited to a *cold core*, which will eventually be overcome, but which leaves an indelible mark on the erotic cathexes of the subjects in question.

The transformation in the psychical life, at the moment of the mother's sudden bereavement when she has become abruptly detached from her infant, is experienced by the child as a catastrophe; because, without any warning signal, love has been lost at one blow. One does not need to give a lengthy description of the narcissistic traumatism that this change represents. One must however point out that it constitutes a premature disillusionment and that it carries in its wake, besides the loss of love, the loss of *meaning*, for the baby disposes of no explication to account for what has happened. Of course, being at the centre of the maternal universe, it is clear that he interprets this deception as the consequence of his drives towards the object. This will be especially serious if the complex of the dead mother occurs at the moment when the child discovers the existence of the third person, the father, and that the new attachment should be interpreted by him as the reason for the mother's detachment. In any case, here there is a premature and unstable triangulation. For either, as I have just said, the withdrawal of the mother's love is attributed to the mother's attachment to the father, or this withdrawal will provoke an early and particularly intense attachment to the father, felt to be the saviour from the conflict taking place between mother and infant. Now, in reality, the father more often than not does not respond to the child's distress. The subject is thus caught between a dead mother and an inaccessible father, either because the latter is principally preoccupied by the state of the mother, without bringing help to the infant, or because he leaves the mother–child couple to cope with this situation alone.

After the child has attempted in vain to repair the mother who is absorbed by her bereavement, which has made him feel the measure of his impotence, after having experienced the loss of his mother's love and the threat of the loss of the mother herself, and after he has fought against anxiety by various active methods, amongst which agitation, insomnia and nocturnal terrors are indications, the ego will deploy a series of defences of a different kind.

The first and most important is a unique movement with two aspects: the *decathexis of the maternal object* and the *unconscious identification with the dead mother*. The decathexis, which is principally affective, but also representative, constitutes a psychical murder of the object, accomplished without hatred. One will understand that the mother's affliction excludes the emergence of any contingency of hatred susceptible of damaging her image even more.

No instinctual destructiveness is to be inferred from this operation of decathexis of the maternal image. Its result is the constitution of *a hole* in the texture of object-relations with the mother, which does not prevent the surrounding cathexes from being maintained, just as the mother's bereavement modifies her fundamental attitude with regard to the child, whom she feels incapable of loving, but whom she continues to love just as she continues to take care of him. However, as one says, 'her heart is not in it'.

The other aspect of the decathexis is the primary mode of identification with the object. This *mirror-identification* is almost obligatory, after reactions of complementarity (artificial gaiety, agitation, etc.) have failed. This reactive symmetry is the only means by which to establish a reunion with the mother – perhaps by way of sympathy. In fact there is no real reparation, but a mimicry, with the aim of continuing to possess the object (whom one can no longer have) by becoming, not like it, but the object itself. This identification, which is the condition of the renouncement to the object and at the same time its conservation in a cannibalistic manner, is unconscious from the start. Here there is a difference from the decathexis, which becomes unconscious later on, because in this second case the withdrawal is retaliatory; it endeavours to get rid of the object, whereas the identification comes about unawares to the ego of the subject and against his will. Here is where its alienating characteristic lies. The ulterior object-relations, the subject, who is prey to the repetition-compulsion, will actively employ the decathexis of an object who is about to bring disappointment, repeating the old defence, but he will remain totally unconscious of his identification with the dead mother, with whom he reunites henceforth in recathecting the traces of the trauma.

The second fact is, as I have pointed out, *the loss of meaning*. The 'construction' of the breast, of which pleasure is the cause, the aim and the guarantor, has collapsed all at once, without reason. Even if one were to imagine the reversal of the situation by the subject, who in a negative megalomania, would attribute the responsibility for the mutation to himself, there is a totally disproportional gap between the fault he could reproach himself for having committed and the intensity of the maternal reaction. At the most, he might imagine this fault to be linked with his manner of being rather than with some forbidden wish; in fact, it becomes forbidden for him to be.

This position, which could induce the child to let himself die, because of the impossibility of diverting destructive aggressivity to the outside, because of the vulnerability of the maternal image, obliges him to find someone responsible for the mother's black mood, though he be a scapegoat. It is the father who is designated to this effect. There is in any case, I repeat, an early triangular situation, because child, mother and the unknown object of the mother's bereavement are present at the same time. The unknown object of the bereavement and the father are then condensed for the infant, creating a precocious Oedipus complex.

This whole situation, arising from the loss of meaning, leads to a second front of defence: *the releasing of secondary hatred*, which is neither primary nor fundamental, brings into play regressive wishes of incorporation, but also anal features which are coloured with manic sadism where it is a matter of dominating, soiling, taking vengeance upon the object, etc. *Auto-erotic excitation* establishes itself in the search for pure sensual pleasure, organ pleasure at the limit, without tenderness, ruthless, which is not necessarily accompanied by sadistic fantasy, but which remains stamped with a reticence to love the object. This is the foundation for hysterical identifications to come. There is a precocious dissociation between the body and the psyche, as between sensuality and tenderness, and a blocking of love. The object is sought after for its capacity to release isolated enjoyment of an erogenous zone (or more than one) without the confluence of a shared enjoyment of two objects, more or less totalized.

Finally, and more particularly, *the quest for lost meaning structures the early development of the fantasmatic and the intellectual capacities of the ego*. The development of a frantic need for play which does not come about as in the freedom for playing, but under the *compulsion to imagine*, just as intellectual development is inscribed in a *compulsion to think*. Performance and auto-reparation go hand in hand to coincide with the same goal: the preservation of a capacity to surmount the dismay over the loss of the breast, by the creation of a patched breast, a piece of cognitive fabric which is destined to mask the hole left by the decathexis, while secondary hatred and erotic excitation teem on the edge of an abyss of emptiness.

The over-cathected intellectual capacity necessarily comprises a considerable part of projection. Contrary to widespread opinion, projection is not always false reasoning. This may be the case but not necessarily. What defines projection is not the true or false character of what is projected but the operation which consists in transferring to the outside scene – the scene of the object – the investigation, even the guessing, of what has had to be rejected and abolished from within. The infant has made the cruel experience of his dependence on the variations of the mother's moods. Henceforth he devotes his efforts to guessing or anticipating.

The compromised unity of the ego which has a hole in it from now on realizes itself either on the level of fantasy, which gives open expression to artistic creation, or on the level of knowledge, which is at the origin of highly productive intellectualization. It is evident that one is witnessing an attempt to master the traumatic situation. But this attempt is doomed to fail. Not that it fails where it has displaced the theatre of operations. These precocious idealized sublimations are the outcome of premature and probably precipitated psychical formations, but I see no reason, apart from bending to a normative ideology, to contest their authenticity. Their failure lies elsewhere.

The sublimations reveal their incapacity to play a stabilizing role in the psychical economy, because the subject remains vulnerable on a particular point, which is his love life. In this area, a wound will awaken a psychical pain and one will witness a resurrection of the dead mother, who, for the entire critical period when she remains in the foreground, dissolves all the subject's sublimatory acquisitions, which are not lost, but which remain momentarily blocked. Sometimes it is love which sets the development of the sublimated acquisitions in motion again, and sometimes it is the latter which attempt to liberate love. Both may combine their efforts for a time, but soon the destructiveness overwhelms the possibilities of the subject who does not dispose of the necessary cathexes to establish a lasting object-relation and to commit himself progressively to a deeper personal involvement which implies concern for the other. Thus, inevitably, it is either the disappointment in the object or that in the ego which puts an end to the experience, with the reappearance of the feeling of failure and incapacity. The patient has the feeling that a malediction weighs upon him, that there is no end to the dead mother's dying, and that it holds him prisoner. Pain, a narcissistic feeling, surfaces again. It is a hurt which is situated on the edge of the wound, colouring all the cathexes, filling in the effects of hatred, of erotic excitement, the loss of the breast. In a state of psychical pain, it is as impossible to hate as to love, impossible to find enjoyment, albeit masochistic, impossible to think; only a feeling of a captivity which dispossesses the ego of itself and alienates it to an unrepresentable figure.

The subject's trajectory evokes a hunt in quest of an unintrojectable object, without the possibility of renouncing it or of losing it, and indeed, the possibility of accepting its introjection into the ego, which is cathected by the dead mother. In all, the subject's objects remain constantly at the limit of the ego, not wholly within, and not quite without. And with good reason, for the place is occupied, in its centre, by the dead mother.

For a long period, the analysis of these subjects will proceed with the examination of the classic conflicts: Oedipus complex, pregenital fixations, anal and oral. Repression reposing on infantile sexuality, on aggressivity, will have been interpreted without cease. Probably some progress has become manifest. But it hardly convinces the analyst, even if the analysand himself seeks comfort by underlining the points on which there would be cause for satisfaction.

In fact, all this psychoanalytic work remains subject to spectacular collapses, where everything again seems to be as on the first day, to the point where the analysand realizes that he can no longer continue to bluff himself and he finds himself forced to admit to the insufficiency of the transferential object: the analyst, in spite of the relational manoeuvres with the supporting objects of lateral transference which had helped him, the patient, to avoid approaching the central core of the conflict.

In these cures, I finally understood that I remained deaf to a certain discourse that my analysands had left me to guess. Behind the eternal complaints about mother's unkindness, or her lack of understanding or her rigidity, I guessed the defensive value of these comments, against intense homosexuality. Feminine homosexuality in both cases, for in the boy it is the feminine part of the psychical personality which expresses itself thus, very often in the search for paternal compensation. But I continued to ask myself why this situation prolonged itself. *My deafness related to the fact that, behind the complaints concerning the mother's doings, her actions, the shadow of her absence was profiled.* In fact the enquiry against X concerned a mother who was absorbed, either with herself or with something else, unreachable without echo, but always sad. A silent mother, even if talkative. When she was present, she remained indifferent, even when she was plying the child with her reproaches. Thus, I was able to represent this situation for myself quite differently.

The dead mother had taken away with her, in the decathexis of which she had been the object, the major portion of the love with which she had been cathected before her bereavement: her look, the tone of her voice, her smell, the memory of her caress. The loss of physical contact carried with it the repression of the memory traces of her touch. She had been buried alive, but her tomb itself had disappeared. The hole that gaped in its place made solitude dreadful, as though the subject ran the risk of being sunk in it, body and possessions. In this connection I now think that the concept of *holding*, of which Winnicott spoke, does not explain the feeling of vertiginous falling that some of our patients experience. This seems to me to be far more in relation to an experience of psychical collapse, which would be to the psyche what fainting is to the physical body. The object has been encapsulated and its trace has been lost through decathexis; primary identification with the dead mother took place, transforming positive identification into negative identification, i.e. identification with the hole left by the decathexis (and not identification with the object), and to this emptiness, which is filled in and suddenly manifests itself through an affective hallucination of the dead mother, as soon as a new object is periodically chosen to occupy this space.

All that can be observed around this nucleus organizes itself with a triple objective:

- to keep the ego alive: through hatred for the object, through the search for exciting pleasure, through the quest for meaning;
- to reanimate the dead mother, to interest her, to distract her, to give her a renewed taste for life, to make her smile and laugh;
- to rivalize with the object of her bereavement in the early triangulation.

This type of patient presents us with serious technical problems which I shall not go into here. On this point, I refer the reader to my paper on the analyst's silence (Green, 1979). I greatly fear that the rule of silence, in these cases, only perpetuates the transference of blank mourning for the mother. I will add that I do not believe that the Kleinian technique of the systematic inter- pretation of destructiveness is of much help here. On the other hand, Winnicott's position, as it is expressed in his article 'The use of an object and relating through identifications' (Winnicott, 1971), seems appropriate to me. But I fear that Winnicott somewhat underestimated the sexual fantasies, especially the primal scene, which I will take up later on.

Frozen love and its vicissitudes: the breast, the Oedipus complex, the primal scene

Ambivalence is a fundamental trait of the cathexes of depressives. What is the case in the dead mother complex? When I described above the affective and representative decathexis of which hatred is the consequence, this descrip- tion was incomplete. What one must understand, in the structure that I have expounded, is that the inability to love only derives from ambivalence, and hence from an overload of hatred, in the measure that what comes first is *love frozen* by the decathexis. The object is in hibernation, as it were, conserved by the cold. This operation comes about unknown to the subject, in the following way. Decathexsis is withdrawal of cathexsis, which takes place (pre)consciously. Repressed hatred is the result of instinctual defusion, all unbinding and thus weakening the erotic-libidinal cathexis, which, as a consequence, frees the destructive cathexes. By withdrawing his cathexes, the subject believes he has brought them back within his ego, for want of being able to displace them onto another object, a substitute object, but he ignores that he has left behind, has alienated, his love for the object, which has fallen into *oubliettes* of primary repression. Consciously, he believes his reserve of love to be intact, available for another love when the occasion arises. He declares himself ready to be attached to another object, if he appears to be friendly and he feels loved by him. He thinks the primary object no longer counts for him. In truth, he will encounter the inability to love, not only because of ambivalence, but because his love is still mortgaged to the dead mother. The subject is rich but he can give nothing in spite of his generosity, for he does not reap enjoyment from it.

In the course of the transference, the defensive sexualization which took place up to now, always involving intense pregenital satisfactions and remark- able sexual performance, comes to a sudden halt, and the analysand finds his sexual life diminishing or fading almost to nothing. According to him, it is a matter neither of inhibition nor of the loss of sexual appetite: it simply that no one is desirable, or, if perchance someone is, it is he or she who is not attracted in return. A profuse, dispersed, multiple, fleeting sexual life no longer brings any satisfaction.

Arrested in their capacity to love, subjects who are under the empire of the dead mother can only aspire to autonomy. *Sharing remains forbidden to them*. Thus, solitude, which was a situation creating anxiety and to be avoided, changes sign. From negative it becomes positive. Having previously been shunned, it is now sought after. The subject nestles into it. He becomes his own mother, but remains prisoner to her economy of survival. He thinks he has got rid of his dead mother. In fact, she only leaves him in peace in the measure that she herself is left in peace. As long as there is no candidate to the succession, she can well let her child survive, certain to be the only one to possess this inaccessible love.

This cold core burns like ice, and numbs like it as well, but, as long as it is felt to be cold, love remains unavailable. These are barely metaphors. These analysands complain of being cold even in the heat. They are cold below the surface of the skin, in their bones; they feel chilled by a funereal shiver, wrapped in their shroud. Everything happens as though the core of love frozen by the dead mother does not prevent the ulterior evolution towards the Oedipus complex, in the same way that the fixation will be ultimately overcome in the life of the individual. These subjects may outwardly have a more or less satisfactory professional life; they marry and have children. For a while all seems well. But soon the repetition of conflicts contributes to turning the two essential sectors of life, love and work, into failure: professional life, even when profoundly absorbing, becomes disappointing, and marital relations lead to profound disturbances in love, sexuality and affective communication. It is in any case this last which is most lacking. As for sexuality, it depends on the later or earlier appearance of the dead mother complex. It may be relatively preserved but only up to a certain point. Love, finally, is never completely satisfied. Thus, at one extreme, it is completely impossible, or, at best, it is somewhat mutilated or inhibited. There must not be too much: too much love, too much pleasure, too much enjoyment, whereas on the contrary *the parental function is hyper-invested*. However, this function is more often than not infiltrated by narcissism: children are loved on condition that they fulfil the narcissistic objectives which the parents have not succeeded in accomplishing themselves.

Thus, if the Oedipus complex is reached and even bypassed, the dead mother complex will give it a particularly dramatic aspect. Fixation on the mother will prevent the girl from ever being able to cathect the imago of the father, without the fear of losing the mother's love, or else if love for the father is deeply repressed, without her being able to avoid transferring onto the father's imago a large part of the characteristics that have been projected onto the mother. Not the dead mother, but her opposite, the phallic mother whose structure I have attempted to describe (Green, 1968). The boy projects a similar imago onto the mother, while the father is the object of a homosexuality which is not very structuring but makes him into an inaccessible being and, as in the familiar descriptions, insignificant or tired, depressed and overwhelmed by this phallic mother. In all cases there is a regression to anality. In anality the subject not only regresses from the Oedipus complex backwards, in every sense of the term, but also protects himself by the anal buttress against the tendency towards oral regression to which one is always thrown back by the dead mother, because the dead mother complex and the metaphoric loss of the breast reverberate each other. One also always finds the use of reality as a defence, as though the subject feels the need to cling to the presence of what is perceived as real and untouched by any projection, because he is far from sure of the distinction between fantasy and reality, which he does his utmost to keep apart. Fantasy must be only fantasy, which means that one witnesses, at the limit, the negation of psychical reality. When reality and fantasy are telescoped together, intense anxiety appears. Subjective and objective are confused, which gives the subject the impression of a threat of psychosis. Order must be maintained at any price, by a structuring anal reference which allows splitting to continue to function, and above all keeps the subject away from what he has learned of his unconscious. This is to say that psychoanalysis allows him to understand others better than to see clearly within himself. Whence the inevitable disappointment with the results of the analysis, though it is strongly cathected, albeit more often narcissistically.

The dead mother refuses to die a second death. Very often, the analyst says to himself: 'This time it's done, the old woman is really dead, he (or she) will finally be able to live and I shall be able to breathe a little.' Then a small traumatism appears in the transference or in life which gives the maternal imago renewed vitality, if I may put it this way. It is because she is a thousand-headed hydra whom one believes one has beheaded with each blow; whereas in fact only one of its heads has been struck off. Where then is the beast's neck?

A habitual preconception expects one to delve to the deepest level: to the primordial breast. This is a mistake: that is not where the fundamental fantasy lies. For, in the same way that it is the relation with the second object in the Oedipus situation that retroactively reveals the complex which affects the primary object, the mother, likewise, it is not by attacking the oral relation face on that one can extirpate the core of the complex. The solution is to be found in the prototype of the Oedipus complex, in the symbolic matrix which allows for its construction. Then the dead mother complex delivers its secret: it is the fantasy of the primal scene.

Contemporary psychoanalysis has understood, many indications attest to it – belatedly, it is true – that if the Oedipus complex remains the indispensable structural reference, the determining conditions for it are not to be sought in its oral, anal or phallic forerunners, seen from the angle of realistic references – for orally, anality or phallicity depend on partly real object relations – nor either in a generalized fantasizing of their structure, 'a la Klein', but in the isomorphic fantasy of the Oedipus complex: that of the primal scene. I emphasize this fantasy of the primal scene to stress the difference here from the Freudian position as it is expounded in the 'Wolf Man' (Freud, 1918), where in the controversy with Jung, Freud searches for proof of its reality. Now, what counts in the primal scene is not that one has witnessed it but precisely the contrary, namely that it has taken place in the absence of the subject.

In the case with which we are concerned, the fantasy of the primal scene is of capital importance. For it is on the occasion of an encounter between a conjuncture and a structure, which brings *two* objects into play, that the subject will be confronted with memory traces in relation to the dead mother. These memory traces have been forcibly repressed by decathexis. They remain, so to speak, in abeyance within the subject, who has only kept a very incomplete memory of the period relative to the complex. Sometimes a screen memory, of an anodyne nature, is all that is left of it. The fantasy of the primal scene will not only recathect these vestiges, but will confer to them, through a new cathexis, new effects which constitute a real *conflagration*, that sets fire to the structure which gives the complex of the dead mother retrospective significance.

Every resurgence of this fantasy constitutes *a projective actualisation*, the projection aiming to assuage the narcissistic wound. By actualized projection I designate a process through which the projection not only rids the subject of his inner tensions by projecting them onto the object, but constitutes a *revivifying* and not a *reminiscence*, an *actual* traumatic and dramatic repetition. What happens to the fantasy of the primal scene in the case that concerns us? On one hand the subject takes account of the insuperable distance that separates him from the mother. This distance makes him realize his impotent rage at being unable to establish contact with the object, in the strictest sense of the term. On the other hand the subject feels himself incapable of awakening this dead mother, of animating her, or rendering life to her. But, on this occasion, instead of his rival being the object who had captivated the dead mother in her experience of bereavement, on the contrary, he becomes the third party who shows himself apt, against all expectation, to return her to life and to give her the pleasure of orgasm.

This is where the revolting aspect of the situation lies, which reactivates the loss of narcissistic omnipotence and awakens the feeling of an incommensurable libidinal infirmity. Of course, in reaction to this situation there will be a series of consequences which may come singly or in groups:

1. The persecution by this fantasy and hatred for the two objects which form a couple to the detriment of the subject.
2. The classic interpretation of the primal scene as a sadistic scene, but where the essential feature is that the mother either has no orgasm and suffers, or else has orgasm in spite of herself, forced to it by the father's violence.
3. A variation of the last situation; when the mother experiences orgasm, she becomes cruel, hypocritical, playing it up, a sort of lewd monster, that makes her the Sphinx of the Oedipus myth, rather than Oedipus' mother.
4. The alternating identification with the two imagos: with the dead mother, whether she remains in her unaltered state or gives herself up to a sadomasochistic type of erotic excitation; with the father, the dead mother's aggressor (necrophilic fantasy), or he who repairs her, through sexual union. More often, depending on the moment, the subject passes from the one to the other of these identifications.
5. Erotic and aggressive delibidinalization of the primal scene to the advantage of intense intellectual activity, which restores narcissism in the face of this confusing situation, where the quest for meaning (which was lost anew) results in the formation of a sexual theory and stimulates an extensive 'intellectual' activity, which re-establishes the wounded narcissistic omnipotence by sacrificing libidinal satisfaction. Another solution: artistic creation, which is the support for a fantasy of auto-satisfaction.
6. The negation, 'en bloc', of the whole fantasy. Ignorance of everything pertaining to sexual relations is highly cathected, making the emptiness of the dead mother and the obliteration of the primal scene coincide for the subject. The fantasy of the primal scene becomes the central axis of the subject's life which overshadows the dead mother complex. This is developed in two directions: forwards and backwards.

Forwards, there is the anticipation of the Oedipus complex, which will then be experienced according to the schema of defences against the anxiety of the primal scene. The three anti-erotic factors, namely hatred, homosexuality and narcissism, will conjugate their effects so that the Oedipus complex is adversely structured.

Backwards, the relation to the breast is the object of a radical reinterpretation. This becomes significant retrospectively. The blank mourning for the dead mother reflects back to the breast which, superficially, is laden with destructive projections. In fact, it is less a question of a bad breast, which is ungiving, than a breast which, even when it does give, is an absent breast (and not lost), absorbed with nostalgia for a relation that is grieved for; a breast which can neither be full nor filling. The consequence of this is that the recathexis of the happy relation to the breast that existed prior to the occurrence of the dead mother complex, is this time affected with the fleeting signal of a catastrophic threat, and, if I dare say so, it is a *false breast*, carried within a *false self*, nourishing a *false baby*. This happiness was only a decoy. 'I have never been loved' becomes a new outcry which the subject will cling to and which he strives to confirm in his subsequent love life. It is evident that one is faced with a situation of mourning which is impossible, and that the metaphoric loss of the breast cannot be worked through for this reason. It is necessary to add a precision concerning oral cannibalistic fantasies. Contrary to what happens in melancholia, here there is no regression to this phase. What one witnesses above all is an identification with the dead mother on the level of the oral relation and with the defences which arise from it, the subject's fearing to the utmost either the ultimate loss of the object or the invasion of emptiness.

The analysis of the transference by means of these three positions will lead to the rediscovery of the early happiness that existed prior to the appearance of the dead mother complex. This takes a great deal of time, and one has to work it over more than once before marking a victory, namely before blank mourning and its resonance with castration anxiety allow one to reach a transferential repetition of a happy relationship with a mother who is alive at last and desirous of the father. This result supposes one has passed through the analysis of the narcissistic wound, which consumed the child in the mother's bereavement.

References

Freud, S. (1918) From the History of an Infantile Neurosis. In *The Standard Edition of the Collected Works*, Vol. 17, pp. 1-122. London: Hogarth and Institute of Psychoanalysis.
Green, A. (1968) 'Sur la mère phallique', *Revue française Psychanalytique* 32.
Green, A. (1979) 'Le silence du psychanalyste', *Topique* 23.
Winnicott, D. (1971) *Playing and Reality*. London: Tavistock; NY: Basic Books; Harmondsworth: Penguin, 1974.

PART III

Representations and Reality

The representation of the fantasy baby rarely coincides with that of the real one that arrives. However, there are circumstances when the discrepancy between the two is heightened. Current-day dilemmas are also exacerbated by medical advances, which have changed the eternal nature of childbearing, enabling infertile couples to conceive and ever-younger prematurely born babies to survive. However, technological input, and particularly antenatal screening, not only reveals the foetus hidden in the interior of the womb but provides information that was previously unknown. While such tests can be helpful in reducing anxieties, they also promote tacit assumptions about 'perfect' babies, raising ethical questions about which baby is entitled to survive. The existential angst of reactions to major life-events such as neonatal loss, a damaged or special-needs baby are documented in this book from several different perspectives. These issues, accompanied by extracts from the diary he kept during his partner's pregnancy, are candidly addressed by psychotherapist (then in training) Glenn Whitney from his own poignant personal experience (Chapter 14). In the following chapter, Dorian Mintzer and her colleagues observe the reactions of five couples hard-hit by the birth of special-needs babies. Using measuring techniques of the baby's adjustment and interviewing the parents, the professional team trace the slow process of adaptation beginning with shock, disappointment, loss of self-esteem and inappropriate handling of the infant to eventual acceptance and restoration of psychic equilibrium in the family. The team describe the impact on the couple's relationships, the wide range of defences employed (denial, avoidance, withdrawal, rationalization etc.) noting that the degree of disturbance is linked to the visibility (particularly facial), correctability and severity of the baby's defect.

Another means of exploring early sources of our adult emotions is through weekly observations of infants and their families in the home. These observations are now a standard part of the training for psychoanalytic psychotherapists (in addition to theoretical courses and personal analyses).

One such observation is offered here by (then) student analyst Francis Grier (Chapter 16) describing in fine detail some intense early experiences within a family and how baby Amanda rediscovers her equilibrium with the help of her mother's sensitivity, using the term 'breast mother' to depict her responsiveness to the, nevertheless, bottle-fed baby. Following this, in Chapter 17, I comment on some issues raised by his observation, particularly fantasies and representations around breastfeeding and the role of an observer in early parenting.

CHAPTER 14

Joy and woe: response to prenatal testing

GLENN WHITNEY

This is a story full of finitude and death but, alas, without an ending. It is also very much a story of life. Our awareness of the biological mechanics of the beginning of new life is enormous and increasing every year. What has been for thousands of years a miraculous mystery is being transformed into a technical intervention – from in-vitro fertilisation to induced labour, total anaesthesia and surgical delivery. As post-menopausal women are implanted with embryonic grandchildren and the multiple foetuses that result from fertility treatments necessitate 'selective reductions,' it becomes clear that philosophy, ethics and psychotherapy are struggling in vain to keep up with science.

As human beings we are privy to certain existential truths unknown to other forms of being. One is that we are 'beings-towards-death' – that we know we will one day die, that our existence is finite. I would argue that we are also aware that we are 'beings-towards-life' – that most humans are capable of reproduction. We are conscious of the full cycle of birth and death in a way that no other being is. Thus after much planning, nutritional rigour, temperature taking and strategically times intercourse, my wife and I were delighted to learn that we created a new being, which began growing in her womb on July 18, 1996.

As an expectant father, without an embodied knowledge of what was happening, the reality of the event was not fully comprehensible to me for several more months. I began keeping a journal of my own response to impending parenthood once this experience became more immediate. I must say that the journal extracts below represent my state of mind at its calmest and most rational. In between entries were moments of huge confusion.

October 14, 1996

Saw our baby on TV today. The first glimpse brought a rush of amazement and exhilaration. I suspected there was something in Conner's stomach, but to see such graphic proof was truly astounding and gave me this powerful feeling of ownership and protectiveness. It also felt like a resounding wake-up call to adulthood. I could see this tiny but already human life form that absolutely depends on Conner for its very survival and I now see how important my support role is ... I'm excited and looking forward to actually having a baby. I can hardly believe we're capable of giving birth to a healthy child. I've been quite neurotic about potential birth defects. We're statistically low-risk, but my mind keeps telling me to watch out. I'm always looking for the worst-case scenario. But I want to be positive and allow myself to be thrilled, which almost all of me is ...

Following this scan we settled into a routine of nervous expectation and screening, in which a sample of Conner's blood was taken to test for hormone levels, which are used to indicate the risk of birth defects. Then things changed quickly and dramatically.

October 31, 1996

I feel shattered. We found out two days ago that our baby has a one in 15 chance of having Down's syndrome. (This is compared to the average women Conner's age having a 1 in 550 chance) ... We are shaken to our very core. We have to contemplate termination of a life that we created and that we have hoped so ardently for ... [The hospital] offered us an amniocentesis[1] test straight away. We have a 3-week wait. It's gruelling so far. We have to learn to let go of the doom. And we learn to suffer and we learn to create meaning from that suffering. This being one of the most difficult things of all ...

In addition to contemplating the birth of a severely handicapped child, we now had to contend with a heightened risk of miscarriage as a result of the amniocentesis. The period in which all this occurred immediately followed a presentation I gave on Viktor Frankl's *Man's Search for Meaning*. His influence was obvious and was a source of strength, helping me realise that difficulties can be transcended, that there is nobility in suffering. At the same time, however, I felt weak and unworthy amid Frankl's exhortations to suffer with dignity. One passage in particular kept running through my head:

But not only creativeness and enjoyment are meaningful. If there is a meaning in life at all, then there must be a meaning in suffering. Suffering is an ineradicable part of life, even as fate and death. Without suffering and death, human life cannot be complete. (Frankl, 1946/84, p. 88)

My wife and I knew that having a child with Down's syndrome would transform our life completely. There is a popular image of them as cheerful and

---

[1] Antenatal test checking foetal cells by extracting amniotic fluid from the womb [Ed.].

surprisingly competent. However, the reading we did following the probability results indicated that only about 10% of all Down's children eventually develop enough mental capacities to enable them to perform even menial labour jobs. At 18 years old most are sent to languish in special homes. Only about 20% achieve enough linguistic competence to be understood by outsiders. Many need lifelong assistance with urination and defecation. Sexual development and expression can be especially problematic (Newton, 1992).

At the same time, the development of some Down's children can proceed along lines approaching 'normality'. They are impeded as much by social stigma as by their chromosomal abnormalities. Some display a high degree of sensitivity and self-awareness not always seen in non-Down's children. Sinason (1993) notes that one of the most important emotional issues to understand with a child with Down's syndrome is the impact of looking clearly different, something usually underestimated by those trying to understand them. She relates one particular case:

> A young girl told me 'When I went on my school holiday I saw someone like me'. In her integrated school there were a few children with physical disabilities, but she was the only child with Down's syndrome. After the holiday she asked her mother for a mirror for her bedroom. She spent a long time examining her face. Eventually she was able to ask why she looked liked the girl on holiday more than her own family. (Sinason, p. 55)

Information like this highlighted the obvious 'humanity' of these children, but also the painful reality of their existence. The difficulties caused by 'differentness' are an extreme form of the anxiety we all feel about fitting in, about being normal. Both my wife and I were teased as children for minor physical dissimilarities; we feared the vastly more severe abuse our Down's child might be subjected to.

We also knew that by having an amniocentesis test, we opened ourselves to the dilemma of having to decide whether to continue the pregnancy or abort it. Sartre's notion of bad faith (1943/91) loomed particularly large during these days. To pretend that this was all out of our hands and the responsibility of the hospital was especially bad faith. To their credit, they were keen to ensure, to the limits of their ability, that we appreciated the implications of having the screening test and the amnio. Still, for most of the medical community and our friends and relatives, a foetus with Down's is a 'problem' to be solved rather than a 'dilemma' to be faced (Spinelli, 1994). For us it was very much the latter.

We both realised that it would be bad faith to take comfort in the technical language of medicine. 'Terminating' or 'aborting' the pregnancy meant killing the baby, and killing the baby because it was deemed physically and mentally defective. It is a choice taken by 90% of those with a Down's positive test result. This statistic did not lend much comfort. If anything, as a budding existentialist, I felt an imperative to somehow 'do better than that.' I wanted to proceed in good faith, but I didn't really understand what that meant apart from facing the full horrors head-on. I do not mean to imply that the majority of expectant parents take the decision to terminate lightly. I'm sure they do not, not the least because termination after an amnio requires that labour be induced and the mother go through the actual delivery process as with a normal birth. This usually lasts 12 to 24 hours. The baby is born alive but dies immediately outside the birth canal because his/her lungs aren't developed enough. One self-help book (Ilse, 1993) we read made much of the notion of 'loving' the baby although it is has been aborted. Parents are encouraged to hold and caress their aborted child, perhaps wash him/her, give him/her a name, have a baptism, etc. The contradiction of killing the child and loving it was and still is too much for me to understand. One woman who went through the experience describes the contradiction well:

> Whenever I saw my pregnant body in the mirror, I felt like throwing up. I could still feel the baby kicking during those six days between getting the results and having the abortion. It was just agony! And now I could take any medications I wanted; after all, I'd be killing this foetus in a few days, so it didn't matter. It was a horrible switch, to go from being careful and protective of this new life to deciding to end it. (Green, 1992)

I became aware of the fact of that I was seeing this baby not as a being in its own right, but what Heidegger would describe as *Bestand* or 'stock' (Heidegger, 1927) This stock was being held in the warehouse of my wife's body awaiting the appropriate amount of ageing. Technology makes it possible to assess its eventual quality in advance. If it makes the grade, it is then delivered to us. The stock serves the function of making us feel productive, loving and socially valued. The realisation that I felt this way to an extent makes me feel nauseous with embarrassment. To what extent is this foetus (in the medical jargon) a '*Dasein*' or '*Bestand*,? I struggled with these questions throughout and still do today.

My next journal entry shows a tentative understanding of the experience, but also gross intellectualisations on my part and a certain amount of defensive disengagement.

November 3, 1996

So here we are on Sunday after five days together of fear and lots of tears. I think we're both feeling a bit more stable and courageous ... I feel more and more certain that having a Down's baby is not right. That it is not necessarily selfish to terminate. Deciding to press on and have the baby despite knowing ahead of time conveys an air of beatitude onto the parents who want to have the child anyway, but for whose benefit? Probably not for their own, probably not for the unborn child's, almost certainly not for society ...

While the extract above paints a picture of calm resolve, we were constantly weighing up counter arguments. We knew that some parents had Down's children and were thankful for the experience. One couple had just written a book about it. Their situation was quite different from ours in that Jamie was their second child and they had not known before birth that he had Down's. Still, the issues they raised were provocative:

> In a time of the zero-sum game and fiscal austerity, will human life soon be judged on the basis of a cost-benefit analysis? Do we insist that citizens make a return on the investment we have made? Do we label citizens productive and unproductive? In a society that combines eugenics with enforced fiscal austerity, will parents who choose to bear a disabled child be seen as selfish or deluded? Will we have the right to measure how much of the national health budget Jamie Berube gets to eat? (Berube, 1996, p. 117)

Time passed and through intense communication with each other and with our friends and relatives our misery seemed to stabilise.

November 10, 1996

We are becoming at peace with ourselves in that we don't feel capable or desirous of bringing a Down's syndrome baby into this world. This is testing all that I believe in as far as whether we are born with a soul. Of course, as a budding social constructionist/existentialist, it doesn't make sense to me to think of this foetus in terms of a fully fledged human being who has made choices and exercised his or her potential. I can fault myself or us for cutting off its potential. I do often. I wonder if I have this right. But I also wonder if we as humans have the right to decide whether we want to have children, when we want to have them and how many we want to have ...

Throughout I felt a nagging sense that to believe I had the right to end this life was bad faith, but that it was also bad faith to pretend as if this was not a choice that we had to make. I was also terrified of the damage that termination could inflict on Conner, on our future fertility and on our marriage generally. I struggled throughout not to delude myself.

November 10, 1996

There is still the terror of the termination – the inevitable turning of Conner's body into a killing field. Yes, in some ways it sounds and feels like murder and we have to face up to that. We are not killing an autonomous, fully functioning human being, but we are preventing it from realising its full potential, however limited that might be. It feels terrible. We sometimes feel selfish and cowardly. Mostly though we feel realistic and forgive ourselves ...

We have taken this decision and we have to live with the consequences of it, regardless of whether anything is actually carried out, whether we need to terminate or not. We have chosen our lives and our future lives over the uncertain, and possibly greatly impaired and painful life of an unborn child. I am still trying to work out how this can be reconciled with my belief in people and my belief in goodness, and my wobbly belief in God.

Then there is what felt to me a significant shift, where I began tentatively to derive meaning from the experience. That in itself was a source of relief. It evoked Nietzsche's axiom: 'He who has a *why* can live with almost any *how*.'

November 13, 1996

... in quiet moments I reflect on the value of life. I have been saying to Conner that we decide to have children because of the richness and joy they bring. It is our decision. When we actually bring them into the world, we owe them everything. They did not choose to be born, nor did they choose not to be born. I'm finding the whole philosophical/theological issue very confusing and challenging to my intellectual convictions, which are hitting against some of my more superstitious beliefs and those I have taken on from society. My own belief is that bringing a Down's baby into the world does very little good for anyone; not for us, for the child, who would struggle and fight an impossible battle to be 'normal' and to keep up with everyone else. The frustration and depression would be huge for the child, and I think for us. Sure, we would learn to live with it, to extract moments of joy, but essentially we would be turned inward as a family to support one child with very limited potential to make positive contributions to the world.

But do we have the right to play God? Where will all this end? With designer babies, with sperm and egg tested before conception? We are moving further and further away from our affinities with the rest of the animal world for whom 'decisions' like these are unthinkable. We are rapidly advancing in medicine without the similar advances in ethics and social wisdom.

We decide to terminate out of love for ourselves. It is so hard to imagine doing it out of love for our child ... It comes back, however, to a philosophical issue – what is our responsibility in this life? Is this our decision to make? Are any decisions 'ours to make'? We are faced with choices everyday. This is one huge choice. It will cause great sorrow, but ultimately it is the least bad one to take.

As the date for our results arrived I felt a sense of calm.

November 18, 1996 2:35 PM

I pray for this foetus's health. I know that it is already very much 'our baby' in our hopes, dreams and expectations. I know it is bad faith to think otherwise.

We are both excited and also scared. The waiting seems to be over. We need to learn to have faith, we need to experience having faith. This has pointed out acutely our lack of spiritual development, in many ways we are quite handicapped in this area; it is we with the problem as much as our child. But we are filled with hope and optimism for our life together being good and rewarding, if not now, then eventually.

November 18, 1996 6:33 PM

Got the results. They came out fine: 'no chromosomal abnormalities detected'. Deep sighs, then some tears followed by relief and joy. We're very happy and thankful. We feel that we can finally put our minds to the task at hand – getting ready to foster new life, to learn and to serve. We're very excited and dedicated to learning from this experience. Thanks be to God.

So there is a happy ending of sorts. And yet as I write this there are three more months before our baby is 'due' to arrive and we don't know what that arrival will bring. We have indeed learned some lessons from this period – particularly the value of facing up in as good faith as possible to the decisions we have to make and inevitably to accept that many things in life are out of our hands. Even in the depths of the experience I felt incredibly alive. I think this was because I tried to be fully and authentically engaged with the world and its possibilities. Above all, I have learned from this how quickly and irrevocably our children become metaphors for ourselves! To contemplate the termination of our much-desired offspring felt at times like self-annihilation. I imagine that feeling was even more intense for Conner. Death pervaded the whole period amid the life we were both hoping for. I am aware, ex-post facto, that a kind of death is implicit no matter what decision we made. Having a child feels like the death of my own childhood. Not having one feels like the death of my future.

There is also a sense that something did indeed die in the process of all this testing and torment, namely a sense of innocence and purity about the whole miracle of birth. We have to face up to the fact that we planned to end our baby's life if he or she had a chromosomal abnormality. Will this turmoil have negative repercussions on our child? What does this say about our acceptance of his/her inevitable imperfections and of our own 'abnormalities'? Will we explain to our child someday the decision we took?

There are no final insights, no absolute answers, only further questions. Yet there is a sense that answers will emerge, highly imperfect and ephemeral ones to be sure. This seems to me an inevitable truth of existential self-analysis and indeed all of Being. As our child's birth nears, it is increasingly clear to me that the extreme emotions felt during this experience are but a hint of what being a parent is all about. I imagine I will turn again and again to the words of William Blake:

> Man was made for Joy and Woe;
> And when this we rightly know
> Thro' the World we safely go.
> Joy & Woe are woven fine,
> A clothing for the soul divine;
> Under every grief and pine
> Runs a joy with silken twine.

Postscript

On April 17, 1997 Oscar-Nichols Middelmann Whitney was born, bursting of good health, after a gruelling 36-hour labour ending in an emergency Caesarean section. Some four years later his parents want to have another baby and are discussing once again how to handle prenatal testing.

References

Berube, M. (1996) *Life As We Know It*. New York: Pantheon.

Frankl, V. (1946/84) *Man's Search for Meaning*. New York: Washington Square Press.

Green, R. (1992) 'Letter to a Genetic Counselor', *Journal of Genetic Counseling*, 1: 55–70.

Heidegger, M. (1927) *Being and Time*, trans. J. Macquarrie and E. Robinson. New York: Harper & Row (1962).

Ilse, S. (1993) *Precious Lives, Painful Choices*. Maple Plain, Minnesota: Wintergreen Press.

Newton, R. (1992) *Down's Syndrome*. London: Little, Brown & Co.

Sartre, J.P. (1943/91) *Being and Nothingness: An Essay on Phenomenological Ontology*, trans. H. Barnes. London: Routledge.

Sinason, V. (1993) *Understanding Your Handicapped Child*. London: The Tavistock Clinic.

Spinelli, E. (1994) *Demystifying Therapy*. London: Constable.

CHAPTER 15

Parenting an infant with a birth defect – the regulation of self-esteem[1]

DORIAN MINTZER, HEIDELISE ALS, EDWARD Z. TRONICK AND
T. BERRY BRAZELTON

This paper examines how five families experienced parenting infants with birth defects. The concept of assault to the parent's self-esteem or narcissistic injury (e.g. Bibring, 1953; Kohut, 1966) is the theoretical framework used to understand the intrapsychic and the external, reality-based aspects of parental reactions. These were influenced by a complex interplay of factors: the severity and correctability of the defect, how they were told about it, and the nature of the medical procedures required; previous expectations for the child and their view of themselves as parents; their prior means of coping with stress, the nature of the marital relationship and their own experiences in the parent–child relationship; the infant's temperament and capacity to interact and be organized; the uncertainty about the short- and long-term, implications of the defect and its impact on the child and on the family, and the role of environmental supports.

While the experience of giving birth to an infant with a defect is similar to other painful experiences, the naturally heightened wish for renewal and self-fulfillment inherent in the expectation of a new life creates special issues. As Anna Freud (1960) said:

> There is no reason to expect that mothers [parents] are automatically equipped for
> the specialized task of bringing up such a child in a manner calculated to minimize

[1] This paper first appeared in *Psychoanalytic Study of the Child*, 39: 561–89 (PSC), Reprinted here by kind permission of Yale University Press. Based on a study submitted in partial fulfillment of the D.W.S./Ph.D. degree, Smith College School for Social Work (Greenberg (Mintzer), 1979). The work was supported by Grant 3312 from the W. T. Grant Foundation and was conducted in part at the facilities of the Mental Retardation Center of the Children's Hospital Medical Center, Boston, Mass. Special thanks go to the families who allowed us to observe and to view them so closely; to Nancy Kozak Meyer, Lois Barclay Murphy, and Shelly S. Ehrlich.

the handicap. On the contrary, the mother's natural hurt and despair concerning her child's defect, the injury to her pride and pleasure in her child will all work toward estranging her from the task of mothering, thereby increasing the initial damage. There is here a specially difficult therapeutic task with the mothers which has been tackled in few places ... There are a whole host of emergency situations of this kind in which the normal mother will feel helpless without guidance. (p. 296)

The specific aim of this study was to observe the adaptational process unfold and to gain a better understanding of how the parents handled their own feelings, especially their self-esteem, and developed pleasure in their infant so they could provide the necessary parenting. A further aim was to learn about the specific kinds of help needed by these families.

Our material was collected by the following means: home visits to obtain clinical information about each parents' history and the ongoing experiences of parenting their infant (Greenberg (Mintzer), 1979b), assessment of the strengths and weaknesses of the neonate using the Neonatal Behavioral Assessment Exam (Brazelton, 1973), observation of the face-to-face interactions between mother, father, and infant to assess the level of reciprocity achieved (Als et al., 1980a; 1980b), and observation of the parents as they watched and discussed the videotaped playbacks of the interactions to note how the parents utilized the research approach and the videotaped interactions.

The families were followed over a period of two years.[2] Home visits began in the first month of the infant's life and continued monthly during the infant's first six months and then bimonthly. Laboratory sessions were held monthly during the infant's first six months and then at bimonthly intervals during the next six months with follow-up visits at 18 and 24 months.

The study families

The parents were all in their thirties and moderately well-educated. All of the infants were first-born and had visible birth defects, which represented a scale of severity, the most severe being family A. The A, B and C families experienced periods of severe to moderate disequilibrium; the D and E families felt injury, but disequilibrium was less severe.

---

[2] The first author has continued with yearly follow-up home visits to learn more about the ongoing adaptational process.

The A family

Al was born with multiple anomalies: cleft lip and palate, hypospadias and a patent ductus arteriosus.[3] He was immediately placed in the hospital special care nursery for observation and discharged two days after his mother.

Al was a cuddly baby with large, compelling eyes, but his facial disfigurement was obvious and painful to his parents. Owing to his anomalies, he had early special feeding needs. He was an active infant, difficult to calm and modulate because of breathing difficulties. He required eight surgical interventions during his first two years, most to repair the lip and palate. After each hospitalization of 6–10 days, Al had to wear a 'butterfly jacket' for four weeks to restrain his arms so he would not pick at the stitches. At age six months Al developed heart congestion because of a patent ductus following restorative surgery for his palate. A few weeks later he underwent open heart surgery. The first of two procedures to correct the hypospadias occurred when Al was 26 months old.

Mrs. A was an overweight, tired-looking woman who worked until the month before Al's birth and did not plan to return to work during Al's early years. She had no prior experiences with crises or loss. Mr. A had nieces with correctable birth defects. Conception was unplanned but wanted and occurred four months after the marriage, with each parent hoping for a daughter. Mrs. A had looked forward to natural childbirth and breast-feeding and was disappointed when she learned that a Caesarean section was required due to cephalopelvic disproportion. She chose delivery on her husband's birthday in order 'to give him a special gift'.

Mr. A learned first about Al's anomalies. He felt his prior wish for a daughter was suddenly unimportant; his concern was for his son to be healthy. He set up a fund to provide for Al's future orthodontal costs; he told his family and friends about Al, giving them the option to visit if they were comfortable. His work and role as provider for his wife and Al helped maintain his self-esteem.

Mr. A and the doctor decided it would be helpful for Mrs. A to be sedated prior to learning about Al. She felt like a failure – not only had she not produced a daughter for her husband, but her son was defective. She initially did not want to look at or hold Al; she cried and felt afraid and ashamed. Despite her protests she did hold him, with the assurance from her husband that Al was a cuddly baby. Mrs. A actively tried to find ways to master her emotions. In spite of her intense reluctance to hold Al and disappointment that she could not breast-feed, she wanted to learn to feed and care for him.

---

[3] Malformed penis and hole in the heart [Ed.].

Her attachment to Al during this early period reflected a negative and burdened bond; both she and Al were devalued. She needed to cover Al's mouth, hide him, and withdraw in order to avoid further injury. Looking tired and disheveled, she blamed Al for her looks. She was angry, guilty, helpless, and depressed. For the lab visits, she dressed Al in pajamas rather than in street outfits. She avoided taking him out; when she had to, she would wrap his face or shield him from view to conceal his defect. She said she felt trapped: she saw herself as too dependent financially on her husband, and Al too was dependent on her. She told us that she would have been content with parenting a dog, that being more pleasurable. Although she had not planned to return to work, she talked about getting a job as a waitress rather than one in her previous managerial position.

During Al's first three months, Mrs. A was hyperattentive to his needs and cues and worried that she was overprotecting him. For example, at night she would anticipate his awakening and be listening for him. She slept in his room, picking him up at the faintest sound, yet viewed herself as dangerous and 'bad'. She felt they needed Mr. A to protect them both. She lacked confidence and competence in feeding Al, feared bathing him when her husband was not at home, and generally sensed that she and Al were happier when Mr. A was present. She said, 'I'm afraid I'll drown him.' Since feeding Al was traumatic, she often waited until Al was very hungry, which further upset him and made feeding even more difficult. At these times she called him 'Monster' and 'The Rat', reflecting her feelings that he represented the monstrous and bad parts of herself and perhaps also the monstrous intensity of her hurt.

During this period when face-to-face interactions were difficult for Mrs. A, she often imitated Al's expressions, distorting her mouth into a grimace-like expression. We found it difficult to know whether this was a normal parenting attempt to mirror and empathize with Al and/or a reaction of hostility. As her anxiety mounted, she tried to use toys as a buffer; with objects, she could distract herself from his face, but often overloaded him by stimulating him more than he could tolerate. When her goal was to help him to be modulated and quiet, she could do this if she avoided looking at his face. She realized that a play situation typically became counterproductive. Al's breathing would grow heavier, he would avert his gaze and begin to gag; Mrs. A was thus denied the satisfaction of being able to play pleasurably with her baby.

Because of breathing difficulty, Al's body was generally tense. Both mother and baby were caught in a bind, since the mother could not find ways to calm him without breaking the surgeon's orders. Although instructed not to hold Al's face against her body, she often assumed this position, relieving his discomfort by holding him face down over her knees and gently patting his back. At times when he was distressed, she would put her fingers into his mouth and jokingly say, 'We'd better not tell the meany surgeon.' This action, although against the surgeon's advice, calmed Al. Mrs. A reported that she felt sorry for Al. These coping responses showed Mrs. A's despair and confusion when Al was upset, since he was denied the normal avenues for self-calming, such as sucking a pacifier, his own hands or her breast. An example of her ambivalence, as well as of her coping attempts, is that she tried to comfort him and to help him organize, but often did so in aggressive or intrusive ways that interfered with her goal. She would calm him by holding him toward her chest, but then, apparently feeling guilty, she would suddenly shift his position, disrupting him; his breathing would again build up and lead to gagging.

Mrs. A's changing nicknames for Al were a clear indication of her emerging positive feelings and her developing capacity to feel pleasure in him. She began to enjoy him at a distance or when not confronted by his face. For example, by the end of Al's second month, she called him 'Little Pumpkin' when she was not directly interacting with him, e.g. when her husband was holding him or when he slept.

It was during Al's third month that Mrs. A was able spontaneously to reflect back on the birth and discovery of Al's defects. She told us that she had been 'pulled in' by his cuddliness and helplessness and felt relieved that he was not a 'monster'. She acknowledged her initial anger, upset, and terror at Al's looks, her sense of failure at not having produced a daughter for her husband, and the humiliation she had felt when she had been on a postpartum floor with mothers who gave birth to normal babies. Her depression and guilt were exacerbated by learning that she was the genetic carrier of the cleft lip and palate defect. Her capacity to share these thoughts suggested that, over and beyond the acute injury to her self-esteem, she was beginning to give up the child she had wished for but did not have. She said, 'There's no time to even think about the C-section, no time to daydream. He's our baby, and we have to find ways to take care of him.' After verbally acknowledging her anger and sense of failure, she behaved less aggressively and intrusively with Al. Her acute anxiety lessened. She became more confident in her capacity to read Al's cues and responded more competently. Although her self-esteem began to improve, it was still vulnerable to Al's periods of disorganization. Mrs. A cared for him appropriately but often still did so ambivalently. For example, she would use endearing terms, but looked and sounded angry and frustrated.

After the first surgery, both parents felt disappointed that Al looked worse with only one side of his lip repaired. Mr. A withdrew from the evening feedings, perhaps needing time to distance himself from Al while struggling with his own feelings. Although Mrs. A reported this shift with some resentment, she also sounded proud, since the change occurred when she felt more competent.

During Al's first $5^1/_2$ months, his parents alternated in their reactions to authority figures. At times, they relied on the doctors and the sense of optimism they conveyed about the outcome of surgery. At other times, Mr. and Mrs. A displaced anger, regarding the doctors as powerful people who performed tests, withheld information, and doubted the parents' competence. During Al's early surgical repairs, the hospital staff and routine inadvertently supported Mrs. A's confusion, regression, withdrawal, avoidance, and self-blame. The surgeon gave the parents a list of 'dos and don'ts' to facilitate the healing process. Mrs. A said that, if anything went wrong, it would be her fault, since at times she 'violated the rules in order to calm Al'. Although the surgeon 'suggested' that the parents stay away during the surgical repairs so that Al would not get upset, cry, and impair the initial healing, he was placed in the hospital's parent-participation unit. When Mrs. A complied with the surgeon's 'suggestion', she felt that the nurses thought her to be a 'bad' mother since she did not feed Al or stay overnight with him during the hospitalizations of his first year.

Once Al's upper lip was repaired at $5^1/_2$ months, both Mr. and Mrs. A reported experiencing more pleasure in being his parents. Although his mouth still looked disfigured to a stranger, his parents were desensitized. They had accomplished one of their goals: Al was 'all fixed up' by Christmas. Mrs. A began to take him out, no longer covering his face to keep it from view, and dressed him in street clothes rather than pajamas. She found feeding less traumatic and did not fear hurting him while bathing him. At times she was able to let him cry, allowing separation and letting him learn to deal with frustration. This shift reflected that she worried less about others viewing her as bad if he cried. Although Mrs. A still looked tired, depressed, and had gained some weight, she began to take pride in her appearance. The competition with Mr. A over who was the better parent began to decrease. Mrs. A left Al with his father for a weekend. She was proud that they had managed well and that Al had missed his mother and was a 'mama's boy'. We understood these changes to mean that Mrs. A was achieving a new equilibrium of her self-esteem.

Mrs. A's emerging ability to view Al as separate from and not just a negative extension of herself was reinforced by the visual feedback from seeing herself and Al on the videotapes. By age six months, he looked happier, fed better, and began to use a walker. He was more assertive and let his mother know that he was independent but still needed her. Responding to his need enhanced her image of being a good mother.

Mother–infant interactions improved significantly after the second surgical repair. Mrs. A felt more affection for Al and became more available emotionally, working hard to respond to him. On many occasions she acted appropriately, although she continued to do some things which he could do for himself. She subjected Al to fewer abrupt position shifts and usually responded confidently to his cues, but she was frustrated and anxious when she did not know what he wanted. She regarded his activity, curiosity, and alertness as his individual, positive personality characteristics. She viewed him as a strong-willed child and expressed the hope that these qualities would help him cope with his problems. She also began to call him 'Scooter' in an endearing way. Both mother and son visibly enjoyed their interactions, and Al's behavior and expressions showed that he sensed he had an impact on his environment. He had progressed to a stage in which he gave clearer cues, but he continued to lag in some developmental areas.

Mr. and Mrs. A experienced a new crisis at six months when Al developed heart congestion necessitating open-heart surgery. They reported depression, helplessness, disbelief, and a 'what next?' attitude. They attempted to minimize the seriousness of surgery but appeared exhausted and worried. They said they realized how important Al had become to them.

During the open-heart surgery, unlike the time of the previous cosmetic-restorative procedures, both parents stayed at the hospital. Al was placed in the intensive care unit, which proved helpful for Mrs. A. Visiting was limited, and the nurses provided the caretaking. Mrs. A felt like a 'good mother'. During this second crisis, her self-esteem did not plummet as it had at Al's birth. She was sad, but her sadness was for Al and his situation. After he had fully recovered, Mrs. A was able to express both sides of her ambivalence. She commented to Al: 'You're a good baby, we'll keep you, but some days, I swear, I'd like to put you out in the snow.' Such ambivalence is experienced by all parents.

When Al was nine months old, Mrs. A no longer displaced rage onto the medical staff but instead talked about her anger appropriately. To defend against the assault to their self-esteem, Al's parents mentally turned his genetic defect into a form of 'specialness' when they learned that he was the first of a few children recognized as having a similar genetic history and that he would be written up in a medical journal. At 11 months, they had reached a level of reorganization that helped to integrate Al into the family so that everyone's needs could be addressed. They arranged for a weekly baby-sitter so they could go out together, and they bought their first home.

At the 12-month visit, Al was alert and sociable, although he had few vocalizations and poor motor coordination. The research team considered referring the family to an infant-stimulation program, but did not. Mrs. A was looking forward to the family's new house and a period of time without hospitalization for Al.

At the 20-month follow-up, Mrs. A no longer felt acutely self-pitying and devalued, but she still looked depressed and tired. Al's palate surgery was completed, the family had moved into their new home, and Mr. A had a new job with a promotion and salary increase. Mrs. A was enjoying her role as homemaker, interior decorator, and mother. She began to talk about returning to work part-time when Al could join a nursery program. She had dropped the idea of being a waitress; now she spoke about getting a job in her field of interest which would not only be stimulating but also increase her sense of competence.

At this follow-up, Al was walking and running with marked awkwardness; he seemed delayed in his social and emotional development, functioning at about a one-year level with limited vocalizations. Although he appeared happy, he was shy in his approach to people and objects, tending to rely on his mother to reach for objects rather than asserting himself. Mrs. A complied and did not try to help Al accomplish the tasks more independently; some symbiotic attachment between mother and child continued.

After this follow-up visit, we referred Al to an infant-stimulation program. We were concerned about the child's development and thought that he would benefit from interacting with other children. We also thought that his parents would benefit from involvement with the staff and with other parents. They accepted the referral and were enthusiastic about the program, wanting to provide Al with as many helpful opportunities as possible. Previously, Mrs. A had not wanted to be in contact with families of children with cleft lip and palate; now she could welcome being involved with the program and was not threatened by the Association for Retarded Children sponsoring it.

Both parents knew that Al had some developmental lags, and they stressed the numerous medical insults in his short life. Both hoped that his development would proceed with most of the surgery behind him. Neither talked about the possibility of retardation. Mr. A, however, was able to evaluate Al's functioning in comparison to younger neighborhood children, which upset Mrs. A. They reported that they had learned to cope with the events of Al's life and would continue to respond to each situation as it came up. Both expressed a hope that Al would find ways to compensate and to have some pleasure in his life.

The B family

Bonnie was born with congenital cataracts in each eye. She was a pretty, cuddly infant: active, excitable, yet robust. She did not focus visually and did not make eye contact with her parents. When excited or upset, she could calm with a pacifier, or when held by Mr. B. The parents had no way of knowing whether her eyes were developed and what kind of sight she would have.

The parents appeared to be nice, conventionally dressed people who looked a little older than their years. Mrs. B had worked until a week prior to

Bonnie's birth and took a leave of absence, assuming she would not return to work during Bonnie's first few years. Conception was planned, wanted, and occurred after seven years of marriage. Mrs. B wanted a daughter and Mr. B preferred a son. Mrs. B was looking forward to natural childbirth. Bonnie was born by Caesarean section after a long, difficult labor. The parents initially thought they had a healthy little girl, but then learned on her second day that Bonnie had severe cataracts. They felt shocked, angry, helpless, and hopeless – 'shot down'. They showed magical thinking, confusion, disbelief, and self-blame. For example, Mrs. B immediately envisioned Bonnie as a blind baby but was afraid to ask the doctor questions lest verbalizing this image would make it come true. Both blamed themselves because of their own poor vision, and they wondered if Mrs. B had done anything during the pregnancy to cause the problem.

The pediatrician told the Bs that Bonnie would need some special attention. Mrs. B wanted to care for Bonnie right away, thinking that, since her baby could not see, she would know people by their touch. This wish to provide mothering and to attach was thwarted because of a postpartum infection that separated her and Bonnie for seven days. Her disequilibrium was reflected in her belief that Bonnie immediately developed a preference for Mr. B and would not like her. When she was finally allowed to touch Bonnie, she was afraid to hold or feed her. She perceived herself as defective and was afraid that she would interact inappropriately with her infant. She regarded Bonnie's crying as an affirmation of her own inadequacy as a mother rather than as a reflection of Bonnie's sensitive state organization. When the Bs consulted two eye doctors and received conflicting recommendations about the timing and number of surgical procedures that Bonnie required, they turned with confusion to their pediatrician for help in the decision. Bonnie underwent a surgical procedure on her right eye when she was $2^1/_2$ months old. Both parents became increasingly anxious as the operation date approached and decided to delay the surgery for a week so she could be baptized beforehand.

After the first surgery on her right eye, the parents were immediately told she would probably have vision in that eye. Two weeks later, the cornea clouded over; the parents learned she would need additional surgery on the same eye. The second procedure, six weeks later, was followed by three weeks with an eye patch. They then learned that this eye had not developed properly prior to birth and that she had no vision in that eye. The parents' hopes and fears kept vacillating. The surgeon was optimistic about her left eye since it was larger. Mr. and Mrs. B felt betrayed by the surgeon and began to lose trust in him. They wondered if he was leading them on with 'false hopes'. Their anxieties and fears persisted until the surgery on her left eye. During Bonnie's first eight months, her parents did not know if they would have a visually impaired or a totally blind child.

Mrs. B was depressed throughout this period. She chose to withdraw by resuming her job prior to when she had planned to do so. This apparently helped her to regain a sense of competence and self-esteem. She needed literally to separate from her infant in order to prove that she herself was not defective. Mrs. B was unable to acknowledge her painful and angry feelings and maintained a brittle, defensive structure of denial and avoidance. As she regained her self-esteem via her professional competence and her ability to arrange for the baby's daily care in her absence, she found some pleasurable ways to interact directly with her infant. For example, she played a game of touching and jostling with Bonnie which had both mother and child smiling and laughing; thus she achieved her wish for a smiling little girl. She gradually arranged her work schedule so that she was flexibly available to take Bonnie to the doctor when needed, which further helped her to feel like a good mother. Mrs. B was overly concerned about her own and her infant's appearance during the period of disequilibrium. She always dressed Bonnie in pretty, delicate outfits, taking pride when people commented on Bonnie's cuteness. Despite her disability, Bonnie progressed developmentally in other areas.

When Mrs. B was emotionally unavailable, Mr. B assumed the primary caretaking role during Bonnie's early months, although he was extremely depressed. He had not planned to provide caretaking for Bonnie, since he viewed the early parenting care as the 'mother's role'. Intermittently, Mrs. B doubted her own competence and at times felt competitive with Mr. B, convincing herself that Bonnie preferred Mr. B since he had provided the early feedings. Mr. B welcomed and supported his wife's increasing attempts to become Bonnie's caretaker, but he also seemed to compete by subtly undermining her, asserting that he was more sensitive to Bonnie than she was. Yet, in the course of restoring her own internal equilibrium, Mrs. B's feelings of competence as a parent grew. The parenting roles gradually shifted, with Mrs. B providing more of the caretaking functions, though they maintained some shared parenting tasks.

When Bonnie was eight months old, just prior to her third surgical procedure, and before they learned that Bonnie would have vision in one eye, Mrs. B began to feel that Bonnie needed her and that she was capable of being Bonnie's mother even if Bonnie were a blind child. Mrs. B decided that, regardless of the outcome of the surgery, she would take a leave of absence from work so that she and Bonnie could 'get to know each other'.

After the cataract on the left eye was removed, the parents were relieved to learn that Bonnie would have some vision in that eye. They wished for dramatic changes in her eyesight after the operation and were disappointed that this did not happen, but reminded themselves that Bonnie's use of vision would develop gradually. Mrs. B took three months off from work to spend time with her daughter during the transition from sightlessness to vision. By age two years Bonnie's motor, verbal, and social skills were well developed, and she clearly knew that she could influence events. She was well-modulated, organized, and calm. She connected words with wishes and could use sentences. She evidenced object constancy, had a good memory, and distinguished circumstances and events in her environment. When Bonnie is older she will undergo surgery to remove the cloudy covering on her right eye so it will look less abnormal.

The C family

Charles was born four weeks prematurely, with three fingers on each hand fused, borderline small for gestational age, and suffering respiratory distress. He appeared to be a very temperamental, labile baby: his movements were jerky; he was wide-eyed, easily overstimulated, and disorganized, similar to many small-for-date full-term infants (Als et al., 1976). He needed continuous help with state modulation and organization. He had four operations to separate his fingers between 14 and 21 months.

Mrs. C, a slim, attractive woman who took pride in her appearance, had planned to work throughout her pregnancy, to take a two-month leave of absence after the baby's birth, and then to return to work. Both Mr. and Mrs. C showed a mixture of easy verbalizations and some denial. While they could talk about previous losses, they could not make connections to current experiences.

Conception was planned and was wanted by Mrs. C, but Mr. C was ambivalent. Each preferred a daughter. Mrs. C had looked forward to natural childbirth and breast-feeding, but was hospitalized in her sixth month of pregnancy because of toxemia. For this reason, she not only missed the pre-birth parents' sessions but did not have the entire pregnancy to prepare psychologically for the baby.

Mrs. C experienced a narcissistic disequilibrium characterized by feelings of guilt, worthlessness, helplessness, hopelessness, and self-blame. She was emotionally labile, either bursting into tears or laughing anxiously. Mr. C said he was more upset about Charles's prematurity than about the hand defect. Although he reported some sadness about the defect, he either denied or minimized concern by stressing that it could be surgically repaired. His sense of shame, however, was evidenced in his wish to put gloves on Charles's hands so his fused fingers would not be noticed.

Mrs. C decided not to breast-feed Charles since she felt like a failure from the complications of pregnancy, premature birth, and her infant's minor birth defect. Her low self-esteem and anxiety interfered with her early attachment to Charles. She was gentle, empathetic, and patient with him, but she did not recognize her own competence as evidenced in her negative comments about herself. She was not confident that she knew what he wanted or how to help him. She blamed herself for his behaviors and responses, indicating aspects of a negative symbiosis (Lax, 1971). For example, commenting that Charles had trouble with his bowel movements, she said: 'It must be my problem, I keep wanting him to do more.' She also said: 'He smiles before he opens his eyes and sees what a mess I am,' and 'When he's alert and smiles, it's as if he's apologizing.'

Gradually, Mrs. C found ways to interact with Charles and to enjoy him during the brief periods when he was awake and alert. Eventually, she was able to help him to extend the awake and alert periods and to reciprocate in his play. Charles worked hard to engage his mother with smiling, tongue motions, a wide range of vocalizations, eye contact, and cycling of his feet and hands. These behaviors helped to elicit Mrs. C's maternal feelings. Charles tolerated more direct touching and bouncing from his father and would smile broadly, which brought pleasure to Mr. C and fostered his attachment to his son.

Mrs. C took pride in her own and in her infant's appearance and did not regress to withdrawal or avoidance as much as Mrs. A and Mrs. B. Unlike these two mothers, she was able to acknowledge and tolerate her sense of failure and disappointment and could ask for help. This may reflect her somewhat higher level of intactness, but it may also have been influenced by her infant's comparatively minor defect which did not interfere with pleasurable feeding or with face-to-face or eye-to-eye contact and required no surgery during his first year. In general, after the initial shock and upset, the disequilibrium of the first three months seemed related primarily to Charles's prematurity and his subsequent neurological immaturity which caused his highly sensitive state organization and temperament, and secondarily to his birth defect. It was during his fourth month, by which time he had compensated fairly well for his prematurity, that his parents began to focus on his fused fingers. Their sense of injury and disappointment were retriggered at this time.

Similar to the B family, the Cs received conflicting recommendations regarding the timing and number of surgical procedures. They felt confused and worried about making the right decision. Mr. C said: 'The birth defect was predetermined, it happened, we had to adjust. Now it's up to us to decide what type of procedure Charles should undergo.' Charles was hospitalized only during the first procedure to separate his fingers. At that time his parents alternated being with him in the hospital. At the parents' request the other surgical procedures were done on an outpatient basis. They felt the additional hospitalizations would be too disruptive for Charles and preferred to provide his care at home. After each surgical intervention Charles had his hands bandaged during the healing process. At age two years Charles had full use of his hands, but his fingers looked abnormal. He was a very active, alert, and engaging child who was functioning within normal developmental limits but with some delay in his speech. He needed a good deal of organizing and structure from his environment because of his sensitive temperament.

The D and E families

Dan was born with a hemangioma[4] on his lip, a lump on his neck, and had large, low-set ears and wide-set eyes. He required no surgery. He was a very calm and well-organized infant with an intense gaze, engaging smile, and vigorous suck.

Ms. D was a large-boned woman who was quiet and somewhat aloof. Mr. D was a small-framed, quiet, and shy man. They had lived together for $4^1/_2$ years but were not married. Conception was unplanned but wanted. Ms. D was looking forward to natural childbirth and breast-feeding her infant. A Caesarean section was performed after a long, difficult labor. Although the mother was isolated from Dan for his first three days because of a post-delivery infection, she was able to breast-feed. She had planned to return to work but chose to stay home.

The E family's infant, Eve, was born with an absent right ear, diagnosed as congenital atresia. At three months, X-ray showed that Eve had an eardrum and 75 percent hearing in that ear. The parents decided not to submit her to surgical reconstruction of the ear canal because of the risks and because she had compensated well for the hearing loss. The plan is to reconstruct an external earlobe when she is older.

The pregnancy was unplanned, and both parents felt ambivalent about it. Mr. E was born and raised in another country, and he and Mrs. E differed in their expectations of child-rearing practices. Moreover, Mrs. E had just lost her job, and Mr. E was unemployed. Each parent preferred a son to carry on the family name. By the end of the pregnancy Mrs. E was looking forward to being a mother and hoped to have natural childbirth. The infant's delivery was uncomplicated, although Mrs. E had had an infection during her last trimester and worried that the antibiotics might hurt the baby.

Eve was a calm, well-organized infant who had a bright, alert, intense gaze, and a vigorous suck. Early on she would engage others with her smile and gaze. By age two years Eve was a bright, active little girl who had compensated well for her 25 percent hearing loss.

The discovery of the infants' defect was less upsetting for Ms. D and Mrs. E. Both had rationalizations for why the defects occurred, thus protecting their self-esteem. Ms. D conceived Dan shortly after the death of a friend's

---

[4] Strawberry-like cluster of vessels. [Ed.]

baby, and she felt that her child was meant to be born and was a replacement child for her friend's dead baby (Cramer, 1976). Mrs. E was able to view her impaired sibling as a model for her own necessary adaptation. In addition, each mother had some of her pre-birth expectations met, which helped them to maintain aspects of their parental ego ideal. For example, both were able to breast-feed. They also gave birth to infants with relatively minor defects which, in spite of being visible, did not directly interfere with the infants' state regulation and facial expression, and did not inhibit their giving cues to elicit supportive responses from their parents. Furthermore, Dan and Eve were calm, well-organized infants and did not demand dramatic early parenting adjustments. Although neither Ms. D nor Mrs. E had difficulty attaching to their infants, they had to overcome initial feelings of self-doubt and assault. These mothers also had to resolve intrapsychic conflicts in order to respond to the thrust for separation from the mother–infant symbiosis toward the middle of the first year (Mahler et al., 1975).

Discussion

The tasks of parenting a child with a defect are similar to those of parenting a normal child, requiring empathy, learning the infant's cues, organizing and expanding alert periods, and supporting the infant in the gradual development of a tolerance for frustration. For Mrs. A, B and C, however, their success at parenting was initially highly problematic. Any interpretation is complicated because of the multiplicity of factors at play, real and intrapsychic. The mothers' reaction was in part caused by experiencing the infants as a negative extension of themselves, which limited the amount of energy they had to devote to the task of parenting. It was also significant that the real aspects of the defect itself and the infants' temperament, capacity to interact and be organized, and developmental progressions or lack of progress affected parental perceptions and reactions and influenced the severity of the mothers' disequilibrium and the adaptational process. These three mothers found it difficult to read and interpret their infants' cues and to trust their perceptions of their babies' capacities. These problems were less extreme for mothers D and E. A key part of the resolution was the re-establishment of self-esteem in these parents – a healing of the narcissistic injury, which often took place outside of the parent–infant interaction.

Aside from the anomaly itself, there is a real and disturbing series of events that must not be lost sight of in understanding parental adaptation and attempts at coping. For example, these parents experienced a combination of Caesarean section, premature birth, separation from the infant because of special tests, the mother's discharge from the hospital without her infant, or specific difficult caretaking needs. These events interfered in the establish-ment of a relationship with the infant as well as disrupted the intrapsychic equilibrium of the parents. The insults to the parents' sense of self were experienced by some as a blow to their self-esteem and as interferences in their attempts to restore their self-esteem (Reich, 1960; Jacobson, 1976). Learning about the defect at the time of birth is particularly stressful because of the normal disequilibrium that a first baby and the tasks of parenthood bring. Medical interventions and uncertainty about the future add even more strain.

There is also the intrapsychic assault. It is influenced not only by the wished-for infant but also by the loss of the parents' hopes and ideals. They suffer the disappointment of not realizing the wished-for relationship with their infant (Joffe and Sandler, 1965). Given the normal narcissistic invest-ment in a child, the infant is usually experienced as an extension of the self but often as a positive part unless disappointment or deviations from expec-tations occur. One of the psychological tasks of any birth is to view the infant as part of the self and partner but also as a separate person (Bibring, 1959; Bibring et al., 1961). When a child is born with a defect, this task is more diffi-cult to accomplish because the child may represent the negative or defective part of the self.

We observed parents go through three stages of reactions and adaptations to the birth defects:

1. initial sense of shock and disappointment reflecting an intensely felt injury to their sense of self-worth;
2. a period of intrapsychic disequilibrium manifested in loss of self-esteem, painful feelings, inadequacy of defenses, and, at times, inappropriate handling of the infant, and
3. restoration of the intrapsychic equilibrium manifested in renewed parental self-esteem, awareness of existing painful feelings but with adequate defenses, and more appropriate meeting of the infants' and of their own needs.

During the period of disequilibrium, the parents' capacity to parent is compromised if they view their infant as a negative part of themselves rather than as a separate person. The adaptive tasks for these parents is to identify positive aspects of the infant and to view the infant as a separate individual, rather than as a representation of their own inadequacies, to grieve the loss of their aspirations and ideals for a child and the wished-for relationship, and then, as they begin to re-establish self-esteem, to understand the special as well as the normal developmental needs of the infant and to find ways to experience pleasure in being a parent given the reality of continuing pain.

A normal infant is an active elicitor of parenting as well as of movement through the normal adaptational process (e.g. Robson, 1967; Bowlby, 1969; Brazelton and Als, 1979). The infant with an anomaly is a weak parental ally in this process. The reactions of Mrs. A and Mrs. B show that the lack or distortion of the presence of normal elicitors of maternal responses, such as the lack of smiling, feeding problems, or the lack of eye-to-eye contact, creates a situation in which the initial mother–infant attachment is at risk. These two infants demanded extra structure from their parents to be helped to stay alert and to control posture and arousal because of their visible facial defect, distortion in the giving of cues, and difficult temperament (Als, 1979; Als et al., 1980a). The infants' gagging and crying overwhelmed these mothers, exacerbating their sense of helplessness and inadequacy, especially during the period of early disequilibrium.

Unfortunately, during the period of disequilibrium, the parents are not yet good allies to their infants. Not only have they experienced a real set of insults, but there is an interaction of their own lowered self-esteem and the severity and visibility of the defect and its effects on their good feelings about themselves and their child. The mothers who experienced the most severe sense of injury and the longest period of disequilibrium suffered many disappointments in their pre-birth expectations as to the sex of the infant, mode of delivery, and manner of desired feeding. These experiences lowered their self-esteem and might have put them at risk for parenting problems even if they had had a normal infant. Sadly, they gave birth to infants with continuously visible facial defects, which made the initial communication between mother and child difficult.

Contrary to the notion that marriages break up with the birth of a child with a defect, we found that a form of balancing reciprocity for coping developed between the adult partners in all but the E family. Bonnie's birth fostered an immediate form of complementarity between Mr. and Mrs. B, a kind of turn-taking which often occurs in families so that the infant's needs are fulfilled. When one parent was emotionally unavailable, the other parent provided the caretaking. In general, one parent assumed the role of 'feeder' and the other of 'player'; these usually, but not necessarily, were patterned on the traditional mother and father roles. In the families in which both parents worked, the parenting tasks were eventually shared more evenly, an accommodation many families reach.

The birth and parenting of an infant with a defect brought most of these couples closer together over time, although periods of marital disorganization occurred when they were at a different stage of the adaptational process. The marital relationship of the Bs in particular underwent a great deal of stress. Both parents experienced their infant as a negative extension of themselves, they had stereotyped notions about parenting, and they lacked the ego strengths of flexibility and adaptability. Mrs. B could not acknowledge or tolerate her feelings of pain and had to withdraw literally in order to restore her self-esteem. Mr. B was depressed and developed hypochondriacal symptoms. He temporarily assumed a full-time maternal role until Mrs. B gradually recovered her self-esteem through her work. Lack of eye-to-eye contact and uncertainty for eight months about the limits of the infant's vision exacerbated the adaptive process. Both Mr. and Mrs. B, however, believed that they eventually emerged from the disequilibrium functioning better as a couple than they had previously.

The turning point in the restoration process of parental self-esteem was when the parents experienced their infants as separate persons and found aspects of the infants which they could identify as personal and individual. The parents' experiences with the infant, which provided feedback from the infant, helped to focus their attention on such positive qualities as compelling eyes, cuddliness, and suck, so that they could enjoy both their child and being the child's parent.

During restoration, as the positive parent–infant attachment developed, the parents began to recognize their infant's cues and were able to protect the infant, adjusting care and handling to their specific baby. This is similar to parents of children without birth defects. These parents were increasingly able to function as the auxiliary ego to help the infant learn to process external stimuli, to contain arousal, and to regulate states. Restoration took place at different times with each family. In the A and B families, there was a time lag in the development of positive attachment and mutuality with their infants, although mutuality occurred, with both parent and infant initiating the interaction. For instance, Bonnie developed specific vocal games with her mother and tactile reaching and holding games with her father. Al vigorously provided his mother with grunts and arm cycling, while with his father he used beseeching looks and cocked his head. In turn, his mother played with him in more arousing ways, while his father tended to pick him up readily and to rock and move him gently. Each infant in this study, similar to infants without defects, found ways to engage each parent successfully within the first months; these responses differed from how they interacted with strangers.

The findings support and extend prior research on the grieving process of parents with a defective child (Solnit and Stark, 1961; Olshansky, 1962; Kennedy, 1969; Johns, 1971; Drotar et al., 1975; Irvin et al., 1976). The parents had to grieve the loss of the wished-for child, for their own self that was disappointed, and for the real baby and his or her difficulties. We observed uniformly that the parents needed first to view the infant as separate and not as a negative extension of self for grief-work to occur. Mrs. A, for example, needed to regain some self-esteem, feel more confident being Al's mother, and begin to view him as separate before she could acknowledge her grief. This finding supports developmental theory that there needs to be a separation between the self and other for mourning to occur. Continued rejection, withdrawal, avoidance, or overprotection suggest that the parent is not yet experiencing the infant as a separate individual. While ongoing sadness continued, by the end of the study the parents were sad for the child and his realistic problems and not feeling mostly self-pity, suggesting some adequate resolution of the injury they sustained.

But, of course, the adaptation was not a smooth process. Throughout the two-year study each family remained concerned about the outcome of surgical procedures, future consequences of the defects, and how the parents would be able to help their child understand and adjust to the defect. When the infants failed to progress according to normal developmental rates or to attain a milestone and when medical procedures were necessary, anxiety, depression, and self-blame were retriggered in the parents. Once the initial intrapsychic balance had been restored, parents handled these anxieties with increasing adequacy and less regression; they were able to identify the patterns of their reactions and to reconstruct their previous handling of the crisis. This process allowed them to acknowledge openly their current pain and anxiety and simultaneously to recognize their developing coping strategies and energies.

Clinical signs of restoration of the equilibrium occurred in some of the following ways:

- mutual interaction patterns as described above;
- integration of the infant into the family so that each member's needs were met; for example, the mothers were able to relinquish the care of the infant to others, freeing time for the spouse or for themselves;
- an end to devaluing the parent and infant; for example, the mothers started taking better care of themselves physically, participated in activities such as travel or socializing without the children, took the infant to visit relatives, or invited grandparents or friends to come and meet the infant;
- allowed arenas for self-esteem regulation; for example, the mothers would resume their job or start an activity to enhance prestige;
- development of a clear picture of the infant as a separate individual; for example, all five sets of parents could describe their infants' strengths and difficulties with increasing specificity, identifying the defect directly and discussing its implications for them and their children.

These families utilized many adaptive maneuvers which testify to the resiliency, motivation, and energy parents have and bring to their child in the face of trauma. For example, Mr. B studied Bonnie's behavior and developed his own 'tests' of her visual acuity to assess if there were any behavioral changes after surgery. To restore their equilibrium, the parents concentrated on the normal aspects of their infant and gradually displaced their concerns from the defect. In this regard, Mr. A commented that Al, who had multiple anomalies, was also left-handed. He worried that 'the world wasn't made for left-handed people'. Most of the parents used maneuvers to protect their self-esteem, such as comparing their baby to those who were 'worse off', setting up a hierarchy of possible defects, and focusing on the competencies of other parents with similar children.

All of the families needed to find allies in the environment. In the B family, religion provided organization and support. In the B and E families, the extended family was reliably called upon for positive feedback and encouragement. At times, all the parents looked to the future, hoping to experience a sense of relief. Often, however, this action stirred up new worries about how life would progress. How would their children feel about themselves as they grew up? How would other people react to them?

The parents also set specific goals. They focused on the reality that some aspects of their infants' defects were correctable, and they attempted to face one day and one defect at a time. Time itself was part of the healing process. As the parents looked back to the initial discovery of the infant's defect, they remembered those early days as a time of crisis and felt that they had gradually grown to a more balanced emotional state.

Clinical implications of this study

The developmental research approach in combination with home visits provided a model for clinical help to parents of infants with birth defects. This model offered a form of intervention which focused on the parent–infant relationship and served to enhance the parents' self-esteem and foster their affection for and mutuality with their infants.

The self-esteem of the parents in this study was directly supported as they engaged as collaborators in the research. They entered into the process of getting to know their infant in the context of helping the research team learn how they negotiated this process, an approach which reinforced their competence. The team provided an emotional bridge for the parents by viewing infant and parents as dyad and triad; yet the team members stressed the separateness and competence of each parent and infant by discussing with the parents the infant's specific competencies as assessed with the Neonatal Behavioral Assessment Scale (Brazelton, 1973) and the videotaped parent–infant interactions (Tronick, 1982).

We found that the tools of data collection could also be used for educative and preventive purposes. Observing the administration of the Brazelton Neonatal Behavioral Assessment Scale by a supportive person helped the parents to see their infant as a separate individual whose limitations were specific. The examination highlighted the possibilities of aiding the infant to contain the effects of the defect and to bring his strengths to bear on fostering his own development.

The experimental laboratory situation of the mother's play with her infant enabled the mother to see how the infant differentiated between her and other people. The fact that the infant was repeatedly videotaped by the research team, despite his defect, altered the parents' perception of the value of their infant and themselves and encouraged them to focus on their infant without having to deny the defect. Mrs. C related that, during the early months when she felt like such a failure, it was reassuring to know that the team thought that Charles was 'quite a baby'. The laboratory experience fostered face-to-face interactions between mother and infant. All of the mothers in this study, including Mrs. A who initially provided the auxiliary ego functions only when not confronted by her infant's face, practiced the face-to-face laboratory interactions at home. This play was facilitated because the researchers helped the parents learn ways to modulate, contain, and understand certain behaviors of their infants. The increased capacity to know, comfort, and stimulate their babies helped the parents to experience pleasure rather than pain.

The home visits gave each parent opportunities to reveal his or her own history and to receive some gratification from interacting with the team members. The parents were encouraged to express their feelings, freeing them to view as allies other professionals involved with their infant. When appropriate, the concept of injury to the sense of self was explained. Mr. B in particular found this helpful and felt relief as he began to explore the intensity of his own pain, feeling of defectiveness, and sense that his infant exposed this defectiveness to the world. Marital therapy or discussions about parent–child interactions and child development were initiated, particularly as the children began to separate and differentiate from the early newborn closeness.

Overall, the research team developed a sequence of interventions:

- First, we focused on helping each parent gain specific knowledge about his child's behavioral organization and style.
- Secondly, parent–infant interactions were discussed, the team often pointing out how the infant needed and responded to the mother and had

learned to differentiate between the parents. This helped to diminish parental competition since the parents saw how they complemented rather than duplicated each other, thus providing richer opportunities for the infant.

- Thirdly, as the observational process continued, the team at times intervened in the parent–infant interactions or addressed specific issues of the parents, such as their sense of injury, need for grieving, options for themselves, or their marital relationship. At other times, child-rearing issues such as limit setting, bedtime procedures, and response to tantrums were discussed. When appropriate, we observed some periods of parent–infant disorganization without intervening, so that the parents could find their own ways to develop mastery.

An awareness of the family system was necessary to determine the kind of intervention that would be helpful, that is to assess whether parents might benefit from affective help, such as identifying and acknowledging feelings, having a cognitive framework within which to understand reactions and adaptations, and/or educative help about child development and parent–child interactions. In this sample parental adaptation included the parents' normal and reality-based sadness for the child and awareness of their own ambivalence. How the adaptational and parenting processes would have progressed for these families if the team had not been involved is impossible to answer. The research team clearly helped to prevent additional crises and helped to maximize parental attachment to the infants. The findings certainly suggest that the parents of firstborn infants with congenital anomalies need empathy and help specific both to their problems and to their own level of ego intactness. Our findings confirm that issues of parental adequacy and restoration of parental self-esteem continue over time. Clinical support, therefore, needs to be ongoing and include all aspects of the child and the family.

The clinician needs to pay special attention to the parents' injury of self-esteem to help the parents reinstitute this self-esteem, develop a healthy self-concept as a parent, and establish a positive relationship with their infant. This parent-centered and parent-infant–centered intervention should occur as early in the newborn's life as possible so that patterns of distortion do not solidify but are transitions to new levels of functioning which yield a strong, positive, and affective relationship between parent and child.

Although the infants in this study had at least partially correctable birth defects, our clinical experience shows that a similar process of injury to the parental self-image and restoration of self-esteem with good-enough and often optimal parenting occurs when the defect is more permanent and pervasive. The lifelong demands on the parents of a child with an uncorrectable defect are most similar to those described for the A family. If one assumes imbalance and injury to parental self-worth when deviations from expectations occur, then a parent–infant approach which stresses the infant's strengths, views the infant as separate, and improves the parents' self-esteem is indicated.

Summary

The birth of an infant with a defect was experienced by the parents in this study as a substantial trauma with intrapsychic and reality-based aspects. Their reactions were influenced by a complex interplay of factors: the severity and correctability of the defect, how they were told about it, and the nature of the medical procedures required, previous expectations for the child and their view of themselves as parents, their prior means of coping with stress, the nature of the marital relationship and their own experiences in the parent-child relationship, the infants' temperament and capacity to interact and be organized, the uncertainty about the short- and long-term implications of the defect and its impact on the child and the family, and the role of environmental supports. The parents experienced a series of assaults to their sense of self that affected self-esteem and interfered with the parenting process. We observed three distinct stages in parents' reactions: an initial sense of shock, disappointment, anger, and self-esteem injury, a period of painful intrapsychic disequilibrium, and the gradual restoration of intrapsychic equilibrium and robustness. During the period of disequilibrium, the parents' capacity to parent may be compromised by their viewing the infant as a negative part of their own self. The adaptive tasks for the parents are to restore their self-esteem, to view the infant as a separate individual, and to find ways to experience pleasure in being parent to this infant.

The study further suggests that the pain parents experience is not only the loss of the psychological image of the wished-for infant. They also need to grieve for their own self that was disappointed, for the loss of the satisfaction of the wish for a certain kind of relationship with the infant, and for the real baby and his or her difficulties. For effective parenting to occur, enough intrapsychic separation between the parent and infant has to have been achieved so that the infant is not viewed as the negative extension of the parent. One of the clinical implications of this study is that the parents' injured self-esteem needs to be addressed prior to the successful initiation of the process of grieving. Another implication is that such parents need help, which should be given early and be continued as an ongoing process. Feelings of sadness for the child and his or her situation are normal and expected as long as the sadness is not a continuation of devaluing the self or the child.

References

Als, H. (1979) Social interaction In *Social Interaction and Communication in Infancy*, ed. I. C. Uzgiris. San Francisco: Jossey Bass, pp. 421–41.

Als, H. (1982) The unfolding of behavioral organization in the face of a biological violation. In *Social Interchange in Infancy*, ed. E.Z. Tronick. Baltimore: University Park Press, pp. 125–60.

Als, H., Tronick, E.Z., Adamson, L. and Brazelton, T.B. (1976) The behavior of the full-term yet underweight newborn infant, *Developmental Medicine and Child Neurology*, 18: 590–602.

Als, H., Tronick, E.Z. and Brazelton, T.B. (1980a) The achievement of affective reciprocity and the beginnings of the development of autonomy, *Journal of American Child Psychiatry* 19: 22–40.

Als, H., Tronick, E.Z. and Brazelton, T.B. (1980b) Stages of early behavioral organization. In *High-Risk Infants and Children*, ed. T.M. Field, S. Goldberg, D. Stern and A. Sostek. New York: Academic Press, pp. 181–204.

Bibring, E. (1953) The meaning of depression. In *Affective Disorders*, ed. P. Greenacre. New York: International University Press, pp. 13–48.

Bibring, G.L. (1959) Some considerations of the psychological processes of pregnancy, *Psychoanalytic Study of the Child*, 14, 113–21.

Bibring, G.L., Dwyer, T.F., Huntington, P.S. and Valenstein, A.F. (1961) A study of the psychological process in pregnancy and of the earliest mother–child relationship, *Psychoanalytic Study of the Child*, 16, 7–92.

Bowlby, J. (1969) *Attachment and Loss*. New York: Basic Books.

Brazelton, T.B. (1973) Neonatal behavioral assessment scale. In *Clinics in Developmental Medicine* no. 50. London: William Heinemann.

Brazelton, T.B. and Als, H. (1979) Four early stages in the development of mother–infant interaction, *Psychoanalytic Study of the Child*, 34, 349–69.

Cramer, B. (1976) A mother's reactions to the birth of a premature baby. In *Maternal-Infant Bonding*, ed. M.H. Klauss and J.H. Kennell. St. Louis: Mosby, pp. 156–66.

Drotar, D., Baskiewitz, B.A., Irvin, N., Kennell, J.H. and Klauss, M.H. (1975) The adaptation of parents to the birth of an infant with a congenital malformation, *Pediatrics* 56: 710–17.

Freud, A. (1960) The child guidance clinic as a center of prophylaxis and enlightenment. In *The Standard Edition of the Complete Psychological Works of Sigmund Freud*, Vol. 5: 281-300.

Greenberg (Mintzer), D. (1979a) Parental reactions when an infant has a birth defect. Read at the Biennial Meetings of the Society for Research in Child Development, San Francisco.

Greenberg (Mintzer), D. (1979b) Parental reactions to an infant with a birth defect. Unpublished doctoral dissertation, Smith College School for Social Work.

Irvin, N., Kennell, J.H. and Klaus, M.H. (1976) Caring for parents of an infant with a congenital malformation. In *Maternal-Infant Bonding, ed. M.H. Klauss and J. H. Kennell, St. Louis: Mosby, pp. 167-208.*

Jacobson, E. (1976) The regulation of self-esteem. In Depression and Human Existence, ed. T. Benedek. New York: Int.U Press 169–81.

Joffe, W.G. and Sandler, J. (1965) Notes on pain, depression, and individuation. *Psychoanalytic Study of the Child*, 20: 394–424.

Johns, N. (1971) Family reactions to the birth of a child with a congenital abnormality. *Medical Journal Australia*, 1: 277–82.

Kennedy, J. (1969) Implications of grief and mourning for mothers of defective infants. Unpublished doctoral dissertation, Smith College School for Social Work.

Kohut, H. (1966) Forms and transformations of narcissism, *Jounal of the American Psychoanalytic Association*, 14: 248–72.

Lax, R. (1971) Some aspects of the interactions between mother and impaired child, *International Journal of Psychoanalysis*, 43: 339–44.

Mahler, M.S., Pine, F. and Bergman, A. (1975) *Psychological Birth of the Infant*. New York: Basic Books.

Mintzer, D. see Greenberg, D.

Olshansky, S. (1962) Chronic sorrow, *Social Casework*, 43:190–3.

Reich, A. (1960) Pathological forms of self-esteem regulation, *Psychoanalytic Study of the Child*,15: 215–32.

Robson, K. (1967) The role of eye-to-eye contact in maternal–infant attachment, *Journal of Child Psychology and Psychiatry* 8: 13–25.

Solnit, A.J. and Stark, M.H. (1961) Mourning and the birth of a defective child, *Psychoanalytic Study of the Child*, 16: 523–37.

Tronick, E.Z. (1982) *Social Interchange in Infancy*, Baltimore: University Park Press.

CHAPTER 16

Amanda: observations and reflections of a bottle-fed baby who found a breast mother[1]

FRANCIS GRIER

When she reached her first birthday, Amanda seemed to me as an observer to be a very healthy baby: full of vitality, warmly engrossed in life, able to complain and make her wishes known very directly, curious, able to struggle with difficulties, and engaged in obviously strong relationships with her mother and siblings: Benjamin aged six and Rachel aged four. It was reported that she was also very involved emotionally with her father, though I did not witness this directly.

This paper is an attempt to trace something of Amanda's development from birth to the age of 12 months from the particular perspective of regular weekly hour-long observations.

I wish to focus on two particular features immediately at the outset: first, as already sketched, Amanda's personality at 12 months had many of the characteristics one might expect from an infant who had had a good relationship with her mother from the beginning of life at the breast. But this was no foregone conclusion in this case, for Amanda was not fed at the breast: she was bottle-fed. (Of course, it goes without saying that many mothers who bottle-feed their babies do so for a huge variety of reasons and often love their babies as deeply as any breast-feeding mothers and are just as successful at communicating their love to their babies; just as the reverse side of the coin is that some breast-feeding mothers can be emotionally quite out of touch with their babies.) What was interesting in this case was that this particular

---

[1] Francis Grier wrote this paper while training at the British Institute of Psychoanalysis. It was presented to the British Psychoanalytical Society on 16.2.00 (with Joan Raphael-Leff as respondent – see Chapter 17, this volume) and later published by the *Journal of Infant Observation*. It is reprinted here with their kind permission and that of the author.

mother's personality contained quite strong features which might be inter-preted as pertaining metaphorically more to the bottle than to the breast: she could be rather cold and aloof, she thoroughly disliked mess, she could be rigidly controlling, and she had somewhat barricaded herself into her house, never opening the windows even on the hottest summer days. Yet gradually she related to her baby less constrictingly, with more spontaneity. So an underlying theme to this paper is an exploration of how the mother was helped in her own maternal development by her baby to be able to give her baby a good 'breast-experience'.

What I think this observation bears out, therefore, is not so much the importance of the experience of the breast in a concrete way – although at the same time I would not want to minimise the fact that the real breast has its own physical and emotional richness, and a child who misses out on that may be missing out on something fundamental – but I am emphasising the importance of *the integrating quality of the mother's mind* behind the breast – what Bion (1962, p. 35) refers to as alpha function.[2]

The second feature of this observation which I would like to underline was the importance of older siblings in Amanda's life. As already mentioned, she had an older brother (six) and sister (four). From the start of her life Amanda was therefore part of a whole family group. Her mother took great care to carve out a special reservation of time and attention for Amanda, but, of course, she had to continue to be available to her other two children as well. Especially since they could both be quite boisterous in character, they impacted strongly on Amanda from the start, both directly through their relationships with her and indirectly through their demands on the mother, who had constantly to be choosing how she spread her energy and attention. And, of course, Amanda in return impacted strongly on them: the family dynamics were for ever altered by her birth. As I shall show, it was particu-larly Rachel who felt most threatened by Amanda's arrival, and with good reason: at one stroke Rachel had for ever lost her place as the youngest and as the only daughter. She regarded Amanda with the utmost suspicion and ambivalence, and it became one of the mother's major tasks to manage the difficult relationship between the sisters – as I hope to illustrate.

I first met with Amanda's parents nine days after her birth. She slept peacefully throughout this encounter. Jane, the mother, described herself as 'an old hand' because this was her third baby, but both she and David, her husband, proceeded to give me accounts of what difficult infants their own mothers had found them to be. Each had been told he or she had screamed incessantly. In later meetings Jane would often talk about her mother and

---

[2] A process through which the emotional experience of sensory data becomes intelligible and is granted meaning.

underline how much she detested mess and noise. It became my impression that Jane really wanted to bring up her children differently, and this she had to learn herself. David seemed to carry for the couple a very overt sense of incapacity to be with children, whilst Jane became 'the expert'. At the very end of my observations David had gone to stay with his family abroad for two weeks, taking the older two children with him. He placed them in a nursery during the weekdays, but bravely took them out himself to the beach at the weekend. He also took his mobile phone, and telephoned his wife almost every 15 minutes to check out how to manage this unknown world of children, e.g. whether or not they could take off their sandals in the sand. Jane overtly enjoyed her role as expert, but I think she also felt rather isolated, with few external or internal figures to help her (as I will explore later in the paper) – particularly as she was also somewhat reclusive.

I learned much later that she had had a thriving career in the City which she had felt impelled to drop after the birth of her first-born. She had not planned on this: she had not expected to find infants and motherhood so overwhelmingly important to her. She had been brought up to be competent, and she now proved herself as competent at bringing up children as at stock-broking, but it seemed that she still felt somewhat insecure and unsupported in her maternal role. This was exacerbated by David's working very long hours and frequently travelling abroad, so that she was often at home alone with the children for long periods. These may have been some of the factors, I came to reflect, which helped her be quite open and welcoming to the unusual idea of having an observer of her baby regularly in her house. For such a reserved woman she treated me with great warmth and clearly regretted the ending of the observations. I think she hoped to find in me, and make unconscious use of me as, a benign figure and presence who could support her and witness the ways in which she was trying – and often succeeding – to give her children, and her third baby in particular, a precious, warm beginning of life, in which she reciprocated the infant's centredness on her by allowing the child to be right at the centre of her life. I got the impression that she felt she had been brought up in her own infancy to be the kind of girl she *ought* to be; she seemed very concerned to try to be open to her own baby's actual personality as it unfolded.

On my second visit, three days later, I was told about the birth.

It had occurred very quickly, within 2½ hours. It had been very painful for Jane. Earlier she had manically hoovered and cleaned the house, and realised that this was a biological sign that the birth was imminent. She related her state of mind: she didn't want a mess. David's mother lived just down the road, but she was anxious not to wake her in the middle of the night. Her other two babies had been born at 'decent times', at 2 and 4 p.m. In the event, she had been able to cook the family supper, put the children to bed, and only afterwards had felt the definitive twinges. She and David had gone to the hospital, and 2½ hours later it was all finished. Her own mother had then come to stay for a week, but Jane had already done all the housework, so they had sat there 'like lemons', not sure what to do.

This account showed me just how identified Jane was with her mother, with such an emphasis on the desirability of birthing neatly, which seemed threatened by the more organic but messy aspects of the beginnings of life. However, by being so organised, even if out of compliance to what she imagined her mother's expectations to be, she lost the chance to be mothered herself. She also explained why she did not breast-feed.

She had tried with Benjamin, but it had been a very difficult, long labour culminating in an emergency Caesarian. She had immediately developed mastitis. The whole experience had been so painful and fearful that she had refused to try ever again. This time her husband had begged her to try again, and she had been sorely tempted, but the memory of the pain had again stopped her.

All this did not seem to augur well for her capacity to enjoy her new baby. However, in the same observation 12-day-old Amanda herself appeared quite happy, peacefully exploring her new world. And when she began to suffer from wind, Jane showed herself well able to attend to her patiently and empathically.

Jane tried holding her in all sorts of different positions, but always with care and respect. Amanda would calm down, become curious, get pain, crumple up; sometimes the pain would intensify and she would yell; sometimes it suddenly went away and she would look around as if to search for it ... She started to search again with her mouth. Occasionally, she would suck at parts of Jane's body through her clothes, including her breast. Jane became disturbed by not knowing how to calm her, and eventually said, 'I just haven't a clue whether she's wanting to burp or to have some milk.' Saying this seemed to help her (Jane), and she then relaxed again. Amanda found a comfortable place between her mother's breasts and neck, and lay there motionless, both (I imagined) loving the warm feel and also the absence of pain. But soon the pain came back, and she yelled.

Jane felt the time had come for the milk, so she prepared it, holding Amanda, talking to her and singing to her, in touch with her discomfort and putting words to it ... She then settled Amanda against her and put the teat in her mouth, and the immediate response of quiet sucking was so sudden that we both laughed. Amanda sucked well for about 5 minutes and then slept, the teat in her mouth, occasionally waking and sucking. Jane sat very quietly with her, attentive, occasionally murmuring a song.

I think this extract from my notes highlights many interesting aspects which were to become regular features of Amanda's personality and the mother–daughter relationship. It shows Amanda's ability to complain and make her wishes known, very directly. Her mother is well in touch, and responds affectionately and empathically. She allows Amanda ready access to her body, despite not giving her the actual breast. Jane does become distressed herself at one point, and it may be that she was able unconsciously to use myself as observer to contain her, so that she could rediscover her equilibrium. Amanda also shows even at this very early stage a high capacity to tolerate frustration. She appears well able to make good use of what she is offered, including her mother's voice, and does not to become upset about what she is denied – in this extract it is so clear that she searches intuitively for the breast for comfort and love as well as for food. Jane effectively allows her to find the comforting breast, even if only through her clothing, and gives her food separately, via the bottle. Amanda immediately settles down when attended to after being distressed – an almost unfailingly regular feature in all future observations. Sometimes when exploring these kinds of interactions in seminar discussions we thought of Amanda as having an experience of a breast-mother without a breast.

In this observation Jane also showed herself able to use and enjoy the experience of observation. She said:

> *'Actually, it is fascinating watching her. I've never really looked at her before like this, with someone else. You can see so much starting to happen.'* ... *As she talked she sounded interested and exploring her baby, as if this was rather new for her; and there was also a sad note in her voice.*

I think this was confirmation already of her hunger for a figure who could help support her in being with and attentive to her baby with a different attitude from prioritising competence. I wondered if the sad note communicated a sense of melancholy at not having received this experience as a baby herself, and possibly a regret that she had been less centred on the emotional life of her two older children when they were babies.

Jane also spoke about

> *how both the other children love Amanda and play with her beautifully. I asked what they thought about her. She said that Benjamin simply loved her, and was thrilled with her ... Rachel, however, had other ideas. She was extremely jealous. But she never took it out on the baby. 'You know who she takes it out on' nodding at herself. But the she quickly spoke up for Rachel, how Jane will get round her jealousy by involving her in looking after Amanda, getting things out of the fridge, etc., particularly her bottles, which Rachel loves to do.*

I saw Benjamin at my third observation, when Amanda was 19 days old, and he was indeed very taken up with Amanda. He played quite gently with her, but then she started to cry, quite softly, and not, I thought, in particular reaction to him. But her crying seemed to make Benjamin quite anxious, and he tried one thing after another – singing soothing songs, then banging a rattle increasingly hard until he was finally walloping it on a chair – to try to get her to stop. Jane intervened and picked Amanda up, and she calmed down, but Benjamin

> *was all over her, kissing her, tickling her, passing his fingers all over her, but often poking her, squeezing her, biting her when he was kissing. I could only admire his ability to stay exactly on the border-line of what his mother would and would not permit, so that she got increasingly exasperated with him. Yet she didn't lose her temper and found him some things of his own to play with at his table, still stroking Amanda. Amanda, I think, rather enjoyed Benjamin's attentions: she was very interested, sometimes excited, sometimes crying ... and looked round for him again.*

The following week, Jane told me

> *how the children never really saw David during the week, because the two elder children go to bed at about 6 p.m. She described how Benjamin continues to adore Amanda, and how he's decided to marry the other little baby girl in his life. This made her laugh. Rachel, on the other hand, is very jealous and rough with Amanda. Jane had made the mistake of telling her not to hit her on the head, which was now Rachel's main ambition in life.*

The rough-and-tumble of family life thus featured in Amanda's life from the start. I only sometimes saw Benjamin, who in fact normally treated her much more gently and considerately than in the above example. Rachel, on the other hand, had a very lively, ambivalent and frequently conflictual relationship with her little sister. She would often be quite rough with Amanda, on occasion directly attacking her. Perhaps she felt particularly hurt and angry about having been robbed of her precious position of youngest. She would try to excite Amanda as much as possible and in these direct engagements always succeeded. I describe some such incidents later in the paper.

Despite her siblings, the early period of Amanda's life was dominated by a real closeness to her mother. The following extract is typical. She was 19 days old:

> *Jane fed Amanda fennel tea. She immediately quietened down and sucked vigorously. Soon she stopped and dozed off. After a short time Jane put her in her rocking-chair, clearly hoping that she would sleep there whilst Jane could get on with her household chores. But Amanda immediately woke and searched in the air with all four limbs and then with her mouth. She whimpered and then cried. Jane came and spoke about her being windy, but I thought it was the closeness to her mother immediately after the feed that she had been relishing and which she felt had been taken abruptly from her. And, indeed, although*

Jane continued to talk about Amanda being colicky, she didn't try to burp her but held her against her breast, in a very natural and tender way, which Amanda clearly loved. She quietened and almost purred. My impression was that Jane knew intuitively that this was what both she and the baby desired and needed but that it wasn't allowed, whereas talk about wind and burps was.

There followed a beautiful quiet time in which for about 10 minutes or so mother and daughter stayed quietly with each other, Jane clearly putting aside for the moment her other pressing domestic duties. They looked at each other adoringly ... Amanda put her hands up and stroked her mother and explored her face, whilst her feet played around. Jane started to talk about the need to feed on the clock, and how it should be 4-hourly, but Amanda needed to be fed 3-hourly during the day and 5-hourly at night, so that's what she did, she said rather decidedly, as though she were in danger of being criticised.

I choose this example because it seems to illustrate both Jane's state of 'primary maternal preoccupation' (Winnicott, 1956) and also her and Amanda's mutual idealisation of each other – the healthy idealisation which Klein (1952) thinks each baby needs to establish in order to establish secure good internal objects. It was obvious that during this period each was in love with the other. But I think it is also clear that Jane has to wrestle with an internal figure who forbids her to enjoy too much pleasure with her daughter, maintaining, for example, that she should feed not organically on demand but to a timed schedule. Winnicott wrote:

> It took me years to realise that a feeding difficulty could often be cured by advising the mother to fit in with the baby absolutely for a few days. I had to discover that this fitting-in with the infant's needs is so pleasurable to the mother that she cannot do it without moral support ... she is scared to do as she deeply wants to do. (Winnicott, 1948)

This difficulty in knowing and enjoying pleasure was of great significance for Jane, and I suspect that another unconscious motivation for having an observer was to help her manage this. I came to feel that a good word to describe Jane was 'austere', because of what I understand to be this word's ambivalent meanings: it simultaneously evokes both simplicity and an anti-warmth, even anti-love quality. A core aspect of Jane's personality appeared to be exactly on this border-line. Her austere simplicity was, I felt, partially helpful to the baby. This would manifest itself in a number of ways. To me she would never gossip. Most of the observations were conducted in virtual silence. There was never once any background music. I only got to know any biographical details about her by chance after about six months of observing, on a day when Amanda slept through almost all of my visit. Jane never asked me personal questions. How this side of her austerity translated into her relationship with Amanda can be illustrated from my visit when Amanda was seven weeks old.

Mother and baby then played together for about 5 minutes, Amanda on Jane's lap, facing her. ... Amanda slowly woke up more and more and started to smile at her mother. Jane always smiled back and made cooing noises. But a lot of their play was almost silent, certainly very quiet. Amanda moved her lips into lots of different positions, particularly often into an O, and Jane would be doing something similar. Amanda was particularly taken with very gently opening her lips from closed, so that they made a soft, smacking sound: Jane laughed softly when Amanda did this and did the same. There was a particular delicacy in their play which could only occur because of the very quiet background. They were constantly in eye contact with each other.

I noticed over the total course of observations that Amanda seemed to be developing a rather musical ear, and perhaps this quiet, attentive background helped her to develop an innate capacity to listen to sounds attentively herself and to react creatively.

However, Jane's austerity also possessed a rather rigid, cold, defensively phobic aspect. As mentioned earlier, she kept all the windows and doors into the garden shut in the hottest summer days. She hated the neighbours' children coming into the garden to fetch lost balls and was pleased when her husband threatened to take the parents to court if the children continued. Sometimes Rachel was obviously tantalised beyond endurance by my concentration on Amanda rather than on her, but Jane would often not do anything to make her frustration easier to bear but simply expected this passionate three-year-old to obey and be compliantly quiet in the wings. The most dramatic example of this came when Amanda was five months and three weeks. It was towards the end of my visit, and Amanda was just beginning to show signs of being tired. This happened often enough, and Jane would usually allow Amanda to get drowsy in her own time, before taking her to bed or allowing her to fall to sleep in her chair. On this occasion, however, Jane immediately took her upstairs, saying ...

'She'll probably cry herself to sleep.' And this was a very exact description of what happened. Jane put Amanda down in her bed ... she turned on a musical box just over Amanda's head. She simply said 'Goodbye,' came out of the room, and shut the door. Amanda started to cry at once, but Jane calmly walked down into the kitchen and took up her game with Rachel. The intercom was off, but for the last 10 minutes of my time Amanda's crying could be clearly heard, constantly, at one point getting into a complete and utter frenzy. I found it devastating to sit there with this as background music, whilst Rachel and her mother played on. I wondered what the experience must be for all three of them, and whether this was a regular occurrence.

This particular incident occurred around the time of Amanda's forthcoming baptism, which was an event causing Jane manifest anxiety. All her relations were going to be there, and the arrangements had to be perfect. She seemed to relax after it (it had gone well – 'Amanda didn't disgrace us!'). I sensed that this aspect of her – was it an identification with an internal, anti-libidinal mother? – was always present to some degree: it was something perfection-istic and indomitable, which partly contributed to her strength and compe-tence, but which I think she dimly knew contributed to her difficulties in, for example, feeling it was legitimate to enjoy her baby. In the example just quoted it was not only Amanda who was attacked but also me as the one who represented interest in the baby; however, I suspect that part of my role was to help protect her baby and herself from this harshly judgmental part of herself.

A similar atmosphere prevailed with regard to nappy changes. During the entire period of observations I only saw one nappy change – and never a single bath. Jane was apparently quite open to my observing these when I had raised the subject with her early on. I felt I needed to do this, particularly on account of being a male observer, since I knew I needed quite specific permission to accompany Jane into the private upstairs rooms of the house. I was surprised, therefore, that when Amanda defecated and needed changing during an observation (she was six weeks old) Jane

> *scooped her up, saying, 'Come here, smelly', and marched her off upstairs. I stayed in the kitchen in some indecision. I wondered whether to call upstairs and ask if I could come, but I decided instead to wait and talk to Jane about it when she returned.*
>
> *Soon she came back with a clean-smelling and beaming Amanda in her arms. When we sat down again, I said I didn't want to be too intrusive, but if that happened again would Jane mind my coming up too? Jane said 'Of course not.'*

This experience left me feeling I might have been too reticent. We discussed this matter in the seminar group, and the consensus was that it was particu-larly important for me as a man to keep clear boundaries between downstairs and upstairs, and that perhaps Jane was more reticent than she was admitting because of Amanda being a girl: perhaps she did not want me to see her daughter's genitals. Might it have been different had her baby been a boy? Time passed by, with some observations in which it was clear that Amanda had defecated and yet in which Jane did not change her, which led me to conclude that she really might have some strong aversion to my observing this. I asked whether I could come to see one of Amanda's baths, offering to change my time, thinking that my visit could take place when other family members were present, but this request Jane flatly rejected. Then she was entertaining friends with babies on a social visit during one session, and one of the other mothers changed her baby daughter's nappy quite openly and calmly in my presence. Soon after this, when Amanda was 23 weeks old, Jane announced during an observation that she was going to change Amanda's nappy. I asked if I could accompany them, and she said 'Yes'. But the change was

> *so well organised that neither mother nor baby seemed to make much of it either positively or negatively. Jane had it all well laid out, with a high changing mat in Amanda's bedroom. Jane was completely exact and precise in her movements. Amanda seemed not at all interested in anything to do with the nappy change. I could not tell that she was pleased or relieved that it had happened other than by the absence of her former complaint ... it seemed as if in no time we were downstairs back in the kitchen.*

So after all this waiting the nappy-change was a non-event! This seemed to be an area where Jane was very similar to her description of her own mother, and her baby responded by being as lifelessly mechanical as she was – so very different from the way they both interacted at most other times.

With regard to sleeping arrangements, Amanda had moved out of her parents' bedroom and into her own room at six weeks with the minimum of fuss. She was apparently always good at sleeping through the night. The whole family tended to get up early – soon after 5 a.m., so there was not much early-morning time in which she might have been on her own. When she was asleep, she sometimes gave evidence of dreaming. When she was 14 weeks old, I had seen her asleep for part of an observation, in which she had two dreams.

> *The first dream appeared to be a bad one. She shifted around and made a crying face, and did slightly cry. It had quite a deep tone of anguish to it, and she seemed distressed. But after a few seconds she relaxed back into a deep and immobile position.*
>
> *About five minutes later she again started to move around, and this time she giggled, smiled and laughed. This also passed after a few seconds, and again she remained still.*

These dreams show her having quite different internal experiences. Their closeness in time bring to mind Freud's comments (1900) about how dreams that occur during the same night arise from the same latent dream-thoughts and should be interpreted together, as a composite unit.

Another area in which the interplay between Amanda and Jane's rigidity, austerity and spontaneity showed itself was in feeding. When Amanda was eight weeks old, she had her first triple vaccination. I visited them six days later. Since the vaccination Amanda had gone off her food, and Jane was spacing out her feeds at four-hourly intervals:

> *otherwise Amanda just takes a little and spits the rest out and is really uncomfortable. If Jane makes her wait longer then Amanda gets really hungry and drinks more, 'but it makes me feel cruel.'*

I noticed Amanda having spasms of pain, for which she always seemed unprepared. Jane lifted her up and gave her fennel tea – she had it all prepared on the table. She sat down with Amanda on her lap. Amanda took the bottle very enthusiastically, and Jane heaved a sigh of relief. Amanda's hands gripped Jane's. But very soon she turned her head away and moved around in pain and discomfort. Jane held her close and sometimes talked to her about how unhappy and miserable she was, rubbed her nose against hers, and at one moment lifted Amanda up so that her face touched Jane's forehead: Amanda clearly loved this and moved her head from side to side, rubbing her cheeks against her mother's forehead for comfort. She would get little periods of comfort but then would be writhing again and beginning to cry: once or twice she would cry out in great pain and shriek. Jane was very attentive to her and, it seemed to me, intuitive; she occasionally got up and walked with her, putting her over her shoulder, talking to her, rubbing her back, holding her face outwards over her arm, which was clearly a position which gave Amanda a lot of relief. Amanda was clearly crying in her anguish to her mother, engaging with her, looking into her face for a response, occasionally pummelling her chest with her fists, sometimes burrowing her head right into her mother's body.

So it surprised me when Jane said, 'Why can't you talk? I wish you could tell me what the problem is. What does "Ahhh Ahhh" mean? I don't know what's wrong with you. What should I do? Is it milk you want? The ultimate answer? Probably not.'

I think this was one of the times when Jane sensed with some anguish that it was the *actual* breast as well as the mind of a breast-mother that her baby needed as the ultimate response to her pain, and it was tough that this was something she had decided not to make available. And, of course, being a male observer, I thought that this was typical of a situation a father can often find himself in, in which when faced with a distressed baby he can offer all the responsiveness of which he's capable, but he realises he doesn't have and can't have the one thing, the female body, which at certain times can feel like the only solution that would actually fit the baby's need. And the extract also illustrates clearly Amanda's capacity to help her mother and to communicate to her mother just what she needed.

When Amanda was 16 weeks old, I observed the following interaction over food. Amanda was happy and giggling, but

gradually a note of complaint entered her communications. To begin with it was just occasionally a look or a noise of pain, but then it increased in frequency. Jane's response was to try to jolly her out of it: she would say, 'Oh, it's time for a niggle, now, is it?' and kiss her, or, 'You're a terror, aren't you? Yes, you are', whilst tickling her stomach or kissing her nose. Amanda let herself be persuaded back into a more happy mood for a while, but then the complaints increased. From time to time she would look at the bottle next to her on the table, which had a small amount of water in it, and Jane would give it to her; but Amanda would always immediately turn away from it, and Jane said, 'It's

*only water, and that's not good enough, is it?' Jane explained to me that
sometimes she and Amanda joined two other mother-and-baby couples, and
this had happened earlier today. That meant that Amanda had been too excited
by the company to finish her milk like she normally does. Jane told me when
her next bottle was due, in about half an hour's time, and my heart sank at the
thought of Jane's holding out till then - but she didn't. She put the napkin to
Amanda's face, and Amanda immediately became very excited. Jane said
'That's it!' got up with Amanda, and took her over to the microwave and put the
milk bottle into it. Amanda clearly knew exactly what was going on, because
she stopped her complaining sounds and instead started beaming and getting
very excited with her breathing and other sounds.*

*Then Jane came over, sat down and put the napkin round Amanda's neck.
All of this seemed to Amanda to take an inordinately long time, and she just sat
there with her mouth wide (WIDE) open ('like a little bird,' said Jane) until Jane
put the bottle in it. The relief was instantaneous.*

It was evident that Amanda could find a way - through, for example, the way
she opened her mouth in this episode - of communicating to her mother
which Jane found endearing.

*For a good 5 minutes Amanda now seemed to immerse herself in the experi-
ence. To begin with she seemed to be sucking vigorously, her arms and hands
moving, but soon she relaxed and seemed to move into a much more sensuous
experience. Both her hands were busy stroking/touching Jane's hands and the
bottle. She shoved one of Jane's hands off, so that the bottle ended up being held
by one of each of their hands. Her feet occasionally moved up and down. Her
eyelids half-closed and closed, and occasionally she moved her eyes around so
that I could see the whites of them. At these (apparently ecstatic) moments she
also raised her arm halfway up and then slowly settled it down again.*

*She rather suddenly came off the bottle, raised her upper body and head so
that she was in a more upright position, and swayed about rather giddily with
a beatific grin for quite a few seconds. 'She's drunk!' said Jane.*

I wonder whether this observation doesn't illustrate how Jane seemed to be
on the cusp between feeling she should impose a rather rigid control and a
conflicting desire to respond more spontaneously to her child, and how
possibly she may have been making unconscious use of the observer to help
her strengthen her resolve to opt for the more responsive side of the conflict.

The same qualities could be seen on my next visit, when Amanda was 17
weeks old. She had a cold and was a bit uncomfortable and unhappy. She had
started to complain, and Jane said it was nearly time for her feed. Again, Jane's
description of her baby stuffing her mouth with her fists show how she could
be amused by Amanda's struggle to wait, and this endeared her baby to her -
helping her *not* to feel persecuted by Amanda.

The feed was different from previous ones I had observed because of Amanda's cold. She could just breathe through her nose, but only just. Constant snuffling and snorting. So it was hard work, involving her whole body working away. She soon got rather tired, but went on sucking well: she was hungry.

Then I was very touched to notice that a private duet had started up between mother's and baby's hands on the bottle: Jane was holding the bottle, and Amanda was stroking her mother's hands with one of hers, to which Jane was responding with one of her fingers. This quiet communication continued underneath the more overt snorting and energetic feeding.

After some minutes Amanda had had enough and dropped the bottle from her mouth with a big milky burp. 'Thank you,' said Jane.

It seems to me that this material illustrates rather movingly the breast quality of many of the bottle feeds I observed.

Jane started Amanda on solids at about 18 weeks. In fact the first time I witnessed this Amanda was less than keen on her solids, but this probably had more to do with her irritation at her mother focusing on Rachel during that observation than with an intrinsic dislike of the solid food itself. But it was noticeable that in that same session Amanda was beginning to 'roar'. It was a strong, rather masculine sound, which was perhaps related both to her father's voice and to the deep strong voice her mother reserved for the occasions when she was reprimanding her older children. On this occasion it was Amanda who seemed to be using it to reprimand her mother for insisting on her eating solids. But there seemed also to be a note of desperation and frustration in the roar. One might suggest that she was anxious that the solids might be *instead* of her bottle. It seemed that she had something like a preconception that weaning was on the cards, and she was defending against this quite vigorously with her roar. Was she even wanting to *become* father? If she were fed solids, she would have to share mother and become part of the family.

Jane eventually got the message, saying, 'It must be milk you're wanting – nothing else will do!' She gave her the bottle, and Amanda held onto it tightly, and, unusually, finished all the milk. Soon afterwards I observed her eating her solids with enthusiasm, and by her 23rd week – the same week as the anti-climactic nappy-change – I noted:

Jane put Amanda's food and a spoon on the table and then put Amanda down in her chair. Jane then fed her, and I want to convey how effortless and seamless, how neat and organised, the meal was. It was over very fast, it seemed to me, with a lack of fuss that seemed almost odd. At the very start Amanda was clearly excited and pleased about dinner-time; in fact, she rooted against Jane's breast through her jumper, as if she were a tiny infant, as Jane put her down in her chair. Jane would then take a spoonful and hold it in front of Amanda, who would then open her mouth wide and take it in. She enjoyed it, it seemed; she

*didn't gulp it greedily nor linger over it; she was clearly hungry and enjoying
herself, and on the whole seemed quite simply to eat one mouthful and then be
ready for the next. Mother was tuned into this, ready with her next spoon (or
was it the other way round?). She fed Amanda very exactly, never spilling
anything and carefully wiped any food from Amanda's lips when there was
even the smallest mess there. And so the meal went on; the first course was
finished, and immediately Jane went to the fridge, got out a fromage frais,
which Amanda ate in the same way, only perhaps lingering a little longer over
the very first mouthful to establish the new taste.*

This engagement over food was very characteristic of much that passed
between mother and daughter: there was a good experience, which clearly
both enjoyed; yet there was also something very organised and efficient about
it, which precluded a fuller pleasure – or too much displeasure. I never saw
Jane allow Amanda time to linger over her meal. She was never allowed to play
with her food. On the whole she was not fed until she showed that she was
properly hungry. On the other hand, Jane spent a lot of time and trouble
cooking Amanda's meals herself, and clearly thought about the preparation of
the food carefully, and I think it mattered to her intensely whether Amanda
enjoyed her cooking or not. Preparing food was perhaps related in her mind
unconsciously to qualities of the breast, i.e. what she herself could provide
from deep within herself. Amanda tended to have a good appetite for food,
and so usually gave her mother the reward of seeing her cooking polished off
with gusto. And just as they never quite had a fully pleasurable eating experience, they never had terrible rows, either. Amanda could not really express
her negative feelings towards her mother by refusing her food. If she tried,
Jane took it that she was not hungry and simply cleared the food away.

By now, Amanda had more full-blooded relationships with her siblings,
particularly Rachel, who, accidentally on purpose, just somehow often used
to come into quite dangerous contact with Amanda. When Amanda was 20
weeks old, for example, Benjamin and Rachel were playing quite boisterously
around her. I noted that

*considering what a nearly chaotic scene was being improvised around her, I
was surprised to notice how on the whole she would follow one element of it at
a time. She would either look at Benjamin, and follow him with her eyes
around the room, or similarly at Rachel, and sometimes she would look around
at her mother and smile at her.*

However:

*Rachel then became more and more excited with a long piece of plastic with
two balls at either end. She was hurling and flailing it about, hitting the kitchen*

surfaces hard. Jane told her off firmly, but then, at a moment when her mother's eyes were elsewhere (all this happened so fast that I'm not sure Rachel could have done this actually purposefully), she swirled the rope near Amanda and one of the balls hit her on the eye. My anxiety had been racing, and I leant forward and said 'Hey!' rather sharply, in a spontaneous reaction. Jane immediately looked round and said 'Out!' to Rachel, whom she marched off out of the room. Benjamin wasn't in the least disconcerted by all this and went on with his playing. Soon he followed the other two out.

Amanda was clearly very shocked by this blow, but to begin with hardly reacted vocally at all. I imagine she was a bit stunned. Certainly her expression had lost all its animation and playfulness. I was slightly behind her so I do not think she knew I was there, and she began to look around, saw there was no-one, and looked rather frightened. Just when she was beginning to whimper, however, Jane came back in with the older children, who were a bit calmer. Amanda was all eyes on Jane and stopped crying. Benjamin and Rachel immediately began to play up again, but Jane rather calmly got out their drawing things, papers and crayons and put them out for them on their special table, and they sat down to draw.

This kind of scene emphasised the act that Amanda from the beginning of life was part of a sibling group with its own dynamics of excitement, love, jealousy and hatred.

When Amanda was 21 weeks old, I recorded that at the very start of my visit, when I saw her

her eyes were shining and she looked full of health; she gave me a big smile and started to wave her arms and feet about. (Somehow she seemed to me older in this observation, as though rather suddenly she wasn't 'just' a small chubby baby anymore.)

It was as though from about this age it was obvious that she was well organised inside herself, with an inner continuity, who could think thoughts and recognise and relate to external figures very well. Perhaps this was partly because of her eating solids and not 'hogging' mother so much – even if she had never literally hogged mother at all.

One of the ways it was possible to see her growing up was in her successively more complex vocalisations. At 20 weeks

Amanda burped, and then made a vocalisation starting right high up and ending with a mixture between a growl and a gargle. Jane explained that this was her new noise, which had at first really alarmed her, because she thought Amanda was trying to make herself sick, but then realised it was just more vocal experimentation.

The following week

> *Jane and Amanda played together, mostly verbally, with Amanda making lots of differently pitched vocalisations, as if practising her scales and arpeggios. Jane mimicked her and occasionally added bits of her own.*

These two examples show both Amanda's own experimentation and also Jane's response, in which she could both support her daughter by being (literally) in tune with her and also occasionally prod her into exploring further. But music could also be an arena for pain. When Amanda was 5¹/₂ months old, I observed her being played with by her sister, Rachel. Amanda became excited, and her noises

> *turned from playful pleasure to excited, manic squeaks. But what really got to her and turned the experience bad was when Rachel attacked her with sound. Rachel would shout or suddenly scream, or whisper, or sing very very high. Amanda began to crumple up. Rachel saw this, and, swift as lightning, caught hold of a toy with bells which she then danced in front of Amanda, who immediately joined in with laughter. Soon Rachel appeared to judge that the danger of Amanda's crying was over, and so started to torment her again with sounds. Amanda looked utterly frightened and miserable, went pale, and closed her eyes.*

At 5 months 3 weeks Amanda was sitting in her baby-seat, but boisterously

> *kicking about and strongly waving her arms ... Jane gave her a rattle, and Amanda thrashed it around, revelling in the sound and the feel. She would often thump it hard on the seat behind her head. Occasionally, she would wallop herself with it ... but she didn't seem to mind that. Most of the time she didn't vocalise, but occasionally she did, and then it was in harmony with her robust mood, a sort of strong 'Oi, Oi, Oi!'*

And so on, until her vocalisations clearly began to be differentiated between ever closer approximations to speech inflections and something more purely tuneful and musical.

From a very early age it was clear that Amanda was aware of different people. When she was just eight weeks old, at the start of my visit

> *Amanda had not taken her eyes off me since I came in through the front door, and now she started on a long period of looking at me and relating to me.*
>
> *She became completely absorbed in getting to know me. For a full half-hour she did nothing else. Sometimes she gazed at me, sometimes stared at me, sometimes watched me with interest ... she would sometimes break into an amazing smile, sometimes seem to have a quiet chuckle to herself, sometimes would frown ... Her mouth was busy working all the time...*
>
> *After 30 minutes [Jane having left the room for about 10 minutes] Amanda started to become disturbed ... Then quite soon things got worse and worse for her ... to begin with as she suffered internal pain she could remain in a communi-*

*cating relationship with me, as it were telling me about it with her eyes and her
complaining noises, but then it escalated so that she was in more and more
pain and she could no longer use me as a good enough substitute or extension
of her mother. Her mother came back ...*

Here, at this very young age, Amanda seems to have been able to feel secure
enough of her solid relationship with her mother to relate closely to another
person, myself, but after some time - quite a long time - she seems to have
begun to feel terrified that she was in danger of losing her link with the
mother and to be swallowed up in or marooned on a strange and alien figure.
At 15 weeks, in the midst of sucking from her bottle:

*she stopped, and cocked an eyebrow at me ... For the next 15 minutes Amanda
flirted outrageously with me ... She would lean towards me, moving all her
body, and gurgle, coo, sing a little, blow bubbles, close her eyes then open just
one, look at me and collapse in giggles. Her eyebrows went up and down, and
she frowned and smiled.*

At 7 months 4 weeks I was told

*That Amanda had recently fallen in love with her father. She would reach out
for him as soon as he came and couldn't bear to be parted from him.*

The following week I was told that, as well as fancying men in general, she
had begun to get frightened of women. For example, she had acted as though
she disliked her grandmother and was frightened by her, and had been particularly coy and loving to her grandfather, although it was her grandmother she
knew well and had had a good relationship with, rather than her grandfather.
Then:

*Jane took two telephone calls, about 5 minutes apart, and I was struck how on
these occasions Amanda immediately stopped whatever she was doing and
looked and listened very intently at the start of the call. After a few seconds she
went back to her play. But then Jane spoke to me for quite a long time ...
Amanda initially took no particular notice ... but after some minutes she began
to stop playing for about 30 seconds at a time and to look carefully either at me
or her mother (in detached, scrutinising mode). Then, after we had been talking
for over 5 minutes, she started to look from one to the other of us. She always
went back to her play and was able to take it up and engage with it, but clearly
she was preoccupied with us, because before long she would again look up and
glance from one to the other. I was struck by how it seemed as though she was
gathering and processing information from her observations ...*

And so this maturational process continued through the weeks. It seemed as
if Amanda was quite comfortable in two situations - either being alone with

her mother in a dyad, or as one of a family group – but she was quite intensely aware of the difference between these and a threesome. Though she came to know me quite well, and would often relate very freely to me, the first moments of my visits were often difficult for her. It was as though she found it hard to move psychically from being in a dyad with her mother to allowing in a third, with all its greater complexity and particularly possibilities of exclusion.

As she gradually became more able to observe and think about more complex relations between others or between herself and others, so she began to notice things about herself. At 8 months 1 week

> *she was humming to herself quite a lot, and sometimes would suddenly break into a high-pitched laugh, which she would then laugh at, and usually Jane and I did as well, in spontaneous reaction. She would then look delighted...*

Her noticing herself laughing seemed to me to be evidence of the beginning of a reflective self (Fonagy et al., 1991), a core component of healthy psychological development.

I will now move to Amanda's physical and emotional development with regard to getting herself upright. By seven months two weeks she was 'sitting straight up on Jane's lap, all on her own, obviously with complete comfort'. It was on this occasion that Jane produced, with some embarrassment, a baby-walker, saying

> *that she always swore that she wouldn't use 'one of these things', but she hadn't been able to stop herself borrowing one from a friend just whilst Amanda was at the stage of toppling over. So she put Amanda in it. At first Amanda didn't seem very pleased, but very soon (less than a minute) she cheered up and started to get interested in the play-things at the front of the baby-walker. In particular she liked to play with the telephone: she made it ring (it had a ring like a bicycle bell) many times, and she tended to look at me with a big grin of triumph each time she did this. 'She's showing off again!' said mother.*

For the next few minutes Amanda gleefully demonstrated her capacity to use and steer the walker with intent. This baby-walker became a major theme of Amanda's life. In time I gathered that in fact both Benjamin and Rachel had used it previously, so that it was very much the family walker rather than one which had been borrowed. Jane clearly had misgivings about whether she should encourage its use and whether I would approve, but in seminar discussion we thought that it might well have been her hatred of dirt and mess that motivated her to use it. She stated on numerous occasions her ambivalence about Amanda crawling: she wanted her to crawl because it was developmental, but she hated the idea of her crawling around the house, getting dirty and opening cupboards, etc. She portrayed herself as having to crawl around after her. The walker seemed a more controllable and organised form of movement, and when in it Amanda could not actually open cupboards – though not for lack of trying.

Rachel's rather rough relationship with her sister continued, but I think the following extract from my notes shows how, as well as sometimes being dominated and defeated by her big sister, Amanda was simultaneously becoming more able to hold her own. She was becoming quite robust herself. For example, when playing with a spinning top, at 8 months 3 weeks:

> *Rachel came back in and immediately stormed Amanda. Jane retreated to a chair, so that she was sitting just above the girls. Rachel put her face right up against, almost into, Amanda's, and roared at her. I got a big shock, but not Amanda, who laughed and laughed, and thrust her head forwards against Rachel's. Rachel kept doing this, until Amanda fell over backwards, her head making a big clonk on the floor. Amanda started crying, but no one seemed too bothered, least of all Rachel who immediately looked for a toy to distract her sister: a musical box. She quickly wound it up and placed it, playing, right next to Amanda, who did immediately stop crying and smiled with pleasure, then joining in the music with 'goo, goo, goo', and again waving her arms. Rachel quickly took it away, to Amanda's consternation, which seemed to be Rachel's desired goal ... Rachel started to blow what felt like an interminable series of raspberries on Amanda's stomach. To begin with Amanda loved this, giggling and laughing and moving around on her cushion, but it was clear that it soon became a persecution: she looked frightened and then panicky. Jane told Rachel to go easy, and so Rachel went off now in search of the top. Jane helped Amanda up, who very soon recovered and was obviously overjoyed at seeing her two favourite objects, sister and top, coming back towards her together.*

But then, about 10 minutes later:

> *Rachel suddenly had had enough and left the room. Amanda was collapsed in a heap on the cushions at Jane's feet. Jane said to her, 'Peace at last.' But then she soon added (to Amanda), 'I can't begin to compete with that, you know.' She lifted Amanda up and put her on her knee. After a short time of relaxing, Amanda looked up and gave her mother a big smile, and then Jane began to play with her, putting her head on her knee and lifting up her legs and clapping them together. Amanda was very squirmy and active, and a couple of times Jane put her down and then lifted her up; it seemed that she was full of life after being with her sister and found it hard to settle down afterwards. 'Has the little terrorist gone then?' Jane asked of her a couple of times. Amanda yawned and began to whimper and then cheered up again.*

This extract is typical of interactions I observed between the sisters throughout my visits. I think they show what a big influence on her personality development her relationship with her brother and sister will have had.

Amanda seemed to be able to cope with Rachel's impingements very well, on the whole: she would, of course, get excited, and sometimes, as in the last example, it would be too much for her. Her mother sometimes surprised me by allowing Rachel's attacks to escalate (which I thought was unhelpful to Rachel as well as to Amanda), but usually Jane would be available to her at such moments, and, after collapsing for a short while into being a tiny baby at the (metaphorical) breast, Amanda would usually recover her good spirits and be ready for the next thing – even if that were sleep. Time and again, if Benjamin and Rachel were playing rowdily or getting into trouble with their mother, she would continue with her own activities apparently entirely unmoved. She had heard it all before. No doubt she will probably be quite able to look after herself when she reaches the school playground. I think that this kind of rather strong, passionate experience with Rachel and her mother ensured that her development continued on all fronts, including, very obviously, her mobility. Amanda learnt astonishingly fast how to use the baby-walker, and soon I found myself referring to it as her car, even her sports car, and both Jane and I talked about her 'zooming around'. However, this inorganic and too facile ease of transportation got her into severe emotional difficulties, especially as instanced above, when she would get herself into a desired position but then not be able to get out of it. Naturally enough, she then felt very frightened and suffocated. I found this particular aspect of the whole observation sequence the hardest to tolerate as an observer: Amanda seemed such a bright girl with such an appetite for life, endowed with such a regularly evinced capacity to struggle with difficulties and to be curious, that to give her something so dangerously easy, which bypassed the more arduous stage of crawling and real walking, seemed quite unnecessary and in danger of damaging or blunting her capacities for hard work and achievement. But in the event I am not sure that these anxieties and judgements of mine were justified. Within the very orbit of her walker experiences, she did indeed work hard, and with success, at controlling it and getting it to do her will. And it didn't, in fact, completely stop her from either crawling or walking. Crawling, as already mentioned, was not particularly encouraged by Jane, but nevertheless Amanda began manoeuvring herself from a sitting to a crawling position, and then to try and move her limbs – so that Jane really found that, like it or not, she just had to help her. And, as for walking, at nine months

Jane told me that Amanda could walk quite well already when Jane held her loosely around her stomach, and she then demonstrated exactly this.

She pulled Amanda up to a standing position, then held her loosely by her hips, and Amanda walked: this was real walking, in the sense that she put her full weight on her legs and lifted each up in turn, etc. I was astonished, as Amanda, steadied by her mother, walked around the kitchen. Rachel had just come in and was opening a colouring book to draw in at the little children's

*table. Amanda aimed and made for this table, and then, lightly supported by
her mother, stood at the side of it and tried to seize the book and the pens in
turn away from her sister, laughing uproariously. Rachel got rather cross, and
took the book onto the floor a little distance away. Amanda immediately
turned round and pursued her, mother in tow. Rachel then went back to the
table: and this happened about four times ...*

The two girls then played rather friendly, teasing games with each other.

*Rachel left the room, and Amanda wanted to follow her; so she walked (with
mother balancing her) right out of the kitchen and into their sitting-room,
where to her great delight she found Rachel. Amanda grinned at her sister and
her arms went up and down with pleasure, and she made a rhythmically
repeating 'Ooh! Ooh! Ooh!' vocalisation. She then walked to Rachel, who sat on
a sofa, and at the last minute Jane picked Amanda up and put her on Rachel's
lap. Both girls loved this, and Rachel stroked Amanda's hair. But then Amanda
grasped a handful of Rachel's hair and pulled hard. Rachel screamed and
rushed off into the kitchen. Jane lifted Amanda back into a walking position
and Amanda followed big sister in hot pursuit. Both hooted and screamed with
excitement when they met up in the kitchen.*

This somewhat manic but good-humoured play between the sisters
continued and developed, without escalating into crisis, as I had so habitually
witnessed on many previous occasions.

This vignette seemed to me a good one with which to end this paper,
because it brings together many important and typical features of this series
of observations. It shows Amanda's sense of 'onward and upward' development and her desire and delight in walking. It also shows Jane facilitating this,
delighting in her child, and it is important to note the persistence of their
mutual adoration. Just as Jane was prepared to spend a lot of time in this and
other observations being Amanda's servant, in the sense of walking behind
her and facilitating her 'walking' wherever she wished to explore, so psychologically she seemed to wish to be right behind her daughter, supporting her
development. For all her cold, defensive austerity, this warmth, love and
longing for her daughter to develop seemed to win as the stronger current.

This picture seems to me to symbolise how Jane had been, fairly consistently, since the beginning of Amanda's life, and perhaps is as good an answer
as any to my opening question as to how it is that a bottle-fed baby like
Amanda can develop into the kind of warm, affectionate, curious and full-
blooded creature that she manifestly is, demonstrating qualities which we
tend to associate with a securely attached breast-fed baby. And, for Rachel,
this scene seems to mark a turning point when Amanda stops just being the
baby to be jealously taunted and becomes instead a genuine playmate, a real
sister. In fact, in this observation and one soon after at which Benjamin was

also present, it was obvious that Amanda had become a third partner in the children's group, no longer 'just' a baby.

References

Bion, W.R. (1962) *Learning from Experience*. London: Wiliam Heinemann, Medical Books; reprinted London: Karnac, 1984.

Fonagy, P. et al. (1991) The Capacity for Understanding Mental States: The Reflective Self in Parent and Child and Its Significance for Security of Attachment. *Infant Mental Health Journal*,12/3.

Freud, S. (1900) *The Interpretation of Dreams*. London: Hogarth, 1953.

Klein, M. (1952) Some Theoretical Conclusions Regarding the Emotional Life of the Infant. In: *Envy and Gratitude*. London: Hogarth, 1975.

Winnicott, D.W. (1948) Paediatrics and Psychiatry. In: *Collected Works: Through Paediatrics to Psychoanalysis*. London: Karnac, 1992.

Winnicott, D.W. (1956) Primary Maternal Preoccupation. In: *Collected Works: Through Paediatrics to Psychoanalysis*. London: Karnac, 1992

CHAPTER 17

Cannibalism and succour: is breast always best? (thoughts on 'Amanda')[1]

JOAN RAPHAEL-LEFF

In my discussion of breastfeeding, I will use Francis Grier's sensitive observation and its carefully crafted presentation to illustrate various themes rather than dwelling minutely on the rich details of the material. In particular I focus on the subtext about breast- as opposed to bottle-feeding and conclude by raising several queries about the practice of infant observation (as this training procedure is curiously named, rather than 'infant-caregiver/s' or 'psychodynamic' observation which acknowledges that 'there is no such thing as a baby' on its own as Donald Winnicott famously observed). And, finally, I touch briefly on a few points about the observer and the observed, the sex of the observer and the introduction of a threesome within the dyad.

Breastfeeding

The first of these issues, then, is the underpinning assumption shared by so many health professionals that bottle-feeding is always second best to breast. In this paper I contend that, *although breastfeeding can be a tender mutual delight for both mother and baby, we must always bear in mind that for some it can be a nightmare in which the 'wild things' predominate*. Clearly, the emotional climate for the 'nursing couple' is reciprocally determined and the feeding experience, whether breast or bottle, is both indication and function of the *quality* of the relationship between them. Thus a bottle-feed may be intensely sensual and intimate (as the delicate 'duet' of Jane and Amanda's finger play shows) while a breastfeed may be mechanical and remote, rejecting or even tyrannizing.

---

[1] An earlier version was presented to the Scientific meeting of the British Psychoanalytic Society on 16.2.00 as an invited response to Frances Grier's paper (see Chapter 16).

Ironically, the psychoanalytic formulation of 'the breast' is modelled more on a theoretical abstraction than on the human body, which tends to sprout not a singular breast but *two* such fleshy articles! I am not quibbling over a mere linguistic mannerism – it seems to me that one of the main differences between breast and skin-to-skin bottle-feeding is the fact that there *are* two breasts, not one. Importantly, unlike the bottle, breastfeeding is distinguished by variations in volume and composition of milk and its accessibility, which differs from beginning of the feed to its mid-point of burping before beginning the *second breast*. We may observe how a breastfed baby develops a sense of trust that s/he can let go of the emptied first breast and more will follow from the second.

In the exquisitely balanced economy of breastfeeding, supply follows demand, as the mother's milk production itself waxes and wanes in accordance with the infant's needs. Within the system that develops around breastfeeding, the baby plays an active part in determining the nature of the interaction. But not only the quantity of milk but its *content* varies. Each feed begins with a thinner, more rapidly delivered thirst-quenching liquid, which only after lengthy and vigorous sucking yields progressively more nutrients. Left to his or her own resources, a breastfeeding infant gauges and sets the duration of the feed, according to degree of hunger, varying the strength of sucking and determining when to stop, rest and mix work and play as the going gets hard in promoting the rich hindmilk.

Conversely, the consistency and flow of bottle milk is *invariable* throughout the feed, and, if the bottle is sufficiently tilted, the strength of suction need not vary from beginning to end. Formula milk is also more dense, sustaining the baby for longer intervals than breastfed babies, who need 'top-ups' every one to three hours. This means that a breastfeeding mother who decides to feed four-hourly and/or regularly curtails the feed by timing it will *have* to introduce bottles as a nutritional supplement. Conversely, the bottle-fed baby 'lasts' longer without maternal intervention, and the baby's intake is objectively quantifiable.

Breast milk has built-in advantages of delivering antibodies and being available 'on tap' rather than necessitating sterilized bottles and teats, scooping and mixing the formula and heating it to the correct temperature. Nevertheless, for many mothers the emotional advantages of bottle-feeding outweigh these considerations – not least that it is a separate, shareable activity and that the amount of milk consumed is *measurable*. This is of considerable importance to women who have doubts about adequacy of their own resources or concerns about nourishing the infant – neither starving nor overstuffing. Indeed, an eating disorder, dread of her pathogenic tendencies, anxieties about the 'thin' quality of her milk or fantasies about its potential poisonousness may have led a woman to introduce bottle-feeding in the first place, either as a supplement to breastfeeding or instead of it. Given the peace of mind it provides – for many mothers (and, consequently, their infants) bottle feels best!

Idealizing as we do, the imagined blissful 'symbiosis' of mother and infant and its corollary of 'primary maternal preoccupation' as Winnicott (1956) called a new mother's reverie, we sometimes tend to ignore the fact that for many parents in the early postnatal days and weeks, particularly with a first baby, the experience is more likely to be that of 'primary maternal *persecution*' as I termed it (Raphael-Leff, 1999). Close encounters with a new infant are highly arousing emotional experiences – rushes of cosy warmth and calm peacefulness often oscillate with moments of sheer panic and high tension provoked by exposure to wordless distress and acute neediness.

In fact, to see this in context, national statistics for 1995 show that, even when women intended to breastfeed, only 66% of mothers put the baby to the breast at birth, dropping to 56% feeding at one week, 42% at six weeks and *only a quarter of women in the United Kingdom still breastfeeding by four months*. Although the incidence of breastfeeding rose from 64% in 1990 to 68% in 1995 to 70% in 2000, the majority of the increase were older first-time mothers in social class I, and only 38% of mothers who had left school at 16. (Social class, geographical region and birth order affect prevalence, incidence and duration with 63% of breastfeeding women in social class I in London still doing so at four months compared to 12% in Northern Ireland.) Most importantly in the context of Jane, the probability of breastfeeding is closely related to experience with previous children, and only 26% of mothers who had not breastfed before tried it with the new baby (Department of Health, 2000).

If a mother does allow the baby to feed off the fluids of her own body, she is permanently 'on call', leaking milk through her clothes to the tune of his or her whims. Not only does she feel in danger of being depleted, but the quality of her nurturing is starkly evident to all in the baby's weight, complexion and level of contentment. In a culture prone to dissociate maternity and sexuality – the Madonna and the Whore – a new mother might be horrified by the erotic intimacy of breastfeeding and the orgasmic uterine contractions it arouses. Whereas some mothers welcome the warm sensuality, revelling vicariously in luscious bodily care, a deprived woman may envy her baby the care her partner or, indeed, she herself lavishes upon the child – envying her own breast, so to speak. Another, may feel 'cannibalized', appalled by the baby's 'rapacious' hunger, and abhorring the infant identified with split-off aspects of the demanding baby she imagines herself to have been. So, despite our view of the bottle as a poor 'substitute' for the 'real' thing (Klein, 1936), we may assume that for some 'nursing couples' it is a lifesaver, as being breastfed reluctantly by a persecuted or endangering mother is hardly conducive to infant mental health.

Intimacy and exposure

In the observations described by Grier, the mother called Jane seems content to have her baby nuzzle contentedly between her breasts. She is sensitively attuned to Amanda's feeding rhythms and possibly, at times, in the absence of the observer, might have bottle-fed her daughter skin to skin. Owing to the paucity of our information about her fantasies, unconscious or otherwise, we can only speculate whether worries such as these informed Amanda's mother's original decision not to breastfeed her daughters. However, the observer points to the pleasure both Jane and Amanda derive from her preparation of food. She appears to protect their intimacy by projecting danger outside their benign circle – by keeping mess efficiently at bay and badness beyond closed windows and the garden fence. Yet at no point do we get the impression of obsessionality in preparing the bottle feed, withdrawing from the baby's touch or withholding of her own bodily contact. Jane claims to have been deterred from breastfeeding by the recalled pain of mastitis (which incidentally is often considered second only to that of passing gall stones). Wariness about breastfeeding is hardly uncommon when it is associated with the excruciating past experience of a hungry little mouth latching onto the cracked and bleeding nipples of an engorged inflamed breast. In addition, given that she contracted mastitis immediately following an emergency Caesarean, not only was Jane recovering from major surgery at the time but presumably still suffering from the long ordeal of her difficult and painful labour with her first-born son.

Although any carer is threatened by the regressive infectiousness of a newborn's primitive feelings, these have a particular impact on the *biological mother*. The mother, as Francis points out, has the female body the father lacks. In my clinical experience it is this very reproductive body that constitutes her vulnerability. In addition to the physical experiences of birth-bruising and bodily pummelling, stitches and hormonal fluctuations, the new mother feels exposed by her infant. In appearance and behaviour, the baby who has come out of her body shows the world what she is capable of producing for better or worse. Conversely, this child who has been inside her seems to know everything about her, all her hidden resources and vices from the inside out. The child may seem critical of her innermost feelings and meagre resources and every whimper may be interpreted as a complaint or accusation of her insufficiency. Retriggering fantasies of her own infancy and poignant yearnings for nurture and merger, caring for a baby also activates powerful preverbal memories of feeling mothered and unmothered.

Not surprisingly in the West, almost half of all mothers (and many caregiving fathers – Ballard and Davies, 1996) experience some form of postnatal disturbance over the course of the first two years of the baby's life. I suggest that the especially acute distress experienced during the early weeks is a function of inexperience, anxiety, sleep deprivation and unmediated contact with *primal substances* such as vernix, amnion, lochia, collostrum, urine, faeces, mucus, vomit and possibly breast milk (what Francis Grier refers to as 'organic mess of the beginning of life'), which plunge a new parent into inchoate flashbacks of their own infancy.

The regressive suction of a tiny baby's primitive emotions disarms adult defences. Close encounters with a preverbal baby revitalize presymbolic experience while caregiving reactivates internalized representation of one's own baby-self with an archaic carer. Thus, at the very moment of total responsibility and greatest demands on their adult capacities, the carer is also most vulnerable to the release of unresolved infantile emotions in themselves.

In my view part of the prevalence of modern-day postnatal distress in lies in the unique combination of post-industrial urban insulation and social stratification which precludes contact with babies. For many a primagravida the baby she takes home from hospital is the first newborn she has encountered. She may never have seen anyone breast feed and has had no practical or emotional preparation for the intensely arousing and demanding dyadic relationship she is about to encounter. Smaller nuclear households and scattered extended families also mean few opportunities to work through one's own early distressing experiences by interacting with infants before parenthood.

So, in re-examining our cherished presumption about breast being the optimal form of feeding, let us not ignore the real world in which, given a choice, many women, in developing societies as well as our modern one, *elect* to forgo the intimacy of this numinous pleasure (often, with dire results in geographical areas lacking clean water to mix with the milk-formula). Nor is this a new occurrence. Before the invention of the feeding-bottle and pasteurized milk, whether due to economic necessity, personal preferences or social beliefs about the 'weak' consistency of urban women's milk (Hufton, 1997), babies were farmed out to wet-nurses. Indeed, history reveals that in fifteenth- to nineteenth-century Europe in cities such as Paris only 5% of babies were breastfed by their own mothers (!) due to discordant lifestyles not only of aristocrats but artisans too. Sadly, at times, of the majority sent to the country or foundling homes to be wet-nursed, owing to a shortage of lactating women, two-thirds died before their first birthday (Badinter, 1981).

Parental orientations

In his paper, Francis Grier tacitly refers to characteristics he sees as more prevalent in bottle feeders – '*the mother's personality contained quite strong features which might be interpreted as pertaining more to the bottle than the breast: she could be rather cold and aloof, she thoroughly disliked mess, she could be rigidly controlling'* and seemingly phobic of invasion. In my own studies (Rapahel-Leff, 1985, 1986), now confirmed by large-scale longitudinal research by others (e.g. Sharp, 2001; Scher, 2001; Scher and Blomberg, 1992, 1999), various clusters have been delineated which may make sense of this. The maternal orientation of *Facilitators* devote themselves to adapting to their idealized babies. They tend to breastfeed on demand, wean late and prefer to mother exclusively, vicariously enjoying the indulgence of their babies. By contrast the orientation I have termed *Regulators*, regard their task as socializing a wild asocial baby, expecting the *baby* to adapt. They feed by schedule, introduce solids early, and, although preferring to bottle feed, some now do breastfeed in the early weeks, not only for the sake of the baby's immunization but because they are told it will hasten return of their pre-pregnant figure. They tend to share caregiving (which in itself necessitates bottle feeding) both for the sake of convenience and, in some cases, to avoid overexposure to a baby unconsciously associated with repudiated aspects of their own baby selves. In large studies, both these groups were found to have higher levels of maternal separation anxiety. The former tend to produce securely attached yet 'fussy and dependent' babies; the latter, a higher rate of ambivalent insecurely attached infants. Internal world changes lead to a third orientation of *Reciprocators* whereby, rather than a set mode of adaptation by either mother or baby, uncertainty is tolerated and each incident negotiated on its own merits. This last pattern of interaction seems based on *empathy, mutual reciprocation and awareness of ambivalence* rather than enacted or denied primary identification as in the former two where fear of hatred and love feature respectively. Finally, a fourth response is a *bi-polar* one where two conflicting orientations vie with each other in the same mother towards the same baby. This discord may reflect clashes between her own internalized parents, conflicts between rigid and responsive facets of herself or introjected stereotypical 'feminine' and 'masculine' aspects or more conscious ideological discrepancies, for instance between feminist and child-centred ideals.

In the case of Jane, her characteristic efficiency and 'cool' detachment common in regulators appears in conjunction with spontaneous warmth, empathic thoughtfulness and facilitating attunement. The result is a moderating *austerity* which the observer attributes to defeat of an internal perfectionistic demand and exacting prohibition on 'too much' pleasurable enjoyment. We can only speculate about connections between this internalized stricture and her own restricting archaic mother. On the basis of the material presented, my evaluation would be that despite (or perhaps by virtue of) her austerity, in her interaction with *this* baby, Jane has successfully overcome the confines of her internal world and is able to 'reciprocate'. If previously conflicted, at this point in time she presents with a seemingly integrated, well-developed capacity to tolerate uncertainty and contain both her baby's anxieties and her own. From the start she respects and responds thoughtfully to Amanda's capacity to communicate her moods, while the baby in turn seems to match and complement her mothers' attentiveness. In the detailed descriptions, Jane appears usefully aware of her own and her children's mixed feelings, able to provide graduated failure and age-appropriate care for each and, while enjoying their lively interaction, prevents over excited or conflictual escalations. Amanda in turn seems lustily engaged with her siblings, secure in her mother's loving and moderating presence and increasingly able to tolerate frustration and absences.

Observer and observed

Which brings me to my final points on psychodynamic infant/carer observations. The practice of year-long observations are often used as training exercises for therapists and healthcare professionals. They serve as lessons in *bearing and processing powerful counter-transferential feelings* without either allowing these to spill over into the emotional atmosphere or dispelling them with critical or remedial action. The observer enters a contract with the family he or she observes that is quite different to that of therapist and patient, or health visitor and client. The observer is *a guest* in the household, a position of a privileged but precarious and indeterminate nature. For a brief hour a week, a portion of life is spread out to be seen, yet the observer must be aware that all personal disclosures by the family are partial and guarded. Furthermore, their fragmentary nature inevitably leads to speculative assumptions by the observer and a desire to close gaps in understanding. Observational reports to the small weekly training group in which these are discussed are also inevitably selective and filtered through the theoretical assumptions of the observer. When a critical standard of idealized maternal excellence is upheld, it further distorts the lens of observation.

There is one training model that regards an observer as a *fly on the wall*. However, once again, the flesh-and-blood reality differs from the ideal, and we now recognize that however retiring his/her manner, an observer is always inevitably both participant and contributor to the process observed. Moreover, he or she invariably introduces potent foreign and self-conscious elements into the works. We may consider the parallels between the erstwhile prescribed non-interactive observer and the 'neutral screen' analyst. Indeed, in many toddler observations, the idea of being silently watched by an unresponsive observer is so bizarre that it may become intolerable to the child who, not uncommonly, demands that the observer 'go away' and stop 'looking' at him or her! Thankfully, Francis makes it clear that at moments of Amanda's funniness or distress he is far from impassive.

Another central question is one of *who agrees to be observed and why*. Reasons for a family accepting an observer may range from loneliness or insecurity through altruism to exhibitionism, and we can by no means take it for granted that these are 'ordinary' households. In Jane's case, the observer speculates with great sensitivity that her motivation was to make unconscious use of him as a benign and supportive presence to counteract her tendency to prioritize 'competence' over intuitive warmth. As a third-time mother, she is also confident enough of her maternal capacities to engage with the experience of observing in her own right without herself becoming either too detached or engrossed in the process.

In conclusion, I will just touch on *the issue of gender*. It seems to me that in observation, as in analysis, the sex of participants is a major factor in the interaction. Here the observer is a man – and one who seems *au fait* with the subtleties of childrearing in a household where the (absent) father 'carries the incapacity' by contrast to his expert wife. Mother and baby are aware of the impact of his maleness, as is the observer in this case. In some observations, the presence of a male observer may inhibit breastfeeding; in others, it may serve as a catalyst to exhibitionism, submission or competitiveness. Likewise a female observer's presence might activate feelings transferred from the mother's past.

Finally, there is Amanda's distinction between dyads and triads and her growing capacity to relate in threesomes, now seen by neonatal researchers to occur in the early months when babies clearly distinguish between communications addressed to themselves or to others. Analysis of video-recordings of interaction in the presence of both parents reveal the infant's intention not to exclude but *to bring in the third* (Fivaz-Depeursinge and Stern, 1999). Thus, in the case of this particular observer, he recognizes that he constitutes *an embodied sexed third presence* rather than an invisible eye, thereby inevitably changing any 'dyadic' processes observed. To my mind, these last points prove the importance of a mindful approach such as Francis Grier displays in his report, cautious about interpreting observations and about ascribing meaning to life as lived in the absence of an observer. Hopefully, pooling findings from unbiased open reports such as these across as many observers as possible may supplement theoretical speculations and complement laboratory research, stimulating us to rethink some of our long-held cherished theories.

References

Badinter, E. (1981) *The Myth of Motherhood – An Historical View of the Maternal Instinct*. London: Souvenir Press.

Ballard, C. and Davies, R (1996) Postnatal depression in fathers, *International Review of Psychiatry*, 8: 65–71.

DOH (2000) *Infant Feeding Survey*. Statistical Press Notice, Department of Health.

Fivaz-Depeursinge, E. and Stern, D. (1999) *L'intersubjectivité dans le triangle père mère/bébé*, University of Lausanne, presentation to Family Therapy conference, Paris, 14.10.99.

Hufton, O. (1997) *The Prospect Before Her: A History of Women in Western Europe 1500–1800*. London: Fontana.

Klein, M. (1936) *Weaning*. Chapter 18 in: Love, Guilt and Reparation and Other Works 1921–1945. London: Hogarth, 1975.

Raphael-Leff, J. (1985) Facilitators and Regulators: vulnerability to postnatal disturbance, *Journal of Psychosomatic Obstetrics & Gynaecology*, 4: 151–68.

Raphael-Leff, J. (1986) Facilitators and Regulators: conscious and unconscious processes in pregnancy and early motherhood, *British Journal of Medical Psychology*, 59: 43–55.

Raphael-Leff, J. (1999) Primary maternal persecution. Chapter 3 in: *Forensic Psychotherapy and Psychopathology Winnicottian Perspectives* Kahr, B. (ed.) Brett Kahr, London: Karnac.

Scher, A. (2001) Facilitators and regulators: maternal orientation as an antecedent of attachment security, *Journal of Reproductive Infant Psychology*, 19: 325–33.

Scher, A. and Blomberg, O. (1992) Facilitators and Regulators: cross cultural and methodological considerations, *British Journal of Medical Psychology*, 65: 327–31.

Scher, A. and Blomberg, O. (1999) Night-waking among one-year-olds: a study of maternal separation anxiety, *Child Care Health & Development*, 25: 295–302.

Sharp, H, and Bramwell, R. (2001) An empirical evaluation of a psychoanalytic model of mothering orientation and the antenatal prediction of postnatal depression, *Archives of Women's Mental Health*, 3: suppl. 2: 14

Winnicott, D.W. (1956) Primary maternal preoccupation. Chapter 24 in: *Through Paediatrics to Psycho-Analysis*, London: Hogarth Press, 1982.

PART IV

Management Issues

This final section addresses not only parental feelings but some of the ways in which working with infants and parents impacts on professionals too. Expectations and transferred feelings are crucial aspects of interchanges between client and therapeutic 'caseworker' and can cause hitches and unexpected glitches in the work relationship. These are clarified in Chapter 18 by Isca Salzberger-Wittenberg, to promote awareness in professionals of the ways in which these subtle feelings affect their work.

A further aid to understanding work with parents and infants is offered by Joanna Hawthorne (Chapter 19), who depicts different capacities and states of consciousness in young babies. She introduces the Brazelton Neonatal Behavioural Assesment Scale, designed to assess the emotional and behavioural characteristics and individuality of newborns, such as their repertoire of responses to human and non-human stimuli. The Scale also tests 18 reflexes, providing a profile of the baby's ability to self-soothe and self-regulate. This tool of systematic observation is used by clinicians and researchers worldwide (for instance Mintzer and her team in Chapter 15 and Murray in Chapter 20 of this book).

We now know from many studies that depressed women tend to be withdrawn and disengaged from their infants or intrusive and hostile, both of these associated with less sensitive and responsive maternal interactions. In turn, maternal depression has been found to predict a child's poor cognitive development. However, not only does the mother's depression affect the baby (persisting long after she is better), but, using the NBAS, Lynne Murray confirms that attributes of a particular infant can be a potent factor in maternal depression. Findings indicate that a mismatch between expectations and reality may lead to depression in samples of both high and low risk for postnatal disturbance. Results from her large-scale prospective study reveal that the newborn's poor motor control and high level of sensitivity and irritability raises the risk of maternal depression almost fivefold!

Maternal disturbance is also the topic of the next two chapters; however, this time it is to do with the trauma of perinatal loss, its affect on her, other children and further pregnancies. Stanford Bourne, Emanuel Lewis and Elizabeth Bryan share their extensive clinical expertise in this area, offering psychodynamic understanding and practical advice on management of death, grieving and subsequent pregnancies. They explore some of the complex feelings these issues raise in both the bereaved and the professionals caring for them. Finally, in the last chapter of the book, Stella Acquarone draws on her extensive experience of infant–parent therapy, focusing here on eating disorders, classifying these and bringing a therapeutic model, management issues and many examples of treatment cases to the discussion. As noted previously, maternal depression, psychiatric difficulties, abusive or neglectful attitude, traumatic pregnancy and/or delivery or family dysfunction may underlie feeding problems. Conversely, oversensitive babies who are difficult to soothe, or temperamentally very different to her, may confuse the mother, leading to cycles of anxiety which exacerbate insecurity.

In conclusion, were we to draw out a common denominator across all the papers in this Reader, it is that the early exchange is potentially fraught with emotional issues for infant and parent/s (and their health carers), triggering unresolved wild things within. Given the different temperamental combinations of parent–infant pairs, each household develops its own 'emotional climate' in which the primary exchange takes shape. An infant arrives equipped with capacities that enable him or her to initiate and participate in dialogic interactions with responsive others. However, when carers are insensitive to the infant's basic rhythms or answer his or her exuberance with austerity or intrusiveness, the infant will initially take on the carer's mood, then become apathetic, rejecting, defiant or compliant to their expectations rather than unself-consciously living out his or her own innate potentialities. Conversely, if the mother's face is the baby's 'mirror', the baby is the parent's emotional 'trigger' and a catalyst to re-emergence of unresolved infantile issues from their own past, reactivating primitive forces and unconscious representations of themselves in the mind of the original carer. With a family, symptoms in an individual are likely to reflect wider interactive dysfunction and sometimes transgenerational transmissions. But, above all, psychoanalytic understanding enables us to contemplate the complexity of meanings behind disturbance – a problem's significance varies according to context; different behavioural manifestations may share common roots, and, conversely, a single symptom may express a variety of conscious and unconscious personal and familial connotations. On the positive side, disturbances in infancy are highly responsive to timely therapeutic intervention, as they are not yet well-established and entrenched and parents are often highly motivated to provide better parenting than they received. As we've seen, it is more difficult to dispel the 'ghosts' that have been around for generations or a disturbance that has remained unchallenged into adulthood.

Returning to our opening metaphor, to some degree we each always do retain wild inscriptions on the archaic apparatus of our psychic 'mystic pad'. However, as the many and varied papers in this book confirm, by developing a capacity for self-awareness and retrospective reflection we lessen the intensity of our own and transmitted unconscious experiences. And, when we find healing, through compassionate understanding, we may even achieve a recurrent, albeit precarious, sense of reconciliation with both human frailty and the wildness within.

CHAPTER 18

Psycho-analytic insight and relationships[1]

ISCA SALZBERGER-WITTENBERG

I Feelings the caseworker brings to the relationship with the client

Although we have to use shorthand terms like 'case-worker' and 'client', I am always thinking of people or a particular person needing help and a particular individual offering help. For the sake of clarity, I shall refer to the caseworker as 'she' and the client as 'he' except where I give case material, and there the sex of the actual person will be indicated.

The first meeting of caseworker and client is a new experience for both; they come together eager, though in different ways, to find out about each other. Although it is a new experience, their relationship and particularly their initial contact will be greatly influenced by the attitude each partner brings to the situation.

It is important for the caseworker to be aware of her feelings so that they do not stand in the way of her really getting to know her client as an individual. Otherwise she may be so preoccupied by her eagerness to be helpful, by what her supervisor or head of department will say, or busy proving to herself how successful she is, that these considerations overshadow the interview and distort her perception and reactions. If these feelings can be worked over beforehand and kept in check if they occur during the interview, the worker will be freer to observe and take in what is going on here and now. The worker must also rid herself of preconceived notions about her client from one interview to the next. Every time is a new beginning, and while there is shared knowledge and experience, the worker needs to be free to see her client afresh, to allow another facet of her client's personality to come forward and permit change and development.

[1]First published in 1970 in Psycho-Analytic Insight and Relationships – A Kleinian Approach by Isca Salzberger-Wittenberg. Routledge and Kefan Paul. Reprinted here by kind permission of the authors and Francis & Taylor who now hold the copyright.

The expectations and fears the caseworker may have are innumerable, and depend on the particular caseworker's personality and experience as well as on the nature of the problem she is faced with. I can only mention a few common ones which I have come across.

Hopeful expectations of the caseworker

To be a helpful parent

Most caseworkers set out to be helpful and see themselves in a good parental role, vis-à-vis their client. Their wish to engage in social work may spring from a deep desire to repair situations and relationships, but in order to achieve this aim, reparative zeal must be geared to what is realistic and of benefit to the client. 'Do-gooder' is now a term of insult, conjuring up a picture of someone rushing in, impatient to show how much good she can do, without full consideration of the needs of the person requiring help. In this extreme form it may sound ridiculous, but there is a danger, especially for the beginner, to have to *prove* to the client (and in the back of her mind to herself) that she is helpful. The need to reassure herself that she is doing something of value may drive the caseworker to give advice when she is not yet fully in possession of the facts, or able to judge what receiving advice may mean to the client. Or she may intervene very actively in his life without defining the limits of her role and in this way mislead her client into believing that she will take on a full and active parental role rather than a professional one. The caseworker must be clear in her own mind as to what she can realistically offer, bearing in mind her caseload and what she can expect of herself.

To be tolerant

Because of her wish to be a helpful parent to her client, the caseworker may entertain an expectation of herself being kind, gentle and tolerant. These qualities are certainly desirable in someone entrusted with the confidence and care of human beings in need of help. But too often gentleness, kindness and tolerance are not distinguished from an attitude which comes close to appeasing or colluding with the client's aggressive feelings and behaviour. We need to distinguish between tolerance based on the ability to acknowledge the client's feelings and being able to bear them, and being so frightened of the client's hostile behaviour and negative feelings that they have to be glossed over or excused in some way. The caseworker in the latter instance is implicitly communicating to the client: this is too bad to be acknowledged, therefore let us ignore it, call it something else or pretend it is not there. Clearly, this is not tolerant at all, and the client will understand that the worker cannot stand hostility, depression, despair. If the caseworker cannot, how can the client?

Here is an example: Mrs X cancelled three appointments with a psychiatric social worker. On every occasion she offered an explanation. Once she said she missed the train, another time she did not feel very well; on the third occasion she forgot. Today she phones half an hour after she was due to come, and talks non-stop for five minutes saying that she just couldn't make it, she was going to come but decided to wait for the bread-van to call. The delivery was late and she tried to get a bus and missed the train. The caseworker sympathises with Mrs X's difficulties in having such a long way to come and asks whether she could expect her next week, offering a choice of time. Mrs X is evasive, says she will see, hopes she can make it. The worker leaves it at that. Mrs X does not come next week. Nor does she ring or write.

It is true that the caseworker was sympathetic, recognising the external difficulties, but was she dealing with the client's feelings? No one mentioned that part of Mrs X did not want to come to the interview and that external factors were used to express inner reasons for staying away. Was the caseworker not evading the dilemma of the client who could not bring herself to the interview because she was in a state of conflict? Some verbal recognition of the difficulties, internal as well as external, might have given the client some trust in the worker's ability to understand her conflicted self and so perhaps enables her to come. But suppose the client decided to stop treatment altogether. It would have been such a relief for her to be helped to say that she did not want to come and to experience the worker as one able to tolerate this. Otherwise she may be left with such guilt feelings at having rejected the 'kind' worker that she may find it impossible to return later when she may be more motivated to seek help.

Some caseworkers feel so guilty about losing a client that they sometimes hang on to him under any circumstances. The adult client has a share in the responsibility for his treatment and the freedom to break it off when he wants to. The caseworker might also remind herself that there are more people wanting to get help than staff to deal with them. (These considerations of course do not apply where there is a statutory obligation to keep up a contact with a caseworker such as in probation or certain child care cases.)

To be understanding

By virtue of her training and experience the caseworker may feel justified in feeling that she has knowledge about human relationships which will help her in understanding her client. She needs to guard, however, against a sense of omniscience and superiority in relation to other human beings. Acquaintance with theories about human beings does not give a key to understanding people but tends to remain unintegrated and to be applied indiscriminately unless such knowledge has become part of one's living experience. Clients are not embodied theories. They are human beings, each with their own complicated and unique personality though they have basic patterns of relationships similar to others.

Here is an example of the danger of applying knowledge indiscriminately. A medical social worker was dealing with a case of encopresis in a boy of seven. In taking the social history she learnt that the mother of the boy had recently started a part-time job. At once she was convinced that this accounted for the boy's encopresis, that he was deprived and insecure because of his mother's absence. In vain the mother tried to explain that she was always at home when the child returned from school and that she didn't work in school holidays. The fact that the mother worked was *ipso facto* interpreted as deprivation and as the reason for the child's illness. This prevented the worker from looking for deeper causes for the child's complaint.

There are two separate misconceptions here: first, that in every case it is wrong and harmful for the child's mother to work; secondly, that the cause of an emotional disturbance lies invariably in the parent. There are two partners to every relationship and all we know at the beginning is that something has gone wrong in the delicate interaction between them. We cannot say what or why until we know much more about each of the partners and the way they interact. Theories are formulated to help us organise our thoughts about the interaction between people and the different parts within the personality, but in no two persons are the manifestations and constellations exactly the same. Each case provides us with an opportunity to discover something new.

The caseworker's fears

Let us now look at some of the fears which beset the caseworker meeting her client. Some anxieties are part and parcel of the price we pay for engaging in such responsible work; for the beginner there is the additional guilt of knowing that the client will credit her with authority and knowledge by virtue of her holding a position in the agency. Will she be able to understand the client's feelings? Will she not do harm to her client? If she allows herself to be receptive will she be invaded by the problems put before her, overwhelmed like the client by depression or fear? How is she to cope with silences in an interview? None of these anxieties can be lightly dismissed. The fact that they are experienced shows that the student is in touch with her feelings and trying to deal with them. Supervision is essential not to do away with such anxieties but to afford a check on whether the caseworker's own problems are interfering and distorting the work process.

There is room only to take up three of the fears I have often come across, while some others will be dealt with in section III. Students sometimes express a fear that in exploring their client's feelings they are 'digging into' and 'doing harm'. Related to this is the notion that psychological insight means looking 'with X-ray eyes' into someone's mind. Each of these statements connotes an aggressive act, something like forcing one's way into the other person without his knowledge, against his wishes and interest. This is not the place to go into the childhood sources of such anxieties. This will be discussed in section II. Here I want to question these assumptions.

Probing and digging into the past

Casework students sometimes say that they do not like 'probing' and 'digging into' the client's past. Indeed, they would be wrong to attempt to do so. I think that the assumption is based on a misconception. The client comes because he is at present in some difficulty. There is therefore no need to dig into the past; the past is only relevant in so far as it is still active and influencing him today. It is therefore something traceable in the here and now, although it may have its roots far back in childhood. Perhaps it is the caseworker's fear of the ongoing emotional relationship to herself that makes her want to explore the past. Here is an example. A young man tells the worker shortly before her holiday that he hates saying goodbye and feels angry at having recently been left by a friend 'high and dry'. It is correct to assume that these feelings were first experienced in babyhood when he might have felt unsupported by a mother's arm and dry in the mouth when she went away, but the client is saying this now because he experiences the separation from the caseworker as being left with his problem, unsupported, in a state of needing more mental feeding. The client is bringing the baby part of himself that operates at that moment in relation to the caseworker.

Doing harm

The fear of doing harm may have various sources: the caseworker may be afraid of what forces she is unleashing when she allows her client's feelings to emerge and afraid of things getting out of control. If these feelings are so readily available to the client – and in casework we do not usually deal with deeply unconscious feelings – one would suppose it is far safer for them to be brought out in the caseworker's presence than burst out somewhere else where they may do more harm. The caseworker might ask herself whether she is afraid of her own reactions and finds some emotions too disturbing and painful or whether she is afraid of not being able to control the client.

The caseworker may fear that she will hurt the client if she says something inappropriate. Unless clients are very disturbed, they are not so vulnerable that a wrong remark would upset their whole balance. She may feel that she is causing suffering by allowing the client to experience painful feelings, but in fact a client will find great relief if he is able to share such feelings. The caseworker's ability to stand emotional pain and to be tolerant will enable the client to incorporate and identify with her and so become more tolerant of himself and others.

To look with X-ray eyes

Does psychological insight really enable us to look into somebody's mind like a machine taking an X-ray picture? This fear is often linked to the idea that the student's personality is transparent to her supervisor. The student will soon discover that the situation in reality is vastly different. At best, we understand only a fraction of what is going on, and we depend at every step on the co-operation of the client. It is both a limitation and an essential condition of the work that it is a joint enterprise and can be hindered, virtually stopped or broken off by the client at any time. (Compare examples in this chapter.) It is true, however, that a person's behaviour, facial expression, voice, manner, posture, etc. tell us a good deal about him, providing clues to those prepared to look and listen. One does not necessarily have to be trained to have such perception and draw inferences from it. Mothers often have acute intuition about their young baby's states of mind and on the basis of this respond to his needs. Such psychological closeness occurs when the mother has sufficiently worked through her own infantile anxieties and is therefore able to accept and carry those of her baby. What we need, in order to understand our clients better, is not a mechanical aid to looking and listening but the ability to be sensitively aware of what it is like to be that other human being, in the effort to overcome the limitations of separateness and differences.

II Feelings the client brings to the relationship

Hopeful expectations

Long before the client meets the caseworker he has ideas about the kind of person he wants her to be and what she is to do for him. The nature of these expectations depends on the client's maturity. In everyone, however, there are some hopes which are unfulfilled, and every new venture tends to arouse our ideal expectations. It is as if we were saying 'this time it is going to be different; this person will give me all I ever longed for'. In as far as our expectations are ideal they are unattainable; in as far as they are reasonable, they have a chance of being met.

To rid himself of pain

Basically, the ideal the client hopes for is that the caseworker will take away all pain. To this end the client may tell the worker what she should do: e.g. 'Get me a house, then my wife will look after the kids properly, and I won't go to the pub any more.' Alternatively, he may treat the caseworker as if she was an oracle: 'Tell us what to do!' 'Tell me who's right!' 'I'll do anything you say.' 'You know what's best.' These attitudes are met with again and again, both in individual work and in groups. The pressure to get the caseworker to give answers and to make decisions arises from the avoidance of emotional pain connected with not-knowing, uncertainty and self-hate and guilt when things go wrong. If the caseworker does not fall in with such demands, she may be told that she gives nothing worthwhile and become the object of hostility.

Another way of ridding himself of his troubles is to pour them out, with no effort to try and understand them. A social worker will say. 'He told me too much in the first interview; he won't come back.' Such intuition implies that the client has used the caseworker as a dustbin, has massively evacuated his problems into her and is likely to become frightened in case the worker will put it all back, reproach him or make him feel ashamed.

To find someone to help carry the burden

If the client is looking for someone temporarily to carry his anxieties, to share his burden and to help him towards finding a solution, this can become the basis of a realistically helpful relationship. 'You are the first person who has taken the trouble to listen to me, who is really interested, who cares' are expressions of gratitude and show how great is the human need to find someone who is a good listener, capable of carrying anxiety and how rarely this need is met.

To be loved

To be loved is every human being's most ardent desire. At the deepest level this means being loved as we are, with all our faults and shortcomings. This requires that someone should understand us in the widest sense of the term and yet not reject us. It is such understanding that the more mature part of the client is striving for. Yet there is always the doubt whether it is possible to be loved if the truth were known, and hence the worker may find herself being seduced into a relationship based on mutual admiration of each other's nice qualities. If this happens, she must ask herself what has happened to the bad aspects of the client and herself. If, because of her own need to be loved and admired, the caseworker allows herself to be idealised, she is not helping the client to face the inevitable frustrations and disappointments of reality. On the contrary, the client will all the more concentrate his anger on someone outside, e.g. the marriage partner.

Fears the client comes with

To be blamed

As the client comes for help because there has been a failure in dealing with himself, his family or the outer world, the notion that he will be criticised is near at hand. He may be full of self-reproaches, 'it's all my fault' (which is unlikely to be so) or adopt a belligerent attitude. 'It's no good investigating me, you will find nothing in my family that accounts for Janet's behaviour' was the opening remark of a mother to the psychiatric social worker. Implicit in this statement is the client's assumption that the purpose of the interview was to attach blame and that it would end in a moral indictment. Feelings of guilt may lead to the withholding of important information or blaming someone else: 'I am sure it is the school'; 'It all started since she has been going out with that boy.'

The client tends to pick on some simple external reason to explain what he dare not or cannot understand. There is a positive aspect to this, however, namely the belief that if the true cause can be discovered some answer might be found.

To be punished

Guilt and a moralistic outlook lead to fear of punishment. Child care officers come across children who feel so guilty and responsible for the breakdown of their parents' marriage that they expect their foster parents to be wicked people to whom they are sent for punishment. Probation officers, as representatives of authority, have a particular problem here. If the probationer has been treated in a punishing way before, this will make him even more sensitive to any hint of punitive attitude in the probation officer. The offender may behave in a way designed to provoke the probation officer to become angry and punitive and then feel justified in believing him to be as irrational and uncontrolled as he is himself.

To be abandoned

Once the client has been able to trust the caseworker enough to tell her about himself he may feel very vulnerable. His hopes have been raised and he fears he will be abandoned by her before his troubles have been sorted out. It may be difficult for the caseworker to appreciate the full weight of her commitment to her client from the beginning. Through the very act of seeing him, she is putting herself forward as a person who accepts responsibility for feelings of trust and dependence. She must remember that the client brings not primarily the adult but the infantile aspects of his personality that are in need of help. As with his parents in the past, he is liable to interpret her actions as if they all refer to him. If she hands him on, is it because his problems are so serious that she cannot cope with them? If she goes on holiday, does she not care? If she leaves her job, has he undermined her ability to work? These are but a few of the many anxieties that may beset the client.

III Transference and countertransference

Transference and its implications for casework

We have seen that caseworker and client alike have expectations about each other even before they meet. Such ideas are based on their past patterns of relationships and we therefore say that they are *transferred* to the present.

Such *transferences* of feelings influence the new relationship in important ways. As Gosling (1968) points out, they affect the way we (a) perceive, (b) interpret the new situations and (c) influence it; for our behaviour, in terms of our assumptions, tends to elicit a response in the partner(s) which fits in with our expectations. An example of (a) was the woman who felt so responsible for her child's problems that she saw the caseworker as highly critical of her, someone who would blame her. An example of (b) is the client who interprets his caseworker's absence as the result of the excessive demands he made on her. An example of (c) is the young offender who, expecting punishment, behaves in such a provocative way to his probation officer that the latter finally does in fact respond in an aggressive and punitive way.

It is most important, therefore, for the caseworker to be aware of the nature of transferred feelings. Knowing that such feelings *are transferred* from the past may help her to look at the situation more objectively. The deep feelings of love, hatred and dependence which the client experiences towards her may have less to do with her personal worth than finding himself in a relationship where such feelings are reactivated. Secondly, such awareness will help the caseworker to resist colluding with or being manipulated by the client to fit in with unrealistic expectations whether they be of someone bad or ideal. In this way, instead of being encouraged to act out his feelings, the client is forced to become aware of them, to compare them to the reality of the situation and to deal with his frustrations.

The concept of transference

We owe the discovery of the phenomena of transference to Sigmund Freud (1895). When he found that hysterical female patients tended to fall in love with their physician, he first regarded this as a nuisance and hindrance to the work of analysis. But he had the brilliance subsequently to arrive at the conclusion that what was happening was that the patient was re-experiencing feelings that she had had previously towards someone else, e.g. the girl towards her father. Such feelings had given rise to conflict, had been suppressed and found an outlet in the hysterical symptom. In the psycho-analytic setting, they surfaced again. Freud later found that all kinds of earlier conflicts involving hate, jealousy, rivalry, etc. entered into the relationship with the analyst. 'A whole series of psychological experiences are revived, not as belonging to the past, but as applying to the physician at the present moment.' Such repetitions made it possible for earlier conflicts to be understood and undergo change. It also enabled Freud, to a large extent, to reconstruct the patient's past. On the basis of many adult analyses, Freud was able to arrive at hypotheses about the sexual development of children. Direct observation of children has since proved these to be correct.

Through Melanie Klein's work (1952) the concept of transference has extended in two directions. First, she widened it to include not only repressed conflicts but the whole range of earlier emotions which enter into a relationship. Secondly, it has deepened in the sense that Klein's analysis of children showed that what is transferred are both more grown-up elements and all the infantile feeling states which persist right through life.

It is in the Kleinian sense that I have applied transference in the foregoing chapters. We shall later need to examine the nature of the 'child and baby feelings' existing within the adult and trace their roots to infancy.

Countertransference

The caseworker, like the client, brings to the situation expectations, fears and problems transferred from the past. For instance, she may see in the client before her some aspect of her mother and consequently feel herself still to be in the position of a little girl, unable to help this adult. Or, faced with a couple, her problems of jealousy in relation to her parents may incline her to support one against the other. She may be overinquisitive, motivated less by the wish to understand and be concerned about her client than driven by the need to intrude into other people's private life as she might have once wanted to enter into the secret life of the parents from which she was excluded, or she may be so frightened of such inclinations that her natural curiosity is inhibited.

There is a common tendency for workers to side with children against their parents because of the wish to blame one's own parents for whatever has gone wrong in one's life. This is, of course, particularly so if the child in fact appears to be rejected or the mother expresses hatred for her child, in spite of the caseworker's theoretical acceptance of a non-critical attitude! We need to dissociate ourselves sufficiently to be able to ask: 'Why does this woman feel like this about this particular child?' and appreciate the mother's difficulties. If we do, we may find that the mother's hostile or even murderous feelings are not so alien to our nature after all, for we harbour in ourselves similar hidden feelings towards siblings or unacceptable childish parts of ourselves. Sometimes a particular problem so closely corresponds to the worker's own, that she is either blind to it or alternatively gets over-involved.

The term *counter-transference* was coined to denote feelings which the worker transfers from the past and inappropriately applies to the client or his problem. Supervision and self-examination are important to check whether clients in general, or particular clients or specific problems, tend to trigger off in the caseworker her own unsolved problems. In so far as they do, this will distort her perception and interfere with her interaction with the client.

In recent years, the term counter-transference has also been used in a different sense namely, to describe the reaction set off in the worker as a result of being receptive to the client's transferred feelings. These emotions, in so far as they correctly mirror the client's, are a most helpful guide to understanding. Often, they give us a clue to the feelings which have remained unexpressed. For instance, a client may evoke great concern in us as if the child in him was crying out for maternal care, although he may tell us repeatedly that he doesn't want any help. Or, for instance, feeling in despair after a client left may be the only clue, that behind the client's outburst of anger there is a hopeless, miserable part of himself. After a holiday, a child sat for weeks behind books apparently completely rejecting me and the treatment. This was her way of communicating to me what she had felt I had done to her in the holiday, and how terrible it was not to be able to get in touch. It becomes pertinent therefore to ask oneself: what does this person make me feel like? and what does this tell me about him, about the nature of the relationship and about the effect he has on others? Further, we need to question ourselves as to whether this is valid intuition, a response in terms of what the client is communicating or whether we are reacting in terms of what we are putting into the situation. Such questioning can lead to greater understanding of oneself, of the client and of the nature of the 'here and now' relationship.

References

Freud, S. (1895) Psychotherapy of Hysteria, *Standard Edition of the Collected Works*, vol.3. London: Hogarth & Institute of Psychoanalysis.

Freud, S. (1905) Fragments of an Analysis of a case of Hysteria, Standard Edition of the Collected Works, Vol 7, London: Hogarth and Institute of Psychoanalysis.

Klein, M. (1952) The origins of transference, *Envy and Gratitude, The Writings of Melanie Klein*, vol.3. London: Hogarth & Institute of Psychoanalysis.

Gosling, R. (1968) What is Transference? The Psychoanalytic Approach Ballier. Tindall & Cassel.

CHAPTER 19

Understanding the language of babies[1]

Joanna Hawthorne

Newborn babies are no longer seen as passive recipients of stimuli but rather as highly sophisticated, complex beings. The relationship between an infant and their parents is a two-way interaction, and parents need to spend time watching their baby and observing her signals in order to understand the individual baby's responses to them and to the environment. The time of birth is a vulnerable time for forming relationships, and a mother's experiences and the support she receives at this time can determine the nature of the relationship she has with her baby (Hawthorne and Richards, 1999). We know that patterns of interaction are set up by three months of age and what a baby experiences in this period, positive or negative, will contribute to his or her understanding and sense of security in the world. We also know that a baby's brain is developing extremely fast during this period and will take in from the environment what it needs for optimal development. But this means that the baby must have positive experiences and responses to their behaviour in order to build up a trusting relationship with their caregivers. If babies habitually encounter inappropriate responses to their behaviour, they will build up a sense of insecurity and unpredictability about their world and carers (Rutter and Hay, 1994).

What can babies do?

At birth, babies have remarkable abilities. They can identify their own mother's or father's voice (and they prefer the sound of the human voice, which has a pitch and loudness in the right range). They can identify their mother's smell, they can distinguish their mother's face from that of a stranger, and they can taste the four basic tastes that adults taste (Cole and Cole, 2001). Babies can turn to a sound, and they can track a moving object with their eyes and head. They show a preference for certain patterns,

---

[1]Written for the CPS Summer School, University of Essex, 2001.

especially contrasts between dark and light, and they like the shape of the human face most of all.

But the need to socialise is a top priority of babies, who can suffer if they are left too long without sufficient interaction with other human beings. Babies have remarkable social skills (Klaus and Klaus, 1998; Murray and Andrews, 2000). Recent research suggests babies may be able to detect the difference between happy and sad expressions. Babies have a powerful gaze, which they use from birth, to engage adults. They entice adults to pay attention to them by crying, then reward them by responding to being soothed. They respond to social interactions with a reciprocity, like a 'social dance', which leads to later conversations and 'give and take' in relationships. Research suggests that the suck–pause feeding rhythm adopted by babies is the prototype for later 'turn-taking' behaviours (Brazelton and Cramer, 1991). Babies can imitate gestures such as sticking out the tongue, frowning, and pouting their lips. They learn that certain actions will bring a reward, such as turning towards a nipple ready to feed when their cheek is stroked. Babies are 'pre-tuned' to enable communication with other human beings.

Behavioural states – asleep and awake

All of the baby's behaviour has to be understood in the context of behavioural states. For instance, the baby will not feed if he is sleepy, or the baby will not want to go to sleep if he is in an alert state, ready to play. Some babies will change from state to state rapidly, which can be challenging to cope with, whereas others wake up slowly, stay alert for a period, then might fuss, and go to sleep. Identifying the baby's state can be very helpful to parents, who learn to predict what might come next, after they get to know their own baby's particular pattern (Brazelton and Nugent, 1995).

Six states of consciousness

1. *Deep sleep* – eyes are firmly closed; breathing is deep and regular with no motor activity; in this state the growth hormones are active.
2, *Active* (light) *sleep* – eyes are firmly closed, but there may be twitches, irregular or shallow breathing, facial movements; it is thought that brain growth and differentiation may occur during active (or rapid eye movement, REM, sleep).
3. *Drowsy state* – eyes may open and close, but look glazed in appearance; arms and legs may move smoothly; breathing is regular but faster and shallower than in sleep; babies in this state may be susceptible to being aroused to a more alert, responsive state.
4. *Alert, awake state* – body and face are relatively quiet and inactive with bright shining eyes. Sights and sounds will produce responses, and in this state the baby can be very rewarding for parents.

5. *Alert but fussy state* – transitional state to crying; available to external stimuli and may be soothed or brought to an alert state by attractive stimuli; if stimuli are too much, may break down to fussiness; movements are jerky, disorganised, and may startle the infant.
6. *Crying* – communicates hunger, pain, boredom, discomfort, tiredness, setting off automatic responses of concern and responsibility in parents; this is the most effective mode for attracting a caregiver (Brazelton and Cramer, 1991).

It is helpful for parents to understand that the baby's brain is not mature enough for the baby to regulate his states (sleep and feeding times), and some babies need more help than others in the early weeks to regulate. Some babies can also soothe themselves more easily than others, which helps them regulate their states. This information can help parents see that their baby's behaviour is spontaneous and that babies cannot manipulate their behaviour or responses.

The Neonatal Behavioural Assessment Scale

One method to systematically observe babies is through use of the Neonatal Behavioural Assessment Scale (NBAS) developed by Dr T. Berry Brazelton in 1973. It is designed to assess the emotional and behavioural characteristics and individuality of newborns. It assesses the newborn's behavioural repertoire as he or she responds to human and non-human stimuli, such as a rattle, bell, red ball as well as the human face and voice. It also assesses 18 reflexes, and in total there are 53 scorable features, some of which are administered and some just observed during the assessment, like startles, tremors, skin colour and other signs of stress or withdrawal, and smiles.

The NBAS is being used increasingly by clinicians as a way of encouraging parents to be more aware of the capacities of their newborn infants, and as a way of identifying concerns about the baby. It provides a profile of the baby's ability to self-soothe and self-regulate, and thereby provides information on caregiving.

The NBAS can be used on any baby from birth to three months old, and on premature babies when they are well and over 35 weeks' gestation. The trained professional can join with the parent in getting to know the baby as a person and validating the parent's observations. Because the baby's behaviour is seen by the professional and the family at the same time, there is a focus of attention on the baby, and this seems to pave the way for an open discussion. The NBAS has been used successfully with postnatally depressed mothers, mothers of premature infants or mothers with particular difficulties in interacting with their babies (Nugent and Brazelton, 1989). Studies where the NBAS has been used as an intervention show increased maternal self-confidence and mother–infant reciprocity scores, and enhanced paternal involvement (Beal, 1986; Britt and Myers, 1994). Parents become aware that, by observing their baby's behaviour, they can tell when their baby is over-stressed, tired, hungry or playful, and provide the appropriate response.

What do babies need?

Babies do not only need food, sleep, and physical warmth; they need an emotionally warm and responsive caregiver to meet their emotional needs. Babies need a sense of being contained and 'held' not only physically but emotionally. The following is a list of what babies need, developed by Brazelton and Cramer (1991).

1. an observer who sees their strengths and helps them with their difficulties
2. warm, responsive interactions with caretakers
3. social interaction providing feedback within the family system
4. vocalisations reinforced by response
5. to be asked questions and told what is happening in order to establish a meaning of what is happening and promote a feeling of security
6. structure and routine, with flexibility
7. interesting things to look at and do
8. a caretaker who understands that individuals develop at their own rate
9. a caretaker who understands development
10. maternal self-confidence, which comes from understanding the baby as an organism with behaviours that can be read, and indicate if the baby is content
11. caretakers who enable babies to develop their full potential by encouraging them to make a success of their actions and helping them with their difficulties

These concepts are vital when we think about helping parent–infant relationships get off to a healthy start.

How health professionals can help

A health professional who is aware of the baby's needs and capacities can enhance the caregiver's responsiveness and alertness to the baby's signals. Professionals can be trained to systematically observe emotional and behavioural characteristics in babies using the Neonatal Behavioural Assessment Scale (NBAS). If we can create an open, non-judgmental environment where parents can express their feelings of ambivalence, joys and concerns, we can help mothers become in tune (or to gain attunement) with their infants. 'Attunement', according to Stern (1985), is 'the performance of behaviours that express the quality of feeling of a shared affect state'.

The mother and baby must be in tune with each other, and the ability of the caregiver to understand changes in the baby enhances the infant's sense of self (Winnicott, 1982). The carer's unconscious and conscious feelings are easily sensed by the infant from birth, via non-verbal cues. The mother brings many past experiences to her relationship with her new baby; the success of the new relationship will depend on many factors including the mother's perceptions of her own mothering, and how she has come to terms with these experiences. If she is at ease, then she will be better able to observe her new baby and meet his or her needs appropriately. If she is not, she may need professional help to understand troubling feelings.

As health professionals, we have an important role to play in helping parents form positive relationships with their babies (Brazelton, 1992). We are in a position to have an influence on a new family at a very sensitive time, and parents will watch how we handle and talk about their baby, and model their interactions with their baby in the same way. We must be sure that we know all the things babies can do, and look at recent research ourselves, so that we can impart accurate information to parents. By using the baby's behaviour as the focus, we can form a therapeutic alliance with the family. Emphasising the wonderful things the baby can do helps parents focus on the strengths of their baby. By helping parents to understand that the baby has a personality and temperament of its own from birth, and will develop certain abilities at certain times, we have found that parents tend to feel less guilty about, and less rejected by, their baby. Parents are also less likely to impute intent to their baby by feeling their baby is out to get them by behaving in a certain way. It is through a positive collaboration between parents and health professionals that we can help family relationships develop in the best possible way.

References

Beal, J.A. (1986) The Brazelton Neonatal Behavioural Assessment Scale: a tool to enhance parental attachment. *Journal Pediatric Nursing*, 1: 170-7.

Brazelton, T.B. (1992) *Touchpoints: Your child's Emotional and Behavioural Development*. Perseus Books.

Brazelton, T.B. and Cramer, B.G. (1991) *The Earliest Relationship*. London: Karnac.

Brazelton, T.B. and Nugent, J.K. (1995) The Neonatal Behavioural Assessment Scale (3rd edn.). *Clinics in Developmental Medicine*,137. MacKeith Press. Distributed by Cambridge University Press.

Britt, G.C. and Myers, B.J. (1994) The effects of Brazelton intervention: a review. *Infant Mental Health Jounal*, 15: 278-92.

Cole, M. and Cole, S.R. (eds) (2001) *The Development of Children*, 4th edn., New York: Worth Publishing.

Hawthorne, J.T. and Richards, M.P.M. (1999) Psychological aspects of neonatal care. In: Roberton, N.R.C. and Rennie, J. (eds), Textbook of Neonatology, 3rd edn. Edinburgh: Churchill-Livingstone.

Klaus, M.H. and Klaus, P.H. (1998) *Your Amazing Newborn*. Perseus Books

Murray, L. and Andrews, L. (2000) *The Social Baby*. Richmond: CP Publishing.

Nugent, J.K. and Brazelton, T.B. (1989) Preventive intervention with infants and families: the NBAS model. *Infant Mental Health Journal* 10: 84–99.

Rutter, M. and Hay, D. (1994) *Development through Life: A Handbook for Clinicians*. Oxford: Blackwell Science Inc.

Stern, D. (1985) *The Interpersonal World of the Infant*. Basic Books, New York.

Winnicott, D.W. (1982) *The Maturational Processes and the Facilitating Environment*. New York: International Universities Press.

CHAPTER 20

The effect of infants'
behaviour on maternal
mental health[1]

LYNNE MURRAY

Most women find becoming a mother a positive experience. Indeed, research in Edinburgh showed that childbirth actually had a psychiatric protective effect (Miller, 1989). The study compared rates of depression following different events, including childbirth, job loss and a single neutral or positive event other than childbirth. It found that birth was closest in impact to the neutral or positive event and that women who had recently delivered were less anxious and depressed than expected.

Nevertheless, several studies have shown that for between 10 and 15 per cent of women childbirth is followed by an episode of clinical depression. The symptoms are indistinguishable from those of depressive disorders arising at other times (Cooper et al., 1991). They include a pervasive depressed mood, a marked increase in levels of anxiety and irritability and a significant impairment of normal daily functioning.

The onset of depression in the year following childbirth most often occurs within the first two months (Cooper et al., 1988) and, although most episodes remit within four months (Cooper et al., 1988; Murray, 1992) several studies have shown that a level of emotional disturbance commonly persists for at least a year (Cooper et al., 1988; Pitt, 1968; Nott, 1987). Several of the British community studies have found that depression in the postnatal months is, like depression at other times, associated with adverse social and economic circumstances such as poor housing and financial difficulties or unemployment (Murray, 1992; Paykel et al., 1980; Cooper and Stein, 1989). In addition, studies in which the quality of a woman's relation-

---

[1] This paper appeared in *Health Visitor* 70/9, September 1997: 334–5 and is reprinted here with kind permission of author and journal.

ship with her partner has been assessed have found a significant association between conflict, or a lack of confiding, in the relationship and depression in the postnatal period (Murray, 1992; Paykel et al., 1980; Kumar and Robson, 1984; Stein et al., 1989; Watson et al., 1984). In fact, lack of confiding relationships in general is common in postnatal depression. The only other antenatal variable to have commonly emerged as predictive of postnatal depression in British studies is a previous history of depressive disorder (Kendell, 1985).

Despite the consistency with which these risk factors have been associated with postnatal depression, predicting who will actually become depressed is far more difficult. Even a predictive index based on the follow-up of several thousand women from late pregnancy through the postpartum period (Cooper et al., 1996) was still far from perfect. Women in adverse circumstances somehow remained well, while others, with ample support and favourable living conditions, experienced depressive mood disorder following delivery.

One possibility is that individual differences between infants may exert an impact on the mother's experience, including the onset of depression. This line of investigation represents something of a shift in emphasis in the work on mother–infant relationships and postnatal depression. The principal concern has been the possible impact of the mother's depression on the infant. Such studies have shown, for example, striking differences in interactive styles between depressed and well mothers during structured face-to-face interactions with their two-to-three-month-old infants (Cohn et al., 1986; Field, 1992; Murray et al., 1996; Murray et al., 1993).

In high-risk samples such differences are marked. Depressed women often appear either withdrawn and disengaged from their infants or intrusive and hostile. In low-risk samples the disturbance is not as extreme, but depression has still been associated with less sensitive and responsive maternal interactions with the infant. These, in turn, have been found to predict a child's poor cognitive development in later infancy and early childhood (Murray et al., 1996). While, undoubtedly, infants are influenced by the care they receive, some studies have suggested that mothers also are affected by their experience of looking after their child. Depressed mothers frequently report that their infants are difficult to manage: they cry a lot, are difficult to settle to sleep and demand attention (Cooper and Murray, 1997; Murray, 1997; Seeley et al., 1996).

Depressed mothers from two Cambridge samples reported sleeping problems with their children. Their infants were hard to settle and required active intervention to get them to sleep – such as pushing the pram up and down. Their infants were also more likely to waken in a distressed state and to cry for prolonged periods. Two further studies suggest that these kinds of factors may affect both maternal depression and the quality of face-to-face interactions with their children. Cutrona and Troutman (1986) found that temperamental difficulties in infants were associated with the persistence of maternal depressed mood. Field et al., (1988) found that when non-depressed nurses interacted with infants of depressed mothers, the nurses' own behaviour became less expressive and positive than when interacting with infants of well women.

These findings are consistent with the idea that an infant's behavioural characteristics may exert a significant influence on maternal mood and behaviour. They are not, however, conclusive. This is because in each of these studies the assessments were carried out when the infants were already two to three months old, and they may have gradually become difficult and unresponsive through being with a depressed mother.

A prospective study

To investigate this prospectively a study was conducted in which the behaviour of infants was examined early in the neonatal period, before the onset of any maternal depression. The mothers were then followed up at eight weeks postpartum, and the association between the characteristics of the infants and maternal mood investigated (Murray, Stanley, Hooper et al., 1996).

A large sample of primiparous women in late pregnancy was screened at the Cambridge Maternity Hospital, using a questionnaire to detect those at raised risk for postnatal depression (Cooper et al., 1996). Women were asked to take part in the study if they had delivered between 38 and 42 weeks, if the infant's birth-weight was > 2500 gm, and the apgar score[2] was at least 8 at five minutes; 238 women at raised risk for depression were invited to take part (of whom 50 (21 %) refused), with a further 46 women at low risk for depression (of whom 3 (6.5%) refused).

Participants were asked to complete two sets of questionnaires in the first postpartum week. One concerned their mood at that time, the 'Blues' questionnaire (Kennerley and Gath, 1989), and the other their perceptions and experience of their infant – the Mother and Baby Scale (Wolke, 1995). When the infants were 10 and 15 days old, they were assessed with a standardised measure of infant behaviour, the Neonatal Behavioural Assessment Scale, or NBAS (Brazelton and Nugent, 1995).[3] This scale gives a profile of an infant's behaviour in response to a range of stimulation, as well

---

[2] Apgar is a screening test done on every newborn immediately following the birth to assess the baby's responsiveness. The top score is 9 [Ed.].
[3] See Chapter 19 this volume [Ed.].

as recording reflexes. It enables the administrator to identify an infant's strengths and difficulties, and in particular its ability to fend off unpleasant environmental events and its capacity to regulate its own state. At the same time each mother's mental state was assessed, and those who were depressed were excluded from the study. At eight weeks postpartum the women were seen again, and a researcher administered a standardised psychiatric interview to determine whether the mother had become depressed since the neonatal examination. Thirty-two per cent of the women at raised risk for depression had become depressed, as had 19 per cent of those in the low-risk sample.

The relationship between the infants' behaviour assessed by the NBAS and the mothers' subsequent mental state was then investigated, and a significant relationship was found. *In cases where the infant's motor control had been rated as poor, the risk of maternal depression was raised almost fivefold.* This applied to women at both high and low risk of depression. *Irritability was the other neonatal characteristic that was found to predict later maternal depression.* This category refers to infants who are highly sensitive to slight stimulation, who respond quickly by becoming distressed and who require considerable help to become calm again. In cases where the mother was already categorised as at increased risk from depression the presence of such behaviour raised the risk more than three-and-a-half times.

In considering the impact of the infant on the mother it is important to show that the neonate's behaviour during the NBAS examination at ten days was not actually caused by the mother's state at that time. This was done by eliminating from the study women who had become depressed by the time the neonatal assessment was carried out.

However, it was also felt important to consider the influence of an infant's behaviour once the mother's general mood (and possibly subclinical depression) had been taken into account, along with her experience and perceptions of her infant. While both severe 'blues' and feelings that the infant was unsettled and irregular did predict later maternal depression, the influence of an infant's behaviour was still highly significant. Two other findings also confirm the view that the behavioural characteristics of infants which were predictive of depression were not actually a function of maternal variables. First, none of the social and personal risk factors assessed in the antenatal screening questionnaire was found to predict an infant's irritability or poor motor control. Indeed, the risk of these occurring was the same in both high- and low-risk women. Secondly, there was scant relationship between the mother's feelings and her perceptions of her infant in the first few postpartum days and her infant's actual behaviour. It is not hard to imagine how an infant with high levels of irritable behaviour may make the task of child care more difficult, particularly in the context of previously existing maternal vulnerability.

Irritable infants may find even simple procedures, such as having a nappy changed, stressful, and calming them places considerable demands on parents. The difficulty for parents of infants with poor motor control is not so immediately obvious, and more research is needed to understand exactly what goes on. One possibility is that these infants find it more difficult to establish and maintain eye contact with their carers, and there may be fewer opportunities for parents to enjoy the normal interpersonal contacts and sense of relationship with the infant that can make child care so rewarding.

Another reason why difficult behaviour in infants may place mothers at risk of depression concerns broader cultural beliefs about infancy. Much of the information parents receive about infant development has tended to give the impression that there is a 'typical' or 'normal' infant – one, for example, who sleeps a lot between meals and is easily comforted. *If an infant does not match this image of the normal baby, a mother may easily feel that this is her fault.* In such cases mothers may be reluctant to avail themselves of support routes, such as mother and baby clinics, because they imagine that they will meet with disapproval or that they will be the only one with an infant who is crying.

These findings highlight the need for healthcare professionals to make parents aware that infants do not necessarily correspond to textbook models and that their response to their baby may be influenced by the child's behaviour. Ways in which healthcare professionals may be effective in helping parents with difficult infants are currently being investigated in an NHS Executive-backed project at Reading.

References

Brazelton, T. and Nugent, J. (1995) Neonatal Behavioral Assessment Scale. London: MacKeith Press.

Cohn J., Matias R., Tronick, E. (1986) Face-to-face interactions of depressed mothers and their infants. In: Tronick, E. and Field, T. (eds.) *Maternal Depression and Infant Disturbance: New Directions for Child Development*, No. 34. San Francisco: Jossey Bass.

Cooper, P., Campbell, E. and Day, A. (1988) Non-psychotic psychiatric disorder after childbirth: a prospective study of prevalence, incidence, course and nature, *British Journal of Psychiatry*, 152: 799–806.

Cooper, P. and Murray, L. (1997) The impact of psychological treatments of postpartum depression on maternal mood and infant development. In Murray, L. and Cooper, P. (eds.) Postpartum Depression and Child Development. New York: Guilford.

Cooper, P., Murray, L. and Hooper, R. (1996) The development and validation of a predictive index for postpartum depression. *Psychological Medicine*, 26: 627–34.

Cooper, P., Murray, L. and Stein, A. (1991) Postnatal depression. In: *The European Handbook of Psychiatry Disorders*. Zaragos: Antropos.

Cooper, P. and Stein, A. (1989) Life events and postnatal depression: the Oxford study. In: Cox, J. and Paykel, E.S. (eds.), *Life Events and Postpartum Psychiatric Disorder*. Southampton: Duphar Laboratories.

Cutrona, C. and Troutman, B. (1986) Social support, infant temperament, and parenting self-efficacy: a mediational model of postpartum depression, *Child Development*, 57: 1507-18.

Field, T. (1992) Infants of depressed mothers, *Development and Psychopathology*, 4: 49-66.

Field, T., Healey, B. and Goldstein, S. (1988) Infants of depressed mothers show depressed behaviour even with non-depressed adults, *Child Development*, 59: 1569-79.

Kendell, R. (1985) Emotional and physical factors in the genesis of puerperal mental disorders, *Journal of Psychosomatic Research*, 29: 3-11.

Kennerley, H. and Gath, D. (1989) Maternity blues: detection and measurement by questionnaire, *British Journal of Psychiatry*, 155: 356-62.

Kumar, R. and Robson, K. (1984) A prospective study of emotional disorders in childbearing women, *British Journal of Psychiatry*, 144: 35-47.

Miller, P. (1989) Life events technology: is it adequate for the task? In: Cox, J. and Paykel, E., Page, M. *Current Approaches to Childbirth as a Life Event*. Southampton: Duphar Laboratories.

Murray, L. (1992) The impact of postnatal depression on infant development, *Journal of Child Psychology and Psychiatry*, 33: 543-61.

Murray, L. (1997) The role of infant irritability in postnatal depression in a Cambridge (UK) community population. In: Nugent, J., Brazelton, T. and Lester, B. (eds.), *The Cultural Context of Infancy, Vol. 3*. Ablex: New Jersey.

Murray, L., Fiori-Cowley, A. and Hooper, R. (1996) The impact of postnatal depression and associated adversity on early mother–infant interactions and later infant outcome, *Child Development*, 67: 2512-26.

Murray, L., Kempton, C. and Woolgar, M. (1993) Depressed mothers' speech to their infants and its relation to infant gender and cognitive development, *Journal of Child Psychology and Psychiatry*, 34: 1083-1101.

Murray, L., Stanley, C. and Hooper, R. (1996) The role of infant factors in postnatal depression and mother–infant interactions, *Developmental Medicine and Child Neurology*, 38: 109-19.

Nott, P. (1987) Extent, timing and persistence of emotional disorders following childbirth, *British Journal of Psychiatry*, 151: 523-7.

Paykel, E., Emms, E. and Fletcher, J. (1980) Life events and social support in puerperal depression, *British Journal of Psychiatry*, 136: 339-46.

Pitt, B. (1968) A typical depression following childbirth, *British Journal of Psychiatry*, 114:1325-35.

Seeley, S., Murray, L. and Cooper, P. (1996) The outcome for mothers and babies of health visitor intervention, *Health Visitor*, 69: 135-8.

Stein, A., Cooper, P. and Day, A. (1989) Social adversity and perinatal complications: their relation to postnatal depression, *British Medical Journal*, 298: 1073-4.

Watson, J., Elliot, S. and Rugg, A. (1984) Psychiatric disorder in pregnancy and the first postnatal year, *British Journal of Psychiatry*, 144: 453-62.

Wolke, D. (1995) Parents' perceptions as guides for conducting NBAS clinical sessions. In: Brazelton, T. and Nugent, J. (eds.), *Neonatal Behavioral Assessment Scale*, 3rd edn. London: MacKeith Press.

CHAPTER 21

Management of perinatal loss of a twin[1]

EMANUEL LEWIS AND ELIZABETH M. BRYAN

The death of a twin during pregnancy or around birth gives rise to a bewildering confusion of thoughts and feelings that can impede mourning and disturb the bereaved mother's care of a surviving twin. Every effort should be made to give the parents and siblings an experience of the dead baby. Photographs especially can reduce confusion and assist reality testing and thus facilitate the grieving process and improve the care of the surviving twin.

Introduction

Death at birth or in the womb, though natural and common events, seem contradictory and against the natural order of life. When birth and death are fused, not only hurt and bitter disappointment but confusion and unreality are felt. After months of growing fullness the mother finds a sudden emptiness. Even after a live birth women may experience an emptiness, but the bereaved mother has far stronger emotions: hurt and shame, failure as a mother, and guilt without reason. She has unmanageable, conflicting feelings of love and hate for her dead baby, for other babies, and for other women in childbirth. Grievances abound and distract her from grieving. Bad feelings about what has been lost have to be disentangled from good ones to avoid idealisation on the one hand and chronic unresolved grievances on the other (Bourne, 1968).

A death at birth is associated with a confusion of thoughts and feelings. As a result the parents' thinking is impaired, their testing of reality is undermined, and bizarre reactions and actions can occur, not only in the bereaved

---

[1] This paper is reprinted with permission of author and publisher. It appeared in 1988 in the *British Medical Journal* 297: 1321–3.

family but also in those who care for them (Cullberg, 1972). For example, a vicar reluctantly allowed a stillborn infant to be buried in his graveyard but insisted that the gravestone should be left blank.

Mourning during pregnancy is hard. For normal mourning it is necessary to hold images of the dead person in the mind until eventually there is resolution of grief and relinquishment. This process could interfere with the similar yet vitally different state of mind required during pregnancy – that of cherishing the idea of the baby inside the mother's body. The mother will feel the baby is endangered by the bad feelings and frightening ideas inevitable in the mourning process.

This same emotional complexity exists when a twin dies during pregnancy or soon after its birth (Bryan, 1986a). When one twin survives and the other dies, not only the bereaved but also those who care for them are faced with contradictory psychological processes. The celebration of the birth of the live baby and the increasing emotional commitment of the mother contrast with the opposing processes of sorrowful relinquishment and of coming to terms with the painful emptiness of stillbirth (Winnicott, 1958; Lewis, 1979a). The dead baby may seem a fantasy, particularly if no tangible memories and mementoes remain. Bad memories get lost rather than relinquished. As a mother's full commitment is necessary for effective nurturing of her new-born live baby, the mourning processes may understandably be postponed; if not resumed later, they may give rise to the various syndromes of *failed mourning*. On the other hand, the mother may grieve compulsively for the dead baby and be unable to devote herself to the care of the live baby. Excessive polarisation of feelings about the live and the dead twin may occur if she starts idealising the dead baby (her 'angel baby'), especially if the surviving twin is difficult to handle or worrying because of behaviour or illness.

Management of dying and death

Every effort must be made to give the parents and siblings an experience of the dead or dying baby, as has been described for singleton stillbirth (Lewis, 1976; 1979b; Klaus and Kennell, 1982). If one twin is likely to die, the family should be encouraged to spend extra time with this one so that precious memories can be created, and the parents may later find comfort in knowing that they have given as much love and care to this baby as they could.

Twins are often premature and often surrounded by medical paraphernalia, and therefore they look unusual to parents. It is thus all the more important that the babies become real to their parents by being named, held, and photographed. Many parents treasure photographs of their dead baby, which can facilitate the testing of reality, create memories, and help sort out confusion between the live and the dead twin. Several types of photographs need to be made of the twins separately and together, dressed and naked, to give as satisfactory and complete a memory as possible of the baby and of the multiple birth. Black and white as well as colour pictures should be available when a baby is discoloured; such photographs may be easier to show to siblings, relatives, and friends.

The parents' sense of confusion and unreality is increased if they have had only a partial experience of the dead baby, especially a stillbirth. Some mothers have said that all they remember seeing was a seemingly disembodied limb, or just a head. Seeing but not holding the dead baby, especially a stillborn or very premature baby, can be tantalising and bewildering. Such muddled feelings are not merely painful, they are psycho-pathogenic.

A malformed baby tends to increase the parents' sense of guilt and confusion, but seeing and holding the baby and obtaining the permanent record of a photograph will help the testing of reality. Without a record many parents tend later to exaggerate the deformity, however severe the malformation has been, and grieving is also impeded in those few parents whose memories minimise the malformations. Spare photographs should always be kept with the medical records. Some parents who initially refuse (or even destroy) photographs may later desperately want one.

Photographs should be as natural a part of death as they are of life. The value of a photograph of the twinship was demonstrated at a meeting of the Twins and Multiple Births Association Bereavement Group, where all the five mothers who had had a stillborn twin said that they wished they could have had a picture of the live and dead twin together. Ten mothers whose babies had died in the neonatal period were all sympathetic to this, whereas several members of the medical profession were clearly disturbed by the idea. Though they themselves may have feelings of failure, medical staff can do much to reassure parents and relatives that no reaction, however mixed, to such a death is abnormal or inappropriate.

Twin motherhood

A mother who has had a multiple pregnancy continues to think of herself as a mother of twins (or more) (Bryan, 1986b). Many mothers who had a higher-order birth deeply resent the labelling of their surviving children as, say, triplets when they were born as members of a quadruplet set. A mother showed her need to be seen as a mother of twins when, while shopping with her 18-month-old surviving daughter, she met a mother with identical twins of the same age. She said, 'I've got twins too.' 'Oh', replied the other mother, 'and where is your other little girl?' 'At home,' the bereaved mother replied.

Trite comments such as 'at least you have one healthy baby' will cause pain and resentment. No parent can be expected to find comfort for the death of one child in the survival of its healthy sibling. Yet parents of a surviving twin are often made to feel guilty about their grief. They should be helped to voice this guilt and to acknowledge their confused feelings. If done sensitively, this can diminish anxiety and help with grieving. Any implications that the death was all for the best, even if logically this may have been so, are deeply hurtful to the mother. One mother who had lost one of her triplets made particular efforts never to look harassed or untidy as she dreaded people saying, 'Well, three would have been too much to cope with.'

The pride of a pregnant mother, especially with twins, can have a darker side, in that there can be a conscious or unconscious sense of triumph over others. This can lead to a fear of provoking destructive envy in those less fortunate. After the loss of a baby there can be a fall from grace into a deep sense of shame. The pride of being an expectant mother of twins is enormous, and the failure to become one is therefore all the greater. One mother of a two-year-old surviving twin said to a group of similarly bereaved mothers, almost as a confession, 'I think I am coming to terms with S's death; I shall never come to terms with not being a mother of twins.' All present agreed.

After their loss some parents are unable to celebrate their surviving baby. One couple who would normally have had their child christened in infancy were unable to face the ceremony until it was suggested four years later that the christening should be combined with a memorial for the stillborn twin. This they could accept.

Mourning may be damagingly suppressed for many years, but it is probably never too late for resolution. At the age of 22 a nurse who was a surviving twin showed her mother an article in a nursing journal describing the difficulties faced by parents who lose a newborn twin. For the first time this mother realised that her feelings had not been unique or strange. Her husband had never mentioned the stillborn boy, but when shown the article he began gradually to talk about his son. The mother was so relieved that the quality of their marriage was transformed.

Birth and death before 28 weeks' gestation

If a twin is born dead before 28 completed weeks of the pregnancy (a miscarriage) and a live-born sibling either survives or dies later, the legal paradox and ambiguity add to the difficulties that pervade perinatal bereavement and impede mourning. This experience is movingly described in a personal paper (Gabrielczyk, 1987).

Vanishing twin syndrome

Now that twin pregnancies can be detected by ultrasound scans as early as the first trimester, it has become clear that a substantial number (perhaps as many as half) of twin conceptions end up as single deliveries (the vanishing twin syndrome). With these early detections the question now arises about whether to tell the parents immediately and risk a later disappointment. Many parents say they would prefer to know. A foetus papyraceus can give rise to considerable anxiety. It is often insufficiently explained to the parents, and later the surviving twin may sense that there was something odd or hidden, unexplained, and distressing about the birth. Vagueness can be more troublesome to the surviving twin than a proper knowledge of the lost foetus. Surviving twins have in any case to come to terms with their unease about survival and identity.

Selective foetocide

The intrauterine killing of an abnormal foetus in a multiple pregnancy is now an option available to parents who would otherwise have to choose between terminating the pregnancy despite the sacrifice of a normal baby or continuing the pregnancy while knowingly carrying an abnormal child. This superficially easy solution may seem bizarre and horrifying to many doctors as well as to parents. There are also uncomfortable ethical issues and uneasy associations with eugenics. Thus it is important to identify and clarify the emotional issues that are raised.

The thought of a live baby lying for many weeks by the side of the dead twin can be very disturbing; as well, the natural tendency to deny and the wish to forget are much easier when no baby has been aborted. Unconscious guilt and anxiety may develop and impair grieving. For many parents the full impact of the bereavement is not felt until the delivery, many weeks later, of a solitary live baby. By this time the maternity staff may have 'forgotten' the twin, and this failure to acknowledge and respect the dead baby may add to the mother's distress. A photograph of the ultrasonic scan showing both babies may he a precious and unique proof to parents that they ever had a multiple pregnancy.

Because of the presence of the survivor, there is an increased awareness of the baby that might have been, unlike a simple termination of pregnancy. The bereaved mother will have the difficult task of grieving for a lost baby during a continuing pregnancy and after a live birth.

Surviving siblings

Young children are immensely interested and emotionally involved in pregnancy and childbirth; fact and their fantasies are bewilderingly entangled (Lewis, 1983). The complexities of death at birth are particularly hard to explain to siblings. These vulnerable bereaved children are commonly left to cope with their anxieties largely on their own. Their parents are too often paralysed by their own confusion and distress to be available for explanation and emotional support of the siblings (Bourne and Lewis, 1984). Furthermore, their rearing of the surviving twin may be impaired. This child must later come to terms with survivor guilt and identity confusions, which can affect personality development.

Double loss

When both twins die, it is an enormous tragedy, but at least the mother's grief will be fully realised. Her feelings may be less confusing than those of a mother who has one live and one dead baby. But both mothers need lasting support while they suffer the profound grief of losing not only the child but also the twin motherhood of which they dreamt.

References

Bourne, S. (1968) The psychological effects of a stillbirth on women and their doctors, *Journal of the Royal College of General Practitioners*, 16: 103-12.

Bryan E. (1986a) The intrauterine hazards of twins, *Archives of Disease in Childhood*, 61:1044-5.

Bryan E. (1986b) The death of a new-born twin: how can support for parents be improved?, *Acta Genet Med Gemellol (Roma)*, 5: 115-18.

Bourne, S. and Lewis, E. (1984) Pregnancy after stillbirth or neonatal death: psychological risks and management, *Lancet*, ii: 31-3.

Cullberg J. (1972) Mental reactions of women to perinatal death. In: Morris, N (ed.), *Psychosomatic Medicine in Obstetrics and Gynaecology*. Basel: Karger, pp. 326-9.

Gabrielczyk, M. (1987) Personal view, *British Medical Journal*, 7: 295-9.

Klaus, M. and Kennell, J. (1982) Caring for the parents of a stillborn or an infant who dies. In: *Parent Infant Bonding*. St Louis: Mosby, pp. 259-92.

Lewis, E. (1976) Management of stillbirth: coping with an unreality, *Lancet*, ii: 619-20.

Lewis, E. (1979a) Two hidden predisposing factors in child abuse, *Child Abuse and Neglect*, 3: 327-30.

Lewis, E. (1979b) Mourning by the family after a stillbirth or early neonatal death, *Archives of Disease in Childhood*, 54: 303-6.

Lewis, E. (1983) Stillbirth: psychological consequences and strategies of management. In: Milunsky, A. (ed.), *Advances in Perinatal Medicine*, Vol. 3. New York: Plenum, pp. 205–45.

Winnicott, D. (1958) Primary maternal preoccupation. In: *Collected Papers: Through Paediatrics to Psycho-Analysis*. London: Tavistock; Hogarth/Institute of Psycho-Analysis, 1978, pp. 300–5.

The Twins and Multiple Births Association, a self-help organisation offering help to parents with live or dead twin, can be contacted at 41 Fortuna Way, Aylesby Park, Grimsby DN37 9SJ, UK. [Equivalent organisations exist in many countries. Ed.]

CHAPTER 22

Pregnancy after stillbirth or neonatal death: psychological risks and management[1]

STANFORD BOURNE AND EMANUEL LEWIS

After a perinatal death everyone hopes the next pregnancy will set things right. In reality neurotic, phobic, depressive or hypochondriacal reactions may continue from the first stillbirth (Culberg, 1972) or may be reactivated after an apparent recovery. The marriage (Meyer and Lewis, 1979), or any member of the family, may bear the brunt. Sequelae are often carried into the next generation, activated decades later by anniversaries or life-events (Guyotat, 1980).

Human pain fades, but mourning of stillbirth and genuine recovery are difficult and require time. If mourning is achieved, another pregnancy will offer consolation and fulfilment. Unfortunately, the new pregnancy very often cuts short the mourning process, predisposing to mental disturbance. Serious and bizarre reactions occur unexpectedly, after the birth of a healthy subsequent baby (Lewis and Page, 1978). Puerperal psychosis requiring admission to a psychiatric unit is uncommon: our clinical impression is that it is more likely to follow the next live birth than the stillbirth itself. We refer throughout to stillbirth, but the paper is applicable to neonatal death which, in comparison, is mitigated by the experience of having a live baby – and a little more time to think.

Theoretical considerations

Normal mourning and its difficulties

Normal recovery from a loss involves taking in what has happened, and sorting out mixed feelings and lost hopes so that memories of the dead

---

[1] This paper first appeared in the Lancet, July 7, 1984: 31–3 and is reprinted with permission of authors and publisher.

recede to a healthy perspective (Parkes, 1972; Bowlby, 1980). At first the inner world is occupied with conscious and unconscious images of the body and mind and illness of the dead, which contributes to the malaise, heaviness, and deadness as well as hypochondria and psychosomatic illness (Freud, 1925; Abraham, 1927). In failed or interrupted mourning, symptoms may become chronic, and in some individuals who make an apparent recovery there is a latent vulnerability to subsequent traumas (Guyotat, 1980).

In a loss such as stillbirth the events and feelings are inherently confusing, but difficulties also stem from bad feelings around the dead person or the surrounding events. One feature that family and professionals find bewildering in an adult is the re-emergence of long-forgotten infantile reactions to loss (Klein, 1959).

Special mourning difficulties after stillbirth

Beyond ordinary pain and disappointment, stillbirth is complicated by extraordinary sensations of confusion and unreality, as birth and death have been fused (Bourne, 1968). After months of expectation and growing fullness, there is sudden emptiness with nothing to show, a stupefying non-event. (Even after a live birth, women have a sense of emptiness and sadness mingled with their joy.) Women complain that, after a stillbirth, people expect them to go on as if nothing had happened. The mother feels the stigmata of disease although she usually has no illness. She feels ashamed, inferior, and guilty without reason. If the baby's body is whisked away to an unknown grave, the reality may be yet harder to grasp.

After a stillbirth, the range of unmanageable feelings (Bourne, 1979) involves conflict of love and hate and other complex emotions about the dead baby, about other women, and about childbirth, and there may also be grievances about the obstetric care. Bad feelings about what has been lost have to be disentangled from good ones to avoid idealisation and chronic unresolved grievances.

Mourning during pregnancy

For normal mourning it is necessary to hold images of the dead person, internalised in the mind's inner world until, eventually, there is resolution, relinquishment. In mourning, the dual processes of 'taking in' the loss and eventually freeing oneself from clinging to the past, 'letting go', could both interfere with the vaguely similar yet vitally different state of mind (Winnicott, 1956) required during pregnancy to cherish the idea of the new baby actually inside the mother's body. The baby will seem to be endangered by bad feelings and frightening ideas, inevitable in the mourning process.

During pregnancy after a stillbirth, it is particularly difficult for a woman to think through mixed feelings towards the dead baby still pictured inside herself whilst at the same time trying to grapple with her thoughts and feelings about the new baby whose safety is her immediate chief concern (Lewis, 1979b). The new pregnancy deprives the mother of time and space for mourning. It is therefore misguided to hurry people into another pregnancy after a stillbirth.

Management

There are techniques to facilitate mourning of a stillbirth (Giles, 1970; Lewis, 1979c; Forrest et al., 1981; Klaus and Kennell, 1982; Bourne, 1983;), but how do we know when mourning is taking an unhealthy course?

The danger signals are intensity or rigidity of symptoms rather than any specific features. If, in either parent, there are persistent immoderate grievances, persistent psychiatric disability, or an unrealistic idealisation of the dead baby or of the cure a new one will bring, then it is probably too soon for another pregnancy. We are, however, reassured if there is sadness and thoughtfulness of more ordinary proportions and also if there is the capacity to recognise some irrational ideas, where they exist, and to speak of them sensibly rather than becoming possessed by them. We urge special alertness where the reaction to the stillbirth seems to have been slight and the next pregnancy supervenes in a few months. The rush to the next pregnancy is hard to resist, especially for older women.

Reassurance and antenatal care

In a pregnancy that follows stillbirth, good obstetric care is reassuring, but the anxieties of the mother and her family should not be smothered. Rather, they should be helped to express their specific anxieties. Questions persistently repeated despite comprehensive answers should suggest that other anxieties, or grievances, lie behind the questions and are being missed.

Obstetricians always take the patient's history, but the wider family obstetric history gets meagre attention. This may collude with trends in precisely those inauspicious families where trouble gets ignored and old hidden traumas then await reactivation. Children grow up with a confusing mixture of half-knowledge in families where there has been a perinatal death in their own sibship or in their parents' sibship (Guyotat, 1980; Lewis, 1983). The girl whose mother had a bad obstetric history may be vulnerable to extra psychological disturbance if she has obstetric troubles herself when she grows up. Reactions may be lessened by awareness of this legacy. Discussion may help a woman to differentiate herself from her mother and to free the events in this generation from those of the preceding one.

Congenital abnormalities and genetic counselling

Congenital abnormalities involve parents in exceptional conflict of revulsion and attachment towards the dead baby, towards themselves and each other. Spooky feelings about heredity and the power of bad thoughts are intensified, and some daylight will help. Issues related to genetic counselling provide opportunity to bring such difficult feelings and irrational fears into the open in addition to the contraceptive or obstetric issues that prompt such discussions or investigations.

The replacement child

Children born after any bereavement are at risk of becoming 'replacement' children (Poznanski, 1972). Infancy and childhood are affected by the parents' anxiety and depression, together with their confused wishes and expectations carried over from unresolved mourning. Later troubles may involve confused identity, gender uncertainty, and sexual difficulties, disturbances of ambition and achievement, and, sometimes, a lifelong sense of nameless guilt as if living in someone else's shoes. All this has a worse twist after a stillbirth than after other deaths. 'Survivor guilt' and all these problems may be worst of all for the survivor of twins where one dies at birth.

We believe it something of a disaster for the next baby to be saddled with the name formerly intended for the one who died, adding to the danger that the new baby is only precariously differentiated from the dead one in the mind of the mother and her family. Also, ideas of reincarnation inflame other problems for the replacement child, adding to expectations that the new baby should make up for the old one. Doctors and midwives are in a good position to pick up these dangers early and should use their influence to stop the name being reused.

It is not at all rare for babies to be born on (or near) anniversaries of other births and deaths in the family. Whether or not these coincidences are predetermined by unconscious parental wishes, fantasies of reincarnation, or other magical thinking, they can certainly become charged with significance in the parents' minds, and this, in our experience, is pathogenic. The identity of one birthday with another, or with a death-day, reinforces the confusion of the new baby with someone else. Those in charge of antenatal care should look out for these coincidences, either in prospect or in retrospect, so as to bring underlying ideas into the open. Parents should be especially warned against starting a new pregnancy three months after a stillbirth. It would usually be too soon, anyway, and it would lead to term around the first anniversary.

Continuity of care

These patients need a kind of mothering and fathering themselves during pregnancy, which can nourish their sense of having good parents within themselves, a basis for healthy self-confidence and optimism and for becoming good parents. They should be aware that someone is ready to share the pain, anxieties, and hopes. The ideal mixture will make the patient feel supported by concerned doctors and nurses and yet not feel infantilised and disabled.

Apart from providing attentive encouragement, the obstetric team should clearly specify its availability – especially for urgent contact. Continuity of care is important, and although one person should be in charge it is prudent to ensure that the mother is familiar with several central people in the team. The necessary integration of support is hard to sustain. In cases of stillbirth, 'teamwork' commonly becomes shared uncare. Flaws in the system and lacunae in attentive concern resonate dangerously with these patients' anxieties about nothingness and empty spaces.

The obstetric team: discussion forum

Unless precautions are built into the team structure the stress on staff can affect the care of these patients. Perinatal death is too uncommon for junior staff to acquire enough clinical experience of it. Staff dysfunction is manifested in the fragmentation of care and responsibility, and the professional deafness, blindness, and amnesia that tend to mark the stillbirth case (Bourne, 1979). Units need a regular forum where each perinatal death is discussed, so that information and awareness are concerted (a safety-net for patients) and where sharing of experiences promotes the welfare and clinical knowledge of doctors and nurses (a safety-net for staff).

Psychotherapy and counselling

During pregnancy, especially after a perinatal death, women are difficult to engage in formal psychotherapy, even when they seem to be clamouring for help and presenting the kind of psychological difficulties that would normally justify referral to psychotherapy. The relationship with the obstetric team is of prime importance and cannot be bypassed by referral to counselling. Whilst psychotherapists may have skill in interpretation, we urge caution. The limited aims of sharing and support are more likely to be successful; forcing the pace in the pursuit of insight leads to hardening of resistance, panic, and breaking off of treatment. Interpretations are easily misconstrued as punishment and as a danger to the new baby. Help in differentiating the new baby from the dead baby is a central task where possible.

When anxieties about the pregnancy are discussed, involvement of both parents and any other children enlarges the information and promotes mutual trust. Siblings need help to sort out their misconceptions. Guilt and other anxieties may appear as exaggerated concern for the foetus or the mother during the next pregnancy. However, a blank lack of anxiety, as with grown-ups, is a danger sign too. Talking about these matters helps children to understand and share their distress; they should not always be excluded or forgotten. Yet it is often a case of working with whoever will come – and this may well be the father rather than the mother. Clinicians inexperienced in seeing families together may feel too awkward for such work.

The puerperium

After a stillbirth, feeding and rearing of the next baby are often difficult and pleasure can be spoiled. Mothering difficulties can be quite severe and either parent may reject the new child. We also think there is some risk of child abuse (Lewis, 1979a). The parents should therefore be warned during pregnancy that they may expect to be puzzled by some of their reactions to their new live baby. They expect to be a bit overanxious, but they need warning of sadness despite their joy; painful memories of the dead baby will be reawakened. They need to realise that they may at times confuse the live baby with memories of the dead baby. Preparation helps parents to be less frightened by their muddled thoughts and feelings. And it sometimes helps if they feel there is 'permission' to be confused and afraid.

When mourning is interrupted by pregnancy, anticipation of later difficulty will prepare for unfinished grieving, postponed until the baby is safely in existence. Effective mourning may then be possible, when psychotherapy may also be timely.

General anaesthesia and Caesarean section

Bewilderment and unreality – prime pathogenic elements – will have been particularly intense if the previous stillbirth occurred during general anaesthesia. Caesarian section will have aggravated bad feelings about the dead baby, and the next one, and the whole experience. The dead baby and the obstetrician are both the subjects of irrational resentment over the fruitless wound, and this will exacerbate any unresolved mourning problems now reactivated in the next pregnancy. After a stillbirth, the irrational anxiety and stigma of being ill or diseased are intensified by the operation. Surgery turns a bereaved mother into 'a patient', in her own eyes and in the eyes of medical staff, and although this licence to be ill may be temporarily comforting it can become disabling if it persists.

It is doubly important to anticipate these specific risks if another Caesarean delivery is likely. The previous experience should be clarified and reclarified during pregnancy; such matters are not disposed of by a few questions and answers; anxieties and memories change focus. If intervention is needed, general anaesthesia is best avoided, especially if there is much likelihood of the next baby dying.

Another stillbirth?

Doctors may collude in unrealistic expectations and in avoiding prognostication. It may seem easier to avoid anxious areas, but this can lead to greater trouble later. If the worst happens again, much has been written (Lewis,1976, 1983; Peppers and Knapp, 1980; Kirkley-Best and Kellner, 1982) on overcoming the abhorrence of stillbirth – parents seeing and holding the dead baby, registering a proper name, keeping photographs, a funeral and a decent marked grave. Careful management helps to preserve the dignity and poignancy of the experience and to initiate the difficult mourning process. Thus, the way may be prepared for recovery in due time.

References

Abraham, K. (1927) *Selected Papers on Psychoanalysis*. London: Maresfield Reprints, 1979: 418-80.

Bourne, S. (1968) The psychological effects of stillbirth on women and their doctors. *Journal of the Royal College of General Practice????*, 16. 103.

Bourne, S. (1979) Coping with perinatal death: After effects and theory. *Midwife Health Visitor Community Nurse*, 15: 59.

Bourne, S. (1979) Coping with perinatal death: management problems and strategies. *Midwife Health Visitor Community Nurse*, 1979; 15: 89.

Bourne, S. (1983) Psychological impact of stillbirth. *Practitioner*, 227: 53-60.

Bowlby, J. (1980) *Loss, Vol 3: Attachment and Loss*. London: Hogarth .

Culberg, J. (1972) Mental reactions of women to perinatal death. In Morris, N. (ed.), *Psychosomatic Medicine in Obstetrics and Gynaecology*. Basel: Karger.

Forrest, G.C., Claridge R.S. and Baum, J.D. (1981) Practical management of perinatal death. *British Medical Journal*, 282: 31-2.

Freud, S. (1925) *Mourning and Melancholia*. London: Hogarth Press and Institute of Psycho-analysis.

Giles, P.F.H. (1970) Reactions of women to perinatal death. *Australia New Zealand Journal of Obstetrics and Gynaecology*, 10: 207.

Guyotat, J. (1980) *Mort/naisance et filiation: etudes de psychopathologie sur le lien de filiation*. Paris: Masson.

Kirkley-Best E. and Kellner K.R. (1982) The forgotten grief: a review of the psychology of stillbirth. *American Journal of Orthopsychiaty*, 52: 420-9.

Klaus, M.H. and Kennell, J. (1982) Caring for the parents of a stillborn or an infant who dies. In: *Parent-Infant Bonding*. St Louis: Mosby.

Klein, M. (1959) Our adult world and its roots in infancy. In: *Envy and Gratitude and Other Works*, 1946-1963. London: Hogarth Press and Institute of Psychoanalysis, 1980: 247-63.

Lewis, E. (1976) Management of stillbirth-coping with an unreality. *Lancet*, ii: 619-20.

Lewis, E. (1979a) Inhibition of mourning by pregnancy: psychopathology and management. *British Medical Journal*, 11: 27.

Lewis, E. (1979b) Mourning by the family after a stillbirth, or neonatal death. *Archives of Disease in Childhood*, 54: 303.

Lewis, E. (1979c) Two hidden predisposing factors in child abuse. *International Journal of Child Abuse*, 3: 327.

Lewis, E. (1983) Stillbirth: psychological consequences and strategies of management. In: Mitunsky A. (ed.), *Advances in Perinatal Medicine*, vol. 3. New York: Plenum.

Lewis, E. and Page A. (1978) Failure to mourn a stillbirth: an overlooked catastrophe. *British Journal of Medical Psychology*, 51:237.

Meyer, R. and Lewis E. (1979) The impact of a stillbirth on a marriage. *Journal of Family Therapy*, 1: 361.

Parkes, C.M. (1972) *Bereavement: Studies of Grief in Adult Life*. London: Tavistock.

Peppers, L.G. and Knapp R.J. (1980) *Motherhood and Mourning*. New York: Praeger.

Poznanski, E.O. (1972) The 'replacement child': a saga of unresolved parental grief. *Journal of Pediatrics*, 81: 1190.

Winnicott, D.W. (1956) Primary maternal preoccupation. In: *Collected Papers. Through Paediatrics to Psycho-analysis*. London: Tavistock,1958.

CHAPTER 23

Feeding disorders

STELLA ACQUARONE

Feeding is a basic interaction which should develop into a pleasurable state that is nourishing mentally, physically and emotionally. The causes of feeding problems may lie in a traumatic past of the relationship: either premature birth, prolonged surgical treatment, a fragile make-up in the baby due to unknown vulnerabilities or unconscious pressures on the mother's mind that do not allow for a relaxed, stimulating relationship to take place.

The diagnostic classification focuses on feeding difficulties as the primary diagnosis. It describes the mother's behaviour that favours, predisposes towards or results from an imbalance in the child's ingestion, retention or assimilation of food.

The Parent-Infant Clinic has had 3,520 referrals of which 704 were due to feeding difficulties. (12% of the these had foreign mothers or families), 4% were babies with disabilities, 3% were due to failure to thrive and 5% also had relationship and sleeping difficulties.

Feeding difficulties can be helped within five to seven sessions quickly and effectively, provided the therapist has personal insight into her own unconscious reactions (usually through having undergone personal psychotherapy), sound knowledge in infant research and development and supervision of such work with parent-infant psychotherapists. The baby with feeding difficulties - like all *failure to thrive* babies - produces fear and anguish in the therapist given the risk of damage to a developing baby, and even of death itself. Professionals often deal with such feelings with denial and employ mechanical distancing manoeuvres with these babies and parents. Such behaviours in the professionals may mirror the internal attitude of the parents in respect to the child, since it is the absence of a nurturing parent in the mind of the infant which does not allow him to thrive.[1]

---

[1] This is graphically shown in the films of R. Spitz (1947) on *Hospitalism and Depression*. In his writings, he differentiates between depression in infancy, as a grief reaction when a baby loses the mother, and 'hospitalism', where the baby has not been able to form an attachment with the mother or any other caregiver and therefore cannot develop emotionally or physically.

Feeding in full context

Feeding is central for development because it:

- satisfies the painful experience of hunger;
- provides an opportunity for creating and developing other pleasant experiences such as affectionate contact, verbal and non-verbal communication with the baby and allows the baby initiative, management of time, negotiation etc.;
- focuses his attention, exploring, creating new strategies and moods;
- mirrors his mental and physical states;
- provides a basis for attunement to each baby's needs;
- when all goes well, the mother can hold and give her baby the experience of changing discomfort into comfort and can adapt to his needs;
- organizes the different sensations and sets a time-routine for the day;
- secures a space and time for this meeting of bodies and souls; and
- helps to lay the foundations for other emotional relationships and developments: neurological, inmunological, cognitive and social.

Feeding is thus one of the richest experiences of infancy. When feeding does not go well, all or most of these aspects of the behaviour are in jeopardy. Babies then must find other forms of enriching encounters with their mothers or carers in order to somehow develop their emotions. So, they may remain awake longer, ask to be held more or try to play at odd times, triggering problems in other areas.

Feeding difficulties are best assessed in the wider context of mother–infant interactions. The importance of look, smell, voice, signalling and touch form a complex yet mysterious field of enrichment in the knowledge of each other and stimulate development of the baby's brain, emotions, cognition, neurobiological and immune systems.

The mother has many internal objects, mental representations of her mother, father, husband, baby and others, with and through which she relates to her baby. The baby has preconceptions of what is going to satisfy the needs, including maternal ones that in the interchange with reality will become proper internal objects, growing conceptions of what is good, what is time, and learning to wait. However, there are circumstances where mother and/or infant cannot send these communications.

A mother's previous depression, psychiatric difficulties, abusive or neglectful attitude, traumatic pregnancy and/or delivery may underlie feeding problems, especially with certain babies who find mood changes in the mother intolerable. Conversely, some babies have a fragile make-up or confuse the mother who feels unable to fathom the baby's individuality given his special sensitivities. A vicious circle may be set up where insecurity leads to further anxiety which is an indicator of failure between them (Winnicott, 1952).

Symbolically, this early and important experience is revisited by the therapist with acceptance of the family's state of vulnerability and fear of what might happen. The therapeutic model is one of holding the mother in our mind and through our psychotherapeutic 'reverie' allowing a new or a past experience to present itself. To mother, mothers need to have access to their own early experience of nurturing which they can recall and identify with internally. Talking – if possible – is helpful in talkative cultures, but the nurturing experience is the key to psychic change. Helping the parents to stay with the baby's experience, to tolerate anxieties which the mother and the baby are feeling, supporting them with love, understanding and endurance are part of the therapeutic skills. The therapist's commitment to helping the baby and faith that the family will succeed are equally important. The therapist needs to proceed with care and respect, with tips or suggestions that allow experimentation and reflection. The triangle of therapist, mother and baby allows perspective, space and safe movement. The father also needs the experience of thinking, acting and modulating communications without persecution, but with care. In this way we reach awareness of inner states, feelings, reactions, painful memories and those that have been rejected.

Types of feeding disorders

Because the psychotherapeutic approaches involved in treatment must be matched to the stage in development of the infant, 11 types of feeding disorders are separated into three groups (with treatment and case examples given for the ones in italics):

Feeding disorders in the first three months

1. *Feeding disorder of homeostasis* (which can lead to failure-to-thrive);

Feeding disorders in the first six months

2. *feeding disorder of culture;*
3. *feeding disorder of attachment* (anorexia nervosa and failure to thrive);
4. *feeding disorder of separation and individuation* (anorexia nervosa and failure to thrive);
5. *selective food refusal* (eats only one thing);
6. *feeding disorder of continuation* (after one year, babies are fed bottle or breast only and present difficulties in moving on to weaning or to more grown-up baby food);

Feeding disorders which occur later

7.   *overeating* (greediness);
8.   *pica disorder* (which can be of two types: wall material or soil – where it would be useful to have an analysis of minerals found to be deficient in children with this disorder – and hair, cotton or fluffy stuff – with the risk of suffocation – which indicates other conflicts);
9.   *rumiation disorder* (where children make themselves regurgitate the food and this is used as a specific comforting technique – not common and requires monitoring of other indications of a failure to accommodate to reality or the ability to take it in);
10. post traumatic feeding disorders; and
11. *feeding disorders in special needs children.*

From three months onward, there may be difficulty in the baby forming an attachment to the mother. From six months onward, when the baby begins to separate or become individualized, there may be a lack of acceptance of the baby's difference and separateness by the mother, especially for young insecure teenage mothers who find separation difficult, and/or in fragile infants.

Psychotherapeutic method

The task of the psychotherapist is first to tune into the mental representations and basic sensory-motor experiences of the baby, describing them to the mother and empathizing with her difficulties to reach her infant. The therapist inwardly notes the cultural backgrounds and context dynamics, whether the mother is in a monogamous relationship with the father or entangled in a polygamous situation. If no common language can be established, can an interpreter be found, or must non-verbal communication, video replay, or modelling techniques be used? At the outset of the consultations, clarify the negative transference. If the therapist is of a different culture, acknowledge this fact. Closely observe what is going on, show an interest in and listen attentively and sensitively to the mother's account of her culture and family customs, reinforcing natural competence, valuing it and feeling connected to the family's immediate and more distant family history. Therapists must pay close attention as well to what is going on inside their own minds, allowing their own counter-transference to guide their enquiries and comments and allowing their maternal responses to be aroused, enabling them to empathize with the mother's mothering and to understand the symbolism that permeates the whole feeding process/ritual. It is important for the therapist to be immersed in the primitiveness of the difficulties being expressed (Acquarone, 1987, 1992, 1995).

Feeding disorder of homeostasis

In the first three months, the baby may have difficulty in self-regulating internally and externally with the mother. A lot of emotional distancing occurs and the baby does not manage to feed properly or enough to grow satisfactorily. Homeostasis disorders refer to these regulatory difficulties due to irritability, distractibility or difficulty in mutual accommodation. Mothers get tired and usually became anxious or guilty, creating a vicious circle.

Sylvia – ten days old

Sylvia was born by Caesarean and weighed two pounds. Extremely irritable, she cried very often and fed very little, very often, and seemed to like to be held all the time. The mother had an infection from the stitches in the womb and felt very weepy. Her husband was working and, when consulted, suggested that her mother be asked to come and help, or a friend. The Caesarean had not been planned or expected and the mother was in shock and annoyed about it. The baby, small, irritable and distrustful, was not a good match with an annoyed mother who was still in pain. Acknowledgment of her feelings and reliving the difficult birth, with recognition of the baby's individuality, allowed this mother to ask for and accept help of her own mother. The grandmother allowed the baby to grow fat in her arms, feeding at her own pace and talked to her daughter, letting her become stronger and more knowledgeable about life, events and babies. By the fifth month Sylvia had established a pattern of feeding and was sleeping well.

Beverly – 15 days old

The mother felt in great conflict about feeding Beverly. The baby recognized her father so well that even when he spoke on the answerphone, she would stop crying. The mother could not console her easily. The mother herself had not been breast-fed but was determined to breast-feed her daughter. With idealized and envied images of her siblings having been breast-fed, she felt left out and unaware of other elements which were interfering with her relationship with her baby. Beverly had had an amniocentesis diagnosis of a chromosome abnormality that was not going to be visible physically but could manifest itself in the future in mild mental retardation and infertility. The mother herself was 45 years old and knew that her chances of having another child were extremely low. Both parents nevertheless decided to continue with the pregnancy but were offered no counselling to deal with their emotional turmoil about the diagnosis and their decision. The mother realized then how much she needed to talk about that traumatic period.

Discussion

Physical and adjustment difficulties don't allow baby Sylvia and her mother to create a rhythm and a pleasure in being together. Beverly's mother idealizes breast-feeding and her envy of her siblings, relationship with her own mother and now her baby's relationship with the father do not allow her to have a pleasurable breast-feeding relationship with her baby. Beverly resents the flow of her mother's anxiety and does not take enough when feeding. Both Sylvia and Beverly present an irregular pattern of behaviour and responses. In babies this may be due to sensory-motor hypersensitivity or difficulties in tolerating frustration, pain, discomfort, silence or otherwise normal experiences. Mothers may be first-time mothers, busy with other children or easily frustrated, and their babies' difficult patterns may not get regulated. These cases will benefit from making a feeding chart for a week, to note whatever feeding is taking place and to help the mother look for a pattern.

Feeding disorders due to cultural conflict

Mothers who have difficulties adjusting to life in a new country and experiencing the anxieties of loss, identity confusion and fear of damage may come to identify the new culture as the aggressor. This paranoid anxiety, acting as a defence against feelings of isolation and of being cut off from traditional customs and beliefs, adversely affects their capacity to form healthy attachments, and their babies' capacity to thrive is therefore, stunted. Furthermore, they may be unaware of what resources and support might be available to their families.

Janet – seven days old

Janet's mother was Turkish, and, from the third day in the maternity ward, she was refusing to suck breast or bottle and was in a constant state of lethargy. The mother had come to London for an arranged marriage, become pregnant and gave birth to the baby. The breast-feeding was producing hormones to contract the uterus which caused a kind of sexual excitement that appeared to disturb the mother, reactivating infantile needs, anxieties and fears. The hospital setting, lack of family to support her and the physical changes in her body were all paralysing her capacity to bond with her baby. As she came to understand her physical sensations and her emotional loss, she began to separate her own feelings from those of her baby and learned to see Janet as an individual in her own right.

Kip – six weeks old

Kip's mother was Ghanaian, the fourth child after three daughters. He was lethargic and not feeding, and he presented a regulatory disorder. The mother had arrived from Africa, pregnant with Kip, to join her husband, leaving the extended family who had helped her to bring up the older children. Kip was extremely difficult to reach, and the mother found it difficult to persevere. She was grieving the loss of her homeland, her culture and the support of her extended family and was suddenly faced with having to cope on her own with four children. Fully talking through all aspects of her grief, she began to consider how she was projecting her paranoid anxieties on to the English community and neighbourhood and how, in this strange new setting, she needed her own confused, angry, primitive baby-self to be held.

Ramish – eight months old

Ramish's mother was Indian, and she was failing to thrive, refusing solids. The mother spoke very little English and had brought apple purée with her. She had been given to understand that the only kind of food she was supposed to give her child were English baby foods (e.g. cereals and baby purées). The mother herself ate spicy food but had been advised against feeding her child with such food. Her confusion about what was right for her child, and feelings of inadequacy in this alien culture, needed to be validated, so that she could then make an informed choice herself.

Alek – thirteen months old

Alek's mother was Russian, and he was failing to thrive. A video showed an angry and oppressive mother holding and feeding her baby. She would sit at home and in the consulting room with the baby on her lap, leaning on her left arm as if he were only three months old. She held the left arm of the baby with her left hand, the baby's right arm placed behind his back. The mother's right arm was busy spooning apple purée into the baby's mouth, as fast as the baby spat it out. No allowances were made for the child to explore, initiate, try, converse or negotiate over the meal. The 'baby within the mother' was feeling similarly tied by lack of language, stifled by unexpressed anger and frustration, feeling trapped and powerless. Alek had been hospitalized many times for various tests, which must have fed the mother's anxieties of being torn between looking after her other two children at home and her duty to her English-born baby. Video replay enabled the mother to better understand and express her feelings about herself and to understand her mental representations of her English baby. Encouraging her in the consulting room to allow her baby more freedom of movement also gave the mother more freedom to explore alternative feeding methods.

Jeran – three years old

Jeran's mother was Arab, and he was only feeding through the bottle, refusing any other feeding methods, and so was causing great concern to the GP and health visitor. The mother would constantly make up stories to explain away the problem and would later admit to having told lies. This lying was her culturally acceptable way of defending herself, although it was clear she was expressing a great deal of anger towards her child. Her own father had abandoned the family when she was seven years old. She was then obliged, instead of going to school, to stay at home and look after her five brothers and sisters. At age 20, her marriage was arranged to a man who already had nine children, and, perhaps taking revenge against the men in her life whom she felt had mistreated her, she was projecting her anger onto her small, helpless male child. When the therapist admitted a sense of failure after no progress, that the mother had been transferring her sense of power-lessness onto the therapist who felt defeated in the counter-transference, the relationship between the mother and her son improved and he began to feed normally. The mother went into long-term individual psychotherapy.

Discussion

In normal development, the baby arouses in the mother mainly positive past experiences. But, in these cases, the paranoid anxieties aroused negative ones such as fear of invasion and disintegration that interfered with the feeding process and created serious difficulties. The anger and resentment at having left their homes in order to follow their husbands (supposedly to serve their own interests, at least initially), tended to make them split and project their negative feelings onto the English-born baby, seen as alien and having to be fed alien food. Therapists may find that these sorts of early inter-ventions can be more effective *without* an interpreter. Encouraging the mother to feel strongly and positively connected to her culture and her own experience of being mothered helps the grieving process. She is better able to move forward from her view of the new surroundings as critical, unfamiliar, different, nasty, faulty, frightening or persecutory to a more positive, self-confident position.

Post-traumatic feeding disorders

Traumatic and post-traumatic feeding disorders can come about as a result of hospitalization or as a consequence of choking on a piece of food or something introduced in the mouth by accident. In the sessions, parents discuss their experience of traumatic events, their anxieties, fears, fantasies or illusions they hold for their baby and their new lives. With patience and firmness, the children reproduce in play (preferably with cuddly toys) or through drawing exactly what happened at the time of the trauma so that it can be fully mastered, once the internal material gets activated or retriggered. A few session are required to work over and over again, and slowly start to find solutions to their difficulty.

Angelica – 20 months old

Angelica was extremely small, did not eat solids at all and fed from the bottle and then very little. She was born prematurely by Caesarean when a radiologist told the parents of a malformation. The mother, 40, and father, 50, planned the pregnancy after ten years of living together. There was complete equality between Angelica and her parents. She had no rules or boundaries, and they were all rolling around aimlessly and seemingly frightened. The traumatic birth in the eighth month and the aftermath had completely reversed their ideal plans and their fun life together. Expecting a malformed baby, they cried and despaired, not believing their change in fate, how monstrous the baby might look. Afterwards, when they saw the baby in the incubator, she was normal and tiny and full of tubes. The radiologist had made a mistake. After the shock, the parents were annoyed and angry, but, even as the months went by, the vision of their child-monster formed on the night of panic continued to handicap Angelica. Angelica struggled alone in her incubator, with no contact from her parents. She endured much physical and emotional upheaval and unwittingly played into her parents' guilt and fantasies. Food was not organized around the table, as the parents could not face food and relationships. The tubes of the baby had been a constant reminder of what they did wrong and of damage to her. Through play with cuddly toys, Angelica revisited dramatic hospital and home situations. In her mind the parents were little and weak, while she was the powerful person who could battle with knives and villains. Night battles surfaced even after the parents had bought cuddly toys which represented the family 'changing', and they played with these at home as well. Another four sessions helped the integration of all the issues, and Angelica began to eat at the table with her parents, who felt really happy again. The next year, the mother was pregnant again, and Angelica resumed her difficulties, this time sleeping. Angelica needed explanations and elaboration of the meaning of her mother's pregnancy, the sickness and babies who grow inside the body, but not in the tummy where food goes. Angelica gradually began to eat everything. Follow-ups showed increased acceptance by the parents of Angelica's individuality and proper mourning of their pre- and postnatal traumatic experience. No problems were reported about the second child.

Disability-related feeding disorders

This variation – only 6 out of 632 – was the lowest reason for referral. They came from maternity and developmental paediatricians and were either diagnosed as disabled at birth or were discovered to be disabled later.

Lisa – five weeks old

The mother was Chinese with a Down's syndrome baby. Extremely angry, she didn't want to collect her baby from the Special Care Baby Unit and was abusive to the staff and her husband. Lisa had very good muscle tone and was good at communicating her affection and states of mind. The mother-in-law had recently died and, according to Chinese custom, the mother was obliged to give first priority to her newly widowed father-in-law. The house was too small for her two older children, the Down's syndrome baby and father-in-law, and she felt depleted of maternal support and mental energy. It took several interviews to separate out the mother's anger, her mixed feelings of confusion and divided loyalty and the individuality of her newborn who was taken home three weeks later. Ten fortnightly home visits were needed in order to help mother and infant to form a healthy attachment that would enable the baby to grow emotionally. This was done by describing her physical and mental boundaries, images, communication of signals and needs and ways of relating to herself. The mother was able to create a space in her own mind for this child, who needed, more than anything else, her care and attention in order to thrive.

Abigail – nine months old

Abigail's mother was an English professional recently diagnosed as suffering from cerebral palsy. The mother transmitted her unspoken anger and frustration to Abigail, who screamed continuously unless she was held in her mother's left arm. The therapist based the treatment approach on Bick's (1968) concept of the skin and its function in object relations,[2] Spitz's (1957) studies on the somatic consequences of emotional starvation in connection with mother's grief, Ferenczi's (1929) idea of an unwelcomed baby's wish to die and Adamson-Macedo's (1984) technique of tactile stimulation for premature and low-birth-weight babies. Getting the mother to think about Abigail's needs opened up a dialogue, communicating via the transference from the baby and counter-transference in the therapist of Abigail's states of mind. The mother was encouraged to establish positive, basic, skin communication by stroking her baby while maintaining a secure empathetic relationship with the therapist, who continued to interpret and translate Abigail's reactions to new needs. Over 18 fortnightly sessions, Abigail's inner world began to develop. It then took another 18 fortnightly sessions to work through the changes of mental representations that the baby and the mother had formed of each other. The mother eventually was in touch with her own feelings, and

---

[2] See Chapter 6 in this volume [Ed.].

she cultivated a secure attachment with Abigail, who was able to continue developing in an emotionally stable manner. Follow-up has shown healthy development of the child at home and school.

Discussion

Often, the therapist needs to expand the scope of psychoanalytic psychotherapy in order to treat physically or mentally handicapped infants by utilizing communications at a sensory-tactile level. This allows the first stage of object relations to take place and helps the mother acknowledge the individuality of her baby in order for them to attach properly. Once Lisa's mother was able to create the mental space needed for therapy to begin, she needed help in becoming aware of and discovering the individuality of her Down's syndrome baby. Lisa herself needed interpersonal communication through skin contact and development of her body boundaries by touch and the verbal expression of concomitant pleasurable positive experiences. Regular sessions over a substantial period of time were required for the mother to gain insight into her own personal difficulties and those of the child.

References

Acquarone, S. (1987) Early interventions in cases of disturbed mother–infant relationships. *Infant Mental Health Journal*, 8:4.

Acquarone, S. (1992) What shall I do to stop him crying? – Psychoanalytic thinking about the treatment of excessively crying infants and their mothers. *Journal of Child Psychotherapy*, 2:1.

Acquarone, S. (1995) Mens sana in corpore sano: Psychotherapy with a cerebral palsy child aged 9 months. *Psychoanalytic Psychotherapy Journal*, 9:1.

Adamson-Macedo, E. (1984) Effects of very early tactile stimulation on very low birthweight infants. Ph.D thesis. University of London, Bedford College, Faculty of Science.

Bick, E. (1968) The experience of the skin in early object relations, *International Journal of Psychoanalysis*, 49:484–6.

Ferenczi, S. (1929) The unwelcomed child and his death instinct. *International Journal of Psychoanalysis*, 10.

Spitz, R. (1957) *Dialogues from Infancy*, selected papers, Emde, R.N. (ed.). New York: International University Press.

Winnicott, D.W. (1952) Anxiety associated with insecurity. In: Collected Papers: *Through Paediatrics to Psychoanalysis*, ch. 8, pp. 97–100, London: Hogarth, 1982.

Glossary of psychoanalytic terms used in these papers

ACTING OUT - impulsive use of action to bypass remembering

AFFECT - feelings attached to an idea

ALPHA-FUNCTION - a term used by British psychoanalyst Bion to indicate a capacity which converts raw sensory data (from internal and external sources) into storable visual, auditory and olfactory impressions.

AMBIVALENCE - coexistence of love and hate towards the same person (in contradictory/split emotions as opposed to mixed feelings)

ANALYSAND - a person in analysis (patient, client)

ANXIETY - a psychosomatic signal of impending subjectively defined danger (may relate to specific concerns i.e. separation or castration, or vary in nature, as in depressive or paranoid anxieties)

ATTACHMENT THEORY - a developmental theory based on the work of British Psychoanalyst John Bowlby which maintains that human babies, like other primates, have an innate capacity to form attachments. Instinctive behaviours of crying, sucking, clinging, smiling and following serve to maintain contact and elicit care with the caregiver.

AUTOEROTIC - the infant's early engagement with his own body experiences

BETA ELEMENTS - Bion's term for undigested raw data that must be evacuated as it cannot be held in mind

CATHEXIS - a term used by Freud to indicate emotional energy invested in part pf oneself, in another person or in an idea

CONDENSATION - an unconscious mode of functioning whereby several different elements coalesce, as in dream images

CONTAINMENT - Bion's concept of maternal care which necessitates receptivity to the baby's anxieties, and a capacity to contain and metabolise these before handing them back to the infant in 'detoxified' and tolerable form

COUNTERTRANSFERENCE - emotional responses of a therapist to a patient which provide clues to unconscious processes in both

DECATHEXIS - loosening of emotional ties

DEFENCES - mechanisms used to protect oneself from realising internal or externally derived painful experiences or threats to one's integrity. The most common defences are *denial, projection, splitting, dissociation, magical or obsessional undoing* and *regression*

DENIAL - refusal to recognise the reality of a traumatic perception

DEPRESSION - ranging from a healthy response to loss to a pathological form of mourning, usually directed at an internal figure both needed and hated

DEPRESSIVE POSITION - a concept originating in Melanie Klein's theories about infantile development. The stage at which a young child realises with concern that the person he loves and hates is one and the same (rather than a 'good' mother and a 'bad' mother). A desire for reparation arises

DISPLACEMENT - process of detaching energy from one idea and its investment in another according to an unconscious associative 'chain'

DISSOCIATION - disconnection between (traumatic) knowledge and the emotional experience it generates

EROTOGENIC (erogenous) ZONES - areas of the body from which erotic sensations arise and/or which serve as the focus for sexual excitations

FREE ASSOCIATION - an uncensored form of communication instigated by Freud and still the fundamental principle of psychoanalysis today. The patient attempts to express any thought that comes into his/her mind. By establishing language as the medium of communication, the aim is to reveal unconscious processes and form new connections

GUILT - an indication of a capacity for concern and internalisation

HOLDING - British psychoanalyst Winnicott's concept of reliable and sensitive care which takes account of the minutia of the growing baby's changing physical and psychological needs at a time of 'absolute dependence', followed by 'graduated failure' which enables the baby to gradually take over these functions

IDENTIFICATION - psychic crossing of bodily boundaries between people, through *primary identification* - fusion/confusion of self and other; *projective identification* - imaginary control over the other by 'inserting' parts of oneself into the other; and *introjective identification*, which like its physical prototype of *incorporation*, is a fantasy form of appropriation by 'taking' the other into the self

INTERNALISATION - process of inner representation of significant relations (as in 'internal objects')

LIBIDINAL PHASES - Freud (and Abraham)'s demarcation of phases of erotogenic loci in infantile sexuality. *Oral* (sucking & biting), *anal* (expulsion & retention), *phallic* (exhibitionistic & anxious) and *genital* sequences of modes of being in a child's development

NARCISSISM - ranges from healthy self-love to excessive emotional self-preoccupation

NEGATIVE THERAPEUTIC REACTION - points in the treatment of a resistant patient when progress is met not with pleasure but a negative reaction

OBJECT - usually used to indicate the <u>human</u> object of a person's affections (as in 'object choice'. For instance, narcissistic choice of someone like oneself; or anaclitic choice based on differences and meeting of needs).

OEDIPUS COMPLEX - Freud's depiction of a young child's desire for one parent coupled with jealous hatred of the other's claim to the loved one's affections

OVER-DETERMINATION - a multiplicity of unconscious elements and levels contributing to the significance of a symptom or idea

PHALLIC MOTHER - fantasy that the mother either possesses phallic powers herself or contains the father's penis inside her

PHOBIA - a situation-specific irrational fear (of closed or open spaces, spiders, etc) which serves to tether 'free-floating' anxiety

PRIMAL SCENE - imaginary or real scene of intercourse between the parents, the meaning and gist of which the child re-interprets according to his/her own sexual preoccupations at each developmental phase

PRIMARY MATERNAL PREOCCUPATION - Winnicott's notion of a mother's state of mind whereby she intuitively understands and meets the baby's needs through identification

PROJECTION - what is rejected in oneself is expelled and attributed to others

SUPER-EGO - Freud's concept for that aspect of the self which acts as conscience, self-critic or censor, seemingly constituted through internalisation of parental prohibitions and demands and sociocultural requirements

TRANSFERENCE - actualisation of unconscious wishes and archaic emotional experiences as these are reactivated by present encounters, and repeated, especially in the analytic situation

TRANSITIONAL OBJECT – Winnicott's concept of a comforting toy or object which provides a dimension that is neither internal nor external, part of the child yet 'not-me' and representative of the caregiver's qualities. In adulthood, playing, creativity and cultural experience take place in a similarly 'intermediate area' – a transitional space.

Subject Index

299

Author Index